HELPFUL HINTS FOR A DAILY QUIET TIME

The purpose of this Quiet Time is to meet the needs of spiritual growth in the life of the Christian in such a way that they learn the art of conducting their own personal investigation into the Bible.
Consider the following helpful hints:

1 Give priority in choosing your quiet time. This will vary with each individual in accordance with his own circumstances.
The time you choose must:
- ■ have top priority over everything else
- ■ be the quietest time possible.
- ■ be a convenient time of the day or night.
- ■ be consistently observed each day.

2 Give attention to the procedure suggested for you to follow. Include the following items.
- ■ Read God's Word.
- ■ Mark your Bible as you read. Here are some suggestions that might be helpful:
  - a. After you read the passage put an exclamation mark next to the verses you completely understand.
  - b. Put a question mark next to verses you do not understand.
  - c. Put an arrow pointing upward next to encouraging verses.
  - d. Put an arrow pointing downward next to verses which challenge you spiritually.
  - e. Put a star next to verses containing important truths or major points.
- ■ Meditate on what you have read (In one sentence, write the main thought). Here are some suggestions as guidelines for meditating on God's Word:

a. Look at the selected passage from God's point of view.

b. Though we encourage quiet time in the morning, some people arrange to have their quiet time at the end of their day. God emphasizes that we need to go to sleep meditating on His Word. "My soul shall be satisfied and my mouth shall praise thee with joyful lips: when I remember thee upon my bed, and meditating on thee in the night watches" (Psalm 63:5,6).

c. Deuteronomy 6:7 lists routine things you do each day during which you should concentrate on the portion of Scripture for that day:
   — when you sit in your house (meals and relaxation)
   — when you walk in the way (to and from school or work)
   — when you lie down (before going to sleep at night)
   — when you rise up (getting ready for the day)

■ Apply some truth to your life. (Use first person pronouns I, me, my, mine). If you have difficulty in finding an application for your life, think of yourself as a Bible SPECTator and ask yourself the following questions:

S – Is there any SIN for me to forsake?

P – Is there any PROMISE for me to claim?

E – Is there any EXAMPLE for me to follow?

C – Is there any COMMAND for me to obey?

T – Is there a TRUTH for me to embrace?

■ Pray for specific things (Use the prayer sheets found in the My Prayer Journal section).

3 Be sure to fill out your quiet time sheets. This will really help you re-member the things the Lord brings to your mind.

4 Purpose to share with someone else each day something you gained from your quiet time. This can be a real blessing for them as well as for you.

PLANT BY
STREAMS OF
WATER
YIELD FRUIT IN
SEASON
LEAF WILL NOT
WITHER

QUIETIME

ONE-YEAR DAILY DEVOTIONAL WITH COMMENTARY

QUIET TIME

ONE-YEAR
DAILY
DEVOTIONAL
WITH
COMMENTARY

Word of Life Local Church Ministries
A division of Word of Life Fellowship, Inc.
Don Lough – Executive Director
Jack Wyrtzen & Harry Bollback - Founders
Ric Garland – VP of Local Church Ministries

USA	Canada
P.O. Box 600	RR#8
Schroon Lake, NY 12870	Owen Sound ON N4K 5W4
talk@wol.org	LCM@wol.ca
1-888-932-5827	1-800-461-3503

Web Address: www.wol.org

Publisher's Acknowledgements
Writers and Contributors:

Bill Boulet	Philippians
Dr. Tom Davis	Nahum, Malachi, John, Ezekiel, Revelation
Gary Ingersoll	Psalms, Exodus, 1 and 2 Kings
Dr. Chuck Scheide	2 Timothy, Ephesians
Dr. Marshall Wicks	Romans, Job, 1 Peter

Editor: Dr. Tom Davis
Associate Editor: Gary Ingersoll
Curriculum Manager: Don Reichard
Cover and page design: Boire Design

ISBN - 978-1-935475-30-9

Printed in the United States of America

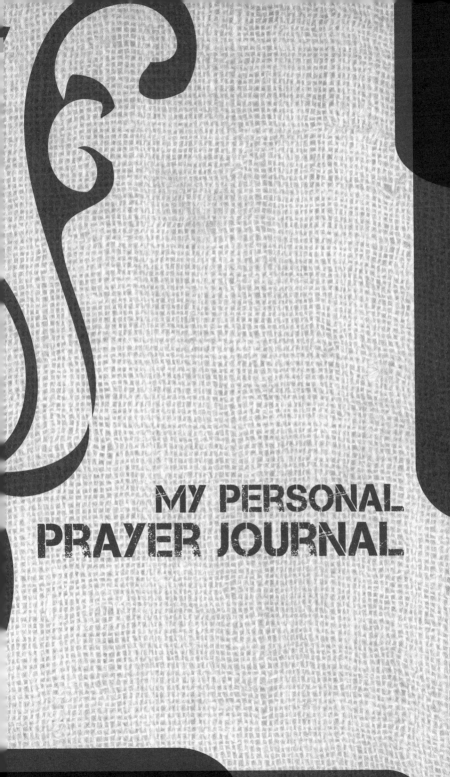

MY PERSONAL
PRAYER JOURNAL

DAILY PRAYER LIST

DATE / REQUEST   **DATE / ANSWER**

DAILY PRAYER LIST

DATE / REQUEST   **DATE / ANSWER**

DAILY PRAYER LIST

DATE / REQUEST   **DATE / ANSWER**

DAILY PRAYER LIST

DATE / REQUEST

DATE / ANSWER

SUNDAY

FAMILY

DATE / REQUEST	DATE / ANSWER

CHRISTIAN FRIENDS

DATE / REQUEST	DATE / ANSWER

UNSAVED FRIENDS

DATE / REQUEST   **DATE / ANSWER**

MISSIONARIES

DATE / REQUEST   **DATE / ANSWER**

MONDAY

FAMILY

DATE / REQUEST

DATE / ANSWER

CHRISTIAN FRIENDS

DATE / REQUEST

DATE / ANSWER

UNSAVED FRIENDS

DATE / REQUEST   **DATE / ANSWER**

MISSIONARIES

DATE / REQUEST   **DATE / ANSWER**

TUESDAY

FAMILY

DATE / REQUEST   **DATE / ANSWER**

CHRISTIAN FRIENDS

DATE / REQUEST   **DATE / ANSWER**

UNSAVED FRIENDS

DATE / REQUEST

DATE / ANSWER

MISSIONARIES

DATE / REQUEST

DATE / ANSWER

WEDNESDAY

FAMILY

DATE / REQUEST	DATE / ANSWER

CHRISTIAN FRIENDS

DATE / REQUEST	DATE / ANSWER

UNSAVED FRIENDS

DATE / REQUEST	DATE / ANSWER

MISSIONARIES

DATE / REQUEST	DATE / ANSWER

THURSDAY

FAMILY

DATE / REQUEST

DATE / ANSWER

CHRISTIAN FRIENDS

DATE / REQUEST

DATE / ANSWER

UNSAVED FRIENDS

DATE / REQUEST	DATE / ANSWER

MISSIONARIES

DATE / REQUEST	DATE / ANSWER

FRIDAY

FAMILY

DATE / REQUEST   DATE / ANSWER

CHRISTIAN FRIENDS

DATE / REQUEST   DATE / ANSWER

FRIDAY

UNSAVED FRIENDS

DATE / REQUEST   **DATE / ANSWER**

MISSIONARIES

DATE / REQUEST   **DATE / ANSWER**

SATURDAY

FAMILY

DATE / REQUEST	DATE / ANSWER

CHRISTIAN FRIENDS

DATE / REQUEST	DATE / ANSWER

UNSAVED FRIENDS

DATE / REQUEST	DATE / ANSWER

MISSIONARIES

DATE / REQUEST	DATE / ANSWER

DAILY PRAISE LIST

DATE / I'M PRAISING GOD FOR...

DAILY PRAISE LIST

DATE / I'M PRAISING GOD FOR...

DAILY PRAISE LIST

DATE / I'M PRAISING GOD FOR...

SOMETHING FOR EVERYONE

Some people just can't get enough! That is why we have
several dimensions in the Word of Life Quiet Time.
Along with the daily reading, content and application
questions for each day, two reading programs are given to
help you understand the Bible better. Choose one or both.

Reading Through the
New Testament Four Times In One Year

Turn the page and discover a schedule that takes you
through the New Testament four times in one year.
This is a great method to help you see the correlation
of the Gospels and other New Testament books.

Reading Through the
Whole Bible In One Year

Turn another page and find a program of several pages that
will guide you through a chronological reading of the
entire Bible. Follow this schedule and you will move from
Genesis through Revelation in one year.

The Choice is Up to You

Whether you have a short quiet time, a quiet time with
more scripture reading or one with a mini-Bible study
each day, we trust your time with God will draw you
closer to Him in every area of your life.

READ THROUGH THE NEW TESTAMENT FOUR TIMES IN ONE YEAR

Weeks 1-13

- Matthew 1-3
- Matthew 4-6
- Matthew 7-9
- Matt. 10-12
- Matt. 13-15
- Matt. 16-18
- Matt. 19-21
- Matt. 22-24
- Matt. 25-26
- Matt. 27-28
- Mark 1-3
- Mark 4-5
- Mark 6-8
- Mark 9-11
- Mark 12-14
- Mark 15-16
- Luke 1-2
- Luke 3-5
- Luke 6-7
- Luke 8-9
- Luke 10-11
- Luke 12-14
- Luke 15-17
- Luke 18-20
- Luke 21-22
- Luke 23-24
- John 1-3
- John 4-5
- John 6-7
- John 8-10
- John 11-12
- John 13-15
- John 16-18
- John 19-21
- Acts 1-3
- Acts 4-6
- Acts 7-8
- Acts 9-11
- Acts 12-15
- Acts 16-18
- Acts 19-21
- Acts 22-24
- Acts 25-26
- Acts 27-28
- Romans 1-3

- Romans 4-6
- Romans 7-9
- Romans 10-12
- Romans 13-16
- 1 Cor. 1-4
- 1 Cor. 5-9
- 1 Cor. 10-12
- 1 Cor. 13-16
- 2 Cor. 1-4
- 2 Cor. 5-8
- 2 Cor. 9-13
- Galatians 1-3
- Galatians 4-6
- Ephesians 1-3
- Ephesians 4-6
- Philippians 1-4
- Colossians 1-4
- 1 Thes. 1-3
- 1 Thes. 4-5
- 2 Thes. 1-3
- 1 Timothy 1-3
- 1 Timothy 4-6
- 2 Timothy 1-4
- Titus 1-3
- Philemon
- Hebrews 1
- Hebrews 2-4
- Hebrews 5-7
- Hebrews 8-10
- Hebrews 11-13
- James 1-3
- James 4-5
- 1 Peter 1-3
- 1 Peter 4-5
- 2 Peter 1-3
- 1 John 1-3
- 1 John 4-5
- 2 Jn, 3 Jn, Jude
- Revelation 1-3
- Revelation 4-6
- Revelation 7-9
- Rev. 10-12
- Rev. 13-15
- Rev. 16-18
- Rev. 19-22

Weeks 14-26

- Matthew 1-3
- Matthew 4-6
- Matthew 7-9
- Matt. 10-12
- Matt. 13-15
- Matt. 16-18
- Matt. 19-21
- Matt. 22-24
- Matt. 25-26
- Matt. 27-28
- Mark 1-3
- Mark 4-5
- Mark 6-8
- Mark 9-11
- Mark 12-14
- Mark 15-16
- Luke 1-2
- Luke 3-5
- Luke 6-7
- Luke 8-9
- Luke 10-11
- Luke 12-14
- Luke 15-17
- Luke 18-20
- Luke 21-22
- Luke 23-24
- John 1-3
- John 4-5
- John 6-7
- John 8-10
- John 11-12
- John 13-15
- John 16-18
- John 19-21
- Acts 1-3
- Acts 4-6
- Acts 7-8
- Acts 9-11
- Acts 12-15
- Acts 16-18
- Acts 19-21
- Acts 22-24
- Acts 25-26
- Acts 27-28
- Romans 1-3

- Romans 4-6
- Romans 7-9
- Romans 10-12
- Romans 13-16
- 1 Cor. 1-4
- 1 Cor. 5-9
- 1 Cor. 10-12
- 1 Cor. 13-16
- 2 Cor. 1-4
- 2 Cor. 5-8
- 2 Cor. 9-13
- Galatians 1-3
- Galatians 4-6
- Ephesians 1-3
- Ephesians 4-6
- Philippians 1-4
- Colossians 1-4
- 1 Thes. 1-3
- 1 Thes. 4-5
- 2 Thes. 1-3
- 1 Timothy 1-3
- 1 Timothy 4-6
- 2 Timothy 1-4
- Titus 1-3
- Philemon
- Hebrews 1
- Hebrews 2-4
- Hebrews 5-7
- Hebrews 8-10
- Hebrews 11-13
- James 1-3
- James 4-5
- 1 Peter 1-3
- 1 Peter 4-5
- 2 Peter 1-3
- 1 John 1-3
- 1 John 4-5
- 2 Jn, 3 Jn, Jude
- Revelation 1-3
- Revelation 4-6
- Revelation 7-9
- Rev. 10-12
- Rev. 13-15
- Rev. 16-18
- Rev. 19-22

READ THROUGH THE NEW TESTAMENT FOUR TIMES IN ONE YEAR

Weeks 27-39

- ☐ Matthew 1-3
- ☐ Matthew 4-6
- ☐ Matthew 7-9
- ☐ Matt. 10-12
- ☐ Matt. 13-15
- ☐ Matt. 16-18
- ☐ Matt. 19-21
- ☐ Matt. 22-24
- ☐ Matt. 25-26
- ☐ Matt. 27-28
- ☐ Mark 1-3
- ☐ Mark 4-5
- ☐ Mark 6-8
- ☐ Mark 9-11
- ☐ Mark 12-14
- ☐ Mark 15-16
- ☐ Luke 1-2
- ☐ Luke 3-5
- ☐ Luke 6-7
- ☐ Luke 8-9
- ☐ Luke 10-11
- ☐ Luke 12-14
- ☐ Luke 15-17
- ☐ Luke 18-20
- ☐ Luke 21-22
- ☐ Luke 23-24
- ☐ John 1-3
- ☐ John 4-5
- ☐ John 6-7
- ☐ John 8-10
- ☐ John 11-12
- ☐ John 13-15
- ☐ John 16-18
- ☐ John 19-21
- ☐ Acts 1-3
- ☐ Acts 4-6
- ☐ Acts 7-8
- ☐ Acts 9-11
- ☐ Acts 12-15
- ☐ Acts 16-18
- ☐ Acts 19-21
- ☐ Acts 22-24
- ☐ Acts 25-26
- ☐ Acts 27-28
- ☐ Romans 1-3

- ☐ Romans 4-6
- ☐ Romans 7-9
- ☐ Romans 10-12
- ☐ Romans 13-16
- ☐ 1 Cor. 1-4
- ☐ 1 Cor. 5-9
- ☐ 1 Cor. 10-12
- ☐ 1 Cor. 13-16
- ☐ 2 Cor. 1-4
- ☐ 2 Cor. 5-8
- ☐ 2 Cor. 9-13
- ☐ Galatians 1-3
- ☐ Galatians 4-6
- ☐ Ephesians 1-3
- ☐ Ephesians 4-6
- ☐ Phil. 1-4
- ☐ Colossians 1-4
- ☐ 1 Thes. 1-3
- ☐ 1 Thes. 4-5
- ☐ 2 Thes. 1-3
- ☐ 1 Timothy 1-3
- ☐ 1 Timothy 4-6
- ☐ 2 Timothy 1-4
- ☐ Titus 1-3
- ☐ Philemon
- ☐ Hebrews 1
- ☐ Hebrews 2-4
- ☐ Hebrews 5-7
- ☐ Hebrews 8-10
- ☐ Hebrews 11-13
- ☐ James 1-3
- ☐ James 4-5
- ☐ 1 Peter 1-3
- ☐ 1 Peter 4-5
- ☐ 2 Peter 1-3
- ☐ 1 John 1-3
- ☐ 1 John 4-5
- ☐ 2 Jn, 3 Jn, Jude
- ☐ Revelation 1-3
- ☐ Revelation 4-6
- ☐ Revelation 7-9
- ☐ Rev. 10-12
- ☐ Rev. 13-15
- ☐ Rev. 16-18
- ☐ Rev. 19-22

Weeks 40-52

- ☐ Matthew 1-3
- ☐ Matthew 4-6
- ☐ Matthew 7-9
- ☐ Matt. 10-12
- ☐ Matt. 13-15
- ☐ Matt. 16-18
- ☐ Matt. 19-21
- ☐ Matt. 22-24
- ☐ Matt. 25-26
- ☐ Matt. 27-28
- ☐ Mark 1-3
- ☐ Mark 4-5
- ☐ Mark 6-8
- ☐ Mark 9-11
- ☐ Mark 12-14
- ☐ Mark 15-16
- ☐ Luke 1-2
- ☐ Luke 3-5
- ☐ Luke 6-7
- ☐ Luke 8-9
- ☐ Luke 10-11
- ☐ Luke 12-14
- ☐ Luke 15-17
- ☐ Luke 18-20
- ☐ Luke 21-22
- ☐ Luke 23-24
- ☐ John 1-3
- ☐ John 4-5
- ☐ John 6-7
- ☐ John 8-10
- ☐ John 11-12
- ☐ John 13-15
- ☐ John 16-18
- ☐ John 19-21
- ☐ Acts 1-3
- ☐ Acts 4-6
- ☐ Acts 7-8
- ☐ Acts 9-11
- ☐ Acts 12-15
- ☐ Acts 16-18
- ☐ Acts 19-21
- ☐ Acts 22-24
- ☐ Acts 25-26
- ☐ Acts 27-28
- ☐ Romans 1-3

- ☐ Romans 4-6
- ☐ Romans 7-9
- ☐ Romans 10-12
- ☐ Romans 13-16
- ☐ 1 Cor. 1-4
- ☐ 1 Cor. 5-9
- ☐ 1 Cor. 10-12
- ☐ 1 Cor. 13-16
- ☐ 2 Cor. 1-4
- ☐ 2 Cor. 5-8
- ☐ 2 Cor. 9-13
- ☐ Galatians 1-3
- ☐ Galatians 4-6
- ☐ Ephesians 1-3
- ☐ Ephesians 4-6
- ☐ Phil. 1-4
- ☐ Colossians 1-4
- ☐ 1 Thes. 1-3
- ☐ 1 Thes. 4-5
- ☐ 2 Thes. 1-3
- ☐ 1 Timothy 1-3
- ☐ 1 Timothy 4-6
- ☐ 2 Timothy 1-4
- ☐ Titus 1-3
- ☐ Philemon
- ☐ Hebrews 1
- ☐ Hebrews 2-4
- ☐ Hebrews 5-7
- ☐ Hebrews 8-10
- ☐ Hebrews 11-13
- ☐ James 1-3
- ☐ James 4-5
- ☐ 1 Peter 1-3
- ☐ 1 Peter 4-5
- ☐ 2 Peter 1-3
- ☐ 1 John 1-3
- ☐ 1 John 4-5
- ☐ 2 Jn, 3 Jn, Jude
- ☐ Revelation 1-3
- ☐ Revelation 4-6
- ☐ Revelation 7-9
- ☐ Rev. 10-12
- ☐ Rev. 13-15
- ☐ Rev. 16-18
- ☐ Rev. 19-22

BIBLE READING SCHEDULE

Read through the Bible in one year! As you complete each daily reading, simply place a check in the appropriate box.

- ☐ 1 Genesis 1-3
- ☐ 2 Genesis 4:1-6:8
- ☐ 3 Genesis 6:9-9:29
- ☐ 4 Genesis 10-11
- ☐ 5 Genesis 12-14
- ☐ 6 Genesis 15-17
- ☐ 7 Genesis 18-19
- ☐ 8 Genesis 20-22
- ☐ 9 Genesis 23-24
- ☐ 10 Genesis 25-26
- ☐ 11 Genesis 27-28
- ☐ 12 Genesis 29-30
- ☐ 13 Genesis 31-32
- ☐ 14 Genesis 33-35
- ☐ 15 Genesis 36-37
- ☐ 16 Genesis 38-40
- ☐ 17 Genesis 41-42
- ☐ 18 Genesis 43-45
- ☐ 19 Genesis 46-47
- ☐ 20 Genesis 48-50
- ☐ 21 Job 1-3
- ☐ 22 Job 4-7
- ☐ 23 Job 8-11
- ☐ 24 Job 12-15
- ☐ 25 Job 16-19
- ☐ 26 Job 20-22
- ☐ 27 Job 23-28
- ☐ 28 Job 29-31
- ☐ 29 Job 32-34
- ☐ 30 Job 35-37
- ☐ 31 Job 38-42
- ☐ 32 Exodus 1-4
- ☐ 33 Exodus 5-8
- ☐ 34 Exodus 9-11
- ☐ 35 Exodus 12-13
- ☐ 36 Exodus 14-15
- ☐ 37 Exodus 16-18
- ☐ 38 Exodus 19-21
- ☐ 39 Exodus 22-24
- ☐ 40 Exodus 25-27
- ☐ 41 Exodus 28-29
- ☐ 42 Exodus 30-31
- ☐ 43 Exodus 32-34
- ☐ 44 Exodus 35-36
- ☐ 45 Exodus 37-38
- ☐ 46 Exodus 39-40
- ☐ 47 Leviticus 1:1-5:13
- ☐ 48 Leviticus 5:14-7:38
- ☐ 49 Leviticus 8-10
- ☐ 50 Leviticus 11-12
- ☐ 51 Leviticus 13-14
- ☐ 52 Leviticus 15-17
- ☐ 53 Leviticus 18-20
- ☐ 54 Leviticus 21-23
- ☐ 55 Leviticus 24-25
- ☐ 56 Leviticus 26-27
- ☐ 57 Numbers 1-2
- ☐ 58 Numbers 3-4
- ☐ 59 Numbers 5-6
- ☐ 60 Numbers 7
- ☐ 61 Numbers 8-10
- ☐ 62 Numbers 11-13
- ☐ 63 Numbers 14-15
- ☐ 64 Numbers 16-18
- ☐ 65 Numbers 19-21
- ☐ 66 Numbers 22-24
- ☐ 67 Numbers 25-26
- ☐ 68 Numbers 27-29
- ☐ 69 Numbers 30-31
- ☐ 70 Numbers 32-33
- ☐ 71 Numbers 34-36
- ☐ 72 Deuteronomy 1-2
- ☐ 73 Deuteronomy 3-4
- ☐ 74 Deuteronomy 5-7
- ☐ 75 Deuteronomy 8-10
- ☐ 76 Deuteronomy 11-13
- ☐ 77 Deuteronomy 14-17
- ☐ 78 Deuteronomy 18-21
- ☐ 79 Deuteronomy 22-25
- ☐ 80 Deuteronomy 26-28
- ☐ 81 Deuteronomy 29:1-31:29
- ☐ 82 Deuteronomy 31:30-34:12
- ☐ 83 Joshua 1-4
- ☐ 84 Joshua 5-8
- ☐ 85 Joshua 9-11
- ☐ 86 Joshua 12-14
- ☐ 87 Joshua 15-17
- ☐ 88 Joshua 18-19
- ☐ 89 Joshua 20-22
- ☐ 90 Joshua 23 - Judges 1
- ☐ 91 Judges 2-5
- ☐ 92 Judges 6-8
- ☐ 93 Judges 9
- ☐ 94 Judges 10-12
- ☐ 95 Judges 13-16
- ☐ 96 Judges 17-19
- ☐ 97 Judges 20-21
- ☐ 98 Ruth
- ☐ 99 1 Samuel 1-3
- ☐ 100 1 Samuel 4-7
- ☐ 101 1 Samuel 8-10
- ☐ 102 1 Samuel 11-13
- ☐ 103 1 Samuel 14-15
- ☐ 104 1 Samuel 16-17

BIBLE READING SCHEDULE

Day 105 - 199

- ☐ 105 1 Samuel 18-19; Psalm 59
- ☐ 106 1 Samuel 20-21; Psalm 56; 34
- ☐ 107 1 Samuel 22-23; 1 Chronicles 12:8-18; Psalm 52; 54; 63; 142
- ☐ 108 1 Samuel 24; Psalm 57; 1 Samuel 25
- ☐ 109 1 Samuel 26-29; 1 Chronicles 12:1-7, 19-22
- ☐ 110 1 Samuel 30-31; 1 Chronicles 10; 2 Samuel 1
- ☐ 111 2 Samuel 2-4
- ☐ 112 2 Samuel 5:1-6:11; 1 Chronicles 11:1-9; 2:23-40; 13:1-14:17
- ☐ 113 2 Samuel 22; Psalm 18
- ☐ 114 1 Chronicles 15-16; 2 Samuel 6:12-23; Psalm 96
- ☐ 115 Psalm 105; 2 Samuel 7; 1 Chronicles 17
- ☐ 116 2 Samuel 8-10; 1 Chronicles 18-19; Psalm 60
- ☐ 117 2 Samuel 11-12; 1 Chronicles 20:1-3; Psalm 51
- ☐ 118 2 Samuel 13-14
- ☐ 119 2 Samuel 15-17
- ☐ 120 Psalm 3; 2 Samuel 18-19
- ☐ 121 2 Samuel 20-21; 23:8-23; 1 Chronicles 20:4-8; 11:10-25
- ☐ 122 2 Samuel 23:24-24:25;
- ☐ 123 1 Chronicles 11:26-47; 21:1-30, 1 Chronicles 22-24
- ☐ 124 Psalm 30; 1 Chronicles 25-26
- ☐ 125 1 Chronicles 27-29
- ☐ 126 Psalms 5-7; 10; 11; 13; 17
- ☐ 127 Psalms 23; 26; 28; 31; 35
- ☐ 128 Psalms 41; 43; 46; 55; 61; 62; 64
- ☐ 129 Psalms 69-71; 77
- ☐ 130 Psalms 83; 86; 88; 91; 95
- ☐ 131 Psalms 108-9; 120-21; 140; 143-44
- ☐ 132 Psalms 1; 14-15; 36-37; 39
- ☐ 133 Psalms 40; 49-50; 73
- ☐ 134 Psalms 76; 82; 84; 90; 92; 112; 115
- ☐ 135 Psalms 8-9; 16; 19; 21; 24; 29
- ☐ 136 Psalms 33; 65-68
- ☐ 137 Psalms 75; 93-94; 97-100
- ☐ 138 Psalms 103-4; 113-14; 117
- ☐ 139 Psalm 119:1-88
- ☐ 140 Psalm 119:89-176
- ☐ 141 Psalms 122; 124; 133-36
- ☐ 142 Psalms 138-39; 145; 148; 150
- ☐ 143 Psalms 4; 12; 20; 25; 32; 38
- ☐ 144 Psalms 42; 53; 58; 81; 101; 111; 130-31; 141; 146
- ☐ 145 Psalms 2; 22; 27
- ☐ 146 Psalms 45; 47-48; 87; 110
- ☐ 147 1 Kings 1:1-2:12; 2 Samuel 23:1-7
- ☐ 148 1 Kings 2:13-3:28; 2 Chronicles 1:1-13
- ☐ 149 1 Kings 5-6; 2 Chronicles 2-3
- ☐ 150 1 Kings 7; 2 Chronicles 4
- ☐ 151 1 Kings 8; 2 Chronicles 5:1-7:10
- ☐ 152 1 Kings 9:1-10:13; 2 Chronicles 7:11-9:12
- ☐ 153 1 Kings 4; 10:14-29; 2 Chronicles 1:14-17; 9:13-28; Psalm 72
- ☐ 154 Proverbs 1-3
- ☐ 155 Proverbs 4-6
- ☐ 156 Proverbs 7-9
- ☐ 157 Proverbs 10-12
- ☐ 158 Proverbs 13-15
- ☐ 159 Proverbs 16-18
- ☐ 160 Proverbs 19-21
- ☐ 161 Proverbs 22-24
- ☐ 162 Proverbs 25-27
- ☐ 163 Proverbs 28-29
- ☐ 164 Proverbs 30-31; Psalm 127
- ☐ 165 Song of Solomon
- ☐ 166 1 Kings 11:1-40; Ecclesiastes 1-2
- ☐ 167 Ecclesiastes 3-7
- ☐ 168 Ecclesiastes 8-12; 1 Kings 11:41-43; 2 Chronicles 9:29-31
- ☐ 169 1 Kings 12; 2 Chronicles 10:1-11:17
- ☐ 170 1 Kings 13-14; 2 Chronicles 11:18-12:16
- ☐ 171 1 Kings 15:1-24; 2 Chronicles 13-16
- ☐ 172 1 Kings 15:25-16:34; 2 Chronicles 17; 1 Kings 17
- ☐ 173 1 Kings 18-19
- ☐ 174 1 Kings 20-21
- ☐ 175 1 Kings 22:1-40; 2 Chronicles 18
- ☐ 176 1 Kings 22:41-53; 2 Kings 1; 2 Chronicles 19:1-21:3
- ☐ 177 2 Kings 2-4
- ☐ 178 2 Kings 5-7
- ☐ 179 2 Kings 8-9; 2 Chronicles 21:4-22:9
- ☐ 180 2 Kings 10-11; 2 Chronicles 22:10-23:21
- ☐ 181 Joel
- ☐ 182 2 Kings 12-13; 2 Chronicles 24
- ☐ 183 2 Kings 14; 2 Chronicles 25; Jonah
- ☐ 184 Hosea 1-7
- ☐ 185 Hosea 8-14
- ☐ 186 2 Kings 15:1-7; 2 Chronicles 26; Amos 1-4
- ☐ 187 Amos 5-9; 2 Kings 15:8-18
- ☐ 188 Isaiah 1-4
- ☐ 189 2 Kings 15:19-38; 2 Chronicles 27; Isaiah 5-6
- ☐ 190 Micah
- ☐ 191 2 Kings 16; 2 Chronicles 28; Isaiah 7-8
- ☐ 192 Isaiah 9-12
- ☐ 193 Isaiah 13-16
- ☐ 194 Isaiah 17-22
- ☐ 195 Isaiah 23-27
- ☐ 196 Isaiah 28-30
- ☐ 197 Isaiah 31-35
- ☐ 198 2 Kings 18:1-8; 2 Chronicles 29-31
- ☐ 199 2 Kings 17; 18:9-37; 2 Chronicles 32:1-19; Isaiah 36

BIBLE READING SCHEDULE

Day 200 - 288

- ☐ 200 2 Kings 19; 2 Chronicles 32:20-23; Isaiah 37
- ☐ 201 2 Kings 20; 2 Chronicles 32:24-33; Isaiah 38-39
- ☐ 202 2 Kings 21:1-18; 2 Chronicles 33:1-20; Isaiah 40
- ☐ 203 Isaiah 41-43
- ☐ 204 Isaiah 44-47
- ☐ 205 Isaiah 48-51
- ☐ 206 Isaiah 52-57
- ☐ 207 Isaiah 58-62
- ☐ 208 Isaiah 63-66
- ☐ 209 2 Kings 21:19-26; 2 Chronicles 33:21-34:7; Zephaniah
- ☐ 210 Jeremiah 1-3
- ☐ 211 Jeremiah 4-6
- ☐ 212 Jeremiah 7-9
- ☐ 213 Jeremiah 10-13
- ☐ 214 Jeremiah 14-16
- ☐ 215 Jeremiah 17-20
- ☐ 216 2 Kings 22:1-23:28; 2 Chronicles 34:8-35:19
- ☐ 217 Nahum; 2 Kings 23:29-37; 2 Chronicles 35:20-36:5; Jeremiah 22:10-17
- ☐ 218 Jeremiah 26; Habakkuk
- ☐ 219 Jeremiah 46-47; 2 Kings 24:1-4, 7; 2 Chronicles 36:6-7; Jeremiah 25, 35
- ☐ 220 Jeremiah 36, 45, 48
- ☐ 221 Jeremiah 49:1-33; Daniel 1-2
- ☐ 222 Jeremiah 22:18-30; 2 Kings 24:5-20; 2 Chronicles 36:8-12; Jeremiah 37:1-2; 52:1-3; 24; 29
- ☐ 223 Jeremiah 27-28, 23
- ☐ 224 Jeremiah 50-51
- ☐ 225 Jeremiah 49:34-39; 34:1-22; Ezekiel 1-3
- ☐ 226 Ezekiel 4-7
- ☐ 227 Ezekiel 8-11
- ☐ 228 Ezekiel 12-14
- ☐ 229 Ezekiel 15-17
- ☐ 230 Ezekiel 18-20
- ☐ 231 Ezekiel 21-23
- ☐ 232 2 Kings 25:1; 2 Chronicles 36:13-16; Jeremiah 39:1; 52:4; Ezekiel 24; Jeremiah 21:1-22:9; 32:1-44
- ☐ 233 Jeremiah 30-31, 33
- ☐ 234 Ezekiel 25; 29:1-16; 30; 31
- ☐ 235 Ezekiel 26-28
- ☐ 236 Jeremiah 37:3-39:10; 52:5-30; 2 Kings 25:2-21; 2 Chronicles 36:17-21
- ☐ 237 2 Kings 25:22; Jeremiah 39:11-40:6; Lamentations 1-3
- ☐ 238 Lamentations 4-5; Obadiah
- ☐ 239 Jeremiah 40:7-44:30; 2 Kings 25:23-26
- ☐ 240 Ezekiel 33:21-36:38
- ☐ 241 Ezekiel 37-39
- ☐ 242 Ezekiel 32:1-33:20; Daniel 3
- ☐ 243 Ezekiel 40-42
- ☐ 244 Ezekiel 43-45
- ☐ 245 Ezekiel 46-48
- ☐ 246 Ezekiel 29:17-21; Daniel 4; Jeremiah 52:31-34; 2 Kings 25:27-30; Psalm 44
- ☐ 247 Psalms 74; 79-80; 89
- ☐ 248 Psalms 85; 102; 106; 123; 137
- ☐ 249 Daniel 7-8; 5
- ☐ 250 Daniel 9; 6
- ☐ 251 2 Chronicles 36:22-23; Ezra 1:1-4:5
- ☐ 252 Daniel 10-12
- ☐ 253 Ezra 4:6-6:13; Haggai
- ☐ 254 Zechariah 1-6
- ☐ 255 Zechariah 7-8; Ezra 6:14-22; Psalm 78
- ☐ 256 Psalms 107; 116; 118
- ☐ 257 Psalms 125-26; 128-29; 132; 147; 149
- ☐ 258 Zechariah 9-14
- ☐ 259 Esther 1-4
- ☐ 260 Esther 5-10
- ☐ 261 Ezra 7-8
- ☐ 262 Ezra 9-10
- ☐ 263 Nehemiah 1-5
- ☐ 264 Nehemiah 6-7
- ☐ 265 Nehemiah 8-10
- ☐ 266 Nehemiah 11-13
- ☐ 267 Malachi
- ☐ 268 1 Chronicles 1-2
- ☐ 269 1 Chronicles 3-5
- ☐ 270 1 Chronicles 6
- ☐ 271 1 Chronicles 7:1-8:27
- ☐ 272 1 Chronicles 8:28-9:44
- ☐ 273 John 1:1-18; Mark 1:1; Luke 1:1-4; 3:23-38; Matthew 1:1-17
- ☐ 274 Luke 1:5-80
- ☐ 275 Matthew 1:18-2:23; Luke 2
- ☐ 276 Matthew 3:1-4:11; Mark 1:2-13; Luke 3:1-23; 4:1-13; John 1:19-34
- ☐ 277 John 1:35-3:36
- ☐ 278 John 4; Matthew 4:12-17; Mark 1:14-15; Luke 4:14-30
- ☐ 279 Mark 1:16-45; Matthew 4:18-25; 8:2-4, 14-17; Luke 4:31-5:16
- ☐ 280 Matthew 9:1-17; Mark 2:1-22; Luke 5:17-39
- ☐ 281 John 5; Matthew 12:1-21; Mark 2:23-3:12; Luke 6:1-11
- ☐ 282 Matthew 5; Mark 3:13-19; Luke 6:12-36
- ☐ 283 Matthew 6-7; Luke 6:37-49
- ☐ 284 Luke 7; Matthew 8:1, 5-13; 11:2-30
- ☐ 285 Matthew 12:22-50; Mark 3:20-35; Luke 8:1-21
- ☐ 286 Mark 4:1-34; Matthew 13:1-53
- ☐ 287 Mark 4:35-5:43; Matthew 8:18, 23-34; 9:18-34; Luke 8:22-56
- ☐ 288 Mark 6:1-30; Matthew 13:54-58; 9:35-11:1; 14:1-12; Luke 9:1-10

BIBLE READING SCHEDULE

Day 289 - 365

- [ ] 289 Matthew 14:13-36; Mark 6:31-56; Luke 9:11-17; John 6:1-21
- [ ] 290 John 6:22-7:1; Matthew 15:1-20; Mark 7:1-23
- [ ] 291 Matthew 15:21-16:20; Mark 7:24-8:30; Luke 9:18-21
- [ ] 292 Matthew 16:21-17:27; Mark 8:31-9:32; Luke 9:22-45
- [ ] 293 Matthew 18; 8:19-22; Mark 9:33-50; Luke 9:46-62; John 7:2-10
- [ ] 294 John 7:11-8:59
- [ ] 295 Luke 10:1-11:36
- [ ] 296 Luke 11:37-13:21
- [ ] 297 John 9-10
- [ ] 298 Luke 13:22-15:32
- [ ] 299 Luke 16:1-17:10; John 11:1-54
- [ ] 300 Luke 17:11-18:17; Matthew 19:1-15; Mark 10:1-16
- [ ] 301 Matthew 19:16-20:28; Mark 10:17-45; Luke 18:18-34
- [ ] 302 Matthew 20:29-34; 26:6-13; Mark 10:46-52; 14:3-9; Luke 18:35-19:28; John 11:55-12:11
- [ ] 303 Matthew 21:1-22; Mark 11:1-26; Luke 19:29-48; John 12:12-50
- [ ] 304 Matthew 21:23-22:14; Mark 11:27-12:12; Luke 20:1-19
- [ ] 305 Matthew 22:15-46; Mark 12:13-37; Luke 20:20-44
- [ ] 306 Matthew 23; Mark 12:38-44; Luke 20:45-21:4
- [ ] 307 Matthew 24:1-31; Mark 13:1-27; Luke 21:5-27
- [ ] 308 Matthew 24:32-26:5, 14-16; Mark 13:28-14:2, 10-11; Luke 21:28-22:6
- [ ] 309 Matthew 26:17-29; Mark 14:12-25; Luke 22:7-38; John 13
- [ ] 310 John 14-16
- [ ] 311 John 17:1-18:1; Matthew 26:30-46; Mark 14:26-42; Luke 22:39-46
- [ ] 312 Matthew 26:47-75; Mark 14:43-72; Luke 22:47-65; John 18:2-27
- [ ] 313 Matthew 27:1-26; Mark 15:1-15; Luke 22:66-23:25; John 18:28-19:16
- [ ] 314 Matthew 27:27-56; Mark 15:16-41; Luke 23:26-49; John 19:17-30
- [ ] 315 Matthew 27:57-28:8; Mark 15:42-16:8; Luke 23:50-24:12; John 19:31-20:10
- [ ] 316 Matthew 28:9-20; Mark 16:9-20; Luke 24:13-53; John 20:11-21:25
- [ ] 317 Acts 1-2
- [ ] 318 Acts 3-5
- [ ] 319 Acts 6:1-8:1
- [ ] 320 Acts 8:2-9:43
- [ ] 321 Acts 10-11
- [ ] 322 Acts 12-13
- [ ] 323 Acts 14-15
- [ ] 324 Galatians 1-3
- [ ] 325 Galatians 4-6
- [ ] 326 James
- [ ] 327 Acts 16:1-18:11
- [ ] 328 1 Thessalonians
- [ ] 329 2 Thessalonians; Acts 18:12-19:22
- [ ] 330 1 Corinthians 1-4
- [ ] 331 1 Corinthians 5-8
- [ ] 332 1 Corinthians 9-11
- [ ] 333 1 Corinthians 12-14
- [ ] 334 1 Corinthians 15-16
- [ ] 335 Acts 19:23-20:1; 2 Corinthians 1-4
- [ ] 336 2 Corinthians 5-9
- [ ] 337 2 Corinthians 10-13
- [ ] 338 Romans 1-3
- [ ] 339 Romans 4-6
- [ ] 340 Romans 7-8
- [ ] 341 Romans 9-11
- [ ] 342 Romans 12-15
- [ ] 343 Romans 16; Acts 20:2-21:16
- [ ] 344 Acts 21:17-23:35
- [ ] 345 Acts 24-26
- [ ] 346 Acts 27-28
- [ ] 347 Ephesians 1-3
- [ ] 348 Ephesians 4-6
- [ ] 349 Colossians
- [ ] 350 Philippians
- [ ] 351 Philemon; 1 Timothy 1-3
- [ ] 352 1 Timothy 4-6; Titus
- [ ] 353 2 Timothy
- [ ] 354 1 Peter
- [ ] 355 Jude; 2 Peter
- [ ] 356 Hebrews 1:1-5:10
- [ ] 357 Hebrews 5:11-9:28
- [ ] 358 Hebrews 10-11
- [ ] 359 Hebrews 12-13; 2 John; 3 John
- [ ] 360 1 John
- [ ] 361 Revelation 1-3
- [ ] 362 Revelation 4-9
- [ ] 363 Revelation 10-14
- [ ] 364 Revelation 15-18
- [ ] 365 Revelation 19-22

Our English word "Psalms" is derived from a Greek word denoting *poems sung to the accompaniment of string instruments*. The English translation of the Hebrew title is "Book of Praises." The book of the Psalms is actually an artistic arrangement of five collections of psalms – each collection ending with a *doxology* Psalm (or, a Psalm of Praise). The superscriptions in the Hebrew text ascribe authorship of seventy-three Psalms to David and twenty-seven to various other writers. Fifty Psalms are anonymous. However, New Testament references and textual content indicate that some of the fifty were authored by David. Truly, David was "raised up on high, the anointed of the God of Jacob" not only to be king, but also as "the sweet psalmist of Israel" (2 Samuel 23:1).

The Psalms contain praise, petition, prophecy, and perspective on the past history of God's people. A number of them are songs about Creation, glorifying the Creator. Others extol the veracity and power of God's Word. The prophetic Psalms are especially intriguing. Sixteen of these are designated *Messianic* because, in whole or in part, they foretell events concerning either the first or the second coming of the Messiah (Greek for "the Christ"). The words of the risen Christ Himself in Luke 24:27 and Luke 24:44 should alert us to search for our Lord in many of the Psalms.

Several Scriptures let us know that the human authors of the Psalms, as well as other Old Testament books, were aware that they were writing under the power and in the wisdom of a Divine Author. See 2 Samuel 23:2, Psalm 102:18, and 1 Peter 1:10-12. If you'll find time to meditate on the words of the Psalms, here are some promises for you. You will be fruitful and prosperous in all that you do (1:2-3). You will sleep well (4:4, 8). Your soul will be satisfied (63:5-6). You will be glad in the Lord (104:34). You will not sin against your God (119:11) but will have respect unto His ways (119:15). You will be wiser than your enemies and understand more than your teachers and elders (119:97-100).

Please note that each year, in the Word of Life Quiet Time, we cover a different portion of the Psalms. In six years you will work your way through all 150 Psalms!

SUNDAY 1

PSALM 104:1-13

WHAT IS THE WRITER SAYING?

HOW CAN I APPLY THIS TO MY LIFE?

Psalm 104 is a sequel to Psalm 103. Both praise God for His blessings to His people. This hymn focuses on the Lord's greatness and power as manifested in His creation. The entire psalm presents us with a poet's meditative thoughts, which loosely follow the Creation story of Genesis:

vv. 1-5 compare with Genesis 1:1-5, the *first day* of Creation;

vv. 6-9 compare with Genesis 1:6-8, the *second day* of Creation;

vv. 10-18 compare with Genesis 1:9-13, the *third day* of Creation.

Since this Psalm is intended to be a meditation on God's greatness, let's consider the key words used here to express His greatness:

- "Clothed with honor and majesty" (v. 1): "Clothed" is a metaphor that pictures God's character and commitment to his people. "Honor" refers to His *authority*, *glory*, and *vigor*, i.e., His active involvement. "Majesty" is a related word that reflects upon the splendor of God's actions that display His *goodness*, *holiness*, and *worthiness* of praise.

- "Who cover Yourself with light <u>as with a garment</u>," (v. 2a). To declare God's garment is light reminds us that God is light (1 John 1:5), God is the Giver of light, both physical and spiritual (Genesis 1:3 & 2 Corinthians 4:6) and that God dwells in light (1 Timothy 6:16). To be *clothed in light* pictures God's character as holy and good. Notice that Jesus, when He was transfigured, was covered in raiment "white as the light" (Matthew 17:2).

- "Who stretchest out the Heavens like a curtain" (v. 2b). The verse's second half is intended to reinforce the first half. Now we see God stretching out His tent-curtains of the heavens which became His dwelling place; God lives in light, thus He has no darkness.

- "The waters … clouds … wind" (v. 3), "angels" (v. 4), "foundations … the deep … mountains" (vv. 5-6). The metaphor is further extended causing us to marvel upon God, the Great Builder, who used these materials to *construct* the Earth as His exclusive, inner chamber where He may personally dwell.

 LIFE STEP Think of it, we are blessed by God's personal interest in our little world in the midst of the vast heavens! So then, how might you today rejoice in the LORD as you walk in His personal *living room*?

MONDAY 1

PSALM 104:14-23

WHAT IS THE WRITER SAYING?

HOW CAN I APPLY THIS TO MY LIFE?

In this second section of the Psalm, the psalmist shifts his view from grand things of God's creation, the heavens, seas, and mountains, to the smaller and more delicate created things that are all around us. These, too, are constantly under God's bountiful care.

It is important to notice that the verbs in yesterday's passage were in the past tense as the psalmist retold what God did in Creation (vv. 5-9; Genesis 1:2-10). Today the verbs are in the present tense (vv. 10-23) because the psalmist is adding an emphasis on the Lord's continuing care of people as he watches over His wonders of creation.

The psalmist is recalling God's marvelous works from the third and fourth days of Creation: First, he considers God's watering and causing to grow the plant life that fills the dry land (Genesis 1:11-13). We are to consider things like fruits, grasses, herbs which become the food for cattle as well as wine, bread and oil which meet our daily needs (vv. 14-18). It is God who "causes" (v. 14) these things to "bring forth food" (v. 14)!

In verses 16-18, the psalmist takes us for a nature walk through the forests and hills which are filled with birds, goats, and other wild animals to remind us that these were "planted" by God and are now watched over by Him. The trees are "full of sap," the birds raise their young in their nests, and the lions find meat and lay down in their dens. All are cared for by God's bountiful providence (*timely care that shows foresight*).

Finally, we are to consider God's work of "appointing" the sun and moon and seasons to guide our days and labors (vv. 19-23, Gen. 1:14-19).

According to Psalm 19:1-4 and Romans 1:19-20, the manifest action of God through His creation speaks to every human being. The observable creation declares, "There is a God who made you and all that surrounds you. Consider His providence. Seek His face."

 LIFE STEP How about conducting a _ten-minute, walking prayer!_ To enable you to reflect on God's providence (timely care that shows foresight) in your life, go outside and walk around the local park. Look closely at God's bountiful care of even the little things in His creation. Certainly, God will take care of you by His continuing timely care!

TUESDAY 1

PSALM 104:24-35

WHAT IS THE WRITER SAYING?

HOW CAN I APPLY THIS TO MY LIFE?

PRAY India – Effective ministry to nearly 400 million youth, many of who are in crisis.

This last half of the psalm loosely continues the psalmist's thoughts upon the fifth and sixth days of the Creation story (Genesis 1:20-23; 1:24-31). The psalmist marvels at the LORD's "manifold works" (*many colored*, thus *diverse*) both in His original Creation and His ongoing care of the world.

"In wisdom" God "made them all" (v. 24): God displayed His *skill*, *insight*, and *craftsmanship* in His creation. Notice the implication of verse 35; not only is His wisdom evident to the godly (vv. 33-34), but the "sinners" and "wicked" should also see God's power. Their failure to recognize God will become, in part, the basis for their judgment by God.

"Full of Thy riches" (v. 24): The earth that God made is a well-supplied storehouse of bountiful foods, beauties and treasures!

"Wait all upon thee" (v. 27): All living things, from the small ("things creeping ") to the great ("leviathan," i.e., great sea creatures like the whales), depend upon their Maker for their food (v. 27).

"You open your hand" (v. 28): Both God's attitude and His thoroughness in providing for His creatures are being pictured here. Since most wild animals can do nothing to prepare their daily food, it is a marvel that year by year their food is prepared for them to eat. God is pictured as a farmer who takes an extra handful of grain from His storage silo so that He might enjoy spreading it upon the ground and then standing aside to watch the wild birds eat from His bounty.

"You renew the face of the earth" (v.30): The word "renew" means either a *renovating or rebuilding something, like a building, which has been damaged*, or a *restoring or revitalizing a thing that has been disrupted, like a relationship or condition*. Think of a forest fire that has swept over a mountain; before long, through scarred landscape, new green life is emerging. Soon the deer return to find fresh food. This, too, is a part of the ongoing care of God!

 LIFE STEP While it is marvelous how God, in many ways, cares for His creatures, what else does the psalmist intend for us to consider here? We must reflect on how God, in many ways, takes care of us! What are some of the "manifold" ways He continues to *care for* and *renew* you?

WEDNESDAY 1

PSALM 105:1-12

WHAT IS THE WRITER SAYING?

HOW CAN I APPLY THIS TO MY LIFE?

PRAY Belgium - Pray that the Word of God might take root deeply within the fabric of Belgian society.

Psalm 105 is a tribute to the Lord for His faithfulness in keeping His "everlasting covenant" (v. 10) to the descendants of Abraham, Isaac and Jacob. The Psalm is looking back to Genesis 12:2-3, where the Lord made a seven-fold promise to Abraham (v. 9a). In Genesis 15 the Lord put the promise in the form of a unilateral, unconditional, permanent covenant. The covenant was confirmed to Isaac (v. 9b; Gen. 26:3-4) and then to Jacob and his descendants (v. 10; Genesis 28:13-14). Though the LORD's covenant was unconditionally forever, there were requirements upon each generation if they were to enjoy the blessings of this covenant (Leviticus 26:3,14). The first five verses of Psalm 105 list twelve stipulations or conditions required in order to assure the blessings:

1. Give thanks unto the Lord. (v. 1).
2. Call upon the name of the Lord.
3. Make His deeds known to other nations.
4. Sing unto the Lord. (v. 2).
5. Talk about His wondrous works (miracles).
6. Glory in His holy name. (v. 3).
7. Seek the Lord with a rejoicing heart.
8. Seek the Lord's strength. (v. 4).
9. Seek His face continually.
10. Remember His works. (v. 5).
11. Remember His wonders.
12. Remember His words.

The Psalmist, in verses 7-12, praises the LORD for *remembering* His covenant with the nation of Israel. While the nation began as just "a few men in number" (v. 12), God had made of them a nation in the "land of Canaan" (v. 11).

LIFE STEP Review the above list. How many of the twelve stipulations apply to you in living a life that pleases our Lord? How can you "give thanks" (Ephesians 5:20)? How are you *seeking* the Lord (Hebrews 11:6)? How can you "remember" His working in your life (Ephesians 2:11-13)?

THURSDAY 1

PSALM 105:13-25

WHAT IS THE WRITER SAYING?

HOW CAN I APPLY THIS TO MY LIFE?

PRAY Korea – For seminary graduates to humbly commit themselves to less prominent, rural pastorates.

Soon after King David established his new capital at Jerusalem, he brought the ark of the covenant there with great ceremony (1 Chronicles 16:1-7). He delivered a medley of psalms to his chief musician, Asaph, for use in the celebration. The medley in 1 Chronicles 16:8-36 is a partial recording of three Psalms: 105:1-15, all of 96, and 106:1, 47-48.

Today's portion of Psalm 105 was intended to be a reminder of God's continued blessings, which had resulted in Israel becoming a strong country with a powerful king. David reminds Israel of God's personal care for her when the nation was just a single family and "strangers" (v. 12, or *foreigners*) in the land God had promised the Israelites (see Hebrews 11:9-16). Through their journeys, they were still under God's special directing of events.

Verses 16-22 continue with a summary of the life of Joseph (Genesis 37-50). The many events that took place in Joseph's life—being sold into slavery (v. 17), cast into prison (v. 18), and then promoted to the Pharaoh's personal administrator of Egypt (vv. 20-21)—were seen as steps in God's directing events to fulfill His plan.

Next we have a summary of the history of Israel in Egypt (vv. 23-25; Exodus 1). At first, the family of Israel had been welcomed guests in Egypt, which allowed for Israel's growth. Eventually, Egypt brought sorrow, slavery, and despair upon their Hebrew guests.

LIFE STEP While most Christians are not in this Hebrew family, we have all been adopted into God's eternal family! Since God has not changed His character, how can you expect His faithful care in your life today? How can you express faith in God when you are faced with hard situations, such as those endured by Joseph?

39

FRIDAY 1

PSALM 105:26-36

WHAT IS THE WRITER SAYING?

HOW CAN I APPLY THIS TO MY LIFE?

PRAY Ghana – For evangelistic outreach in the northern region, which has had less exposure to the Gospel.

Let's begin by noting that today's passage is bracketed by Israel *entering* (v. 23) and *leaving* (v. 38) Egypt. This continues the narrative of God's ongoing care and direction in history, which resulted in His transforming Israel into a great nation. Israel had entered Egypt by God's command, and with God's promise that He would "surely bring you up again" (Genesis 46:3-4).

Today's passage looks at how God raised up Moses and Aaron (v. 26) to do God's "signs…and wonders" (v. 27) in Egypt so Israel could go to the land God had promised her (v. 42).

The ordering of eight of the ten plagues presented here is interesting: We begin with the ninth (v. 28a) and an observation concerning the whole process; that is, Egypt's continuing defiance of God's command to let His people go (verse 28b in context probably means *they did not respond to His word*). Since all ten plagues can be symbolized as a *dark* time of God's wrath upon the Egyptians, the ninth plague of "darkness" is artfully presented first. Our text then backtracks through the plagues to recount the steps that lead to this observation: the first (v. 29), second (v. 30), fourth and third (v. 31), seventh (vv. 32-33), eighth (vv. 34-35), and then the grim climax of the tenth (v. 36) (see Exodus 7-12).

The purpose of this passage was to remind the reader that God had repeatedly shown His loving care for His people. These events were evidences of God's power over the events of history as He brought about His will in the world. They were to cause believers to thank God and look on Him with admiration and reverence as they realized how God brought His blessings.

LIFE STEP Think back through the various stages of God's powerful workings in your own life. What has God done that should cause you to thank and praise Him for His timely care for you?

SATURDAY 1

PSALM 105:37-45

WHAT IS THE WRITER SAYING?

HOW CAN I APPLY THIS TO MY LIFE?

PRAY Aruba – Pray that the gospel radio broadcasts going out in the Papiamento language will yield fruit.

Today's passage is a summary of the fifth stage of God's continued blessings upon Israel. In these verses the psalmist recounts seven ways that the Lord provided for the new nation of Israel:
- God provided the people, who were slaves, with "silver and gold," as prophesied to Moses (v. 37a; Exodus 3:21-22). This was their wages for the years of slavery (Exodus 12:35-36).
- He gave them the physical strength needed for their journey (v. 37b).
- He gave them the cloud by day for a covering from the heat of the desert sun (v. 39a–apparently like an umbrella!) and for assurance of His presence. He gave them fire by night as a source of light, guidance, and protection (v. 39b; Exodus 14:20-21; 40:34-38).
- He provided quail for meat (v. 40a; Exodus 16:13).
- He also provided manna for bread (v. 40b; Exodus 16:15).
- He provided water from a rock in the desert (v. 41; Exodus 17:6).
- He fulfilled His promise to bring Israel from Egypt to the land promised to Abraham (vv. 42, 44).

The reasons for God's miraculous provision of blessing include: first, that God Himself would keep the promises in His word (vv. 8, 42), and second, that God would become the ruler of this new kingdom, where they would seek Him (v. 4) and keep His commandments (v. 45).

The Psalm climaxes with the observation that Israel was filled with joy and gladness (v. 43) because of God's great faithfulness. It concludes with a call for all readers to respond with their own praise to the Lord (v. 45b) for His continuing goodness to them.

 LIFE STEP God still wants a people on earth today who will carefully study the history of His working in the world and then who will make it their purpose to live in a manner that pleases Him. How can you, by your conduct today, bring praise to the Lord?

SUNDAY 2

PSALM 106:1-15

WHAT IS THE WRITER SAYING?

HOW CAN I APPLY THIS TO MY LIFE?

PRAY Mexico – Effective ministry to youth through Christian camping, outreach activities, and social aid.

This Psalm begins with a *praise* (v. 1a), a *proclamation* (vv. 1b-3), and a *prayer* (vv. 4-5). It ends with a *prayer* (v. 47), a *proclamation* (v. 48a), and a *praise* (v. 48b). Between the Psalm's introduction (vv. 1-5) and conclusion (vv. 47-48) there is a three-part review of Israel's history:

- Israel's sinful failure to consider God *in Egypt* (vv. 7-12).
- Israel's sinful failure to consider God *in the wilderness* (vv. 13-33).
- Israel's sinful failure to consider God *in the land* (vv. 34-46).

The psalmist, as the nation's representative, is offering a prayer of confession and repentance (vv. 6-7– notice the use of "we"). "We have sinned" points to the failure of meeting God's standard of righteousness. "We have committed iniquity" is saying they did what was inherently wrong. "We have done wickedly" means their deeds were the opposite of godliness.

The psalmist points out the source of Israel's past sinful conduct: their "fathers" (v. 7), who had failed to consider God's wondrous works (seen in vv. 8-11).

When the psalmist says "our fathers *understood* not" (v. 7), he is saying:

- They failed to *look carefully* at the implications of God's wonderful deeds. Thus they did not *gain insight* into God's character.
- They failed to *wisely consider* the lessons to be learned. Thus they did not gain a right *perspective*.
- They failed to *prudently act* upon the foundational truths presented. Thus they did not *prosper* in their future endeavors.

 LIFE STEP How do you respond to God's care for you? Are you learning from your own spiritual failures and sin? What would God want you to "understand"? What has God done for you that needs your careful look? What lessons have been presented for your own wise consideration? How can you act prudently the next time around?

MONDAY 2

PSALM 106:16-31

WHAT IS THE WRITER SAYING?

HOW CAN I APPLY THIS TO MY LIFE?

Today we look at the second of three divisions in this Psalm: The people of Israel's sinful failure to consider God *in the wilderness*.

- In verses 13-14, their sin of lust refers to a *desire* or *craving* for things they had in Egypt that were no longer available, particularly tasty fruits and vegetables (see Numbers 11:4-5).
- They envied Moses and Aaron (v. 16). Numbers 16:1-3 points specifically to Korah, a Levite, who with 250 princes of Israel accused Moses and Aaron of taking the leadership they wanted for themselves.

- The people exchanged their knowledge of the true God so they could worship a grass-eating ox-god (vv. 19-22; Exodus 32:4)!
- They refused to believe God would care for them if they took the land God had promised them (vv. 24-25; Numbers 13:27-14:4).
- They even worshipped the god of the Moabites, Baalpeor (vv. 28-29; Numbers 25:1-3).

In all these ways, Israel was not believing God's word (v. 24), which led to their "murmuring" against God (*grumbling and complaining*, v. 25).

 LIFE STEP "Now all these things happened unto them for examples: and they are written for our admonition" (1 Corinthians 10:11). With these examples, we have to ask ourselves: How should I act if I believe God will care for me as I seek to live for Him? How can I faithfully follow His Word as a guide for my actions?

TUESDAY 2

PSALM 106:32-48

WHAT IS THE WRITER SAYING?

HOW CAN I APPLY THIS TO MY LIFE?

PRAY Nigeria – A renewing of the minds of converted Muslims and protection since many face persecution.

Today we look at the final part of the Psalm's history of Israel: *Israel's history in the land* (vv. 34-46). Here Israel is committing the sin of disobedience with regard to *not destroying the Canaanites* (v. 34; per Deuteronomy 7:1-2), whose land the Israelites had conquered. Instead, Israel "mingled among" the Canaanites (v. 35; Judges 3:5-6). Sadly, Israel's sin became a "snare" that drew them into greater sins. Soon Israel was learning about the Canaanites' gods (vv. 35-36), worshipping their idols (v. 36; Judges 2:11-12), and even sacrificing their children to the demons associated with these idols (vv. 37-38). They became spiritual adulterers (v. 39) who incurred the "wrath of the LORD" (v. 40).

Verses 35-45 summarize the repeating history ("many times," v. 43) of Israel during the time of the Judges; that is, a continuing cycle of rebellion, retribution, repentance, restoration, and then rest (see Judges 2:10-19).

Despite Israel's continual unfaithfulness and sin, the Psalm says the Lord saved His people again and again (v. 43), showing His heart of mercy and commitment to His own faithfulness (vv. 44-46), as well as His worthiness of our praise (v. 48).

The petition in verse 47 brings this history lesson to a climax: show Your mercy again and save us. The words "gather us from among the heathen" suggest that the Psalm is from a time after Israel had been dispersed from the Promised Land. As a result, it also looks forward to that final re-gathering when Israel will receive her Messiah, saying "Blessed is he that comes in the name of the Lord" (Luke 13:35).

 LIFE STEP Has your life been a continuing cycle of sin, suffering, and repentance, followed by God's deliverance? The psalmist wants you to remember that God will be faithful and willing to show mercy. Of what sin do you need to repent so that God might demonstrate His mercy to you?

WEDNESDAY 2

PSALM 107:1-16

WHAT IS THE WRITER SAYING?

HOW CAN I APPLY THIS TO MY LIFE?

PRAY Costa Rica – For God to keep the school doors open for the Gospel to be preached .

Psalms 105, 106, and 107 form a trilogy. Each begins with a *call to thanksgiving* and then an exhortation to make known the wondrous works of the Lord. All three look at Israel's history from different perspectives: Israel being given a land (Psalm 105), Israel being exiled from their land (Psalm 106), and re-gathering Israel from exile (Psalm 107). Although there have been limited re-gatherings, verse 3 looks to the ultimate re-gathering, when all the people of Israel will return to the land (Isaiah 43:5-6; Jeremiah 31:8-10). The introduction (vv. 1-3) calls us to give thanks to God (v. 1). The same Hebrew word for mercy (v. 1) is used in the conclusion, where we are to observe (v. 43) the loving-kindness of the Lord.

In the first stanza of the psalm (vv. 4-9), Israel is likened to a *wanderer* in a spiritual wilderness–alone, with no place of her own. The second stanza (vv. 10-16) likens Israel to a *prisoner* in a dungeon, being punished for her rebellion against God. No one is concerned about her sad state.

The same pattern is found in both: a *plight* (vv. 5, 12), a *plea* (vv. 6, 13), a *provision* (vv. 7, 14), and a *praise* (vv. 8-9, 15-16).

The words "mercy" (v. 1), "goodness," and "loving-kindness" all come from the Hebrew word *hesed*, which is widely used in the Old Testament to declare an important aspect of God's love: His persistent desire to show abundant kindness and be bountifully good to His people (see Exodus 20:6).

LIFE STEP In your trials and troubles, do you take the time to see that God has also shown you His goodness and loving-kindness? Since the Lord also desires for you to reflect His "goodness" and "loving-kindness" to others (Hosea 6:6), how can you act towards someone else in a good and kind way today?

THURSDAY 2

PSALM 107:17-32

WHAT IS THE WRITER SAYING?

HOW CAN I APPLY THIS TO MY LIFE?

PRAY Pray for the youth of your church to be godly testimonies at school and in their communities.

Psalm 107:17-18 gives the third poetic picture (already seen: the wilderness wanderer and the prisoner)—a *foolish person* who has become so sick that he cannot eat and is near death. A *fool* is one who attempts to run his life without regard for God's Word. They live on "transgression" (v. 17, *conduct against the law*) and "iniquities" (*actions that are inherently wrong*, such as cruelty and arrogance).

The fourth picture (vv. 23-27) is that of *seamen* doing regular, honest business (v. 23) when a storm suddenly comes and threatens to destroy all with its powerful winds and waves.

These mariners have learned to "see" (v. 24, *to look at so as to gain or perceive an insight*) that it is the Lord Who allows such storms—and it is He Who, in due course, will make the storm calm (v. 29). Thus, such great storms are a summons to trust God! The men in this psalm respond to the storms of life by crying out to God (v. 28), then rejoicing because they know God will guide them (v. 30).

How do you respond to unexpected and overwhelming storms in your life? Will you *see* that such events are a summons to prayer? How can you trust and wait for the Lord to guide you to peaceful havens? Have you taken the time to praise God for His goodness to you?

FRIDAY 2

PSALM 107:33-43

WHAT IS THE WRITER SAYING?

HOW CAN I APPLY THIS TO MY LIFE?

PRAY Puerto Rico - Pray for wise governance that works for the best interests of the islands' inhabitants.

The Psalm so far has illustrated God's goodness in response to various cries of distress from His people. Verse 43 says a wise person will note these situations and know that God is always working changes in the world, whether for blessing or judgment. God works in the natural world (vv. 33-38), with the contrast of barrenness and fruitfulness, as well as the inner spiritual world (vv. 39-42), with the contrast of chastisement and prosperity.

When the psalmist tells those who want to be wise to observe the workings of God, he is implying that many people never see God's work in their own lives. A righteous and wise person will understand that God has considered everything beforehand so He may provide for our needs (or if our situation calls for it, our chastisement!). "Righteous" (v. 42) refers to. As applied here, the righteous person chooses to do what is right and pleasing before God's eyes, knowing that God Himself sees and responds! Such a straight life is foundational to becoming a wise person.

LIFE STEP The psalmist has reminded us that the Lord has complete control of our lives. But the writer has also shown us that our conduct influences how He chooses to *work* in our lives. What choices are before you today, and what will be your straight and level response? Take a few minutes and look closely at how God has been working in your own inner spiritual world.

SATURDAY 2

PSALM 108:1-13

WHAT IS THE WRITER SAYING?

HOW CAN I APPLY THIS TO MY LIFE?

PRAY Bulgaria – Pray for biblical, wise and humble Christian leaders – who can train others to use the gifts they have.

Psalm 108 is a composite psalm. It begins with praises from Psalm 57:7-11, which was recording a personal plea to God from David while he fled from King Saul. His plea turns to praise when faith overcomes fear. Psalm 108:6-13 repeats Psalm 60:5-12, from when David was king. His armies had suffered an earlier defeat by Edom, and so Psalm 60 was a national plea for God's help as Israel prepared to attack Edom again. David says he is trusting in God to grant him victory.

The three stanzas of Psalm 108 are thus a refashioning of earlier material to form a liturgical psalm used in public worship. Each stanza of Psalm 108 contains a prayer: that God would be lifted up in glory above all else (vv. 1-5), that God's people would be delivered, as God promised (vv. 6-9), and that God would help those in crisis (vv. 10-13).

Each stanza also brings a truth about God into view: God's unfailing love is the highest thing (vv. 1-5); God has spoken, thus committing Himself to give help (vv. 6-9); and God's power alone is sufficient to meet the crisis (vv. 10-13). The three stanzas teach us how to praise, pray, and plan. Our hearts must be fixed, like an arrow focused on a target, on praise (vv. 1-5); our prayers must be declarations of faith in the promises of God (vv. 6-9); and our plans depend on God for success, since only through Him can we act valiantly—that is, with His strength to be righteous in behavior, strong in influence, and known by virtue (vv. 10-13).

LIFE STEP Like the Israelites, who refashioned these verses into a psalm of reflection, we should also reflect upon these verses! How has God shown his unfailing love to you? What promises has He made that apply to a current trouble in your life? How can you, with God's help, plan to act valiantly in response to your troubling situations?

SUNDAY 3

PSALM 114:1-8

WHAT IS THE WRITER SAYING?

HOW CAN I APPLY THIS TO MY LIFE?

PRAY Slovakia – For a clear expounding of God's Word that results in obedience to His authority.

This Psalm has the character of a *playful* nursery rhyme, with familiar poetic devices including rhythmic parallelism, imagination, and surprise. It highlights Israel's early history, touching on the crossing of the Red Sea (v. 3a; Exodus 14), the crossing of the Jordan River (v. 3; Joshua 3), the quaking of Mount Sinai (v. 4; Exodus 19:18), and God's provision of water in the wilderness (v. 8; Exodus 17:1-7; Numbers 20:11).

Using personification (giving the qualities of people to objects), the psalmist lightheartedly asks the Red Sea, the Jordan River, and Mount Sinai why they responded to the Lord as they did, that is, *fleeing away* in fear (v. 5a), *turning around* as if to get out of the Lord's way (v. 5b), and *skipping* as if full of joy due to the Lord's presence (v. 6). These playful images are intended to have us see that all creation recognizes the Creator's presence and willingly obeys Him. These parts of creation were all amazed and awestruck in the presence of the One who could set aside the natural laws that governed them. As a result, we are to consider how we ourselves respond to the Lord's presence in our lives!

On a more serious note, the psalmist closes with instructions before getting answers from these parts of nature. He tells the earth to tremble in His presence since He has the power to transform the earth's rocks into lakes and springs of pure, refreshing water so He can accommodate the needs of His people.

LIFE STEP What mighty obstacles or barriers stand before you? What sea or mountain of troubles is keeping you from doing what God wants you to do? Have you forgotten that such things are controlled by God? If all creation recognizes the Lord's presence and obeys Him, how can you find faith and courage in God's almighty strength to see you through your current difficulties?

MONDAY 3

PSALM 115:1-18

WHAT IS THE WRITER SAYING?

HOW CAN I APPLY THIS TO MY LIFE?

PRAY Germany – For God to remove the blindness of humanism and hostility toward Christianity.

The first verse of this worship Psalm is addressed to the Lord in the hearing of an assembled audience of Jewish worshippers. They are not gathered to glorify themselves, but to give glory to the true God. After denouncing the gods of the heathen people around them (vv. 2-8), the worship leader exhorts his listeners to trust the Lord (vv. 9-11), receive His blessings (vv. 12-16), and in return, praise Him (vv. 17-18).

In verse 2, the worship leader poses a question asked by the heathen nations, "Where is their God?" – a question that appears six times in the Old Testament. To the heathen, Israel seemed to worship no one (consider the empty space between the two winged cherubim atop the mercy seat of the ark of the covenant). The audience confidently responds, "Our God is in Heaven" (v. 3)! This God, Who is above all that He created, does whatever

He pleases because He is above and much greater than the men He created. In contrast, the idols of the heathen can do nothing (vv. 5-7). Anything made (v. 4) is inferior to its maker, and idols are therefore inferior to the men who made them.

The three-fold exhortation to all who fear the Lord—"trust in the Lord" (vv. 9-11)— is fortified by a three-fold assurance that He is trustworthy as "their help and their shield" (vv. 9-11). Just because God cannot be seen does not mean He is not active in bringing blessings into the lives of those who fear Him. The God of Heaven is "mindful" of His people (v. 12), which is the idea of *remembering*. This indicates that God continues to bring His people into His thoughts in order to pay attention to their needs and bring them help, protection, and preservation.

LIFE STEP What a wonderful thought, that God always keeps us in mind! Since He is paying attention to your needs, how about taking a few minutes to list several areas of your life that need God's "help" and shielding? Trust Him to do something!

PSALM 116:1-14

WHAT IS THE WRITER SAYING?

HOW CAN I APPLY THIS TO MY LIFE?

The use of the first person singular shows that this Psalm is a personal testimony. While this Psalm is anonymous, it has a striking resemblance to the experience of King Hezekiah (Isaiah 38), whose life was threatened by sickness.

The writer starts by saying, "I love the Lord," a unique expression. Such a love is foundational for a believer's walk (Deuteronomy 6:5; Mark 12:30). This love is credited to God, Who delivered the psalmist as an answer to his prayers (v. 4) when he was hunted by death.

This Psalm is also intended to be a means of instructing God's "people" (v. 18), so they would also consider their own love for the Lord.

- In verse 5, the word used for "gracious" is one only applied to God throughout the Old Testament. He is the One Who is inclined to show acts of favor to His people, who have no real claim for such gracious treatment.

- In verses 7-12, God also gives bountiful (v. 7) benefits to individuals! This is to say, God rewards faithfulness by dealing out acts of goodness. If King Hezekiah is writing, then he is referring to the fifteen years added to his life (Isaiah 38:5). The psalmist then says he will give self-dedication (v. 13a), worship (v. 13b), and payment of vows (vv. 14, 18) back to God.

- In verse 8, God recovers (or rescues) us from our many troubles, whether it is death, tears, or falling (*to be tripped by wickedness so as to bring about a downfall*). "Delivered" also carries a subsequent idea of *equipping*, like making strong for battle.

LIFE STEP Why do you "love the Lord?" Because He is good, He protects, deals kindly, rescues, and even equips? Is there something in your life filling you with "tears" or threatening to cause you to fall into sin? How can you ask God for deliverance today?

WEDNESDAY 3

PSALM 116:15 - 117:2

WHAT IS THE WRITER SAYING?

HOW CAN I APPLY THIS TO MY LIFE?

PRAY For lives to be transformed as the Word of God is proclaimed around the world.

Verse 15 is of great comfort to those facing death because it says God does not take lightly the death of His own. "Precious" can refer to valuable jewels and is used here to say that a godly person is held by God as a great treasure. "In the sight of the LORD" refers to providential oversight of the Lord (Psalm 33:18) and promises that a godly person will not die except under circumstances that God oversees, and at a time and manner that will best accomplish His purposes. Death does not come as a surprise to God, for He has made full preparations beforehand for the transition of his saints ("holy ones") to their "life after death" (Psalm 49:15; John 14:2-3; Revelation 14:13).

Psalm 117 is the shortest chapter of the Bible. It is also the Bible's middle chapter, with 594 chapters preceding it and 594 following it.

This little gem has a large call to praise. It is a simple reminder of four great truths:
- Since the earliest time God has made known to the Jews that He intended to make His mercy and truth available to "all ye nations" through Abraham (Genesis 22:18). Romans 15:11 quotes from this Psalm as part of Paul's proof that God's purpose all along has been for the Gentiles, along with the Jews, to partake in God's mercy through the death of Jesus Christ.
- Two times "all people" are commanded to praise God.
- With a look back through history, God's unfailing love (v. 2a, "merciful kindness") for His people has always been displayed.
- With a look forward, God's "truth" (v. 2b) will continue to endure forever! We can place our faith in God's total dependability.

LIFE STEP Have you become one of God's holy ones through faith in the finished work of Christ? If so, how can you express your complete faith in His total dependability to care for you right now?

THURSDAY 3

PSALM 118:1-14

WHAT IS THE WRITER SAYING?

HOW CAN I APPLY THIS TO MY LIFE?

PRAY Kyrgyzstan - Pray the people of Kyrgyzstan continue to have the chance to hear of the Lord Jesus Christ.

Psalm 118 completes a section of hymns (Psalms 113-118) that are recited during the Jewish Passover, or Seder Meal (Matthew 26:30). Originally this Psalm was arranged to be sung in celebration of the laying of the foundation of the rebuilt temple (Ezra 3:1-4, 11).

Subsequently, it was used by worshippers as a processional when ascending Mt. Zion for annual feasts at the temple. Note that today's portion of Psalm 118 concerns the start (vv. 1-4) of the processional and then its journey (vv. 5-18). Tomorrow's passage considers its arrival at the temple (vv. 19-29).

The Psalm calls three times for an expression of thanks for God's enduring mercy. The basis for these calls is two great themes:

- All Israel declares, as if the people were one, its personal experience of God's help (v. 7) in moving Israel from a narrow, confined place (the literal meaning of "distress" in verse 5 is *personal anguish from being 'bound up' on a constricting path*) to a "large place."

- Israel had known the fear of being compassed about by enemies and the disappointment of its people failing to measure up to the confidences placed in them. It had learned that trusting the Lord was the better way (vv. 8-14).

Verse 14 is from the song of Moses (Exodus 15:2), which was Israel's victory song to the Lord, Who saved them from Pharaoh's army at a narrow, confined place next to the Red Sea. It will be Israel's victory song in the coming messianic kingdom (Isaiah 12:2) and the victory song for the tribulation saints, and finally, all nations (Revelation 15:3-4).

LIFE STEP
What great work of God in your life should be the subject of your victory song? How can you express thanks for His enduring mercy and help in your life? How can God be your strength as you face the next distressing situation that seems to be binding up your life?

FRIDAY 3

PSALM 118:15-29

WHAT IS THE WRITER SAYING?

HOW CAN I APPLY THIS TO MY LIFE?

PRAY Ukraine – Christian camps. For God to give youth a passion to live for Him and reach their land.

Martin Luther said Psalm 118 was to him the dearest of all Scripture passages. Verse 22 is quoted six times in the New Testament, as is the first half of verse 26, which looks forward to the first (Matthew 21:9) and second comings (Matthew 23:39) of Christ.

As discussed yesterday, this Psalm was sung as Jews made their way up to the temple. In today's passage we see these worshippers arriving at the temple's gates, here called the "gates of righteousness" (v. 19) and "gate of the LORD" (v. 20). These titles speak of the entrance's purpose of bringing sinful worshippers into a "righteous" (v. 20b) relationship with their holy God. The worshippers understood that the only *gate* to salvation from death was to be found here (vv. 14-17, 21b). Notice that they entered the *gate* with their sacrifice for the altar (v. 27), which is an Old Testament picture of the coming Lamb of God, Jesus Christ, who would become the Redeemer as He became God's perfect sacrifice for sin.

The word "stone" (v. 22) is used metaphorically throughout Scripture for Christ (Acts 4:11). To the church, Christ is the "chief cornerstone" (see Ephesians 2:19-22 and 1 Peter 2:4-6). Christ was also a "stumbling stone" as the Jewish people rejected Him as the Messiah. Daniel prophesied of a "smiting stone" that would destroy the Gentile world powers at the end of this age (Daniel 2:34).

 LIFE STEP The concern that these Jewish worshippers had for their "righteous" standing before God reminds us that we, too, must be concerned about our standing before God today. Have you asked Jesus to become your sacrifice for sin? This is your only gate to God's salvation from sin and death! Do you keep the gate between you and your Lord open by regularly confessing your sin (1 John 1:9), so that Jesus will wash you of all unrighteousness?

SATURDAY 3

PSALM 119:1-8

WHAT IS THE WRITER SAYING?

HOW CAN I APPLY THIS TO MY LIFE?

PRAY Denmark - Pray for wisdom for all who seek to transform Danish churches and make them relevant to secular Danes.

This Psalm is the longest chapter in the Bible (176 verses) and the most elaborate alphabetical acrostic psalm. It is arranged in twenty two sections of eight verses. The Psalm is largely a collection of simple but profound meditations on the Word of God.

It is important to note that the first three verses are addressed to the readers, while all the remaining verses (173!) are addressed to God. And so in the first three verses we find the key to understanding this Psalm. It begins by explaining that through "keeping" (vv. 2, 4, 5, 8; *diligently guarding*) God's word and "walking" (vv. 1, 3; *a consistent doing of a lifestyle*) according to God's teaching, we can have a "blessed" life (vv. 1-2). This word "blessed" means *happy because he is guided, he is able to make progress, or he is able to go straight.*

Let's consider the intentions of this "blessed" person:

- He wants to walk in the "way" that is undefiled, that is, a life that is not blemished by sin but complete in truth and uprightness (v. 1).

- He wants to "seek God with his whole heart" (v. 2).
- He wants to "do no iniquity " but rather "walk in God's ways" (v. 3).
- He "diligently" works at keeping God's "precepts" (i.e., *instruction in how God wants things ordered*) (v. 4).

Now notice that the author recognized that he fails to live up to his own standards of conduct. Thus his need to study God's word:

- "*O* that my ways" were steadfast (v. 5) – The author grieves over his failure to conduct his "ways" in an upright, fixed manner.
- "*Then* I shall not be ashamed" (v. 6) – The author realizes his continuing inability to "keep" God's law and so he looks to the future when he has learned how to apply God's commandments.
- "... *when* I have learned Your righteous judgments" (v. 7) – The author knows that his life cannot truly give praise to God until God has instructed him in the Lord's *rules of life.*

 LIFE STEP The key word in this first section of Psalm 119 is "keep" (vv. 2, 4, 5, 8). It means *to continually observe.* Look back at these verses and see what we are called to "keep" as we follow God.

SUNDAY 4

PSALM 119:9-16

WHAT IS THE WRITER SAYING?

HOW CAN I APPLY THIS TO MY LIFE?

PRAY Portugal – To see lasting changes in the hearts and lives of those attending Christian camps.

This second stanza presents us with the Psalm's first question, *how can a young man stay pure in his path*? The psalmist recounts to the Lord four ways in which he had sought to conduct his life *in the past* (that is, since his own days as a young man):

- He had sought the Lord with his whole heart. He had not only obeyed God's word but sought abiding fellowship with God (v. 10a).
- He had sought to memorize, meditate upon, and study God's Word (v. 11, in obedience to the command in verse 4).
- He had sought to publicly declare God's message (v. 13).
- He had chosen God's ways to be more important than riches (v. 14).

Yet the psalmist also humbly acknowledges that he had fallen short of his goal of a pure life conducted *day by day in the present*!

- As an older man, he recognized that he still needed God's continuing enablement to keep him from wandering into sin (v. 10b).

- As an older man who had long memorized, meditated upon, and studied God's Word, he recognized that he by himself could not fully understand or apply God's message. He needed God Himself to "*teach*" him God's ways! Here, "*teaching*" indicates a style of teaching where the teacher trains his student by repeated *prodding* of the student in the correct response or direction.

Lastly, the psalmist tells of his *intended conduct in the future*:

- He will *meditate* on God's Word (*to think upon, to consider how to apply*), thereby respecting to the ways of the Lord (v. 15).
- He will remember God's words by finding *delight* in heeding God's Word (v. 16). His greatest joy would be the further understanding of God's Word and the accompanying application of it to his life!

LIFE STEP The psalmist has given us a pattern for a growing walk with our Lord. By studying, memorizing, and meditating upon God's Word, we can have God's help in enabling us not to wander into sin and to delight in keeping the Lord's ways! How can God's Word keep you from sin?

MONDAY 4

PSALM 119:17-24

WHAT IS THE WRITER SAYING?

HOW CAN I APPLY THIS TO MY LIFE?

PRAY Taiwan – For believers to accept a more active and committed role in their local church bodies.

In each of the eight verses of this section, the psalmist employs one of the eight designations for God's Word. But he doesn't use all eight of the Hebrew nouns. "Ways" and "precepts" are omitted; "commandments" and "testimonies" are used twice.

By saying "deal bountifully" (v. 17), the psalmist is asking that he be classified among the blessed ones of verse 2. In verse 18, the psalmist is saying that except for the spiritual sight and insight given by the Lord, it is not possible for earth-dwellers to see the wondrous truths in God's Word (John 3:2; 1 Corinthians 2:9-12). Like Abraham, we must consider ourselves "strangers and pilgrims on the earth" if we are to see and embrace His promises and deep truths (Hebrews 11:13). We must at all times have a longing for His Word that can only be satisfied by a Spirit-supplied knowledge of His wonders.

Since God has rebuked people who err from His commandments (v. 21) and condemned them, the psalmist asks to be separated from them. Even though the leaders of society have verbally abused him, he continues to keep God's testimonies.

In verses 15-16 the psalmist announced his intent to meditate and delight in God's Word. In verses 23-24, meditation and delight have become the pattern for his life and are his counselors.

LIFE STEP As I hide God's Word in my heart (v. 11), He will open my eyes, that I may behold wondrous things (v. 18). As I meditate and take delight, I will become unconcerned about those who hold me in contempt and speak against me. They are blind leaders of the blind (Matthew 15:14), and they will all fall into the ditch of eternal damnation.

TUESDAY 4

PSALM 119:25-32

WHAT IS THE WRITER SAYING?

HOW CAN I APPLY THIS TO MY LIFE?

PRAY Albania - Pray for the continual growth and training of leadership in the young Albanian church.

In the first half of this section, the psalmist sends four petitions to the Lord: "Quicken (enliven) thou me," "teach me," "make me to understand," and "strengthen thou me." By adding the information in these four verses to that given in verses 22-23, we deduce the following: after suffering reproach and contempt from people in high office, he experienced severe bodily affliction. (He speaks more of his affliction later in the Psalm.) He has spoken to the Lord about his deep despair, and he is confident God heard his plea. Although he has physical and emotional relapses (vv. 25, 28), he is growing spiritually by calling upon his Lord and trusting in His Word.

In verse 29, the psalmist asks to be separated from those who have chosen the path of lies, and to receive grace from God to live by His law. He has chosen the way of truth and follows that path by constantly keeping the Lord's judgments (ordinances) in his mind. During his time of trial, the psalmist has tenaciously clung to the Lord's testimonies and asks God for vindication because of this (v. 31). Verse 32 lets us know that he is on the road to victory and that he has regained his confidence.

LIFE STEP What are your thoughts about what it means to have an enlarged heart? The psalmist believes that such a heart can only come from God. What does verse 32 say one will do when the Lord enlarges His heart?

WEDNESDAY 4

PSALM 119:33-40

WHAT IS THE WRITER SAYING?

HOW CAN I APPLY THIS TO MY LIFE?

PRAY Kenya – Continued growth for Kenya, which has the highest percentage of believers in all of Africa.

In these eight verses, the psalmist requests nine petitions of the Lord (two in verse 37). We have already heard the psalmist utter the plea "Teach me, O LORD" twice before (vv. 12, 26). This time he pledges to observe what he is taught for the rest of his life. In the previous section, he followed his plea to be taught with a request for understanding, so he would be effective in proclaiming the wondrous works of the Lord to others. Here he asks for understanding of the teaching so he can observe the law of God wholeheartedly. It is one thing to receive instructions but another to comprehend the teaching sufficiently to be able to use it. That comprehension comes through meditation (vv. 15, 23).

The requests in verses 33-34 have to do with the activity of the mind. Verse 35 is a plea that the feet walk in the right pathway. The petition of verse 36 speaks of the heart—the innermost desires. The first petition of verse 37 seeks direction for the use of the eyes. The second asks for fervor of spirit in life's journey.

The psalmist wants the Word so established in his being that he will fear God rather than seek the approval of man. Since the judgments and precepts of the Lord are good, the psalmist longs for the life-giving righteousness they produce in one's life.

 Notice the order in which the psalmist presents his petitions. That which enters our minds occupies our thinking, which in turn determines our walk. Our hearts' desires determine what we will covet. What we see with our eyes attracts us to the vanities of this world. The establishment of the Word produces the righteousness that may be offensive to man but is a delight to God (v. 11).

THURSDAY 4

PSALM 119:41-48

WHAT IS THE WRITER SAYING?

HOW CAN I APPLY THIS TO MY LIFE?

PRAY Israel - Pray for the peace of Jerusalem in obedience to Psalm 122:6

In each of the forty verses already considered in Psalm 119 we have seen at least one of the eight synonyms used to designate the Word. Except for three or four verses later in the psalm, that pattern continues. In this section, verses 43 and 48 each have two, and the others one, for a total of ten.

Notice how the psalmist's experience (vv. 41-42) parallels our own salvation. It is from the Lord's mercy (Titus 3:5), by God's Word (1 Peter 1:23), and through faith in the Word (Ephesians 2:8) that we are saved. The psalmist trusts in the Word (v. 42), hopes in the Word (v. 43), and seeks the Word (v. 45) because he loves the Word (v. 47). He resolves to observe the Word always (v. 44). As a result, he will walk at liberty, that is, his path will be free from the stumbling stones of a sinful life. He will also have the boldness to proclaim God's Word and meditate in it.

Six times in this Psalm the writer speaks of his delight in God's Word. He is aware that the Word saved him. He is very grateful for the Word. He knows that he grows by the Word and needs to feed on it each day. He reveres the Word because of Whose Word it is. He is cognizant of the instruction and admonition he receives from the Word. He senses the comfort the Word brings into his life. He trusts and hopes in the promises of the Word.

Here is the question for us: Do we delight in the Word? One definition of "delight" is *enraptured attention.*

LIFE STEP The Bible instructs us to hear the Word, read the Word, study the Word, memorize the Word, and meditate upon the Word. How pleased our Lord would be if we did all of this in an aura of enraptured attention!

FRIDAY 4

PSALM 119:49-56

WHAT IS THE WRITER SAYING?

HOW CAN I APPLY THIS TO MY LIFE?

PRAY For others as they go on short term mission trips to share the gospel.

The glad message of this section is that, throughout God's Word, there is comfort in times of affliction. Romans 15:4 echoes this point: "For whatsoever things were written aforetime were written for our learning, that we through patience and comfort of the scriptures might have hope." Later, the psalmist says this again: "Thou hast caused me to hope" (v. 49) and "I have hoped in thy word" (v. 74). Hope is appropriated by trusting the promises of God in His Word (Titus 1:2: "In hope of eternal life, which God, that cannot lie, promised..."). Hope in the Bible is not the type of hope that we talk about in everyday conversation: "My lawn is dying—I hope it rains today" or "I hope to pass this exam." Those are wishes that may or may not come to pass, but scriptural hope is the present appropriation of a future, joyous certainty, such as Hebrews 6:19: "Which hope we have as an anchor of the soul, both *sure* and *steadfast*... ."

Think of a seven-year-old girl ten days before Christmas. She sees her name on a package from her grandmother. She doesn't wait until Christmas to become elated—she exults every day in anticipation. Hope is about the future, but it is expressed in the present. Right now, we are "looking for that blessed hope, and the glorious appearing of the great God and our Saviour, Jesus Christ" (Titus 2:13)—"wherefore comfort one another with these words" (1 Thessalonians 4:18). The apostle Paul called all of his afflictions "light" and "for a moment" (2 Corinthians 4:17). He was taking comfort in the trustworthiness of God's promises. His way of finding this hope is seen in Romans 15:13: "Now the God of hope fill you with all joy and peace in believing, that ye may abound in hope."

 LIFE STEP Hope is not for enjoyment in Heaven, for there all hope will have become reality. There certainly is no hope in Hell. Hope is for now. If you are not, in this life, getting your share of hope by rejoicing in the certainty of God's promises, you are missing this great provision from God!

SATURDAY 4

PSALM 119:65-72

WHAT IS THE WRITER SAYING?

HOW CAN I APPLY THIS TO MY LIFE?

PRAY Benin - Pray for more trained pastors to meet the spiritual needs of the growing Christian population in this extremely poor country.

This section advances two themes that we have been following in Psalm 119 – the desire of the psalmist to be taught, and of his affliction. The word "judgment" in verse 66 means *discernment*. It is not related to the word *judgments*, which was used eighteen times in Psalm 119 as one of the eight designations for God's Word. In vv. 25-40, the psalmist asked to be taught so he could understand God's ways. This would enable him to "talk of His wondrous works" and "go in the path of His commandments." His thirst for teaching was from a desire to use knowledge with discernment.

Affliction was what led the psalmist to his desire for learning (v. 71); therefore, it was good for him to be afflicted. What he received because of affliction was better "than thousands of gold and silver" (v. 72). The Bible has other examples of people who have benefited from affliction:

Because Joseph was afflicted, he preserved a posterity for a nation (Genesis 45:7; Acts 7:10).
Because Hannah was afflicted, she was exalted in the Lord and gave birth to Samuel, who became judge and prophet (1 Samuel 1).
Because Job was afflicted, the Lord gave him "twice as much as he had before" (Job 42:10).
Because Paul was afflicted, his "strength was made perfect in weakness" (2 Corinthians 12:7-10).
Because our Lord Jesus Christ was afflicted (Isaiah 53:4-7), we have life "purchased with his own blood" (Acts 20:28).

 LIFE STEP It is a great day when we truly learn that every affliction "worketh for us a far more exceeding and eternal weight of glory" (2 Corinthians 4:17). We will then say with the psalmist, "It is good for me that I have been afflicted." We will say with Paul, "I take pleasure in infirmities, in reproaches, in necessities, in persecutions, in distresses for Christ's sake" (2 Corinthians 12:10).

SUNDAY 5

PSALM 119:81-88

WHAT IS THE WRITER SAYING?

HOW CAN I APPLY THIS TO MY LIFE?

PRAY Hungary – Effective outreach and godly teachers in public schools where Christianity is welcome.

"My soul faints." "My eyes fail." "They persecute me." "Help me!" The words are those of one who is deeply depressed by sore oppression. The psalmist appears to have reached a low point. "When will you comfort me?" He's saying, "I may not have many days left to serve You, so when will You execute judgment on my persecutors?" His faith is wavering because he sees no action from God against his oppressors.

Actually, the psalmist is on the way up. Although his reaction to oppression is pulling him down, he will be lifted up by his course of action: His hope is founded on the Word. He is seeking comfort from "the Father of mercies, and the God of all comfort; Who comforteth us in all our tribulation" (2 Corinthians 1:3-4). He is calling to memory what he has read in God's Word. He is proclaiming God's faithfulness and His loving-kindness while still observing His precepts and testimonies.

The psalmist is in greater need of having his faith stabilized than he is of seeing judgment upon his persecutors. The Word in which he delights and upon which he meditates (vv. 77-78) will produce that faith for him (Romans 10:17). That faith will then permit him to see what is not visible. Then he will find rest for his soul (Psalm 37:7; Matthew 11:29). His prayers will be answered to his complete satisfaction, although not necessarily according to his thinking.

 LIFE STEP It is a work of the indwelling Holy Spirit to bring us to our knees when we have a pressing need. However, what the loving Father chooses to provide us with may not be what we asked for. There may be a more urgent need that we did not comprehend. He will supply according to that need.

MONDAY 5

PSALM 119:97-104
WHAT IS THE WRITER SAYING?

HOW CAN I APPLY THIS TO MY LIFE?

PRAY Australia – For churches to have strong, sound leadership that produces committed believers.

This is the first stanza in which the psalmist asks nothing of God—there are no petitions. Also, he begins emphasizing the word *love* in describing his dedication to God's Word. Look again at Deuteronomy 10:12. Before this, the psalmist has been centering on fearing God in order to walk in His ways. The Word of God next teaches him to love God and His Word in order "to serve the LORD thy God with all thy heart and with all thy soul."

Love of the Word is evidenced by continually meditating on it. Through meditation, the psalmist entered into the benefits of the Word as well as the obligations. He became more focused on the promises in the Word than on the afflictions by his enemies, because meditation made him wiser than his enemies (v. 98).

These verses focus on the importance of each individual personally seeking knowledge through God's Word. Teachers of the Word are helpful, but one gains insight and understanding through meditation (v. 99). Experience brings a degree of understanding and wisdom, although it can sometimes be a hard teacher. Yet getting understanding and wisdom is sweet like honey when there is a love relationship with the Word. Jeremiah 15:16 says, "Thy words were found, and I did eat them, and thy Word was unto me the joy and rejoicing of mine heart." Psalm 19:10-11 adds, "More to be desired are they than gold, yea, than much fine gold: sweeter also than honey and the honeycomb. Moreover by them is thy servant warned: and in keeping of them there is great reward."

LIFE STEP Is there a way to acquire spiritual understanding other than by meditation on God's Word? Can a cow chew its cud without first eating something? Is it possible to meditate without first hiding the Word in the heart?

TUESDAY 5

PSALM 119:113-120

WHAT IS THE WRITER SAYING?

HOW CAN I APPLY THIS TO MY LIFE?

PRAY Nicaragua – For a mighty work of salvation to occur among this country's military forces.

"I hate." "I love." "I hope." "I am afraid." In this section, the psalmist lets us know that he is a person of emotions. Twice in the eight verses he describes his emotion towards God's Word as one of love. Does God have emotions? Of course. He loves (John 3:16), and love is an element of His essence (1 John 4:8). He is love and is able to bestow His ability to love (1 John 4:19). "The God of love" is one of His names (2 Corinthians 13:11).

The psalmist expresses his hatred for every false way (v. 104), for wrong thinking (v. 113), and for lying (v. 163). Does God hate? The Bible tells of objects and behaviors that God hates (seven are listed in Proverbs 6:16-19), but never in Scriptures is He seen as the God of hate. Another name for God is "the God of hope" (Romans 15:13). He does not need *to* hope but rather *is* hope, since hope is the *present* appropriation of a *future* joyous certainty (Hebrews 6:18-20). It is a gift from God for us "to lay hold upon" in this life while looking forward to a time with Him. There is no need for hope in Heaven—all that we hope for will be realized.

The psalmist also has the emotion of fear. When we are properly in awe of God and revere His Word, we don't need to fear anything else. When considering the emotion of fear, we should keep in mind the promise of 1 John 4:18. There is a fear that complements love in order to keep us in a right relationship with God, and there is a fear that torments.

LIFE STEP We are creatures of emotion. Only the Holy Spirit, through the Word of God, can properly channel those emotions. The psalmist expresses emotions such as "delight" and "love" towards God's Word. We need to frequently take inventory of our emotions toward God and His Word and make sure we have the correct attitude.

65

WEDNESDAY 5

PSALM 119:121-128

WHAT IS THE WRITER SAYING?

HOW CAN I APPLY THIS TO MY LIFE?

PRAY Sweden - Pray for a national spiritual awakening and for the re-evangelization of Sweden.

Some suggest that "judgment" in verses 84 and 121, as well as "faithfulness" in verse 90, does not designate the Word of God. Clearly, verses 122 and 132 contain no synonym for the Word. Otherwise, every verse in Psalm 119 names God's Word in some form.

A major portion of the psalm consists of petitions asking for the Lord's ministry on behalf of the psalmist. There are six such petitions in verses 121-125. Verse 122, however, is the only place in the psalm where he asks the Lord to be "surety" for him. A "surety" is *one who assumes the obligation of someone else's failure* (Proverbs 6:1). At the cross, Jesus did this by making full payment to God for our obligation to Him (the penalty of our sin). As our surety, He paid for what we owed but couldn't pay. If my true heart's desire is to please God, He will receive my imperfect service because Jesus Christ, my Mediator, makes up for my lack each day (Hebrews 7:22, 8:6).

The psalmist often submits reasons to God for why his petitions should be answered. He does this three times in verses 121-125. The Lord should grant his petitions because of his righteousness, because of God's mercy, and because, as a servant, he is entitled to be taught knowledge with understanding.

The psalmist knows the Lord will certainly deal with those who live as though there is no word from God. From observation, he believes the time has come for God to act.

LIFE STEP From our present-day vantage point, we can conclude with the psalmist that world society has "made void Thy law," and it is time for God to act. Until He does, we should follow the example of the psalmist—loving God's commandments more than riches and esteeming His precepts while hating every false way.

THURSDAY 5

PSALM 119:137-144

WHAT IS THE WRITER SAYING?

HOW CAN I APPLY THIS TO MY LIFE?

PRAY New Zealand – Bold and vibrant witness of those ministering in secondary schools and universities.

The Hebrew word for *righteous* begins with the letter TSADHE, therefore, it is not surprising that this section begins with "righteous" and that the theme of the section is God's righteousness. The words "righteous," "upright," and "righteousness" appear six times in the eight verses.

Our God is a righteous God; therefore, His Word is righteous (v. 137). Our God is a faithful God; therefore, His Word is faithful (v. 138). Our God is a pure God; therefore, His Word is pure (v. 140). Our God is a God of truth; therefore, His Word is truth (v. 142). Our God is an eternal God; therefore, His Word is eternal (vv. 142-144). These are all sufficient causes for the psalmist to be consumed with zeal and love for the Word. The trouble and anguish that have taken hold of him are overridden by his delight in the Word and its promises.

Throughout the entire Psalm, the psalmist continues to cry out for more learning, more knowledge, and more understanding. "Give me understanding that I may learn" (v. 73). "Give me understanding that I may know" (v. 125). "Give me understanding and I shall live" (v. 144). Instruction, knowledge, and understanding are pre-requisites for the psalmist if he is to live. Since he knows the Word is the source of understanding (v. 130), his zeal and love for the Word become more intense.

LIFE STEP As you read verse after verse about the psalmist's zeal and love for the Word, and his delight in it, something should be happening inside of you. Measure your zeal, love, and delight against his. What does God's Word mean to you?

FRIDAY 5

PSALM 119:153-160

WHAT IS THE WRITER SAYING?

HOW CAN I APPLY THIS TO MY LIFE?

PRAY Cuba – For a greater influx of resource materials and more educational opportunities for pastors.

There is a Hebrew word that is used three times in this section and sixteen times altogether in Psalm 119. Nine of those times the psalmist uses the word in petitioning the Lord. The King James Version renders the petition "quicken me." Some other English language Bibles translate it "revive me." Just what is the psalmist asking the Lord to do for him when he urgently cries, "Quicken me?" In verses 154 and 156, he adds "according to Thy Word" (*judgments*). He expects to receive what he asks for because he is beseeching a God Who is merciful and kind to those who love His precepts. When the psalmist makes the same plea in verses 37 and 40, the context implies that he is asking for spiritual renewal and spiritual fervor. In verses 88 and 107 he seems to have his physical well-being in mind. His thought appears to be, "My enemies are after me—keep me alive so that I can praise You." Considering the use of the same word in verses 50 and 93, we can conclude that the psalmist is primarily concerned about his spiritual connection with the Lord. His heart's desire is for God to use His Word to do whatever is necessary to infuse and maintain vibrancy in his relationship with them.

The psalmist grieves for those who transgress because they don't observe the Word, while instead he is sustained by placing his confidence in that which is both true and everlasting.

LIFE STEP Nothing in this world is everlasting except for the Word of God and the souls of human beings. In what should we invest our time and other resources, then? Human society places much emphasis upon preparation for the future. For what future should we be preparing?

SATURDAY 5

PSALM 119:169-176

WHAT IS THE WRITER SAYING?

HOW CAN I APPLY THIS TO MY LIFE?

PRAY Romania – For dynamic youth ministries that will inspire and teach teens how to live for Christ.

At first reading, this section appears to be a step backward from the lofty spiritual attainments of the previous verses. Actually, the psalmist is summarizing the spiritual journey he has taken. He has come from saying "my soul cleaveth unto the dust" (v. 25), "my soul melteth for heaviness" (v. 28), and "I went astray" (v. 67), to declaring "I rejoice at Thy word" (v. 162), "seven times a day do I praise Thee" (v. 164), "great peace have they which love thy law" (v. 165), and "I love them (Thy testimonies) exceedingly" (v. 167). In Psalm 119, the psalmist has reflected on the ups and downs of his spiritual growth, even if not in chronological order.

Here in the final section, he relates those reflections to his desires for a continued spiritual relationship with the Lord through His Word. The Word has affected his desires (vv. 169-170), his speech (vv. 171-172), his choices (v. 173), and his emotions (v. 174)—his entire life (v. 175).

Late in his ministry, after a life of dedicated service, the apostle Paul said that he still had not attained; he continued to press forward (Philippians 3:12-14). The psalmist acknowledges this same idea. In his desperate condition, having "gone astray like a lost sheep," he still needed a seeking shepherd, lest he forget the Lord's commandments.

 LIFE STEP "All we like sheep have gone astray; we have turned everyone to his own way; and the LORD hath laid on Him the iniquity of us all" (Isaiah 53:6). We are included in the "all" at the beginning of this verse; therefore, how glad we are that we are also included in the "all" at the end of the verse. "For you *were* like sheep going astray" (1 Peter 2:25). The shepherd being sought in verse 176 is available to us, too.

Throughout this brief but exciting epistle, the Apostle Paul makes reference to the fact that he is in prison (1:7, 13-14). Only three of Paul's many imprisonments (Ephesus, Caesarea, and Rome) are of sufficient duration to allow the composition of an epistle such as this one. While there is a case to be made for Caesarea, a number of factors have led most biblical scholars to accept Rome as Paul's writing location. This imprisonment is referenced in Acts 28:16, 30-31, and the early church almost unanimously identified this epistle with Rome. The phrases "the palace" (1:13) and "Caesar's household" (4:22) would best fit the city of Rome. We may, therefore, deem this letter to have been written shortly after A.D. 60 from Rome.

The occasion for writing seems to be a most congenial one. Paul had recently received a gift from the Philippian believers. The gift was delivered by Epaphroditus who, shortly thereafter, became seriously ill. Upon Epaphroditus's recovery, Paul takes the opportunity to send a short thank you note to the Philippians and also includes an update on his own circumstances.

The epistle itself is a celebration of the joy that is found in serving others. The key verse is Philippians 2:3. The following is a suggested outline:

Theme: Joy through others-mindedness

1. Joy through suffering
2. Joy through service
3. Joy through sacrifice
4. Joy through submission

As we progress in this study, we will see the relationship between denying self and true joy. When we put ourselves first, we always diminish our ability to appreciate and enjoy life.

SUNDAY 6

PHILIPPIANS 1:1-7

WHAT IS THE WRITER SAYING?

HOW CAN I APPLY THIS TO MY LIFE?

PRAY For the missionaries from your church to find favor with the governments of the foreign countries in which they serve.

Paul is a prisoner, under house arrest. Timothy was able to visit with him, which is why Paul includes him in the salutation. This book is written to the "saints," a word only used for believers in the Lord Jesus Christ. All believers are saints—the word means *set apart ones*. From the same Greek word we also get the word *holy*.

Notice the three groups of people that are mentioned in verse 1. The first group is the whole church, comprised of all of those who have trusted Christ. The second group is the bishops—a word used interchangeably in Scripture for pastors and elders. The third group is the deacons, servants who served the body. This shows that there are two offices in the church: pastors (elders/bishops) and deacons.

In verse 2, Paul gives the common greeting of the day. If you were to say "hello" to a Greek, you would say "grace to you." If you were to say "hello" to a Jew, you would say "peace to you." Paul wants us to know that God is the source of both.

As we read this text, it is obvious the apostle is thankful for the faithfulness of these dear people. Every time he thought of them, he thanked God, doing so with a joyous spirit (v. 4). He was able to do so because these people were faithful to the Gospel. In verse 6, Paul gives a great statement of assurance for every Christian. He is confident that the One Who saved them would continue to work in their lives, not until the next time they sinned, but until the return of Jesus! The promise is that He "will perform" the work, not you!

LIFE STEP The God Who saved you is the One Who will continue to work in your life until Jesus returns. That should bring security to your life. Thank the Lord today for keeping you secure in Christ!

PHILIPPIANS 1:8-14

WHAT IS THE WRITER SAYING?

HOW CAN I APPLY THIS TO MY LIFE?

PRAY Canada – Pray for Bible institute ministry teams to have a lasting impact in local churches.

Sometimes we may think of the Apostle Paul as kind of a superman, without natural feelings. Notice in today's section that Paul had deep feelings for the people at Philippi and missed them. But not being there physically did not mean he could not have a ministry in their lives— he could still have the ministry of prayer. There are three major prayer requests here that can be a model for us in praying for one another. Paul's first request is that their "love may abound" (v. 9). Notice he says that he prays their love would grow, and that it also should be directed by knowledge and judgment. Love without knowledge will just lead to sentimentalism. And there are many who make terrible decisions based on love without judgment.

The second request is that the Philippians would make excellent decisions (v. 10). Paul knew that if they made good choices, they would be able to live the type of life that could be used by the Lord at any time.

The last request is that they would serve the Lord with all of their being ("being filled with the fruits of righteousness"). The motive of the prayer of Paul (that God would be glorified through the lives of the people) is seen at the end of verse 11. Paul was continually motivated by the glory of God.

In verse 12, Paul makes a shift in his thinking. He begins to let them know what is going on in his life. He knows that the people are discouraged because he is in prison, but he wants them to know that good things are still happening (see vv. 13-14).

LIFE STEP These three prayer requests can guide our prayers for others. Write them as a guide in the prayer section of your quiet time, and pray these requests for your friends.

TUESDAY 6

PHILIPPIANS 1:15-21

WHAT IS THE WRITER SAYING?

HOW CAN I APPLY THIS TO MY LIFE?

PRAY Spain – For an end to the government's selective restriction and closure of Christian radio stations.

During Paul's imprisonment, some men were "supposing to add affliction" by preaching the Gospel. How could that be? Apparently they claimed that Paul had failed the Lord and that God put him in prison as a punishment. They thought his troubles were a sign that the hand of God was no longer on his ministry, and now the mantle had passed on to them. They did this because of "envy" (v. 15)—they were jealous of Paul and the respect believers had for him. Others, however, did preach the Gospel with the correct motive of love. What is amazing here is the attitude of the apostle. Notice in verse 18 that he is willing to rejoice that the Gospel is being preached, even from people who were opposing him and seeking to hurt his testimony! This is a spirit of humility and a wonderful example to the church of Jesus Christ. The major issue to Paul is not that he receives credit, but that Jesus is being preached!

In verse 19, Paul shows he has confidence that all the things that had happened to him would work out in the end for his good. If he continued to live, he would preach the Gospel; if he died, it would be for the glory of God. The statement he makes in verse 21 is one of the most oftquoted in the Bible. For the apostle, to live was to exalt Christ, to preach Christ, to honor Christ, and to emulate Christ. But what if he died in prison? That would be even better according to Paul, for he would be with the Lord, and that was great gain.

LIFE STEP Differences with other believers in doctrine and practice are bound to occur, but we must disagree agreeably so the reputation of the Gospel is not hurt in the process.

PHILIPPIANS 1:22-30

WHAT IS THE WRITER SAYING?

HOW CAN I APPLY THIS TO MY LIFE?

In verse 22, Paul says that if he continued to live, it would mean more ministry. We see here the struggle the apostle was having. He knew going to Heaven meant no more suffering, no more sorrow, and no more prisons! However, it also meant no more ministry with the people he dearly loved in Christ. This was a great conflict of passion for him (v. 23). He deeply desired to see the Lord face to face and to worship Him in glory. Yet he realized that the people needed his ministry to be able to grow in Christ. He apparently believed that the Lord was going to keep him alive to be able to minister to them (v. 25). He was willing to stay and minister if it meant that God would be glorified in a deeper way. His heart's desire was to see them again, but in verse 27 he encourages them that even if he is not able to see them, he wants to hear that they are living lives that are honoring to Christ.

Notice the emphasis on unity in the body. One of the continuing critiques of Christianity is that people do not get along. Jesus prayed for the unity of the church in John 17. One of the by-products of unity is that there will be no fear when others oppose you, for you have the godly on your side (v. 28). Paul closes this paragraph with a promise, but not one that you will hear many Christians claiming today! Just as we are given the gift of faith to believe in Christ, we are given the honor to suffer for His name, just as Paul did (vv. 29-30).

LIFE STEP When you suffer for Christ, it is a fulfillment of the promise of God! Let's thank God that we are worthy to suffer for His name's sake and maintain a positive attitude.

74

PHILIPPIANS 2:1-8

WHAT IS THE WRITER SAYING?

HOW CAN I APPLY THIS TO MY LIFE?

PRAY Papua New Guinea – Effectiveness of literacy ministries that enable nationals to study God's Word.

Attitude. One of the most important decisions we make every day concerns our attitude. Paul knew our decisions are many times a result of our attitudes. In this text, we see the attitude Jesus had (v. 5), which should be the attitude all believers have who are in Christ Jesus.

In verse 1, Paul lists three blessings the people had because of their relationship with Christ. They had the comfort of love, the fellowship of the Spirit, and tender compassion from God. In light of that, each of us should have the same love, the same mind, and the same purpose (v. 2). What is that purpose? Paul first shares what it is not. Our purpose is not to live for ourselves (v. 3) in any way at all. Our purpose is to live for others! As a matter of fact, Paul says that each person is to esteem others to be more important than himself.

The key to this is humility. Humility is not thinking poorly of one's self, as some assume. Humility is thinking of others as being more important than us. The result is that each person looks out for the interests of others (v. 4). This attitude was the attitude of Jesus. He saw the need of the human race, lost in sin. He esteemed our redemption to be more important than His comfort in Heaven! He "made himself of no reputation," or emptied Himself, laying aside the independent use of His attributes so He could become fully man. What a step of humility! Not only did He become a man, He then died on the cross for man.

LIFE STEP Some people don't see a reason to treat others well because they think they are better or more important than others. Jesus was surely better than us and yet He humbled Himself. Ask God for opportunities to imitate Christ today.

FRIDAY 6

PHILIPPIANS 2:9-16

WHAT IS THE WRITER SAYING?

HOW CAN I APPLY THIS TO MY LIFE?

PRAY United Kingdom – For God to create a thirst for and a commitment to God's word in the hearts of youth.

There is a fear in many people that if they humble themselves, others will take advantage of them. That may indeed happen. However, if we humble ourselves, God will also exalt us in His time. Jesus illustrates that truth in this passage, where His humbling led to ultimate glorification. Notice in verses 9-11 that God the Father has given to the Son a name that is above every name. Some falsely assume that name is Jesus. But there have been many people with the name Jesus, so that cannot be it. In verse 9, the phrase literally means "the name which belongs to Jesus." This name is revealed in verse 11, where it says that every tongue will confess that Jesus is "Lord"! That name—"Lord" (Jehovah or Yahweh)—is the divine name for Jesus and is the same name used for God way back in Exodus 3.

Verse 12 is a point of transition. We see it with the use of the word *wherefore*. Paul is, in effect, saying, *In light of the humility of Jesus, which caused Him to pay the price for our sin, we are to 'work out' our own salvation!* What does that mean? We are to live our salvation out— to live like we are saved! But we are not to do it in our own power; God is the One Who works in us (v. 13), and He is the One Who gives us the power to do His will. We just need to live it out.

In verses 14-15, we see a number of ways we are to "work out" our salvation, while holding to the Word of life. The goal is to rejoice at the end, knowing we have done what God has asked.

LIFE STEP After all Christ has done for you, isn't it amazing that He wants to do even more? In what ways can you "work out" your salvation today, showing the world you are happy to serve Christ as a sign of His saving you?

SATURDAY 6

PHILIPPIANS 2:17-23

WHAT IS THE WRITER SAYING?

HOW CAN I APPLY THIS TO MY LIFE?

PRAY Laos – Pray for the pastors of the Lao Evangelical Church that they might handle the growth of both established congregations with love amd humility.

Earlier Paul shared the principle of looking at others as more important than ourselves. He illustrated this with the life of Jesus, and now he is going to illustrate that truth with three more people: himself (vv. 17-18), Timothy (vv. 19-23), and Epaphroditus (vv. 25-30).

The Apostle Paul is an obvious illustration of putting others' needs above his own. He was willing to do that even to the point of death. In verse 17 the phrase "offered upon the sacrifice" literally means *to be poured out as a drink offering*. A drink offering was made only of the purest wine. To purify the wine, you would pour the wine into a vessel and let it sit for a while. The dregs (impurities) would go to the bottom, and then the good wine would be carefully poured into yet another vessel, leaving the dregs behind.

The process would be repeated until the wine was totally pure. Paul is saying that he had been poured from the vessel of one trial to another and another, and now he was ready to be poured out before the Lord, for the trials the Lord takes us through are to purify us. What a beautiful picture this is!

The second illustration is that of Timothy. He was willing to come to them, putting their needs above his own comfort or his own desires. Notice the opposite in verse 21 — "all seek their own." Seeking our own is the opposite of seeking Christ's desire for our lives, which is to serve Him by ministering to others. It is sad to think that of all the people Paul may have had around him, only two were willing to put others' needs before their own.

 Are you going through some trials right now? God is making you pure and helping you focus on others. Make a list of people you need to put above yourself.

SUNDAY 7

PHILIPPIANS 2:24-30

WHAT IS THE WRITER SAYING?

HOW CAN I APPLY THIS TO MY LIFE?

PRAY Poland – For the salvation of many who are taking English classes taught by missionaries.

Paul had confidence that he was going to be able to visit the people at Philippi soon. We are not sure why he felt he would be getting out of prison, but it is obvious he sensed he was. He wanted to get this letter to them, so he said he would send Epaphroditus, who was originally from that area. Paul defines his dear friend in verse 25 as a brother, a companion in labor, and a fellow soldier of Christ. He had ministered to Paul's needs during his time in prison. His ministry to the apostle was so selfless that he got sick and was near death. The people at Philippi had heard he was sick and obviously were upset about it.

As a sign of what a completely selfless man he was, Epaphroditus was burdened because he had caused them to be upset. He is a tremendous illustration of the selfless servant that has been the topic of this chapter. In verse 27, Paul says that God had mercy on both Epaphroditus and himself. *Mercy* is a misunderstood word.

It means to withhold misery or to take it away, and in this case God took away the illness of His servant Epaphroditus. The Philippians would not know this until Epaphroditus showed up in Philippi with the letter from Paul in his hand.

We can only imagine the joyous reunion when Epaphroditus returned home. Paul knew all the people would rejoice and would love to see him again. This is a great mark of servants of God—they have a deep capacity to rejoice when others in the family of God rejoice. Paul was more concerned that they were ministered to rather than himself. In this way, Paul is illustrating the principle of verses 1-4 as well.

LIFE STEP Do you rejoice when others experience blessings from God? There are times when we are better at sorrowing than we are at rejoicing. Find someone who is being blessed and celebrate with them this week!

PHILIPPIANS 3:1-6

WHAT IS THE WRITER SAYING?

HOW CAN I APPLY THIS TO MY LIFE?

PRAY Dominican Republic – For church leaders and their congregation to be good witnesses in tense and inequitable situations.

When you see the word "finally" here, you might think that Paul is wrapping up his thoughts and is almost finished. But then he goes on for two more chapters. You may be thinking, "Typical preacher!" Actually, the phrase means *as for the rest of the matters*, so he is winding down and still has a ways to go.

The warning (vv. 1-3) was concerning the Judaizers. These were people who believed in Jesus Christ but did not think one was saved by faith alone, but by faith plus becoming a Jew. The sign of that was circumcision. But Paul said circumcision has no saving benefit—it was simply cutting the flesh. There was no saving benefit in being circumcised. God does not look at the external ceremonies; He looks at the heart!

These people were telling those who believed in Christ that it was vital to believe, but you also had to keep the law and be a Jew—so, you were saved by faith plus works in their system. The circumcision the Lord is looking for is that of the heart being open to Christ (v. 3—"worship God in the spirit").

In verse 3, we have a great description of a Christian. There are three marks: first, a Christian is someone who worships God in the spirit, or the inner man. Second, he rejoices in Christ, and third, he has no confidence in the flesh. These three marks should be seen in the life of each person who has put his or her faith in Jesus Christ, as opposed to the outward circumcision that was being called for by these converted Jews. Paul goes on to say that if being a good Jew got one into Heaven, he would have been first in line. The list Paul gives in verses 5-6 would be impressive to any Jew.

LIFE STEP The three characteristics Paul lists in verse 3 should mark your life. One way to keep these before you is to write them down on a card and rehearse them daily. Ask God to help you worship in the spirit, rejoice in Christ, and to have no confidence in the flesh.

TUESDAY 7

PHILIPPIANS 3:7-14

WHAT IS THE WRITER SAYING?

HOW CAN I APPLY THIS TO MY LIFE?

PRAY For the perseverance of fellow believers and unashamed boldness for those who preach the Gospel (Ephesians 6:18-19).

Paul possessed all the requirements of a fine, upstanding Jewish man in his culture. Did he lean on those as part of salvation? Absolutely not! He counted them as loss for Christ, that is, he left them all behind. He gave up trusting in his ability to keep the law, or in Judaism, to save him, and put all his trust in Christ alone to save. The point is obvious. You cannot believe in Jesus alone for salvation and believe that somehow you have to do good works to be saved as well.

These two ways are mutually exclusive. A person is either saved by faith in Christ alone, or they are saved by faith in Christ plus keeping the law. Paul illustrates that we are saved by faith alone. Well, what about all the good things Paul did before he trusted Christ? Paul says that he counted them as *refuse*. The Greek word used here means excrement, which is the worst of all refuse. This reminds us of the words of Isaiah when he said that all our righteousness is as filthy rags. This does not mean these things are bad in themselves; it means they have no saving value at all. The righteousness we have now is the righteousness of Christ that was given to us when we trusted in Him (see v. 9).

Instead of having zeal for the law, Paul now has zeal to know God with all of his heart, soul, and mind. Notice the drive the apostle has to follow Christ. In verses 12 and 14, he emphasizes that his passion in life was to press on to serve Christ. The word "press" in verse 14 means *to strain with all of one's might to reach the goal*. It was used of a runner who stretched to reach the finish line.

LIFE STEP Think of sprinters at the end of the 100-meter dash. They strain and stretch to reach the goal. Are you straining to reach the goal of Christ-likeness?

PHILIPPIANS 3:15-21

WHAT IS THE WRITER SAYING?

HOW CAN I APPLY THIS TO MY LIFE?

In verses 15-16, the apostle is calling for unity of purpose in the body of Christ. The word "perfect" in verse 15 means *to be mature*. Those who are mature in the faith should mimic Paul's desire of Christ-likeness. There will be some areas of differences, but we surely can agree on the need to be more like Christ. Since God has saved us and given us a great position in Christ, the apostle tells the readers to live up to this higher calling. In other words, if you are a Christian, you should act like one! What if someone who calls himself a Christian is not walking according to the Word and not seeking to be like Christ? In verses 17-18, Paul says they are enemies of the cross. This is an interesting assessment. In 1 John 2:3-4, we see the same principle.

There are people all over the world who claim to be Christians, but they are not living according to His Word. They are liars and enemies of the cross, driven by their own passions and not by passion for God (v. 19). They put their minds on earthly things. Mature Christians, however, put their attention on Jesus. Notice the emphasis on the return of Jesus in verses 20-21. There are trials and burdens in this world. Temptations seek to draw us away from the Lord. We must remember that our eternal home is in Heaven, and Jesus can come at any time to take us to that home.

LIFE STEP If our citizenship is in Heaven, we should live according to Heaven's values. We should seek to *lay up for ourselves treasures in Heaven* (Matthew 6:20), not ones here on the earth. Do we live for things, or do we live for Jesus?

THURSDAY 7

PHILIPPIANS 4:1-7

WHAT IS THE WRITER SAYING?

HOW CAN I APPLY THIS TO MY LIFE?

PRAY Algeria – Pray the Algerian church, which has grown due to evangelism, will respond to increased threats and intimidations with faith and perseverance.

Paul has great labels for his readers. They are "dearly beloved"; they are "longed for"; and they are his "joy and crown." Paul had a deep affection for the Philippians.

Think about what Paul has been emphasizing. We are not to live for ourselves, but for the Lord. As we live for the Lord, we are to esteem others more important than ourselves. I am sure that as this was being read, many people were saying, "Amen!" Now he applies this to two women in the church who were obviously having a conflict (vv. 2-3). They are encouraged to apply this principle to their conflict and to rejoice in Christ instead of living in conflict (v. 4).

In verse 5, he tells them to let their moderation, or gentleness, be known to all. They were to stop the conflict and learn to be gentle so all would see. Paul addresses a byproduct of conflict—worry—in the next two verses.

In verse 6, he tells them to replace worry with believing prayer. Notice the progression here. When you worry, go to God in worship (prayer here is a worship word in the Greek), bring others' needs to God (supplication), and thank God for all He has done in your life. Then you bring your own request before God. When we worship, we focus on God, not the problem. As we do that, the problem shrinks in comparison to our great God. The result? The peace of God will keep your heart and mind.

LIFE STEP Are you a worrywart? Write verses 6-7 on a card, and carry it with you everywhere you go. When you worry, take it out, read, and pray!

FRIDAY 7

PHILIPPIANS 4:8-13

WHAT IS THE WRITER SAYING?

HOW CAN I APPLY THIS TO MY LIFE?

PRAY Haiti – Pray that the Haitians who call themselves Christian might experience the transforming nature of a personal relationship with Christ.

Doctors tell us that we are what we eat. The Bible teaches us that we are what we think (Proverbs 23:7)! Whatever you allow into your mind will affect you deeply. What kinds of things should you think about? Paul gives a representative list of the kinds of things we should think on as Christians. Not only should we think about biblical principles, but we should also obey them (v. 9). The result of thinking biblically is that the peace of God will be with you. The concept of peace is that of having a stable attitude in life, knowing God is in control. In Isaiah 26:3, we are told that peace is a result of thinking on God and trusting in Him.

Paul thanks the Philippians for the gift they sent to him. It meant much to him that these dear people sacrificed to help him. He was rejoicing over their love for him. You might be thinking, *it is easy to rejoice when you have just received a gift*! How true, yet in verses 11-12, Paul says that even when he was going without, he still was content in God. Notice that he had "learned" to be content; it did not come naturally. He learned that when he was in need, he was to trust in the Lord, and the Lord would give him all the strength he needed to make it through the trial (v. 13). It was part of Paul's life to enjoy plenty at one time, and to endure suffering at another. He had full confidence that God was in control.

 LIFE STEP Put verse 8 on your television and computer. Whenever you see something that does not match that list, turn it off! Also, ask God to help you be content with whatever you have. Don't live to get more things. Live to know God better.

SATURDAY 7

PHILIPPIANS 4:14-23

WHAT IS THE WRITER SAYING?

HOW CAN I APPLY THIS TO MY LIFE?

PRAY Italy – For missionaries working in a culture that is spiritually ritualistic, apathetic and cynical.

Paul expresses his deep appreciation for the generous gifts the Philippians sent. They were examples of Paul's principle that we should esteem others' needs to be more important than our own. Their poverty made their generosity even more impressive. Paul also mentions their selflessness in 2 Corinthians 8:1-6. They were so poor that when they gave him the gift, they had nothing left for themselves. Paul tried to give it back, but they would not let him do that. Paul called their gift a "sacrifice acceptable, wellpleasing to God" (v. 18).

Notice the context of verse 19. When you give to meet someone's need in such a way that you have little left over for yourself, you don't have to worry. God will supply all your needs in response to your sacrificial giving! How much does God have at His disposal? Only everything there is in the universe! Who deserves the glory when our needs are met? God and God alone (v. 20). The last three verses are a general closing, but if you read them quickly, you will miss a great blessing. Notice something in verse 22? There were saints in Caesar's household. How did they come to know the Lord? A good assumption is that they were fruit of Paul's imprisonment. Remember Philippians 1:21, for him to live was Christ!

LIFE STEP Pray that God will give you an opportunity to share Christ with someone today.

Like Genesis, the Book of Exodus is a record of *beginnings*. Genesis is a historical summary given to us by Moses of the beginning of the heavens and the earth, angels and demons, earthly life and mankind, sin and God's plan of redemption for sinful men, as well as the story of the start of the family which God intended to use to bring redemption and salvation to lost people. Exodus continues this historical summary of *beginnings* (notice that its first word is "*Now*" ("and" in Hebrew) which presents its role as the continuation of the story of Genesis).

Exodus is a dramatic story of the growth of the *redemption family* of Abraham into the nation of slaves which God "saved" out of "the hands of the Egyptians" (Exodus 14:30). So then Exodus is the story of the *beginnings* of the nation of Israel, which was delivered by God from bondage in Egypt. Events in Exodus are then referred to throughout the Old and New Testament as the defining work of God - His saving Israel. This would then become the defining picture for us Christians of God's spiritually saving us from our bondage to sin and His subsequent making of us into a new *special people*, the church.

Moses was the human author of the first five books of Bible, often called the "Pentateuch" (meaning *five books*), or simply the Law of Moses. The significance of Moses' life and ministry is that God had decided to choose the Hebrew descendants of Abraham as a kingdom of priests that would eventually reach out to all of humanity. God had selected Moses to be the key person in bringing about these objectives. The people of Israel were to be the bearers of His holy Word, the biological line of the Messiah, and the priests of God to represent Him to the surrounding Gentile nations. Unfortunately, they rarely were spiritual people who could be a testimony to the Gentiles.

A helpful chart that shows the relationship of Exodus to the rest of the Pentateuch is given below:

- Genesis 1-11 – Creation, Fall, Flood, Scattering; Redemption plan revealed.
- Genesis 12-50 – A Family is Called Out; Abraham, Isaac, Jacob, Joseph.
- Exodus 1-15 – Preparing to Leave Egypt: Bondage, Plagues, & Deliverance through the Red Sea.
- Exodus 16-18 – Traveling from Egypt to Mount Sinai; God provides food, water, and protection
- Exodus 19-40 – Leviticus, & Numbers 1-10: Instructions at Mount Sinai: The spiritual equipping of a special people.
- Numbers 10-21 – Wilderness Wanderings: Death of a faithless generation.
- Numbers 22-36, Deut. 1-34 – Encamped across the River from the Promised Land; Spiritual equipping of the second generation.

SUNDAY 8

EXODUS 1:1-14

WHAT IS THE WRITER SAYING?

HOW CAN I APPLY THIS TO MY LIFE?

PRAY Greece – Pray that the few Greek evangelicals will have a witness in a society where the majority claim to be Christian yet do not have a relationship with Jesus.

Moses, the writer of the Books of Genesis and Exodus, wanted us to see them together. Graham Scroggie suggests that in Genesis the "divine purpose of God is revealed," while in Exodus "the divine performance is exhibited." Genesis shows God's promise, while Exodus shows God fulfilling His promises.

Chapter 1 explains how the children of Israel went from being honored guests living on the best lands in Egypt (1876 B.C.; Genesis 45:18; 47:6) to being slaves. The situation changed when an Asiatic army, called the Hyksos, conquered the northern half of Egypt in 1730 B.C. It was a Hyksos king, being concerned about the Hebrews' growing numbers, who decided to make slaves of the Hebrews. The Hyksos were afraid that when war broke out between the Hyksos and the Egyptians of the south, the Hebrews would join their friends, the Egyptians.

In 1584 B.C., the Egyptians were able to drive out the Hyksos (as the Hyksos had feared!), yet the Egyptians continued the enslavement of the Hebrews, due in part to their growing hatred of all foreigners and especially people from Asia. So the children of Israel continued to be slaves under taskmasters who afflicted them with heavy burdens.

Chapter 1 also shows God's promised blessing to Israel even while Israel was in bondage. Verses 7, 12 and 20 are the keys to the chapter, showing Israel's tremendous increase in numbers (note the repeating phrase, "multiplied and waxed mighty"). During the 430 years the family of Abraham was in Egypt, they multiplied from only seventy people to a nation of about 600,000 men above the age of twenty (Numbers 1:46). To increase this much, they doubled their population every twenty five years.

LIFE STEP In several places in the Bible we are reminded that life is filled with both times of blessing and affliction. The Bible also makes it clear, and it is illustrated here in Exodus 1, that God is present during both. Are you in a time of life that is filled with blessings? Then make a list of things for which you can thank God. Are you in a time of life that has afflictions? Then make a list of how God is strengthening, comforting, and blessing you in the midst of the hard times.

MONDAY 8

EXODUS 1:15-22

WHAT IS THE WRITER SAYING?

HOW CAN I APPLY THIS TO MY LIFE?

PRAY Bermuda – For unity among believers so that their testimony will be clear and unhindered.

Because the king of Egypt feared their growing numbers, he commanded that the Hebrew boy babies be killed at their birth. In spite of his commands, the Hebrew midwives let the boy babies live. God was pleased with the midwives and He "dealt well" with them (v. 20a). Note that He also continued to cause Israel to grow in numbers (v. 20b).

Just think: if all the males had been destroyed, there would have been no Jewish line and therefore no King David and no Son of David (who would be Jesus, the promised Savior of mankind)! The example given for us here is that of the faithful midwives' refusal to do the evil bidding of Pharaoh. The secret weapon in this passage is the fact that the midwives "*feared God*" (v. 17). Yes, Pharaoh could have had the midwives killed, but the midwives did not stop doing what was right because of fear of Pharaoh's judgment. Rather, they feared God, for they knew that ultimately they would stand before God to give an account of their choices in life. They were careful to do what was right, proper, and God-pleasing rather than what was expedient.

Do we fear the Lord? The *idea* of fearing God includes knowing we will ultimately stand before God to give an account for our choices in life. Yet the *emphasis* of fearing God means we will act in all our ways with God in view, having an intense desire to please Him in all we do. Even though the midwives were putting themselves in jeopardy, they acted with the Lord in view. God loves to see this in us. This is important to Him.

LIFE STEP We, like the midwives, can expect to face hard choices and even life-threatening choices. We, like the midwives, must choose to do what is right, and not just expedient. We can then trust God to "deal well" with us when we make the hard, but right, choices. What hard choices do you face today? Write God a note explaining decisions that need to be made. Then ask Him for the wisdom to choose the correct path and the strength to do the right thing.

TUESDAY 8

EXODUS 2:1-10

WHAT IS THE WRITER SAYING?

HOW CAN I APPLY THIS TO MY LIFE?

PRAY Guatemala – For the growth and maturity of the churches in the nation.

The great story of baby Moses being hid in the bulrushes is seen in this passage. The mother of Moses saw that he was a beautiful child. Acts 7:20 helps us here by commenting upon this Exodus passage. The literal Greek of Acts 7:20 tells us he was "beautiful unto God." C.A. Coates writes, "They beheld in him a beauty that was in relation to God, and that must be preserved for God's pleasure and service." The testimony of Moses' mother speaks to every parent. Every believing parent should recognize that his child is special.

Another New Testament commentary (Hebrews 11:23) tells us the parents acted *in faith* by hiding Moses. Their *faith* is seen in their hiding him for three months and then placing him in the ark of bulrushes. *Faith* is the opposite of fear; "they were not afraid of the king's commandment" (Hebrews 11:23).

Each of us must examine his own heart to see if he consistently trusts the Lord in difficult circumstances. Not only are we saved by faith (Ephesians 2:8-9), but we must continue to walk by faith each day (2 Corinthians 5:7). Our daily walk of faith demands that we "stand fast in the faith" (1 Corinthians 16:13). We cannot please God without this faith (Hebrews 11:6).

"The beginning of anxiety is the end of faith, and the beginning of true faith is the end of anxiety.
Faith is: dead to doubts, dumb to discouragement, blind to impossibilities." (Anonymous)

LIFE STEP What evil thing, person, or thought is going to ask you today to choose a path of living that takes you away from God? What choices will you need to make so you will not follow the evil but rather will stand fast in your faith, just like the mother of Moses did!

EXODUS 2:11-25

WHAT IS THE WRITER SAYING?

HOW CAN I APPLY THIS TO MY LIFE?

PRAY For teens to be saved at evangelistic events being held around the country.

Today's passage picks up the story of Moses forty years later (v. 11). We find Moses, while still living in comfort as a son of a daughter of Pharaoh, slaying an Egyptian task-master who had been "smiting" a Hebrew slave. First, we should remember that it is never right to do wrong to get right results. Moses was right in seeing the injustice and being concerned about it. He was not right in the impetuous response of slaying the hard-hearted Egyptian taskmaster. Notice that Moses "*looked this way and that*" (v. 12) before he killed the Egyptian. He knew his intended deed was wrong and he had hoped to keep his deed hidden!

The real lesson to be learned from today's passage comes from observing New Testament comments related to Moses' fleeing from Pharaoh (see Hebrews 11:27). Apparently, Moses had been living the privileged life of a prince of Egypt at Thebes and he had given little interest to his oppressed brethren who toiled as slaves, one hundred miles north in Goshen. But then, when he was forty years old, God changed all that, for "*it came into [Moses'] heart to visit his brethren, the children of Israel*" (Acts 7:23). God had been preparing Moses to be God's agent in the freeing of God's people. Now God was setting into motion his plan for Moses! Stephen goes on to say about Moses, after Moses had killed the Egyptian, "*For he supposed his brethren would have understood how that God by his hand would deliver them*" (Acts 7:25). Sadly God's own people did not yet understand that God intended to deliver them from their slavery by means of Moses (v. 14).

When Moses became aware that his murder of the Egyptian was known by others, including Pharaoh, any hope of continuing to hide his true nationality as an Israelite was also gone. This left Moses without hope of defending himself against charges that would be brought against him. And so, Moses saw that his only option was to flee the country (v. 15b).

LIFE STEP It is not uncommon for the Lord to direct a person away from one endeavor in life to another so that He might use that person as an agent to fulfill His will. Are you such a person? Is God *"bringing to your heart"* an interest in a cause that had not formerly been there? Will you take some time to talk it out with God? What does He want you to do?

THURSDAY 8

EXODUS 3:1-12

WHAT IS THE WRITER SAYING?

HOW CAN I APPLY THIS TO MY LIFE?

PRAY Austria – Each student receives their own free copy of the Bible at school. Pray that they would study it and accept its truths.

Moses' life can be divided into three periods. For forty years he was in Egypt, educated by the Egyptians "in all the wisdom of the Egyptians" (Acts 7:22a). Apparently during this time Moses became an accomplished diplomat for the Egyptians, for Stephen also says that Moses "was mighty in words and deeds" (Acts 7:22b).

The second forty years he was on the backside of the desert, being prepared by God as a shepherd to lead Israel out of their bondage. The third forty years were spent leading the Hebrews out of Egypt toward the Promised Land.

In our present passage, Moses is keeping sheep (v. 1) near the end of the second period of his life. The angel of the Lord appears to him in a flame of fire and speaks to him (vv. 2-4). The angelic creature reveals himself to Moses as the God of Abraham, Isaac, and Jacob. Moses is in the presence of the Lord!

From the Lord's statement to Moses, we learn six things about the Lord:

1. God is aware of the needs of individuals and groups of people. He said, "I have surely seen the affliction of my people" (v. 7). How wonderful to know the Lord sees our needs and cares for us.
2. He knows the details of that need (v. 7b), even knowing the wicked deeds of those who oppose people.
3. He promises to act on their behalf and deliver His people. "I am come down to deliver them" (v. 8a).
4. He wants to direct them into the land of plenty (v. 8b).
5. The Lord has a plan He will execute to bring about His will. In Exodus God's plan was to send Moses. "I will send thee" (v. 10).
6. Finally, with the Lord's sending comes the accompanying divine promise. "I will be with thee" (v. 12).

 LIFE STEP We have the same God as Moses! God also sees our need, hears our prayers, and will respond when we ask for His help. When He sends us to accomplish a task He also promises to equip us! His directions are always coupled with power to do them! So, what do you need from God to accomplish what He has directed you to do with your life?

FRIDAY 8

EXODUS 3:13-22

WHAT IS THE WRITER SAYING?

HOW CAN I APPLY THIS TO MY LIFE?

PRAY Netherlands Antilles – For hearts to be open as the missionaries and pastors share the Good News with them.

When the Lord commissioned Moses, Moses was reluctant. His first question was, "What shall I say unto them?" (v. 13). He was afraid that the Israelites wouldn't know Who God is. He imagined them saying, "Which god are you talking about, Moses? What is his name?" Immediately the Lord responds to Moses' question by identifying Himself as, "I Am that I Am" (v. 14).

We live today in a world where all gods are considered equally relevant (or irrelevant) and have something to contribute to society. Our world also believes that nothing, including God and His Word, is unchanging and absolute. God's answer to these errors is found in this name God gave Moses. There is one

God and He is eternal and unchanging. He is the self-existing One. God is a personal, all-powerful God Who took the first steps to establish a relationship with Moses.

Notice that this same God has in our day taken the first steps to establish a personal relationship with each of us (John 3:16)! How privileged we are to know in a personal way this great *I Am* and to be sent, as Moses was, to do His bidding ("... so send I you," John 20:21). Note the "I will"s mentioned here in Exodus 3:17, 20 and 21. The God Who sent Moses also sends us. He also promises to be with us and show us the strength of His hand; "I will stretch out my hand" (v. 20).

 LIFE STEP On this memorable day, God revealed to Moses a great insight about Himself. We now, like Moses before us, must build our lives around this insight that God is a personal, eternal, unchanging, all-powerful God who is also interested in each of us! Since this is true, what problems do you face today that you can personally talk over with God who desires to be your Heavenly Father?

SATURDAY 8

EXODUS 4:1-17

WHAT IS THE WRITER SAYING?

HOW CAN I APPLY THIS TO MY LIFE?

PRAY Uganda – For believing Ugandans living abroad to be called back to minister among their people.

No one will believe me! is the declaration Moses makes as we begin this chapter. It is like Moses was pointing to the people and claiming there was no way they would listen to him. He feared that he lacked any credibility before the children of Israel. After all, for forty years as a prince of Egypt he had shown them no particular interest. Then for another forty years, Moses had fled the country and hid from Pharaoh as a shepherd in the land of the Midianites! God responds by giving three signs that Moses could use to deal with the people: namely, a rod that became a snake (vv. 3-5), a hand that became leprous (vv. 6-7), and water that turned to blood (vv. 8-9).

Concerning the first sign, turning Moses' rod into a serpent (vv. 2-4), we note that it was just a shepherd's rod. Not much — an ordinary walking stick, but mighty when empowered by the Lord.

The question "What is that in thine hand?" is a good one for us to consider. It is amazing that the Lord takes the simple, the ordinary, the *not-so-impressive*, and uses it in great and often unexpected ways for His glory. Often God is not looking for self-confident, greatly-talented, super-personality people. In the Bible, we see that God commonly takes ordinary people who are surrendered to Him and who are willing to turn over to God their *ordinary shepherd's rods* to be His instruments. God took what Moses had and used it to accomplish His purpose. As a result, his shepherd's staff became the mighty "rod of God" (v. 20). Moses' second objection was that he was not eloquent. Perhaps he stuttered. What a relief to know that God can take a *not-so-eloquent person* and use his mouth and voice to His glory.

LIFE STEP What is in your hand? What personal resources, however humble, do you have? Will you willingly give these over to Him with the awareness that He can use you? Will you renew your commitment to Him today and yield yourself (your body, your talents, your skills, your gifts) to Him? Since the God of Moses is your God, too, how might He want to use you?

SUNDAY 9

EXODUS 4:18-31

WHAT IS THE WRITER SAYING?

HOW CAN I APPLY THIS TO MY LIFE?

PRAY For young people in your church to see the need and commit to full time Christian service.

For many years, Moses had been working with his father-in-law, Jethro, in the land of Midian (present-day northern Saudi Arabia). The Lord assured Moses that those in Egypt who had sought his life were dead (v. 19). Now Moses was to return. So Moses was ready to go back to Egypt and be used of God to deliver the Hebrews from bondage. Note how respectful Moses is to his father-in-law: "Let me go, I pray thee" (v. 18). This is a good lesson for each of us in our dealings with relatives and loved ones (and older people in general)!

The announcement of the Lord that He would *harden* Pharaoh's *heart* is a difficult saying to understand (v. 21). There are several statements in Scripture concerning God hardening Pharaoh's heart. These are balanced by additional statements in which is stated that Pharaoh hardened his own heart. 1 Samuel 6:6 indicates that Pharaoh was to blame for hardening his own heart. So, both divine sovereignty and human responsibility are here. Remember, these are two sides to one *coin*. While it is true that God in His sovereignty directed this great king to resist God's plan, yet at the same time Pharaoh, of his own will and purposes, hardened his own heart against the announced will of God. God intended for all to see, Egyptians, Israelites, and surrounding nations (see 7:3), that God and not the mightiest of kings ruled in this world. Yet Pharaoh exercised his own will too; Pharaoh "refuseth" (7:14), he was *unyielding* (7:22), his heart *became hard* as the LORD had predicted (8:15, 19), and he *stubbornly refused* (13:15).

Did you notice the surprising statement that the Lord was ready to kill Moses (v. 24)? The reason is obvious. Moses had failed to obey the Lord's command concerning the circumcising of his own children (Genesis 17:10-14). Apparently his Midianite wife, Zipporah, found this disgusting (v. 25) and Moses had deferred to her wishes by refusing to comply with God's command. Now his disobedience almost killed him!

 LIFE STEP Are we willing to be obedient to the Lord even when it is not the popular thing to do? God's will is of primary importance every step of the way. He will see us through when we simply obey Him. What commands of the Lord do you need to work on putting into practice this week in your daily walk? How can you be faithful in obeying the Lord?

EXODUS 5:1-12

WHAT IS THE WRITER SAYING?

HOW CAN I APPLY THIS TO MY LIFE?

PRAY Czech Republic – Crime, sexual immorality, substance abuse, and suicide are prevalent. Pray that people would turn to God during these dark times.

Remember that the Israelites had for a long time been in bondage as slaves to the Pharaoh (king) of Egypt. But God is about to redeem (*to buy back from slavery*) His people from their cruel affliction (Exodus 4:31). When Moses and Aaron deliver the Lord's message to Pharaoh, Pharaoh responds in two ways. First Pharaoh responds, "Who is the Lord, that I should obey...?" (v. 2) This shows us that Pharaoh did not recognize God as the Authority of his life that needed to be obeyed. Second, Pharaoh intensified the burdens that had already existed upon his slaves, the people of Israel (v. 7). This shows that Pharaoh believed his commands were a higher demand upon his slaves than was the command of their God to come into the wilderness to worship Him.

Later in the Bible, this bondage of Israel to Egypt is used as a picture (often called a *type*) of the bondage of all people to the evil world system of Satan. It was from this bondage that Jesus came to redeem us when He died upon the Cross to save us!

When we witness to others about the Lord Jesus, we are talking about the wonderful Savior Who desires to deliver them from their slavery to sin and Satan! The best news is that this deliverance is available free to all who will ask Jesus to redeem them. Don't be surprised if Satan, the lord of this evil world, opposes you and seeks to "blind the minds" (2 Corinthians 4:3-4) of those to whom you witness. Just remember, "Greater is he that is in you, than he that is in the world" (1 John 4:4).

 LIFE STEP You, like Israel when they were slaves in Egypt, can expect the resisting power of Satan to the commands of God in your life! When you face a command from God, you must respond in a way *opposite* to Pharaoh's response. Pray that (1) your responses to life today reflect recognition that God is the Authority in your life; and (2) you are willing to submit to His demands upon your time, talents, choices, and rights.

TUESDAY 9

EXODUS 5:13-23

WHAT IS THE WRITER SAYING?

HOW CAN I APPLY THIS TO MY LIFE?

PRAY Russia – Pray for the balancing of strong government with democratic accountability and respect of basic freedoms.

Conditions are worsening as we read this paragraph. Rather than the people being liberated, the chains of bondage are heavier than ever. But should we be surprised? Didn't the Lord tell Moses that he would be running into relentless opposition? Yes, it's one thing to know that opposition could (and will) come, but it's another thing to experience the awful reality of the forceful hand of an enemy.

So, when Moses and Aaron come out from a conference with Pharaoh (v. 20), a committee of Hebrews is waiting to protest the *no straw policy* that had been laid on them. The complaint is clear. They blamed it on Moses saying, *You have made us offensive in the eyes of Pharaoh and his servants* (v. 21). Moses listened but didn't even reprove them for their

attitude. He knows of their heavy burden and, while he might have reminded them that this could be expected, he simply "returned unto the Lord." What a good thing to do when you have questions or when you have opposition not only from your enemies but even from your friends. Just "return unto the Lord"—take your burdens to the Lord and leave them there.

So our passage ends with Moses going to the Lord with a heavy heart. He said, *Why have you so badly treated this people? Why is it that you have sent me? Why is it that things have only become worse and still there is no deliverance* (vv. 22-23)? As we will see in tomorrow's passage, the Lord certainly listened to His servant and gave him immediate assurance.

 LIFE STEP Have there been times in your life when you found yourself praying and asking the Lord why things were working out in a difficult manner? The Lord has a ready ear to hear our cry and to intervene for us. But remember, He makes no mistakes, yet His timing is not always our timing. What opposition are you now facing that needs to be taken to the Lord?

WEDNESDAY 9

EXODUS 6:1-13

WHAT IS THE WRITER SAYING?

HOW CAN I APPLY THIS TO MY LIFE?

PRAY Cayman Islands – For Christians to continue to hold fast to the Christian values in the midst of wealth and materialism.

Today's passage is the recording of a *double message* from God. First, the LORD tells Moses, "*what I will do to Pharaoh*" (v. 1). The second is the longer message with several "*I will's*" of God for Israel concerning what He would do for Israel:

- *I will* bring Israel out from bondage to Egypt (v. 6)
- *I will* redeem you with My powerful arm (v. 6b)
- *I will* take Israel for My people (v 7)
- *I will* be your God; you will know I am the LORD your God (v. 7b)
- *I will* bring you into the land that will be your heritage (v. 8)

The LORD includes in His second message three "I have"s:

- *I have* established My covenant with Israel (v. 4)
- *I have* heard the groans of Israel under their hard oppression (5a)
- *I have* remembered My covenant with Israel (v. 5b)

The LORD then concludes by answering an assumed question, "How do we know that these things will come to pass?" God simply declares "*I am the LORD*" or, as the Hebrew says, "*I am Jehovah.*"

Our passage also presents a puzzling statement, "*But by my name Jehovah was I not known to them*" (v. 3). But careful study reveals that the name *Jehovah* is found several times in events centuries before in the time of Abraham, Isaac, and Jacob (see Genesis 9:26; 12:8; 13:4). So we must conclude that while Israel knew the name *Jehovah*, they didn't fully understand what that name implied to God's people. That is why God also says that He was revealed earlier as God Almighty, which is the Hebrew name "El-Shaddai," *the Powerful One who provides and sustains.* But now God was going to reveal Himself to Moses according to the intent of the name, "Jehovah," *the Promise-Keeper who will redeem Israel and be personally known by them.*

LIFE STEP When we remember that we Christians also have many *"I will"* promises from God in the New Testament (for example, John 14:14, 16, 18, 21), we are led to ask, "What 'will dos' can I expect from the Lord Jesus in my daily life so that He can allow me to see that He is my personal friend who keeps His promises?" Take a minute to write a thank-you note to the Lord for showing Himself to be your friend who keeps His promises!

THURSDAY 9

EXODUS 6:28 - 7:13

WHAT IS THE WRITER SAYING?

HOW CAN I APPLY THIS TO MY LIFE?

PRAY Nepal – Pray that positive strides by the gospel may be made quickly in the window of opportunity provided by the new government and new constitution.

Do you ever feel the years are passing and you aren't making the progress you should? Be encouraged with our present passage. Moses is eighty years old, and he is just beginning the most important ministry of his life! It has taken that long for God to get Moses ready! Moses needed forty years to learn to be the administrative leader of a great people but he also needed another forty years to learn to shepherd God's people while watching over sheep and goats in the land of the Midianites.

In this passage, Moses and Aaron go to Pharaoh. Aaron casts down his rod and it becomes a serpent. Pharaoh is not impressed! He calls his sorcerers and they do the same thing. But what amazes all present is when Aaron's rod (now a snake) swallows up all their snakes! We learn that while Satan, who empowered the magicians, was powerful, the Lord is far more powerful and able to easily defeat the opposition.

We also see in this passage that God is warning Moses that the way ahead would not be easy or quick (7:3-5). The LORD knew that it was going to take some time for the Egyptians to "know that I am the LORD." The LORD was going to challenge and show Himself powerfully victorious over the many aspects of Egyptian religious life and the many gods of the Egyptians.

As a result Moses must guard his heart against discouragement, fear (6:30), and impatience while he pursued his responsibilities as God's ambassador to Pharaoh. Moses and Aaron must remember that they were on the winning side; they were doing the work of the truly powerful One, Jehovah. Moses and Aaron didn't need to fear Pharaoh or his magicians, for all these would, like the magician's snakes, soon be defeated.

 LIFE STEP We must choose to live with the faith of Moses and Aaron by remembering God is the powerful One who gives our "snakes" victory over the "snakes" of God's enemies! What tasks are before you today for which you need God's strength to succeed? Spend some time in prayer asking God to help you with your fears and to display His great strength!

97

FRIDAY 9

EXODUS 7:14-25

WHAT IS THE WRITER SAYING?

HOW CAN I APPLY THIS TO MY LIFE?

We now begin a study of the judgments, or *plagues*, which the LORD brought upon the Egyptians. It should be noted that these ten plagues covered a period of nine months, with the first plague coming at the time of the annual rise of the Nile (July-August). The tenth is commemorated by the Jewish feast of Passover which occurs in the month of April.

We are told that Pharaoh's heart was *hardened*. Literally, it means that Pharaoh was *dull, stupid, and stiff*, thus implying that Pharaoh's continued refusal was a *stupid* response to the overwhelming economic catastrophe being wrought upon the Egyptians by God's *judgments*. First we see the hand of the Lord on the Nile River that had been the source of Egypt's greatness. Opinions differ as to whether this was real blood or water the color of blood (likely from red clay in the annual flood waters). The problem presented by this plague was not the composition of the river water, but its results: the death of fish in it (vv. 18a, 21a) with the resulting smell, and lack of drinking water (vv. 18b, 21b, 24).

This plague challenged the Egyptian gods of the Nile, Hapi and Isis, as well as Khnum, the river's ram-god guardian. This miracle from God's hand should have brought the Egyptians to recognize Jehovah as the true God. But it didn't. The magicians managed to imitate the miracle (v. 22). The text says Pharaoh *did not* "set his heart to this" (v. 23). This means Pharaoh considered what action to take next and yet he chose to "set his heart" against the LORD who had demonstrated Himself to be the true God!

LIFE STEP Remember, Moses and Aaron also saw the power of the true God! Moses and Aaron were going to be used for more special things, so this demonstration from God also reinforced their faith. Similarly, what has God done in your life to demonstrate His love for you and His power to care for you as your Heavenly Father? Take a minute and write a note to God telling Him you have "set your heart" (v. 23) towards Him!

SATURDAY 9

EXODUS 8:1-15

WHAT IS THE WRITER SAYING?

HOW CAN I APPLY THIS TO MY LIFE?

PRAY North Korea – For opportunities to be given to godly Chinese businessmen so they may use their easy access to North Korea to share the Gospel.

Frogs, frogs everywhere! In the house, in the bedroom, on the bed, in the servants' houses, in the kitchen, covering the land. What a mess! The best the magicians of Egypt could do was to duplicate the miracle which would only add to the problem (v. 7). They could not do what was needed—diminish the number of frogs! But this was a mess that could have been avoided if the Egyptians would have chosen to yield to the command and demand of the Lord.

It is important to note that the frog was a sacred animal associated with the frog-headed goddess, Heqet. The ancient Egyptians believed Heqet was a water-goddess of the Nile, and was responsible for its annual flooding that provided a rich grain crop. It is interesting to note that at certain times of the year all along the Nile, thousands of frogs would appear. The Egyptians saw these many frogs as proof of a blessing and promise from Heqet, the fertility goddess, of the continued fruitfulness of the Nile.

So, by this second plague, Jehovah was challenging Heqet, goddess of the Egyptians! It was as if God were saying, "So you Egyptians believe Heqet blesses you with frogs to show she is in control of the Nile's fruitfulness. Thus you believe you should obey Heqet and ignore My commands! Well then, let's see which god truly controls the Nile frogs!"

We also note that Pharaoh calls for Moses and Aaron and requests that they pray on Pharaoh's behalf to the LORD to take away the frogs (v. 8a, an admission of the LORD's superiority over Heqet!). Pharaoh also promises to let the Hebrew slaves go if the LORD removed the frogs (v. 8b). Sadly Pharaoh, once he saw that the frogs were dying off, changes his mind and refuses to release the children of Israel.

 LIFE STEP The Lord is in control. Yes, He is a God of mercy and love, but He also hates sin and will challenge any god you put ahead of Him. (For us Christians, a false god is anything we obey instead of obeying the true God and His Word, the Bible.) Write a note to the Lord Jehovah expressing why He is your God and the One you will choose to obey.

EXODUS 8:16-32

WHAT IS THE WRITER SAYING?

HOW CAN I APPLY THIS TO MY LIFE?

The contest between the Lord and Pharaoh (and Pharaoh's gods) continues. This time it is the plague of gnats (lice) and flies. Notice that, while the demon-empowered magicians were powerful, this was a miracle-plague they could not replicate. They tried, but could not create lice (v. 18). The lice were spread "in all their coasts" (from border to border) (Psalm 105:31).

Note that one of the many gods that the Egyptians worshipped was Geb, the god over the dust (or dirt) of the earth. Geb was believed to bring life from the silt of the Nile River which became dust when the flood water receded each year. He was usually portrayed with dark green skin, the color of vegetation, and with leaves growing out of his skin. Clearly the true God of life, Jehovah, is challenging the Egyptian god, Geb, by bringing forth life (lice and flies) from the dust of the earth!

Ultimately the magicians recognized this as the "finger of God" (v. 19), a figure of speech that pictures the vastness of God's power, of which a finger would be just a part (see Exodus 31:18; Psalm 8:3; Luke 11:20).

Understand the compromise that Pharaoh proposed! Inundated by the gnats and flies, he seeks a compromise and says, "Go ye, sacrifice to your God in the land" (v. 25). He adds, "Ye shall not go very far away" (v. 28). Pharaoh was pleading for the children of Israel to intercede in prayer for the Egyptians to relieve them from the swarms of gnats and flies (v. 29).

Moses also insisted upon a spiritual principle that the worship of the LORD would also require the Israelites to remove themselves from the detestable practices of the Egyptians. Have you ever been accused of being "narrow" because you seek to stay far from the evil things of the world? Then you get the idea of Pharaoh's suggestion to stay close to the repulsive things of Egyptian idol worship.

LIFE STEP Similarly, Christians are to fully break with sin (1 John 2:15-16). Compromise with evil practices is not pleasing to the Lord; "… friendship of the world is enmity with God" (James 4:4). Are there things in your life that keep you "not far away" from sin? What temptations are there in your life from which you need to be "three days' journey" away so that in a weak moment you don't again go back to them?

EXODUS 9:1-12

WHAT IS THE WRITER SAYING?

HOW CAN I APPLY THIS TO MY LIFE?

PRAY Guatemala – For the rapid and accurate completion of the several Bible translation projects in progress.

Two more plagues (5 and 6) from the LORD upon the Egyptians are presented in today's passage: a pestilence upon Egyptian livestock, verses 1-7, and a plague of festering boils upon the Egyptians, verses 8-12. The text says that all the cattle of Egypt died, with the qualification that the cattle of the Israelites did not. Since Exodus 9:19 and12:29 speaks of further danger for Egyptian cattle, the Egyptians must have purchased some of the Israelite's cattle in the meantime.

While reading this paragraph did you notice God's care of His people? Israel, a pastoral people, was spared the effects of these catastrophic plagues (vv. 4, 6). The LORD's carefulness to make a distinction between His people, Israel, and the Egyptians provided additional evidence that Jehovah was indeed sending the plagues. This was not some natural disease that had infected the cattle – this was a judgment from the LORD! This came as a surprise to Pharaoh who sent officials to Goshen to verify if Israelite cattle had been equally plagued (v. 7).

We should note that cattle were also very important in Egyptian religion. The goddess of joy and motherhood was *Hathor*, the Mistress of Life. She was always depicted with cow horns, sometimes with cow ears, and even as an entire cow. She was often considered to be the mother of the Pharaoh, who in turn was often called "*son of Hathor.*" Clearly, Hathor, Mistress of Life, could not stop Jehovah, Creator and Sustainer of life, from destroying the cattle of Egypt!

Again we read that "the Lord hardened the heart of Pharaoh" (v. 12). After a series of plagues, after opportunities to turn to God, and after a constant refusal to heed God's command, it is as though God finally says, "Enough Pharaoh, I am the true God Who shall be obeyed." Pharaoh discovered that this was a very dangerous way to live!

LIFE STEP God's people were protected by God from this disastrous plague. This is a picture to Christians of our walk in the Spirit, for such a walk results in the believer being preserved by our faithful God. When times are tough and difficult, remember that the Lord cares for and protects His people. Consider someone you know who needs the protecting hand of God. Take some time to pray for this person in need.

TUESDAY 10

EXODUS 9:13-26

WHAT IS THE WRITER SAYING?

HOW CAN I APPLY THIS TO MY LIFE?

PRAY Give thanks for all God has given to you.

Today we consider the seventh plague. The LORD again tells Moses to demand of Pharaoh that he release of the Hebrew slaves (v. 13). If Pharaoh again refused the following would happen:

- The LORD says "I will ...send all my plagues" (v. 14a). This is to be understood to mean that the next plagues would be greater in devastation than all six of the earlier, lesser plagues.

- This plague would be so awesome that the power of the Lord and His name would be reported "throughout all the earth" (v. 16). Notice God had a world-wide mission in view even back then. All the people of the earth would know that He alone was the great and true God.

- If Pharaoh continued to *exalt himself against God's people* (v. 17; *Pharaoh raising himself up like a god who reigns over Israel*), then the true God would bring upon Egypt the most terrifying hailstorm in all of Egypt's history (v. 18).

- This plague was to be so disastrous that for the first time the LORD included a warning to seek shelter ahead of time (v. 19). Again, this advanced warning reinforced the Egyptian's understanding that this was God's judgment and not just a rare but natural weather event.

- Finally, this plague would clearly show that the Egyptian gods could not begin to stand against the power of the LORD; neither *Nut*, the sky goddess, nor *Set*, the storm god, could hold back the hail storm Jehovah was bringing. Also, *Osiris*, the god of bountiful crops, could not protect the maturing crops (especially flax and barley, v. 31a).

There are *two vital lessons* to be learned here: <u>First</u>, the LORD would be known by all and would to be obeyed by all; all the Egyptians, all the Israelites, and all the peoples of the earth! <u>Second,</u> the LORD gives gracious warnings of judgment to as many as will listen to Him.

LIFE STEP The Lord continues to desire that *none should perish (destroyed by God's judgment,* 2 Peter 3:9). God always wants sinners to repent of their sin and turn to God seeking His mercy and forgiveness! How about taking a minute and making a short list of people you know that need to be warned of God's coming judgment upon their sin?

EXODUS 9:27-35

WHAT IS THE WRITER SAYING?

HOW CAN I APPLY THIS TO MY LIFE?

PRAY Ecuador – Development of close relationships between existing churches and new missionaries.

This passage begins with a confession on the part of Pharaoh. Several important things are said in Pharaoh's confession:

- Pharaoh has admitted that God is the true and righteous God!
- Pharaoh confesses that he and the Egyptians are wicked people who have sinned and were deserving of God's judgment (v. 27).
- Pharaoh, for the third time, asks for the removal of the LORD's judgment with a personal promise to correct his ways and let the Hebrews go to worship the LORD (8:8, 28).

But sadly, such is not the case. As soon as the hail and thunder ceased, Pharaoh's fear of God also ceased (v. 34). Yes, they were truly frightened when thunder and hail poured out and fire ran along the ground (v. 23), but Moses could see they had no real intention of obeying God and complying with God's command after the storm ceased (v. 30). While Pharaoh is crying to Moses, *Ask the Lord to make it stop!* Pharaoh does so with a heart that is unchanged (v. 28). We read, "And when Pharaoh saw that the rain… [had] ceased, he sinned yet more…, he and his servants" (v. 34).

What does one do when people mouth the right words but have no intention to change? Well, let's notice what Moses did. He left the city and went into the presence of the Lord in prayer (v. 29). He was aware that Pharaoh was less than sincere, in spite of what he said (v. 30). Yet, Moses still asked the Lord to stop the hail so Pharaoh and the Egyptians, even in his half-hearted confession, would know that "the earth is the Lord's" (v. 29).

Did you notice how Moses responded to the dishonesty of Pharaoh? Moses saw that Pharaoh was seeking to avoid his punishment for sin and was not seeking to turn from his sin! Yet Moses did what honored God and what would demonstrate that "the earth is the Lord's."

 LIFE STEP No doubt you, like Moses, come in contact with people who are dishonest, deceitful, or half-hearted in their actions toward God. Write a note to God asking Him to show you how you can be used by God to help your friend who needs to see that "the earth is the Lord's."

THURSDAY 10

EXODUS 10:1-15

WHAT IS THE WRITER SAYING?

HOW CAN I APPLY THIS TO MY LIFE?

PRAY Philippines – Safety of missionaries working within the reach of Muslim extremists in Mindanao.

In today's paragraph, we have the eighth plague—locusts. Have you ever wondered why the Lord would have Moses announce the plagues on Pharaoh when the Lord knew, as did Moses, that Pharaoh and the Egyptians would not listen? In these verses, we learn that a *plague* to Egypt was also to be a *sign* to Israel (v. 2). Not only was the Lord interested in changing Pharaoh's mind, the events were also to be great signs or lessons from the Lord that would be told to Moses' (and Israel's) children and grandchildren. The Lord would use this historical event and His divine intervention to educate God's people. So, one purpose of the plagues was, "that ye (Moses and the Hebrews) may know how that I am the Lord" (v. 2).

First, we must notice that Pharaoh's own advisors by now were convinced that they were being *destroyed* by the LORD God of Israel (v. 7)! So they sought to convince Pharaoh to let the Hebrew slaves leave Egypt and go into the wilderness to serve this all-powerful God.

Notice that Pharaoh again offers a compromising solution to the demand of the Lord that Pharaoh let the Hebrews go. He says, "Go, serve the Lord your God: but who are they that shall go?" (v. 8) Earlier it had been, "Go, but not very far away" (Exodus 8:28). Now it is, *Go, but I will limit who is allowed to go.*

Now, notice that Moses understood the implied meaning of the offered compromise – just the men may go, but not the women, children or the grandparents, nor the flocks and herds (their source of income; v. 9)! The point of this wicked king is clear to Moses: *You men can go if you insist, but I will make it so you must return* (v. 10). Pharaoh desired to maintain control over Israel and ensure that his slaves would return after a time of worship.

LIFE STEP It is God's will that we turn our backs on similar compromises we face. The point for us is that there is to be no bargaining with the world! How would the world around you want you to compromise God's standard of holy separation in your daily life?

FRIDAY '10

EXODUS 10:16-29

WHAT IS THE WRITER SAYING?

HOW CAN I APPLY THIS TO MY LIFE?

PRAY Korea – For the message of the gospel to penetrate North Korea's isolation from the modern world.

Darkness is the subject of this ninth plague. This time, without warning or demands upon Pharaoh, God brought a plague of darkness to all the land of Egypt for three days. Scripture say that it was "thick" and could be "felt." Perhaps it was like a super-dense fog or perhaps the words are explaining that the Egyptians could only get around by "feeling" their way about their homes (vv. 22-23).

Clearly this plague was intended to be an overwhelming display of Jehovah's power as the true Master of the sun and heavens! Pharaoh and the Egyptians had exalted to the highest position their gods of the sun, whether that is Ra, the sun-god, usually depicted with a sun-disk resting on his head, or Horus, the heavens-god, usually depicted with a falcon head. Now God brings darkness to show that the sun-idol of light is powerless.

Don't miss the most wonderful of contrasts given here. While darkness was engulfing the Egyptians, "all the children of Israel had light in their dwellings" (v. 23). Unlike the powerless god of the Egyptians, God gave His people light during the darkness of this plague. Again, the LORD had marked out a difference between those who feared and worshipped God and those who had turned to other false and weak gods to aid them.

Scripture says a lot about light and darkness. Of greatest importance is the declaration by Christ, "I am the light of the world: he that followeth me shall not walk in darkness, but shall have the light of life" (John 8:12). A.C. Gaebelein writes, "The suspense must have been frightful. What was to come next? God waited, and in the silence and darkness He appealed to their conscience. How slow God is to judge. In infinite patience He waited before He dealt the final blow to Egypt."

Determine that you are going to "walk in the light, as he is in the light" (1John 1:7). There are many things that attract our attention. Some of these can easily gain the focus of our lives and, as such, these will become modern-day *sun-gods* for us. Is there any *sun-god* upon which you are focusing that is replacing your attention to God?

EXODUS 11:1-10

WHAT IS THE WRITER SAYING?

HOW CAN I APPLY THIS TO MY LIFE?

Remember that in Exodus 10:29, Moses was threatened that if he ever saw Pharaoh's face again, Moses would die. Moses apparently knew that the tenth and greatest plague, the death of the firstborn, was about to take place. So Moses turns Pharaoh's words back on Pharaoh as a dire warning of the yet-to-be-announced tenth plague. When Moses said, "I will see thy face again no more" (v. 29), Moses was not declaring that he was quitting because he feared Pharaoh. Rather Moses was declaring that Pharaoh was about to die! Apparently we are to understand the words, "And the Lord said," of verse 1 to mean, *The Lord had already said*, since in Exodus 10:29, Moses speaks with knowledge of the events of Exodus 11:1.

Note that the Lord intervened, giving the Hebrew slaves favor in the sight of the Egyptians (v. 3). After all the plagues, there was great respect for Israel (and likely a great fear of Israel's God, Jehovah) among the common people of Egypt! Also note that Moses was considered "very great in the land of Egypt" in the sight of Pharaoh's advisors and among the Egyptian people. No doubt many Egyptians (even Pharaoh's own advisors) had come to know that the God of Moses was very great and their own gods were powerless!

Verse 7 says, "Against any of the children of Israel shall not a dog move his tongue." This is an obscure, ancient saying which means, *A dog shall not even growl against an Israelite*. It is declaring that not even the slightest harm would come to Israel as they go through this last plague.

LIFE STEP Knowing the Lord is pleased to bring comfort to His people who go through troubles for His purposes, we must ask ourselves, "Does this problem, hardship, or trial cause me to worry and fret or do I trust in the Lord to not even let 'a dog move his tongue' against me?" What is a current trouble you need to place before God?

SUNDAY 11

EXODUS 12:1-13

WHAT IS THE WRITER SAYING?

HOW CAN I APPLY THIS TO MY LIFE?

In this passage we have the establishment of a holiday that was to remember the birth of a nation, Israel. The LORD told Moses that this first Passover meal was to be Israel's "beginning of months" (v. 2), which is to say Israel started a new calendar with this first Passover as *day one* (this was over 3455 years ago!).

The LORD also required that the Passover lamb be slain and its blood applied to each home's entrance doorframe as a declaration that all within were trusting by faith that God would spare them from His judgment upon the firstborn in Egypt. When He saw their demonstration of faith in God upon the doorposts, He would pass over them (v. 13).

Here we also have the first use of the term "all the congregation of Israel." It refers to the gathering together of all people of faith in Israel for the purpose of worshipping the LORD. While the Israelites in this passage were meeting in many houses throughout Goshen in Egypt, they understood that they all were meeting together to worship the Lord.

Of course, later passages of Scripture tell us that the lamb here was a "type" or picture of God's coming Lamb, the Lord Jesus (John 1:29). Note that they took four days (vv. 3, 6) to examine the lamb to be sure it was without blemish. Likewise, Christ would be our "without blemish" Passover Lamb (1 Corinthians 5:7). Just as God accepted the blood on the door posts of the homes where the Hebrews trusted by faith in God's protection from the judgment upon the first-born, so it is for us Christians today; God the Father accepts the blood of Christ as payment for our debt of sin. Our responsibility is to trust by faith in Christ's blood to spare us from God's coming judgment upon sin. On the day we accept Christ as our Savior it becomes our "beginning of months." We become a part of God's heavenly nation operating under God's eternal *calendar*!

 LIFE STEP The Lamb of God, Christ Jesus, is precious to us; precious in that He died to redeem us; precious in that we find in Him our daily satisfaction. If you have already asked Jesus to save you from the coming judgment upon your sins, take a moment to mentally feast upon the wonders of your new life in Christ.

MONDAY '11

EXODUS 12:14-24

WHAT IS THE WRITER SAYING?

HOW CAN I APPLY THIS TO MY LIFE?

PRAY South Africa – Boldness for pastors in a society that no longer holds to moral absolutes, and where the media has pushed abortion, pornography, and gambling.

Today we continue to read about Israel's new annual memorial (v. 14), the Passover, which was to be practiced by all future generations. Closely associated with the Passover meal there was to be a week where the Hebrews ate only *unleavened bread* (vv. 15, 18); bread dough was to be made without the yeast, or "leaven," that normally causes the dough to rise, resulting in a flat bread. Also, the Hebrews were to prepare for their annual *week of unleavened bread* by "putting away" (*a cleansing to remove any remnant of a thing*) all leaven that was found within their houses (vv. 15, 19).

We must note that these two memorials, the *Passover meal* and the *Week of Unleavened Bread*, were to be a *double teaching tool* that illustrated for Hebrew families how a person of faith was to live. First there was a picture of being saved from God's soon-coming judgment upon sin. Then there was a continuing picture of how people of faith were to live each day; their life was to be free from the corrupting effects of sin (a spiritual leaven). The lesson was that people of faith were privileged to eat God's *holy cuisine*, a life not corrupted by sin! Families were to teach their children that sin in a person's life was like a small piece of leaven that permeates an entire loaf of bread. Thus there must be a search through a person's conduct so that there can be a "putting away" or a *cleansing to remove any remnant* of the sin that had formerly been a part of his life!

Clearly, the New Testament likens leaven to sin in the life of a believer, "Purge out therefore the old leaven, that ye may be a new lump ... Therefore let us keep the feast ... with the unleavened bread of sincerity and truth" (1 Corinthians 5:7-8). For a Christian, putting away sin should be characteristic of his walk after his salvation.

 LIFE STEP We Christians also need to examine our lives allowing the Holy Spirit to bring sin to light. Then we need to confess it and remove it from our lives (1 John 1:9). Will you do some *house cleaning* of your own? What "leaven" of sin is hidden in the back room of your life that needs to be removed?

TUESDAY 11

EXODUS 12:25-36

WHAT IS THE WRITER SAYING?

HOW CAN I APPLY THIS TO MY LIFE?

PRAY Thailand – For believers to be wise stewards of the new prosperity that their society is experiencing.

Today's passage begins by making it apparent that the Lord was interested in the future generation of Hebrews keeping the work of God's redemption before the people of God. Children were to be reminded of His great work for them (vv. 26-27). Note the obedience of God's people; they "bowed the head" (v. 27), which is to say they submitted to God's instructions and then they "did as the Lord had commanded" (v. 28).

The devastating climax of the ten plagues is here presented with the death of all the firstborn throughout the land of Egypt, from Pharaoh's family down to the lowest prisoner (v. 29). The hour of the judgment was midnight, the darkest hour in the middle of the night, to emphasize the Egyptian's inability to escape from the LORD's righteous judgment and to emphasize the terror of God's righteous judgment upon sin. God did not pass over those houses in Egypt where there was no blood applied to the door-posts. With every house in Egypt devastated by the death of at least one first-born (v. 30b), a "great cry" arose across Egypt.

The Egyptians were now terrified of the God of their Hebrew slaves, "We be all dead men" (v. 33b). They were convinced that their keeping the Hebrew slaves any longer would result in every Egyptian being killed by the LORD. (Also note that they found no hope in or help from any of their own false gods). As a result they were *urgent to send the Hebrews out of the land* (v. 33a). They even gave the Hebrews their jewelry, silver, gold, and clothing to aid the Hebrews on their journey out of Egypt (v. 35).

Now that the Passover was finished, God's people began their long-awaited journey out of bondage (v. 31). They were to leave Egypt behind and follow the Lord.

LIFE STEP Simply put, this is precisely what we Christians must do after we have been saved from our sin. We leave the world (Egypt for us becomes a type or picture of the world). We must remove the "leaven" of sin from every corner of our lives. And we now look for specific directions as to where the Lord wants us to go. Consider how the Lord wants you to "rise up …and go" (v. 31) in your daily walk of service for Him.

EXODUS 12:37-51

WHAT IS THE WRITER SAYING?

HOW CAN I APPLY THIS TO MY LIFE?

The Hebrews' journey out of Egypt has begun. The Hebrews, who were concentrated in the "*land of Rameses*" (see Genesis 47:11), which was a part of the Nile River delta (v. 37a), began to move out of Egypt by heading to Succoth, a town on the eastern edge of Egypt (not yet in the desert areas of the Sinai Peninsula). The number of Hebrew men gathered was about 600,000 (v. 37b). If the women and children were added to this count, the total would easily exceed two million.

Notice the "mixed multitude" (v. 38) or *people of many races* that gathered with them. Apparently, slaves and other non-Egyptians took this opportunity to leave Egypt. Some Egyptians had been impressed with the miracles they saw and had no doubt become genuine believers in the true God, Jehovah. Apparently these desired to worship the LORD along with the Hebrews in the wilderness. Some of the Egyptians had intermarried with the Jews. Others of this mixed multitude were fearful to remain in Egypt after the ten plagues. But overall, this mixed multitude was to be a thorn to the Israelites in the years to come. In about two years, the mixed multitude would become the first to complain about the manna which was given to Israel for daily food (Numbers 11:4).

The time element given here (v. 41) began with Joseph's family going into Egypt (1876 B.C., Genesis 47:4-12). Note that these four hundred years in Egypt are what God told Abraham would take place (Genesis 15:13).

Our text also tells us that there is a lesson to be learned here! Since God had been "vigilant" (v. 42a; KJV uses "observed"; *keenly watchful* from a root word for *watchman*), the Hebrews in years to come were to be just as *keenly vigilant* in keeping watch over their worship of the LORD and in their teaching their children of God's faithfulness to Israel (v. 42b).

 LIFE STEP The lesson applies to us Christians! The Lord has also shown Himself to be *vigilant* in watching over us; first to bring us to salvation and then to daily guide us in our walk and service for Him. Make a list of some the ways the Lord has been *vigilant* in His care for you!

THURSDAY 11

EXODUS 13:1-10

WHAT IS THE WRITER SAYING?

HOW CAN I APPLY THIS TO MY LIFE?

PRAY No interference from civil authorities in the cities where street evangelism takes place.

Today's passage is a mingling of two subjects; concerning the firstborn (vv. 1-2), concerning the Feast of Unleavened Bread (vv. 3-10), and then back again to concerning the firstborn (vv. 11-16)! Yet Moses saw these two subjects linked to one theme, that is, instructions that parents were to give, from year to year (v. 10), to their firstborn sons (vv. 2, 8, 14). So we have a *double-remembrance* (v. 3) that was to be explained to every "son" (v. 8), presumably focusing on the firstborn sons (v. 2) who would inherit the family's property and become responsible to lead the next generation in *remembering* the *strong hand of the LORD*.

• First, Hebrew families, when they have firstborn, both "of man and of beast," were to "remember" (v. 3) that God saved all of Israel's first-born *with a strong hand* (vv. 3, 9) when the Hebrews came out of Egypt and as a result all of

these were to be sanctified (consecrated & dedicated as belonging to God).

• Second, Hebrew families were to "remember" God's *bringing them out* of Egypt (v. 3b) by having a seven-day "memorial" (v.9), the Feast of Unleavened Bread. A key part of this annual holiday was the removal of all leaven from their homes. Since, on the day the Hebrews left Egypt, all their "leaven" (a dough-ball containing yeast held over from the previous day's batch of dough) was *Egyptian leaven* this memorial was to display a *breaking away* from all connection to all the sinfulness of the Egyptians. After seven days without leaven, new bread with leaven would picture the pure and consecrated life provided by the LORD to Hebrews whom He had freed.

Also, like Israel, we are to remember that we are now on a journey.

LIFE STEP Just as it was important for Israel to remember their salvation from "bondage" to the Egyptians (v. 3), so is it important for us Christians to remember that we have been saved from our bondage to our sin. Once a person is saved, his Christian life must be foremost a walk with God that focuses on inner purity and dedication to the Lord. So then, what spiritual "leaven" do you need to sweep out of your inner house?

EXODUS 13:11-22

WHAT IS THE WRITER SAYING?

HOW CAN I APPLY THIS TO MY LIFE?

PRAY Haiti – Pray for a spiritual outpouring of faith in God in the aftermath of the earthquake also shook the nation and moved the entire world.

The first subject in today's passage deals with redeeming the firstborn. This was to be a constant reminder that God had redeemed Israel from slavery. In the ancient world, someone was said to have been "redeemed" when a price was paid to obtain a captive's release or a slave's freedom. Remember that God had redeemed all Israel from slavery by means of the LORD's strong hand (v. 14b) which was displayed in the tenth plague (v. 15), the death of all the Egyptian firstborn animals and sons. Thus it was God's right to demand that He be repaid by Israel with the sacrifice of a lamb for all Israel's free firstborn.

The second subject in today's passage displays the wisdom of the Lord. The Lord commanded Israel not to take the shortest way with the best roads to the Promised Land (v. 17a, which went through the land of the Philistines). The Lord knew Israel was not ready for war with the powerful Philistines. Since their confidence in the Lord was still weak, they would have been demoralized by war with the Philistines. Then they would have changed their minds about following the Lord and desired to return to Egypt (v. 17b). Notice that God knew their weaknesses and frailties. God wisely chose the long way around through a hard desert (v. 18). For Israel, the good road was not the good choice for the strengthening of Israel's trust in the Lord.

Yet we also are reminded that the LORD provided continuous guidance for His people while they were in the hard desert places by means of the pillar of cloud and the pillar of fire (vv. 21-22)!

LIFE STEP

How wonderful to know that our steps are also ordered of the Lord and that He is directing our paths (Proverbs 3:5-6). Don't be surprised if He directs your steps the long way around to His intended goal for your life! Perhaps the Lord has directed your life's path through a hard desert so you can be spiritually strengthened as you learn to trust in Him for your daily needs. Consider the things you need from the Lord so you may follow the hard desert path He has chosen for you.

EXODUS 14:1-14

WHAT IS THE WRITER SAYING?

HOW CAN I APPLY THIS TO MY LIFE?

PRAY Azerbaijan – Pray for the Azeri church to become an effective witness to non-Christians.

We are not surprised that Pharaoh would pursue Israel after making his promise to let them go again. Nor are we surprised to learn the Lord intended to turn around Israel's impossible situation so He would be honored through it (v. 4). Notice that Israel was to stop fearing the problems and start seeing the care of God for His people (v. 13).

When Pharaoh came after Israel, the Hebrews knew they were in an impossible situation (v. 3). Now the big question was, how would Israel react to the situation? Would they put their trust in the Lord to protect them? Their reaction is disappointing. They had just seen God's protection as they went through the ten plagues upon the Egyptians. Yet they had not learned that they could trust God for protection during this next trial. Rather their reaction was fear and apprehension (v. 10). They attacked Moses and reminded him they were skeptics in the first place (v. 12). They even suggested that their past life as slaves was better than this (v. 12). They thought their choice was to serve the Egyptians or die in the wilderness (v. 12b). How short-sighted they were!

There was another choice that they failed to consider. It was to "stand still, and see the salvation of the LORD" (v. 13). Remember, God said, "Fear ye not, stand still and see ..." (v. 13). The LORD declares to Israel that He Himself was going to fight for them (v. 14a). As the Egyptian chariots sped towards them (v. 10), Moses says, "you shall see them again no more forever" (v. 13b). God was going to bring upon the Egyptian army an eleventh plague, their destruction in the Red Sea.

LIFE STEP The lesson for us? Our ability to trust God for our next difficult situation is based upon His past faithfulness. Remember you have not two, but rather three choices! When you face your next spiritual battle, don't surrender to the enemy, and don't die in spiritual defeat, rather trust the Lord to give you spiritual victory!

EXODUS 14:15-31

WHAT IS THE WRITER SAYING?

HOW CAN I APPLY THIS TO MY LIFE?

PRAY Mexico – For discipleship programs that would effectively teach how the Bible impacts family life.

This is a day of victory for Israel. They were told to stand still and see the salvation of the Lord (v. 13). The terrible horses and chariots of Egypt were closing in behind them. The cloud (a demonstration of the personal presence of God), which normally moved before the host of Israel to lead them, now moves behind them for their protection. The cloud acted as a wall that blocked the progress of the Egyptians.

So Israel crossed the Red Sea as God caused it to go back by a strong east wind. Again, having been redeemed from their slavery, they were enjoying another phase of God's protection. This corresponds to the believer's ongoing victory after he has been saved. We must not only rest in the finished work of the Lord to provide us with salvation, but we must also rest in the fact of His presence with us to give protection.

Be sure to notice that what seemed impossible to Israel was more than possible with the Lord in His power. He parts the Red Sea and causes the Egyptians' chariot wheels to fall off (v. 25). He allows Israel to cross and then He destroys the incapacitated Egyptian army.

We read, "The Lord *saved* Israel that day" (v. 30). The Hebrew word "saved" is from the same root as the name *Joshua* or *Jesus*. When we say, "Jesus saves," we are stating the truth about the redemptive work of Christ. In effect we are saying, "The Rescuer rescues!" We also read, "... and the people feared the LORD, and *believed* the LORD" (v. 31). The Hebrew word "believed" here does not imply an initial faith in God but rather indicates a *maturing confidence and trust* in God as their *sure and reliable foundation.*

 LIFE STEP

In Hebrews 11 we read, "By faith they passed through the Red Sea, as by dry land" (Hebrews 11:29). Yes, it was the power and might of the Lord, and the *faith* of a humble people that resulted in such victory. In what issue or trouble do you need to exercise this kind of *confident trust* in the Lord? Yes, the Lord *saved you* eternally, but are you continuing to *trust* Him to be reliable in *saving* you in daily trials?

EXODUS 15:1-13

WHAT IS THE WRITER SAYING?

HOW CAN I APPLY THIS TO MY LIFE?

PRAY Switzerland – Pray that many may find a personal relationship with Jesus and come to assurance of salvation in every community.

This is the first song mentioned in the Bible. It is not surprising to find God's people singing here after they had been saved through the Red Sea. As believers, we also should sing concerning the death and resurrection of Christ. We have been redeemed as well, only it is from drowning in our sin. Thus we, too, can sing, "I will declare thy name unto my brethren: in the midst of the congregation will I praise thee" (Psalm 22:22).

The essence of Moses' song is seen in verse 2. Moses and all those who had crossed the Red Sea with him declare, "The Lord is *my* strength and song..., and *my* salvation." Indeed, we can add, "*My* God." The song summarizes the account of their deliverance (vv. 4-10). Notice that this song is personal. Dear friend, is He that personal to you? Can you say, "The Lord is *my God*?" Do you draw from His strength on a daily basis (Isaiah 41:10)? Is he *your song* (Psalm 40:3) and do you reflect the joy of the Lord, singing praises for all He has done? Finally is He *your salvation* (1 Timothy 1:15)? Not only has He saved us from sin's penalty, He is presently saving us from sin's power!

A key word in this song is *mercy*. Just like Israel, we are saved by His mercy, for He is "rich in mercy" (Ephesians 2:4). Remember, His mercy extends in a daily direction.

Notice the list of things that Moses points out of the character of God: God is my strength, song, and salvation (v. 2); He is glorious and excellent (vv. 6-7); God is unlike all the gods of Egypt, He is holy, fearful, and a doer of wonders (v. 11); God is merciful, a redeemer, and a guide (v. 13).

 LIFE STEP Not only do we look to Him as our Redeemer (and sing about it), but we may also look to Him as the One Who goes before us and guides us in the way we should go. So, in what areas do you need to trust Him today? Take time to explain to our Lord how you cannot see ahead on the path you are traveling, and then ask Him to lead you through it.

TUESDAY '12

EXODUS 15:14-27

WHAT IS THE WRITER SAYING?

HOW CAN I APPLY THIS TO MY LIFE?

PRAY Romania – For Romanians who will go as missionaries to countries inaccessible to other foreigners.

The first part of today's passage is the conclusion of Moses' song to Israel and it is prophetic in character; notice the nine future-looking occurrences of "shall" in verses 14-18. The nations that are listed (Philistia, Edom, Moab, Canaan) are future opponents of Israel in the land they would soon go on to possess. But there is a *far view* here, too, as we consider the Lord's "*for ever and ever*" (v. 18) work of *re-planting* Israel (vv. 17-18).

The second half of today's passage deals with Israel's journey away from their Red Sea crossing into the Wilderness of Shur for three days (v. 22). Finally they arrived at the pool of Marah (likely one of the pools in the Sinai Peninsula along its eastern shore of the Gulf of Suez), but they could not drink its water as it was bitter. No doubt their initial joy upon seeing the pool became bitter disappointment when they found the waters to be undrinkable. This is often

what happens spiritually to believers. We begin moving forward in our Christian walk only to be disappointed when we walk into bitter events along our spiritual path.

Notice that God gave them this "bitter" disappointment to *prove them* (v. 25b), i.e., *to test so as to know the quality of their faith*). God already knew how to fix the problem; a special tree was cast into the pool to sweeten it. The point is that Israel could have prayed for help instead of murmuring against God's servant, Moses (v. 24). The passage then gives us a spiritual insight: if we diligently follow God's ways, He will *heal* the *bitter pools* along our life's spiritual path. His hand will sustain us.

Don't miss the final step on this trail. After the bitter pool of Marah, they traveled to the twelve wells of Elim – the place of refreshing. How wonderful for us that God's refreshing "Elims" often follow the bitter "Marahs."

 LIFE STEP Yes, there will be bitter "Marahs" in life as you continue on your spiritual walk. But trust in the Lord; He can make sweet the bitter "Marahs" of your spiritual life. Remember, if you keep traveling on His path, He will likely bring you to refreshing places like the oasis of Elim.

WEDNESDAY '12

EXODUS 16:1-13

WHAT IS THE WRITER SAYING?

HOW CAN I APPLY THIS TO MY LIFE?

PRAY Columbia – Pray for the safety and accuracy of those participating in Bible translation projects.

It is hard to believe the children of Israel had been redeemed by the Lord from their slavery, saved from the disasters of the plagues, delivered from an awful enemy, and yet they turned quickly to complaining against the Lord. Well, hard to believe until we remember the many times we, as Christians, complain even though we, too, have been greatly blessed.

After the Passover, after the deliverance at the Red Sea, and after the balmy refreshment of Elim, we find Israel grumbling (the meaning of *murmuring* found eight times in our passage). Grumbling is one of the first signs of a carnal, selfish heart. After all God had done, they still wished they had not taken this journey! The only answer from God was patience, grace, and a response of abundance of manna. He rained "bread from heaven" as He sent them manna (v. 4).

Be sure to note that they were told to collect the manna every morning. This was to be a part of the lesson God had for them. God's care comes one day at a time for us, too—you cannot store it up. Every day is a new lesson about trust in God's provision for you for that day. This is an important lesson for each of us in our wilderness journeys. Each of us must daily feast on the Lord and find our satisfaction in Him. Jesus said, "I am the bread of life; he that cometh to me shall never hunger; and he that believeth on me shall never thirst" (John 6:35).

 What a great lesson this is for us! Every morning, God will provide the "food" you need to sustain you through the day. Every day you need to collect your feast from the Lord. This is accomplished as you read and meditate upon His Word and then trust in His daily care. Oh yes, that is what you are doing right now! Keep it up.

EXODUS 16:14-22

WHAT IS THE WRITER SAYING?

HOW CAN I APPLY THIS TO MY LIFE?

In our passage today we have the LORD's response to the *murmurings* of Israel as they continued into the wilderness; the LORD sent them manna (v. 15)! It is interesting that the name given to this food was not a description of the food, for instance they could have called it, "haspas," which is the Hebrew word translated in verse 14 as *small, round things*. Actually the name, *manna*, is a description to the people's reaction to seeing the "small round things" appear after the morning's dew (v. 14). "Manna" is really a one-word question meaning *what is it?*

Notice Moses' description of the daily manna. When asked about it, Moses said, "This is the bread which the Lord hath given you to eat" (v.15). In the Psalms we read, "And had rained down manna upon them to eat, and had given them the corn of heaven. Man did eat angels' food: he sent them meat to the full" (Psalm 78:24-25). It was gathered every morning according to their need (v. 21).

There is a wonderful passage in the Book of Numbers that helps us here. We read, "And when the dew fell upon the camp in the night, the manna fell upon it" (Numbers 11:9). Someone has suggested that *the dew prepares a clean place for the manna to fall*.

When we taste and feed on the Word of God, the Bible, we are feasting on our *morning manna from Heaven*. God has personally given us the Bible so we can eat of it and be filled with our spiritual food for the day. Just like in the ancient days of Israel, we cannot depend on yesterday's "eating" of the Word as being sufficient for today. Just like Israel, we must gather and eat of our "bread from Heaven" every morning, every day!

 LIFE STEP Just think about it. God Himself, like the morning dew, was already there and waiting for you this morning as you arose and began to eat a feast from the Bible! Consider what He wants you to learn from His Word today that will sustain you through some challenging event you will face later today. Let us never forget the way He supplies us.

FRIDAY '12

EXODUS 16:23-36

WHAT IS THE WRITER SAYING?

HOW CAN I APPLY THIS TO MY LIFE?

PRAY Bulgaria – Pray for reconciliation among believers concerning past conflicts and compromises.

One of the best descriptions of manna is found in today's passage: "it was like coriander seed, white; and the taste of it was like wafers made with honey" (v. 31). The coriander plant looks like carrot tops and its seed is an aromatic herb used to season foods in the same way poppy or sesame seeds are used today. This was the Lord's provision and, as we have learned, it was to be collected daily by every person and eaten to the full. Any leftovers would spoil by the next morning!

Notice that a special condition applied to the Friday collection of manna. Two days' worth was collected so as to provide food for Saturday, their Sabbath Day of rest. The Friday collection did not spoil on Saturday.

Also notice that "some of the people" did not collect a double portion on Friday and so they were found out in the fields trying to collect manna on Saturday, which was to be the seventh-day of Sabbath (v. 27a). Their negligence in preparing for the LORD's required day of rest resulted in their *finding none* (v. 27b) on the Sabbath! Their actions resulted in God's rebuke (vv. 28-29).

Also note that this was such a unique miracle of God's provision that Moses commanded an "omer" (about two quarts) of manna be collected in a pot and placed permanently on display for all of Israel's children to see and remember how God had fed this first generation for forty years in the wilderness (v. 32). Later the pot of manna was collected with other items of remembrance to keep inside the ark (Hebrews 9:4), which itself was placed under the mercy seat in the tabernacle.

LIFE STEP In a similar way, it is often a good thing for us Christians to keep a few little reminders of the great things God has done in our lives. This writer has kept the small half of a stick from a campfire meeting where he dedicated his life to the service of the Lord Jesus. The larger half he tossed into the fire indicating his desire to serve the Lord. The kept half stays in a pencil jar on his desk to remember his decision. What could you display (perhaps something as simple as a photo on a mirror) to remind yourself of some special blessings from the Lord?

SATURDAY 12

WHAT IS THE WRITER SAYING?

HOW CAN I APPLY THIS TO MY LIFE?

PRAY
Praise God for sending His Son to be our Savior.

God's people, Israel, continued their journey in the wilderness. God had been gracious by not only redeeming them from slavery in Egypt, but providing manna for their food in the wilderness. Rather than seeing the past mercies of the Lord as reason for trusting God to provide for their present needs, they again sink into unbelief. They are out of water and they complain to Moses. In desperation, Moses looks to the Lord and is told to strike the rock in Horeb (v. 6). When he does so, water comes out. Next we see Amalek fighting with Israel at Rephidim (vv. 8-16). Again, the provision of the Lord was apparent to all, especially to the army of Israel and its commander, Joshua. The Lord commanded Moses to stand on top of the hill with the rod of God in his raised hands. When he weakened and "let down his hand," Joshua and the army began to lose. When Aaron and Hur assisted Moses by holding up his arms, Joshua and the army began to win. It was apparent to all that day that the LORD had caused Israel to win the victory. No doubt Joshua, as commander of the army, had a plan for the battle, no doubt each soldier of Israel fought hard, yet all knew that their trust and dependence on God had resulted in God granting them victory.

An important side-note here: Joshua is mentioned here for the first time in the Bible. Clearly, Joshua, while unknown to us readers, was known and respected by Moses and the children of Israel. Clearly, the army trusted Joshua's military leadership. (Hebrew tradition says Joshua had been an assistant to an Egyptian general and thus understood military tactics.) Clearly, Joshua was already a man of faith who trusted in the LORD's battle plan of looking on the "rod of God" (v. 9) for victory.

LIFE STEP
The battle with the Amalekites gives us a picture of the battles we face today. Yes, God expects us to plan and prepare for the spiritual battles that await us. Yet, success in those battles comes as we trust in God and depend on His strength to give us victory. What spiritual battles will you face today or in the near future? He has been faithful to help His people in the past. How can you expect His help in your present trial?

EXODUS 19:1-13

WHAT IS THE WRITER SAYING?

HOW CAN I APPLY THIS TO MY LIFE?

PRAY Estonia – Pray for the truth and light of Christ to be established in this new marketplaceof religious feedom and.options.

God's people have now come to the wilderness of Sinai (likely in the southern part of the Sinai Peninsula). Here the law would be given. Here Moses and God meet. Here the Lord reminds Israel of His grace.

Note the three areas of love and protection that are seen here. First, He delivered them from Egypt and "bore them on eagle's wings" bringing them to Himself (v. 4). Second, He calls them a "peculiar treasure" (v. 5) which in Hebrew is a single word meaning *a special possession that is unique*. And finally, God now intends to make of them a "kingdom of priests, and a holy nation" (v. 6). Grace is reflected here.

The metaphor of the eagle (v. 4) is amplified in Deuteronomy 32. There we read: "As an eagle stirreth up her nest, fluttereth over her young, spreadeth abroad her wings, taketh them, beareth them on her wings: So the Lord alone did lead him, and there was no strange god with him" (Deuteronomy 32:11-12). Young eagles just learning to fly were supported on the wings of the parent eagles and taught to fly. This is a picture of the ongoing work of God in the lives of believers in all ages; He Himself will teach His children to fly spiritually!

Notice the new element that is added to Israel's responsibility. All they needed to do for their salvation from slavery in Egypt was to trust in God's deliverance. Now that they were God's people, God expected them to learn how to walk daily by faith in obedience to God's holy ways. The response of the children of Israel to the LORD's commands to them was "All that the LORD has spoken we will do" (v. 8).

LIFE STEP An important lesson is presented quietly here. While your initial salvation was a simple matter of trusting God to save you from your sin, your ongoing daily walk in God's holy ways will involve a considerable amount of *wing-strengthening*. God is going to *stir up your nest* and begin to teach you to spiritually *fly like an eagle*. Perhaps you should talk to Him about strengthening your "wings!"

EXODUS 19:14-25

WHAT IS THE WRITER SAYING?

HOW CAN I APPLY THIS TO MY LIFE?

PRAY Nigeria – For committed Christian leaders that will follow through with real preparation of Bible lessons and true discipleship.

The Israelites didn't realize their true condition and spiritual weakness. Up to this point, they had seen time and again God's graciousness. Now God was going to teach them of His holiness and the fact that, given their state as unholy, He was unapproachable. Israel would soon become aware that without help from God, they were helpless to deal with their sin and thus unable to come near to God. It is important to understand something of the holiness of God demonstrated here. Note the thunder and lightning, the thick cloud on the mount, and the presence of the voice of the trumpet (v. 16). Because of God's presence, the mountain was a holy place. As a result, the people could not approach it without endangering their lives (v. 25).

There is a *twin truth* here about God. The Lord is a holy, righteous God of truth on one hand and a merciful, loving God on the other. There is no contradiction in this *twin truth*. Just note that Exodus 19 is emphasizing the holy God who is so unapproachable. Later in Exodus, we learn that through God's provision of the blood sacrifice, the Lord is able to show His love and mercy. From our vantage point, "mercy and truth are met together; righteousness and peace have kissed each other" (Psalm 85:10). Where did they meet? At the cross! There at the cross, God was both the just Judge of sin (as a holy God) and the Justifier (as a loving God Who paid our debt of sin) of him that believes (Romans 3:26).

LIFE STEP Praise the Lord Jesus for He has "redeemed us from the curse of the law, being made a curse for us" (Galatians 3:13). Before we were saved, we, too, were unable to approach God, the Holy One. Since we have been saved, we have free access to our Father, the Loving One.

TUESDAY 13

EXODUS 20:1-17

WHAT IS THE WRITER SAYING?

HOW CAN I APPLY THIS TO MY LIFE?

PRAY Lebanon – Pray that Lebanese believers might regain a vision for others and for other lands – the war has caused too many to become insular.

This famous chapter in the Bible gives us the Ten Commandments. These commandments were an introduction to the law-code that God was going to give Israel. It was the moral foundation for an entire set of instructions that would follow on how the Israelites were to live holy lives before God and how Israel was to worship God. The commandments reflected the holy character of God. While everything about God is not seen here, everything God commands here reflects His character.

Secondly, it is important to stress that the Israelites never earned their salvation by keeping the Ten Commandments; their redemption had been a gift from God. Remember, God had already saved Israel from slavery in Egypt. Rather, the law was to teach them how to live now that they had been called to be the holy people of God. The people of Israel understood that their seeking to keep the Law was their loving response to God (Deuteronomy 6:5), in that God had already demonstrated His love for Israel when they were just slaves (Deuteronomy 4:37)!

It is also important for us Christians to note two things. First, just like Israel, keeping the Ten Commandments does not save us! Second, the moral foundation provided by the Ten Commandments is reaffirmed by the New Testament's repeating of the principles of the Ten Commandments—with the exception of the Sabbath. (In honor of Christ's resurrection, Christians worship on the first day of the week, not on Saturday, the Sabbath day which is the last of the week.) So then, the Ten Commandments are also intended to provide Christians with the foundation for their holy walk before God.

 LIFE STEP We need to allow the Holy Spirit to be God's instrument to build holy principles of living into our daily walk. What foundational area to your Christian walk do you need to allow the Holy Spirit to strengthen?

WEDNESDAY 13

EXODUS 24:3-12

WHAT IS THE WRITER SAYING?

HOW CAN I APPLY THIS TO MY LIFE?

PRAY Ukraine – For believers willing to translate biblical resource material into the Ukrainian language.

In this passage, we see the formal ceremony at which Israel accepted the covenant given to them by God (v. 3). Afterward, Moses wrote out a permanent record of the agreement. Next, Moses built an altar and had young men prepare oxen for offerings which sealed the agreement. This was their way of solemnly binding themselves to God's covenant.

After the ceremony, one of the most amazing events in the entire Old Testament takes place! Moses ascends Mount Sinai with Aaron, Nadab, and Abihu (the two sons of Aaron, the priest) and seventy elders of Israel. And there they "saw the God of Israel" and they "did eat and drink" on the mount with God (vv.10-11)! Note that it was customary after covenant agreements for the leaders of the two sides to meet in a shared meal.

At first glance, their *seeing God* seems to contradict Exodus 33:20, which says no man can see God's face and live! From passages like Numbers 12:8, Ezekiel 1:26, and Isaiah 6:1, we understand they saw only some form, shadow, or similitude of the Lord.

Another hint is given by the dazzling description of the work of sapphire stone (a deep blue, clear gemstone) under God's feet. Apparently they were in God's presence but they were willing only to look at the blue-stone footstool under the throne upon which God sat. (See Ezekiel 1:26; where we are given the description of a complete sapphire throne!) Yet even this lowly footstool was amazing! Don't miss the little note Moses adds about their not dying, as they might expect, during this meal with God!

 LIFE STEP While this is an amazing passage, we are reminded that Scripture says, "… and truly our fellowship is with the Father, and with his Son Jesus Christ" (1 John 1:3). Think of it as you are doing your Quiet Time. You are having a meal with God while He sits upon His sapphire throne! He enjoys His meal with you; be sure to talk to Him!

THURSDAY 13

EXODUS 24:15 - 25:9

WHAT IS THE WRITER SAYING?

HOW CAN I APPLY THIS TO MY LIFE?

PRAY Venezuela – Boldness for Bible school students getting hands-on experience ministering to the lost.

Moses had been invited up onto the mount to be with the Lord, where God would give him the particulars regarding the tabernacle and all the instruments that were to be a part of their worship at the tabernacle. What an experience it must have been!

The tabernacle was to provide three things. *First*, it would be a special place where God could "dwell among" Israel (v. 8). *Second*, it provided a means for a sinful people to approach their holy God. (Through the sacrifices at the tabernacle, God forgave sinners; Leviticus 4:20, 26). *Third*, it provided a place for God to "commune" (*to enjoy the company of another; to talk together with a friend*) with His people (Exodus 25:22).

Notice the holiness of God was manifested by the "devouring fire on the top of the mount" (v. 17). We have no doubt that the sight of this was truly terrifying to the children of Israel down at the base of the mountain. We are not to miss the point being made here. God, Who was the source of the "devouring fire," had arranged for Moses to come up the mountain into the flames so that God might explain to Moses how the children of Israel could make for Him a tabernacle. This tabernacle, for the next four hundred years of Old Testament history, was going to be a place where God would forgive the sins of Israel and provide Israel with a way to commune with God and not be devoured by the flames of His holiness!

 LIFE STEP Today we do not have a tabernacle, but we do have the same provisions that were provided by the tabernacle. Jesus Himself became the sacrifice through which our sins were paid for. Through Jesus, we now can enjoy an even better communion with God than did Moses and Israel in the Old Testament (see Hebrews 8:6). You have a great privilege of communing with God! How might you now spend a few minutes just enjoying the company of God?

EXODUS 25:10-22

WHAT IS THE WRITER SAYING?

HOW CAN I APPLY THIS TO MY LIFE?

Today's passage describes the ark of the covenant. This was the item of furniture to be held in the tabernacle. This box was about four feet long, two and a half feet wide, and two and a half feet deep. Within the ark were placed Aaron's rod, a pot of manna, and the two tablets of the Ten Commandments.

Over the ark was placed a second item like a lid (v. 21), called the mercy seat. On top of the mercy seat were two cherubim (winged angels) facing each other with their wings arched up over their heads. The high priest was to bring into the tabernacle blood taken from a sacrificed animal. He would sprinkle the blood onto the space between the cherubim. This, of course, was a picture of the presence of the invisible God and His provision for the forgiveness of Israel's sin (see Hebrews 9:1-10).

Without the mercy seat over the ark, the ark would have been reduced to a judgment seat with the condemning tablets of the Law inside. The ark alone would only remind us of His just judgment upon our sin. But with the mercy seat over the ark, God was declaring that He would accept the blood of a sacrificed substitute as payment for a person's sin. The phrase "mercy seat" means a *place of propitiation*, that is, a place where God's justice was satisfied. In the New Testament we learn that Jesus became our propitiation (Romans 3:25). So then, today we do not need to bring an animal to be our sacrificed substitute. Rather Jesus on the Cross was our sacrificed Substitute.

LIFE STEP Your relationship to this lesson is simple: either (1) you have already asked Jesus to be your sacrificed Substitute, resulting in your being forgiven by God of His coming judgment upon your sin; or (2) you have not asked Jesus to be your sacrificed Substitute and you still face His coming judgment upon you and your sin!

EXODUS 31:12 - 32:6

WHAT IS THE WRITER SAYING?

HOW CAN I APPLY THIS TO MY LIFE?

PRAY Peru – Funding for more scholarships that will make Bible training accessible to the poor.

We open today with a paragraph about God's requirement that Israel keep the last day of the week, Saturday, as a Sabbath Day. "Sabbath" means *to cease* and refers to a day when the children of Israel ceased from their normal work. The Sabbath Day was to be "holy to the Lord" (v. 15), meaning it was to be used to worship God, study His Word, and fellowship with His people. Today, Christians worship on Sunday, in honor of the resurrection of Christ on the first day of the week. While the Lord's Day (Sunday) is not a "Christian Sabbath," it is also to be a day set aside for the worship of the Lord, to study God's Word, and to fellowship with God's people! Chapter 32 gives the account of Israel's great sin of idolatry while Moses was on Mt. Sinai. The people became impatient with Moses on Mount Sinai. They demanded that Aaron make them a new god they could see. Aaron collected gold from the people and fashioned a golden calf. Aaron then pronounced a feast day to proclaim this new god to be their new Lord!

It is important to look at Aaron's actions. Aaron was with Moses during the ten plagues and at the Red Sea. He held up Moses' arms in the battle with the Amalekites. Yet he quickly abandons God. We must ask why Aaron did not reason with Israel to discourage them from this great sin. Why did Aaron not warn Israel of a judgment of God upon such a sin? And why did Aaron not pray to God to help him and protect him?

LIFE STEP A right and true concept of God can be obtained only from the Word of God–the Bible. We need to conform to His will rather than seeking to conform Him to our own value system or desire. A daily walk with Christ, led by the Holy Spirit, will guard us against the awful examples we have seen in these verses.

EXODUS 32:7-20

WHAT IS THE WRITER SAYING?

HOW CAN I APPLY THIS TO MY LIFE?

PRAY Praise God that He supplies all our needs according to His riches in glory by Christ Jesus (Philippians 4:19).

The blatant idolatry seen in this chapter shows how inconsistent a man who has had the truth can be. When Moses returned from Mount Sinai and saw the awful condition of the people, he became "hot" with anger and cast down the two tablets of stone upon which God had written the Ten Commandments. The severity of their sin is seen by the language used by the Lord. Note that instead of calling them "my people," He said they were "thy people" (v. 7). They had become "corrupted," which is the same Hebrew word used to describe man's awful sin in Noah's day (Genesis 6:12). The meaning is *to go to ruin or destruction*. Note that they were "stiff-necked" to God, failing to bow before Him in submission (v. 9), and yet they readily bowed to the golden calf in submission (v. 8).

Moses becomes the mediator between Israel and the Lord. He approaches God as an advocate (vv. 11-14) who makes intercession for the Hebrews. What a picture of the One who stands between us and God, the Lord Jesus Christ! "For there is one God, and one mediator between God and men, the man Christ Jesus" (1 Timothy 2:5). We are often stiff-necked and fail to submit to His will. While God was merciful to them and spared them, they were still disciplined. So it is with us when we step out of God's will and insist on going our own way.

 LIFE STEP In our world today we don't have idols of stone, wood, and gold. Today we have other kinds of idols. Our idols can be anything that takes our loyalty away from God. Our idols include anything we worship instead of God; things like our cars, boats, sports teams, or careers. God has said in 1 John 5:21, "Little children, keep yourselves from idols." Do a little personal survey: are there things in your life you serve instead of serving God?

MONDAY '14

EXODUS 33:12-23

WHAT IS THE WRITER SAYING?

HOW CAN I APPLY THIS TO MY LIFE?

PRAY Argentina – For the salvation of the president and the stabilization of this country's economic and judicial systems.

This paragraph relates a series of prayer requests from Moses. Earlier in chapter 33, the Lord had threatened to leave Israel, for they were a "stiff-necked people" (v. 3). Since Moses was the leader of Israel he needed to know God's intent, so Moses makes a request, "Show me now thy way, that I may know thee, that I may find grace in thy sight: and consider that this nation is thy people" (v. 13). God's response is to promise Moses His "presence" (v. 14). Literally "presence" is an ancient saying meaning *God would be fully manifested to His people*.

Next, Moses seeks greater assurance of God's continued care of Israel (vv. 15-16). Moses says he will not move forward until God consents to *distinguish* (the meaning here of "separated") Israel by going forward with them. After all,

Moses knew the only thing that had distinguished Israel from other nations had been God's care of them! God responds, "I will do this thing" (v. 17). (He will go with them to make them distinct!) Now Moses asks for a personal favor. Moses asks to see the full glory of the Lord, which is to say, *Show me all your goodness*. Moses desired complete fellowship with God. God replies that He will allow Moses to see all that a mortal, sinful man can see without dying in the presence of God's holiness. So the Lord put Moses in a cleft of the rock. Next, God covered the cleft with His hand as He passed by. Finally, His hand is removed so Moses could see the "back parts" (v. 23) of God's presence, likely a way of describing the *aftereffects of God's presence*.

LIFE STEP Did you notice that even Moses in his lifetime could not fully see God or fully know the goodness of God? Yet, Moses made it his first priority to get to know God as best as he could during his life! So, how well do you know God? What can you do this week, this year, to get to know God better? How can you make this goal your first priority?

TUESDAY '14

EXODUS 34:1-17

WHAT IS THE WRITER SAYING?

HOW CAN I APPLY THIS TO MY LIFE?

PRAY Indonesia – For missionaries to reach every inhabited island to share the Gospel.

Today's passage opens with the cutting of a second set of stone tablets containing the Ten Commandments. Be sure to note that the second set contained the same words (v. 1). Neither God's character nor His Word had changed, only the stone carrying the Word changed!

God now comes and stands next to Moses to proclaim three important matters: (1) He declares an important insight into His character; (2) then He announces a covenant concerning what He is going to do; and (3) He renews a list of demands upon His people as their response to Him.

Concerning the first, God now "proclaimed the name of the Lord" (v. 5). "Proclaim" here means *a description* of His essential nature so that He could be fully known. We are to understand there are two focal points to His character (vv. 6-7): God's *loving-kindness* and God's *justice*. Notice that God's *loving-kindness* is divided into seven descriptors: merciful (*to extend care*), gracious, longsuffering, good, abundant in truth, mercy (*faithful not to desert those He loves*), and forgiving.

Yet, God's *justice* is not to be forgotten! Two descriptions are given: (1) God will, with truth, judge the guilty; and (2) God visits sin "unto the third and to the fourth generation," an ancient idiom meaning *God will continually be a righteous Judge who will pronounce deserved sentences upon sin.*

Finally, be sure to note that God intended us to see that our holy God does not punish until the sinner despises God's generous mercy!

Listed above are things that deserve thoughtful consideration. Which aspect of God's character has been commonly displayed to you in your life? Which aspect of God's character does God need to reveal more clearly to you so you may have a closer walk with Him?

WEDNESDAY 14

EXODUS 34:18-35

WHAT IS THE WRITER SAYING?

HOW CAN I APPLY THIS TO MY LIFE?

Today's passage completes the story of Moses' forty days on Mount Sinai with the Lord. It goes on to tell the story of Moses' shining face. We read that when Moses finished receiving the Law from the Lord and then came down from the mount, the "skin of his face shone" (vv. 29-30). When Aaron and the people of Israel saw Moses' shining face, they were afraid (v. 30). After Moses had put a veil on his face and called them to him, Moses told them what God had said in the Law.

If you will turn to 2 Corinthians 3:7-8, you will find Paul alluding to this incident when he writes: "But if the ministration of death, written and engraved in stones, was glorious, (Paul is referring to the Law which Moses here received) so that the children of Israel could not steadfastly behold the face of Moses for the glory of his countenance; which glory was to be done away: How shall not the ministration of the spirit be rather glorious?" Paul makes it clear that both the Law and the shining of Moses' face had been glorious things that have been done away. He is also pointing out that this new work of the Holy Spirit is even more glorious. We are being "changed into the same image" (the glorious image of Christ) (2 Corinthians 3:18). This is being done by the Holy Spirit as He applies the Word of God to our lives.

LIFE STEP How reassuring it is that the glory of Christ can be reflected in our lives as the Holy Spirit applies the Word to our lives! The Holy Spirit intends to make your life more glorious than the shining face of Moses!

Will you accept a challenge? If Moses was gloriously changed after forty days with the Lord, will you spend four minutes listing out things God would want to change about you and your life to make you more glorious?

EXODUS 40:1-16

WHAT IS THE WRITER SAYING?

HOW CAN I APPLY THIS TO MY LIFE?

PRAY Slovakia – For believers to overcome apathy and be consumed by a passion to please Christ.

(*It would be helpful to you if you found a picture of the tabernacle to use as a guide as you read this passage.*)

Earlier in Exodus, the instructions for building several of the pieces that made up the tabernacle (which was to be a portable shrine where Israel would worship God) were given. In this chapter, we find the tabernacle pieces have been built and are now assembled. Each part of the tabernacle taught Israel of the future coming Lamb of God, the Lord Jesus Christ, Who would be the perfect substitute Sacrifice for our sin.

In the heart of the tabernacle is the Holy of Holies. In this small room was the ark covered by the mercy seat. (Here God received Israel's offerings for forgiveness!) In the Holy Place were the table of bread, the lamp stand, and the altar of incense (vv. 4-5). (The outer room of the tabernacle "tent" was separated from the Holy of Holies by a veil.) The table of bread speaks of Jesus as "the bread of life" (John 6:35). The lamp stand speaks of Jesus as the "light of the world" (John 8:12). The altar of incense pictures the work of Christ Who now intercedes for us in heaven (Hebrews 7:25). Outside the tabernacle tent was a courtyard where we find the laver of water. This was used by the priests and pictures our cleansing with the water of the Word (Ephesians 5:25-26). The altar of burnt offerings was the large brazen altar where the sacrifices were made in the courtyard outside the tabernacle tent.

 LIFE STEP If the order of these pieces is reversed, beginning at the brazen altar and working inwardly to the mercy seat, we have a picture of what goes on as we come to God. First, we were redeemed by a substitute sacrifice. (Christ is our Substitute!) Then, we are washed daily, we feast on the bread of life, we reflect the light of Christ, and we enjoy the work of Christ as our High Priest. Finally, we can fellowship with God.

FRIDAY '14

EXODUS 40:17-27

WHAT IS THE WRITER SAYING?

HOW CAN I APPLY THIS TO MY LIFE?

PRAY Bolivia – For caring youth ministry in a land where 80% of children are living in extreme poverty.

As we continue to study the tabernacle, we need to be reminded that the Lord is working in shadows. In Hebrews 10:1 we read that the Law was a shadow. Later we read that the tabernacle was not the very image but was a remembrance (Heb. 10:1-3). (It was to remind Israel that God was going to provide His own perfect Sacrifice.) Hebrews 9:23 tells us that the tabernacle contained patterns of things that were to come later. So as we read about the tabernacle, we see glimpses of Christ.

Remember in Luke 24, after His resurrection, Christ teaches His disciples by opening the Bible and "beginning at Moses and all the prophets, He expounded unto them in all the Scripture the things concerning Himself" (v. 27). How did He do this? Well, He probably told them about the tabernacle and how it spoke of Him, His person, and His work. So, this study in Exodus has been a blueprint pointing to the coming Messiah.

God did not desire to just appear before Israel, but rather God desired to dwell with them. In Psalm 29:9 we read, "In his temple doth every one speak of his glory." So, the purpose of the tabernacle was to reveal His glory.

Today we approach Him personally. We do so, not in patterns, or figures, or types, or shadows, but as we are, aware that Jesus is the fulfillment of these promised Old Testament patterns. He is not a shadow but the fulfillment. Not the type but the reality. Unlike the holy priests of the tabernacle who could enter the Holy of Holies only once per year, we may come daily into the Holy of Holies and commune with God!

 Because Christ has completed the tabernacle patterns, you now have full access to God! Exercise your privilege as a priest of God. Perhaps you could write out the names of some people near to you that you could then uphold in prayer to God, asking Him to meet their needs.

EXODUS 40:28-38

WHAT IS THE WRITER SAYING?

HOW CAN I APPLY THIS TO MY LIFE?

PRAY United States – 35% of all foreign missionaries are American. Pray that these missionaries would be able to work in partnership with local churches.

We have come to the final paragraph in the final chapter of Exodus. In chapter 39 we read, "And Moses did look upon all the work, and behold, they had done it as the Lord had commanded" (v. 43). Now Moses sees the tabernacle assembled. "So Moses finished the work" (Exodus 40:33).

We read that a cloud covered the tent and the glory of the Lord filled the tabernacle. When the cloud was "taken up" from over the tabernacle they "went onward in all their journeys" (v. 36). It was a cloud by day and a fire by night (v. 38). The cloud was a constant reminder of the presence of God with His people. In its movements, God made known His will to Israel. We have no such cloud to declare the will of God to us, but we have the internal presence of the Holy Spirit. The Spirit guides us through the Word, which He uses to direct and guide.

Exodus began with a groan from the Hebrews who were slaves. The first part ended with Israel's song of redemption; the slaves had been redeemed and set free. The second part of the book began with a meeting of God in the wilderness. Now, this second part ends with the Shekinah Glory of the Lord filling the tabernacle. God had heard Israel's cry. God had saved Israel from their bondage. God had proclaimed how Israel could come before God to receive forgiveness of sins and fellowship with their God, and then Israel did as God had directed.

LIFE STEP Exodus points out that the first priority of Israel in their new life as a free nation was to prepare for fellowship with God through the service of the tabernacle. In a similar way, how can you make it your priority to get to know God better and to fellowship daily with Him?

Second Timothy is one of three books known as the Pastoral Epistles, the other two being 1 Timothy and Titus. They were written by the older Apostle Paul (in his sixties) to two younger men, Timothy and Titus (probably in their thirties). These young men were serving in pastoral-like roles, Timothy in Ephesus and Titus in Crete. Paul wanted to tell them how to "behave" themselves "in the house of God, which is the church of the living God" (1 Timothy 3:15).

Three themes resonate throughout all three: (1) church organization, (2) sound doctrine, and (3) consistent Christian living. While all three books touch on all three themes, each book has its particular emphasis, and those three themes follow the order in which they have been placed in most Bibles (though not written in that order—Titus was written before 2 Timothy). 1 Timothy emphasizes church organization; 2 Timothy, sound doctrine; and Titus, consistent Christian living. Charles Erdman offers this summation of these three themes: "Church government is not an end in itself; it is of value only as it secures sound doctrine; and doctrine is of value only as it applies to real life." The point is this: you *organize* (1 Timothy) so that you can teach *sound doctrine* (2 Timothy), and you teach *sound doctrine* so that *consistent Christian living* (Titus) can result.

Timothy was Paul's representative at the church in Ephesus. During Paul's first missionary journey (Acts 13-14), he and Barnabas preached the Gospel in the cities of Lystra and Derbe (Acts 14:1-20). Timothy, who had a Greek father and Jewish mother, responded to the message, leading Paul to address him as "my son in the faith" – my own *born-one in the faith* (1 Timothy 1:2; 2 Timothy 1:2). The Book of Acts, as well as Paul's own letters, make it clear that Timothy was a capable, trustworthy individual. He could be sent ahead or left behind to carry on the apostle's work (19:22; 20:4). There is some indication that Timothy was somewhat timid in nature (2 Timothy 1:6-7), easily discouraged or frightened (1 Corinthians 16:10-11; 2 Timothy 1:8), and prone to sickness (1 Timothy 5:23). Nevertheless, Paul placed great trust in him. His recommendation to the Philippian church is clear: "I have no man likeminded" (Philippians 2:20).

2 Timothy was written from prison where Paul was awaiting execution. It is the last known writing we have from the great apostle's pen, and in effect it was his *last will and testament*, the most personal of all his letters. It is believed by many that Paul was arrested and placed in prison when Nero began his campaign of persecution shortly after Rome burned down in A.D. 64. Nero blamed the Christians for starting the fire. (After all, had they not predicted the world would come to an end in a great fire?) He also executed many of them in extremely cruel fashion, including Peter, who, according to one of the early church fathers, was crucified upside down. As Paul authors this second letter to his son-in-the-faith, Timothy, he was very much aware of his apparently soon-to-come death (by beheading).

This letter, even more so than the other Pastoral Epistles, is marked by the open sharing of feelings and thoughts. The major emphases of the book would include: (1) *Encouragement to be faithful...* Timothy was somewhat timid and Paul, reminded of his *tears* (1:4), used this letter to challenge him to *hang in there.* Paul was well aware that the Christian life is not played out on a ball field, but lived out on a battlefield, and that one of the essential characteristics of a faithful servant of Jesus Christ is endurance in the midst of difficulties. (2) *To turn over leadership to Timothy...* generations come and go, and knowing his time was short Paul wanted to be sure that leadership for the next generation was in place. Jack Wyrtzen, founder of Word of Life Fellowship, often remarked, "It is the responsibility of each generation to reach its generation for Christ." (3) *Paul's final and definitive testimony...* a reminder to Timothy that he (Paul) had finished well, and an underlying, not-so-gentle hint that he (Timothy), too, should desire a similar finish.

Major theological emphases would include: (1) the coming apostasy of the last days, detailed in chapter 3. Paul warns Timothy that there will be difficult days ahead for believers, and so he passes on instruction as to how Christians are to behave and respond. Jesus had predicted such times would come (John 15:18-25; 16:33; 17:15-18). Paul himself had written earlier of those coming days (1 Thessalonians 3:1-8), and warned the Ephesian elders of them (Acts 20:29). (2) The importance, value and application of Scripture, scattered throughout the book, including 1:13; 2:2, 15; 3:14-17; 4:2-4. Paul was encouraging Timothy not only to pass on the truths of Scripture to the generations that follow, but also to pass on the basis of those truths, the inspired (God-breathed) Word of God. It is, as many conservative local church constitutions state: "The final authority (the supreme standard) for all faith (what we believe) and practice (how we behave)."

SUNDAY '15

2 TIMOTHY 1:1-7

WHAT IS THE WRITER SAYING?

HOW CAN I APPLY THIS TO MY LIFE?

PRAY Ghana – For trained and spiritually mature men to accept a role in church leadership.

Paul, as in his earlier letter to Timothy, introduces himself as *an apostle of Jesus Christ*, a title unnecessary if this letter was for Timothy's eyes only, for Timothy certainly knew Paul's position. Nevertheless, as in his other *pastorals*, Paul was providing Timothy with the credentials necessary to carry out his task of leading the church of Ephesus. While some might choose to downplay the words of their young pastor, they could hardly do the same with the words of one who was clearly recognized as *one sent from God*, with a message to deliver. Adding the words *by the will of God*, Paul makes it clear that he understood his apostleship was an assignment from God.

This letter is the most personal of all that Paul wrote. Written from a Roman dungeon, it was Paul's *last will and testament*, and was the final book from his pen. He addresses Timothy as his *dearly beloved son* (or his own born-one), and thereby makes it clear that he and Timothy had a very special relationship, that of father and son *in the faith* (see 1 Timothy 1:2). The relationship produced both deep concern as well as thanksgiving in Paul's heart for his young protégé (vv. 3-4).

Concerned that Timothy's apparently timid nature could hinder his ministry (see *tears*, v. 4), Paul reminded him of *his faith* (v. 5) and of *his gifting* (v. 6). That gifting enabled Timothy to carry out his ministry; it was already present, not something to be added to his character, and was to be *rekindled*. Broadening the thought of gifting, Paul challenges Timothy to remember that neither he nor Paul (*us* in verse 7) had been given "the spirit of fear; but of *power…love*, and of a *sound mind*" (v. 7).

 LIFE STEP Timothy had Paul's letters; we have much more, the entire Word of God. He was gifted; so are we. Let us see to it that we use what we have been given (and it is not *fear*) to perform our service for the Lord.

MONDAY '15

2 TIMOTHY 1:8-12

WHAT IS THE WRITER SAYING?

HOW CAN I APPLY THIS TO MY LIFE?

PRAY Australia – Godly workers to reach youth through religious instruction classes offered in public schools.

Paul encourages his young follower to be a "partaker of the afflictions of the gospel" (v. 8). Paul is concerned that Timothy's timidity could cause enough shame for him to back away from an effective ministry, as well as from Paul (as a prisoner) himself. Suffering is part of the believer's calling and when it comes, should be accepted as part of God's will. Furthermore, when it comes, it will be accompanied by the *power of God*, always available for encouragement and strength.

Verse 8, which ends with *God*, is followed by the work of God in salvation, ("hath saved…and called us"). He does so "not according to our works, but according to his own purpose and grace (v. 9)." That purpose, once hidden, is now revealed through Paul. God did not eliminate death through the cross, but He did disarm it. For the believer, its sting is gone (see 1 Corinthians 15:55-57) and Christ has brought "life and immortality" (v. 10) — the condition of never dying — to light (they were in the shadows in the Old Testament).

The believer is called to holiness (v. 9; 1 Peter 1:15-16). Writing to persecuted believers, Peter advocated holy living — lives consecrated to God, and lives consistent with our true identity and position in Christ (1 Peter 2:10-11). Paul's challenge to Timothy is similar, using himself as an example. He had suffered many things for the cause of the Gospel (vv. 11-12) but was never ashamed. Why? because "I know whom I have believed (a continuing attitude of belief with trust), and am persuaded that he is able to keep that which I have committed unto him" (Paul's entire existence) (v. 12). God had committed the Gospel to Paul (1 Timothy 1:11); he was passing it on to Timothy (1 Timothy 6:20; 2 Timothy 4:7), who was to pass it on to faithful men…(and) others also (2 Timothy 2:2).

LIFE STEP The believer has a choice when suffering comes: to back away in shame from his commitment to Christ hoping to avoid pain, or to accept it as part of God's purpose in his life and meet it head on with the provided power of God.

TUESDAY 15

2 TIMOTHY 1:13-18

WHAT IS THE WRITER SAYING?

HOW CAN I APPLY THIS TO MY LIFE?

In verse 12, Paul used himself as an example of one who steadfastly remained faithful to his commitment. In verses 13-14, Timothy is exhorted to maintain a similar commitment. He is to "hold fast the form of sound words." *Form* can mean *example* or *pattern* (1 Timothy 1:16). Paul both preached and lived the Gospel, establishing a pattern for others to follow (1 Corinthians 11:1). *Sound* comes from a Greek word that gives us our English word *hygiene*, meaning *healthy*. *Words* means *teaching* (in Titus 1:9 it is "sound doctrine," also 1 Timothy 1:10). Taken together the challenge is to provide *healthy teaching*, for the opposite (see 2 Timothy 2:17) could result in a crippling disease.

"That good thing which was committed unto thee" (v. 14), refers to the Gospel (1 Timothy 6:20). Having received it, Timothy was to *keep* it, and was reminded that only by the power of the Spirit could he do so. *Keep* means to *guard*, and coupled with 1 Timothy 6:20 ("keep that which is committed to thy trust"), means the Gospel has been placed on deposit with Timothy (a banking analogy). It is to be guarded, kept, and available for use on demand.

This letter is being written from a prison dungeon where Paul is waiting for his trial and potential beheading. His circumstances are dire. Desertion by fellow believers was escalating. The *some* of 1 Timothy (1:6; 1:19; 5:15; 6:10; 6:21) have become the hyperbolic "all" of 2 Timothy (1:15; 4:16), many being led astray by *Phygellus* and *Hermogenes*. Yet even in troubled times God provides relief, and He does so here in the person of *Onesiphorus* (*one who brings profit or benefit*). This godly man was probably a deacon in Ephesus when Paul was there, for verse 18 can be translated: "…and in how many things he fully played the deacon…" He came to Rome, searched hard for Paul, found him and served him without fear or shame (v. 16).

 LIFE STEP Onesiphorus was unashamed and unafraid to serve Christ and his fellow believers. We should do likewise.

WEDNESDAY 15

2 TIMOTHY 2:1-7

WHAT IS THE WRITER SAYING?

HOW CAN I APPLY THIS TO MY LIFE?

"Thou therefore, my son (an expression of strong affection), be strong in the grace (undeserved divine help) that is in Christ Jesus" (v.1). With these words Paul both exhorts and challenges Timothy to be faithful to his calling, while at the same time drawing a contrast between that which he desires for his young *son-in-the-faith*, and the defectors of the previous chapter (1:15). They had turned their backs upon Paul and the Gospel ministry, but by depending on *the grace that is in Christ Jesus* and its accompanying power, and not upon his own abilities, Timothy would not have to repeat their error nor experience their fate.

Next begins a series of pictures demonstrating the characteristics of a faithful servant of Jesus Christ. He is to first be faithful as a *teacher* (v. 2). That which he has heard he is to pass on to others. In fact, Timothy is to be part of an endless chain of passing on truth to succeeding generations (namely, God to Paul to Timothy to faithful men to others also). This is the same procedure laid out by Christ in the Great Commission (Matthew 28:19-20), that of making disciples (discipleship).

In verses 3-6 Paul gives three additional illustrations of faithfulness to demonstrate to Timothy the seriousness of his task. The *first* is that of a *soldier*, and as such he is to (a) endure hardness; (b) not entangle himself with the affairs of this life (not that they are wrong – just don't get caught up in them); and (c) seek to please his commander, and for the believer that is Jesus Christ. The *second* illustration is that of an *athlete*. He is to "strive for masteries" (contend in the athletic games), but to do so according to the rulebook. To receive the victor's crown, his life and ministry must follow biblical directives. The *third* illustration is that of a hardworking *farmer*. Only through strenuous, diligent effort will a bountiful harvest result.

LIFE STEP We should follow Paul's example and ask the Lord to give us understanding to please Him in our regular everyday activities and in the special projects that we attempt for Him.

2 TIMOTHY 2:8-14

WHAT IS THE WRITER SAYING?

HOW CAN I APPLY THIS TO MY LIFE?

Here Paul directs the readers' thoughts, as well as ours, to Jesus Christ and His resurrection. *Of the seed of David* points to His *humanity* and the fulfillment of the promises God made to David (see 2 Samuel 7:16). *Raised from the dead* focuses attention on the *deity* of Christ, and the power of God demonstrated in the resurrection (see Romans 1:1-4). To Paul, the paramount truth of the Gospel (he called it *my Gospel* – Romans 2:16; 16:25; 1 Corinthians 15:1) was the Resurrection. That Gospel of his (v. 8) is what brought about his present distress (v. 9). He is chained like a common criminal, because he preached it. Yet "the Word of God is not bound" (v. 9). In prison he could still preach the Word. In fact, he often had a *captive audience* — the Roman soldiers to whom he was chained. That being the case, he was able to "endure all things for the elect's sakes." He wanted to see the salvation resulting in these who believed, culminating in eternal glory, salvation's final state (v. 10).

In verses 11-13 we have the longest of the five *faithful sayings* contained in the Pastoral Epistles (1 Timothy 1:15; 3:1; 4:9; 2 Timothy 2:11-13; Titus 3:8). These were probably *prophetic sayings* by the New Testament prophets in the early church before the New Testament was written. They summarized key doctrinal beliefs. The theme here is Christ's death and resurrection, and our union with Christ in those significant historical events (v. 11). "If we suffer (better: endure), we shall also reign with him," but, "if we deny (fail to endure) him, he also will deny us (the reign or reward that could have been)" (v. 12). Then comes a contrast of God's faithfulness versus man's unfaithfulness (v. 13). The latter can never cancel the former. For Christ to abandon His own would be contrary to His nature (see John 10:27-30; Hebrews 10:23; 13:5). Paul's charge to Timothy continues in verse 14. *Don't get caught up in fighting over words!* The result is *no profit* and *the subverting (turning upside down) of the hearers.*

LIFE STEP God faithfully fulfilled His promise by sending the Redeemer. Pause now to thank Him for His faithfulness and recommit yourself to be faithful to Him. Consider that He also promised to send His Son back some day!

FRIDAY '15

2 TIMOTHY 2:15-19

WHAT IS THE WRITER SAYING?

HOW CAN I APPLY THIS TO MY LIFE?

PRAY Congo, Democratic Republic of Congo – Pray for revival among believers in this war-torn, nominally Christian nation.

Yesterday Paul concluded that Christians should avoid contentious arguments over the obscure, mystical meanings of words. Positively, however, (v. 15) "study (be eager, zealous, diligent) to shew (present oneself for service) thyself approved (accepted after testing) unto God, a workman that needeth not to be ashamed, rightly dividing (cutting straight) the word of truth." Proper preaching, says Paul, goes straight ahead, never veering left or right, always *correctly handling* the Word, never twisting or changing the truth. Therefore, the teaching is not to be the subjective opinions of men but the objective statements of God.

Having been attacked by false teachers, Timothy was warned to: (a) *Stick to the essentials*. Don't argue over empty words and philosophies (v. 16) (b) *Rightly divide the Word*. Failing to do so gives room to false teachers to promote false doctrines which, unchecked, destroy like gangrene (Greek – *gangraina*, a malignant sore that eats away healthy tissue) (v. 17). These false teachers (two are named) *erred* (wandered away) *concerning the truth* (v. 18), probably teaching there was no bodily resurrection, that the resurrection of believers had already occurred in a spiritual sense. Early Gnosticism emphasized a spiritual resurrection over a future bodily resurrection. Unchecked, this sort of *spiritualization* will destroy weaker believers. Here, a denial of the literal bodily resurrection harms a key part of Paul's Gospel. Elsewhere, application of this same kind of symbolic interpretation can ruin other doctrines such as the millennial reign of Christ or punishment of the unsaved in an eternal Lake of Fire.

"Nevertheless" (v. 19) — in spite of the efforts of the false teachers — "the foundation of God standeth sure." Exchanging his negative tone for a note of encouragement, Paul (based on the tense of the verb) indicates that he saw the truth of God standing firm, not only in the past, but also in the present (see Isaiah 40:8). Armed with that truth, and knowing to Whom we belong, the challenge is to live a life of purity.

 LIFE STEP Pray for those whose job it is to preach the Word of God. The souls of their listeners may be dependent upon their rightly dividing the Word of Truth. Always carefully study and explain Scripture yourself.

SATURDAY '15

2 TIMOTHY 2:20-26

WHAT IS THE WRITER SAYING?

HOW CAN I APPLY THIS TO MY LIFE?

PRAY Papua New Guinea – For Christian youth camps to see significant salvation and consecration decisions.

Verse 20 talks about *a great house*. It is referring to the church, *the household of God* (1Timothy 3:15). In this house are two general types of vessels: those of honor and much value (*gold and silver*), and those of dishonor and little value (*wood and earth* – pottery). The emphasis is not on the usefulness of the vessels (for the latter are probably more useful than the former which only come out for special occasions) but rather the value or quality of the vessel. Wood and pottery will eventually chip and break and must be replaced (a picture of false teachers whose worthlessness is recognized and leads to removal). This is not true with gold or silver. Their value is retained.

The honored vessel is to purge himself from those who are dishonored (v. 21). Contamination must be avoided. The results of doing so: (1) he is *sanctified* – set apart for a holy purpose; (2) he is *meet* – profitable for the master's use (*master* in Greek is despot – strong term denoting God's total authority); and (3) *prepared (ready) for every good work*. Having avoided contamination, the honored vessel is to maintain his value by staying clean. This is a two-step process. *Negatively – Flee*: avoid, shun *youthful lusts* (sexual, but also pride, ego, power, love of money, etc.) *Positively – Follow*: pursue after, *righteousness, faith, charity, peace* (1 Timothy 6:11). Both steps are vital. To fail in either will render one's ministry useless.

Paul then cautions Timothy to *avoid* "foolish and unlearned (stupid) questions (arguments)…they do gender (breed) strifes (quarrels)." He had given similar instructions earlier (1 Timothy 1:4, 7; 4:7; 6:20; 2 Timothy 2:16). He then calls Timothy the *servant (doulos) of the Lord*, and as such he has no will of his own. He is to be governed by his master in every respect. Verses 23-26 explain how to deal with problems in God's house so that strife and contention are avoided.

 LIFE STEP What specific items do we need to *flee, follow,* and *avoid* today?

SUNDAY '16

2 TIMOTHY 3:1-7

WHAT IS THE WRITER SAYING?

HOW CAN I APPLY THIS TO MY LIFE?

PRAY Chile – For future church leaders to be called from among those saved at evangelistic activities.

Chapter three illustrates the urgency of chapter two's exhortation. The theme is "the last days" (v. 1) and the character of men in those days. Those *last days* began with the life and ministry of Christ (Hebrews 1:2), and will continue until Christ returns. They will be difficult days marked by *apostasy* (a falling away – the act of professed Christians who deliberately reject the revealed truth of the deity of Christ and the effectiveness of His cross work). As Christ's return draws closer, man's evil characteristics (vv. 2-5, 8) will intensify (v. 13). Civilized behavior will completely break down.

This includes *lovers of their own selves* and *covetous*, the *twin sins* from which all the others flow. See how this naturally leads to *unthankful, unholy, high-minded* (conceited) and *lovers of pleasure more than lovers of God. Without natural affection* and *disobedient to parents* suggest the breaking up of society as God intended it to be. Striking one's father was as bad as murder in Roman law; abusing a parent in Greek culture caused disinheritance; and honoring parents was the fifth of the Jews' Ten Commandments. Today's broken families and dysfunctional homes show how rapidly we are moving away from God's standards and how rapidly we seem to be moving to the end of the age. All of the age-end characteristics can be found on the pages of today's newspapers, further indication that Christ's return must be drawing near.

Accompanying all of the above is *a form of godliness*, but that is all that it is — a form — for the true power of godliness is missing. The apostate religionists of the last days go through the motions and maintain their external forms, but they have not experienced the dynamic power of true Christianity that results in changed lives. From such Paul says, *turn away*.

 LIFE STEP The dark days in which we live have only two remedies: the Gospel of Jesus Christ unto salvation or the return of Christ in judgment. Help your friends and loved ones escape the second by receiving the first.

MONDAY '16

2 TIMOTHY 3:8-12

WHAT IS THE WRITER SAYING?

HOW CAN I APPLY THIS TO MY LIFE?

PRAY Nicaragua – For gifted Bible teachers committed to the development of future church leaders.

Paul uses Jannes and Jambres (not mentioned in the Old Testament by name, but identified in Jewish tradition as enemies of Moses) as examples of men in the past that resisted God's truth. They were *men of corrupt minds*, similar to the apostates of Paul's day (and ours) who cannot understand truth (see Romans 1:21-22; Ephesians 4:17-18; 1 Timothy 6:5), and *reprobate concerning the faith* (v. 8). Like Jannes and Jambres, this new group of truth-deniers will not get very far for "their folly shall be manifest unto all" (v. 9). Truth always triumphs in the end.

Verse 10 begins a new section containing Paul's final advice to Timothy. To encourage him to *hang in there*, he gives a strong word of personal testimony. He begins with "But thou…," demonstrating the difference between Timothy and the men Paul just referenced, and continues "hast fully known (you've observed)" and notes that which his observation revealed — a life-style (that of Paul's)

worth emulating. It begins with doctrine (teaching), goes on to *manner of life* (conduct), *purpose* (chief aim), and *faith* (the Gospel). To underscore that none of the above came easily, he mentions some personal characteristics that are vital when persecution comes to those who desire to live godly lives (v. 12): "longsuffering, charity, patience (endurance)." He reminds Timothy that he had endured numerous persecutions, but out of them all, the Lord delivered him (v. 11; see Acts 14:19-20; Psalm 34:17).

Paul moves from his own experiences to a word of encouragement by noting that persecution, in some sense at least, is what all non-compromising believers can expect. God does not always deliver His children from persecution but, as Paul has demonstrated and as Scripture testifies, He promises to be with them when they go through it (Matthew 28:20b).

 LIFE STEP Endurance demonstrates the seriousness of our commitment to Christ. No pain, no gain, so keep on keeping on!

TUESDAY 16

2 TIMOTHY 3:13-17

WHAT IS THE WRITER SAYING?

HOW CAN I APPLY THIS TO MY LIFE?

Verse 13 is a transitional verse linking Paul's charge to Timothy (v. 14ff), and the importance behind it to the offenders described earlier in the chapter. *Therefore, Timothy, remember what you've learned, and who taught you* (your mother, grandmother and Paul). The ladies taught him the Old Testament and pointed him to the Messiah. Paul came along and provided the information that Christ indeed was the Messiah, and Timothy responded in faith.

Verses 14-17 are the key verses in 2 Timothy, demonstrating the unparalleled value of the Scriptures. Its words bring about salvation (v. 15) and equip us for productive Christian living (v. 17). Its effectiveness is because "all Scripture is given by inspiration of God" (a compound word in the Greek meaning *God-breathed*). Inspiration — the out-breathing of God — was the process that produced the product: the Word

of God. Because it is God's Word, it is *profitable* (v. 16). It takes the believer and guides all his footsteps, from start to finish. One writer (Guy King) describes those steps this way: (1) FORWARD STEPS – *doctrine*, teaching. How to move ahead in the Christian life. (2) FALSE STEPS – *reproof*. The pointing out of one's faults. (3) FALTERING STEPS – *correction*. Learning not only how we have gone wrong, but how to get right (see Psalm 119:9; John 7:17). (4) FIRST STEPS – *instruction*. This word was used for the training of a child. That training is to be *in righteousness*. For all these purposes, the Holy Scriptures are both highly profitable and highly effective. By *faith* Timothy became a *child (teknon – born one) of God* (1 Timothy 1:2). Now, by utilizing the Scriptures, he has grown into a *man of God*. The result is *good works* (v. 17).

 LIFE STEP The title *man of God* or *woman of God* would be reserved for prophets and notable spiritual leaders in the Old Testament. However, it can be used of all believers today. Let's strive to live up to it!

WEDNESDAY '16

2 TIMOTHY 4:1-4

WHAT IS THE WRITER SAYING?

HOW CAN I APPLY THIS TO MY LIFE?

This is the last chapter we have from the pen of the Apostle Paul. As he begins to bring this letter to a close, Paul's appeal to Timothy to *hang in there* comes into clear focus. To support his appeal he reminds Timothy that Jesus will one day return in judgment (v. 1) and he is answerable to the Lord as to how he carries out his ministry. This idea of judgment is a primary theme of the apostle, especially as it relates to the life and ministry of believers (see 1 Corinthians 3:11-17; 5:10).

The ministry Timothy is to have is spelled out in verse 2 where five exhortations are given. The final four flow quite naturally out of the first, which is: (1) "Preach the Word," for the Word is the foundation of any ministry. It is to be done (2) with urgency: "instant in season, out of season…" Whether the time is convenient or inconvenient, or circumstances favorable or unfavorable…just do it! (3) Included should be reproof (*to correct, convince*); show them how they have done wrong. (4) Rebuke — show them how wrong they were to do wrong. Finally, (5) exhort – show them that they must right the wrong and not repeat it. There is an implication in this *Preach the Word* command. It is not preach about the Word, or even from the Word, but preach the Word, which implies knowledge. This makes study (remember 2:15) of the Word vital. All of these exhortations are to be accompanied with *long-suffering* (great patience) and *doctrine* (careful instruction) (v. 2).

Why the command? Because the time will come (v. 3) when men will not want the Word. They will want to hear what makes them feel good, (*having itching ears*). Given time those *itching ears*, which are satisfied with shallow religious entertainment, will soon become deaf ears, as they turn away from the truth to man-made fables (v. 4).

 Preach the Word. The instruction is to Timothy, but applies to us as well. Faithfully pass on the Word of God. There is no other source of power for the successful life.

THURSDAY '16

2 TIMOTHY 4:5-8

WHAT IS THE WRITER SAYING?

HOW CAN I APPLY THIS TO MY LIFE?

PRAY Pray for an unsaved friend or family member.

Earlier (v. 2) Timothy is told to "preach the Word." Why? "...the time will come" when men will not want "sound doctrine" (v. 3) or "truth," but will turn to "fables" (v. 4). In light of that, Timothy is given four instructions in verse 5: "*Watch*" – be sober in judgment. "*Endure afflictions*" – the work of the ministry is not without its price. "*Do the work of an evangelist*" – remember to evangelize the lost (a difficult, but still required, task for someone timid). "*Make full proof of thy ministry*" – accomplish the purpose to which you've been called. Those instructions are valid not only for Timothy, but for all of God's children.

In verses 6-8, Paul makes it clear it is time for him to move on and pass the torch to others. His reflective words form perhaps the greatest *exit testimony* ever recorded. He has come to the end of his life with no regrets. He goes on (v. 6) to illustrate in two ways his victorious view of death. First, "I am now ready to be offered" (poured out like a drink offering). He considered his life and ministry an offering to God (Romans 15:16; Philippians 2:17). Second, "the time of my departure is at hand." It is time to set sail, take down the tent and move on (see 2 Peter 1:14-15).

He then uses three illustrations (v. 7) that demonstrate his finishing well. "I have fought a good fight," which is the act of a soldier (2:3-4). "I have finished my course," which is the goal of an athlete (2:5). "I have kept the faith," which is the responsibility of a steward of the Gospel. Having done so (1 Timothy 1:11), Paul expects the same from Timothy (1 Timothy 6:20, 2 Timothy 1:14).

"Henceforth," (v. 8) a reward is waiting, the end result of a lifetime of faithful service to Christ *the righteous judge*, who when He returns, would bring with Him rewards for those who served God faithfully during their earthly existence (Matthew 5:10-12).

 LIFE STEP What a joy to have no regrets and to know that you have done what God asks of you. Follow Paul's example! Long to hear, "Well done, good and faithful servant" (Matthew 25:23).

FRIDAY '16

2 TIMOTHY 4:9-15

WHAT IS THE WRITER SAYING?

HOW CAN I APPLY THIS TO MY LIFE?

PRAY United Kingdom – For God to raise up a new generation of vibrant, doctrinally sound Bible teachers.

Following his *exit* testimony (vv. 6-8), Paul requests Timothy to "come shortly unto me (v. 9)," and "come before winter" (v. 21), implying that when winter comes, travel will be more difficult, so an early arrival would be preferable. "The cloak that I left at Troas with Carpus, when thou comest, bring with thee" (v. 13), for it will provide some comfort in the cold surroundings of his prison cell.

Paul then begins to list some of his co-workers (he always recognized their importance and was grateful for their assistance). The first one mentioned, however; triggered unpleasant memories. *Demas*, who at one time had been one of Paul's trusted co-workers (see Colossians 4:14; Philemon 24), had deserted him for what the world had to offer (v. 10) and, apparently, when he was most needed. *Crescens* was off to Galatia on ministry and *Titus* to Dalmatia as Paul's representative. "Only Luke is with me" (v. 11), but for one afflicted with some physical problem as was Paul (2 Corinthians 12:7-9), who better to have as a companion than a medical doctor? *And bring John Mark.* This was the young man who had earlier deserted Paul but had since proved himself (Colossians 4:10). He was now *profitable* for the ministry (v. 11).

Besides the cloak, Paul requests his *books* and *parchments*. The *books* may have been some of Paul's own writings, and *parchments* Paul's personal copies of Old Testament Scriptures. In verses 14-15 Paul refers to an *Alexander*, who in some way did Paul *evil*. Regardless of how it was done, Paul shows no bitterness or *get-even* attitude. At the same time, Paul cautions Timothy to be on guard against him.

LIFE STEP The performance of one's co-workers can make or break the ministry being performed. Thank God for those who serve faithfully with you, and pray that, like John Mark, you also will be *ministry-profitable* to others.

SATURDAY 16

2 TIMOTHY 4:16-22

WHAT IS THE WRITER SAYING?

HOW CAN I APPLY THIS TO MY LIFE?

PRAY Uruguay – For God to reveal truth in a land where spiritists and cultists outnumber true believers.

In this passage, the forgiving attitude of Christ is seen in Paul. Although many had abandoned him, he asked the Lord not to hold them accountable for their actions (v. 16). He writes, "At my first answer" (trial court defense)—the preliminary hearing prior to trial—"no man stood with me." No one appeared to serve as defense attorney, though that was a common practice. Furthermore, "all men forsook me." Those who could have testified for him were also absent. Yet Paul, in spite of their abandonment, like Christ (Luke 23:34) and Stephen (Acts 7:60) before him, exhibits the grace of God he himself had experienced (1 Timothy 1:12-15).

Left alone (but not alone – "the Lord stood with me," v. 17), Paul conducted his own defense and took the opportunity to preach the Gospel – "that by me the preaching might be fully known."

He left nothing out. Even as he said to the Ephesian elders in Acts 20:27, "I... declare unto you all the counsel of God," he used this opportunity to preach the complete Gospel about which he had written (1 Corinthians 15:1-4). His defense was unusual; it said little about him, but much about the Lord, "that all the Gentiles might hear." The Lord again (2 Corinthians 11:16-33), delivered him "out of the mouth of the lion," an expression in Paul's day to express deliverance from extreme danger and a familiar biblical image (see Psalm 22:21; Daniel 6:22).

Paul extends final greetings (vv. 19-22), naming nine of his co-workers. His benediction (v. 22) is two-fold. *Personal* to Timothy: "The Lord Jesus Christ be with thy spirit." *Corporately* to all believers: "Grace be with you (all). Amen."

LIFE STEP Grace—the key word of Paul's life. He had experienced it, and he passed it along to others. Do our family and close friends consider us to be men and women marked by grace and graciousness?

The prophet's name means *comfort*. The name for the city of Capernaum on the northern shore of the Sea of Galilee translates *village of Nahum*. He wrote around 620 B.C. and condemned Assyria, the nation which deported the ten northern tribes in 722 B.C. and attacked Judea in 701 B.C. The great Assyrian king, Ashurbanipal, ruled for forty-two years (669-627 B.C.) but Nineveh fell just fourteen years later! Nahum foretells the destruction of the capital of Assyria, Nineveh, which was fulfilled in 612 B.C. when Nebuchadnezzar's father Nabopolassar (a Babylonian) and Cyaxares (a Mede) defeated it.

As predicted in Nahum 2:6, a flood helped wash away part of the city wall. It was so utterly destroyed that the site was lost to history until found by archaeologists in the 19th century. Nahum also mentions the fall of Thebes ('No') in Egypt, which happened in 663 B.C. (Nahum 3:8). An outline for this short book:

God's Might	1
Nineveh Judged	2
Nineveh Condemned	3

In Christ's day, the Pharisees rather sarcastically asked if any prophet comes from Galilee, because in their day the Galilean region was considered *backward* and they had no respect for Jesus's ministry or background. Not one, but two important prophets actually did come from Galilee – Nahum and Jonah. Furthermore, the Pharisees overlooked the promise of Isaiah that the Galilean region would see "a great light" (Isaiah 9:1-2).

The author of the Book of Malachi is called *Malachi*, which means *the messenger of Jehovah*. Either this was the man's given name or it is the title for an unnamed prophet who is functioning as God's messenger. The book is dated to the period of 450-400 B.C. Ezra's revival (Ezra 7) is dated 458 B.C. Nehemiah ministered 445-433 B.C. and ?-425 BC. Since Nehemiah 5, 10, and 13 have similar themes, it is felt that Malachi also ministered at this time. Notice: 1) Criticism of the laxity of the priests (1:6); 2) Mixed marriages (2:10-11) and 3); Neglected tithes (3). Malachi is distinguished by the following features:

1) It has been about one hundred years since the return of some of the Jews from the Babylonian captivity. Things have not gone as planned. To begin with, only a small percentage of the Jews returned from Babylon (probably less than three percent!) In Ezra 1-6, Haggai, and Zechariah, we see the struggles they experienced getting the temple built and their Jewish national life re-established. As time passed, with few Jews joining them and the exciting prophecies of the coming Messiah in Zechariah not materializing, perhaps discouragement and spiritual apathy set in.

2) This is the last prophetic voice from heaven for the four hundred years leading up to the actual birth of Messiah. God has always provided adequate information for His people to be without excuse for not obeying and believing that all He has promised will come to pass. On the other hand, it is only normal for humans to prefer a current supernatural communication as opposed to reading information given centuries earlier. We have no real knowledge of time spans between supernatural communications prior to Abraham. Starting with Abraham, we see 13 years of silence between God's first and second communication with him. God spoke with the other patriarchs, but then the heavens were silent for the 400 years of enslavement in Egypt. Now the heavens would fall silent again for another 400 years. This does not mean that nothing significant took place on earth. Actually, great political and military activity took place that set the stage for the coming of Christ under the great Roman Empire *in the fullness of time*, as Galatians 4:4 says! Even while Paul was enjoying supernatural revelation, he anticipated another silence (1 Corinthians 13:8). Here we are in the 21st century since Christ walked the planet. We, too, have experienced silence, but we, too, wait for the heavens to open once again!

3) Malachi is in the form of twenty-three questions. Each question is preceded by an accusation by Jehovah of a particular wrong behavior followed by Israel's hypothetical protesting question. The defensive question is then refuted by Jehovah. (cf. 1:2).

4) Malachi criticizes ritualistic/hypocritical worship. Therefore, the theme of the book could be called *challenge to true worship*.

NAHUM 1:1-15

WHAT IS THE WRITER SAYING?

HOW CAN I APPLY THIS TO MY LIFE?

The word *burden* can also be translated *oracle*. It is a heavy prophecy, fraught with gloom and doom. Nineveh was the capital of Assyria, situated on the Tigris River. Assyria was the most ferocious empire in the ancient world, piling up human heads and impaling the citizens of conquered cities alive on wooden stakes. Jonah was dispatched to evangelize Nineveh, much to his chagrin. Amazingly, the people of his day, including the king, repented and judgment was temporarily averted. Unfortunately, the revival did not last and by Nahum's day, 100 years later, God announces that the judgment will fall. It didn't fall for another 100 years, but fall eventually it did. Nahum is called an *Elkoshite*, which refers to his hometown. Unfortunately, no one knows where it was located. The strongest tradition places Elkosh in the extreme southern portion of Judea in the territory of the tribe of Simeon. Verse 4 refers to places normally known for their beautiful vegetation. Bashan was located on the high plateau of what today is called the Golan Heights. It was famous for its good grazing lands and luxurious cattle (Amos 4:1). Carmel (*orchard*) was famous for its olive trees. It is the mountainous ridge overlooking the Valley of Armageddon. Elijah challenged Baal (the agricultural god) on Carmel. Lebanon (*white mountain*) was well watered and in addition to the flowers mentioned, was also famous for the beautiful cedars of Lebanon. The Tigris River flooded and broke down Nineveh's walls enabling her quick defeat (v. 8). Verse 11 refers to the wicked exploits of Sennacherib (who attacked King Hezekiah in 701 B.C.).

LIFE STEP Paul quotes verse 15 in Romans 10:15 and applies it to missionary work. Have you thanked the owner of the "feet" who brought you the message of salvation? Are your "feet" taking the message to others?

MONDAY 17

MALACHI 1:1-14

WHAT IS THE WRITER SAYING?

HOW CAN I APPLY THIS TO MY LIFE?

PRAY Portugal – Pray for more open doors with local churches and for more workers to help teaching and discipling students.

The Lord affirms His love, but the Israelites of Malachi's day question it. The Lord answers with an explanation of His choice of Jacob over his *older* twin brother, Esau. His *hate* of Esau's descendants is in the sense that they are not the *chosen people*. Individuals from that line, however, can experience God's love in salvation and in fact, unbelievers among the chosen people will also experience God's wrath. Amalek was a grandson of Esau and the Amalekites were Israel's first enemy as they came out of Egypt. The descendants of Esau became the nation of Edom (*red*, in honor of Esau.). They frequently caused Israel trouble, especially harassing her when attacked by other enemies. They were displaced from their territory by the Nabateans around 400 B.C. The last known Edomites in history were the Idumeans from which the family of the Herods came. *Lord of hosts* (Jehovah Sabaoth) occurs twenty times in Malachi. After a brief statement about Jehovah's love for Israel, Malachi launches into a long section describing Israel's contempt for God (1:6–3:15). Certainly all the people are guilty, but notice that the religious leaders (the priests) are rebuked! *Polluted* (1:7) occurs just eleven times in the Old Testament, but three of those occurrences are here in the little book of Malachi. It is used in Daniel 1:8 (translated *defile*) to refer to Nebuchadnezzar's pagan food. They had *profaned* the Lord's Table. *Profane* means *to treat as common*. The root of the word refers to a doorstep that everyone entering the room steps on. In English, the word *vulgar* carries the same connotation. The law required an unblemished *male* animal, these people were bringing damaged *female* animals (v. 14, in Hebrew).

LIFE STEP No matter how dark the hour or confusing the situation, the proper response is to trust the Lord and demonstrate that trust by continued obedience to God's revealed will!

TUESDAY '17

MALACHI 2:1-9

WHAT IS THE WRITER SAYING?

HOW CAN I APPLY THIS TO MY LIFE?

PRAY Spain – For godly men to write, develop, and produce more Christian literature in the Basque language.

One of the chief functions of the priest was to be a *pastor* to the people. They were to help the people confess and make atonement for sin. They were to lead them in worship. They were to bless them, both in the general performing of these duties and in a verbal blessing similar to our practice of closing a worship service with a benediction. The *curse* that God would send would most likely be agricultural since that was one of the main reasons the people sought the Lord's favor and the priests lived off of the food they brought as offerings. Having successful descendants to carry on the family name in honor was important. The innards of the sacrificial animals, including the manure, were to be burned outside of the camp (Exodus 29:14). Instead, God says he will smear the refuse on these hypocritical priests and they will be carried outside the camp of Israel! In verse 4, God refers to a covenant with Levi. This was not with the man *Levi* but the tribe (Exodus 29:9 — Aaron was descended from Levi, see Exodus 2:1). In Numbers 25, a Levite by the name of Phinehas defended God's honor by killing an Israelite who grossly sinned against God. God responded by promising Phinehas that his descendants would enjoy a perpetual priesthood. Eventually his family line became the high priestly line and, in fact, in Ezekiel that same line is promised the priesthood in the Messianic Temple. Therefore *Levi* here refers to his descendants and, in particular, his illustrious descendant, Phinehas. Instruction in the law was one of the responsibilities of the priests. These had miserably failed and would be judged. *Contemptible* (2:9) is the same word they used to despise the Lord's Table (1:7). They would be treated as they had treated the Lord.

 LIFE STEP If we expect God's blessings then we must do things His way.

155

WEDNESDAY '17

MALACHI 2:10-17

WHAT IS THE WRITER SAYING?

HOW CAN I APPLY THIS TO MY LIFE?

PRAY Armenia – Pray that Armenian Christians, who have a spiritual legacy of more than 1,700 years, might become sources of light to the surrounding region.

Verse 10 establishes the principle of loyalty to the community of the *chosen people*. The Israelites had one father, Abraham. By definition, they also were to have one God, the God of Abraham. By marrying foreign wives, they were violating this brotherhood both biologically and religiously (as the foreign wives worshipped other gods). This phenomenon can be stated: "Marry me; marry my religion." It is the *covenant of our fathers* (plural) in the sense that it takes faithfulness down through the generations to maintain the spiritual purity. Deuteronomy 7 lists the nations with which the Israelites were not to establish marriage contracts. The only exceptions were in situations where the pagan women converted to Jehovah (like Ruth). *Dealt treacherously* (2:11) occurs five times in 2:10-16. It usually is used of adultery. Israel was already *married* to Jehovah. By marrying pagan women and worshipping their gods, they were committing spiritual adultery. Ironically, the Hebrew word for *married* is the word *Baal*—the same word as the pagan god of agriculture! God also condemns Israel for her contempt of Him as demonstrated in *divorce* (2:13 16) and then in *impiety* (2:17). Verse 16 implies that these Jewish men were divorcing their older Jewish wives in order to marry younger pagans. Verse 13 indicates that these carnal men were so dull that it didn't occur to them that their treacherous treatment of their wives had any effect on their relationship with God. Ignorantly they plead with Him to bless their crops not realizing that He had withdrawn His pleasure from them because of their sinful behavior. The original purpose for the *chosen people* was to remain spiritually dedicated to Jehovah (v. 15).

LIFE STEP Love transcends physical beauty. Love is a command, not an emotion. As we obey the command, the emotion follows.

THURSDAY '17

MALACHI 3:1-6

WHAT IS THE WRITER SAYING?

HOW CAN I APPLY THIS TO MY LIFE?

PRAY Israel – Pray that many more of the ultra-Orthodox Jews, the modern Pharisees, may become like Nicodemus, a process that is already happening.

My Messenger is *Malaki* in Hebrew (as also in Malachi 1:1). Here it applies to the *forerunner* of the Messiah, who by Jewish and Christian tradition is the prophet Elijah. In Christ's first coming, the role of the forerunner was played by John the Baptist. While John came in the *spirit and power of Elijah* he was not Elijah. (Matthew 11:14 "If you are willing to receive it, he is Elijah..." 17:11 "Elijah is coming." 17:12 "Elijah has come already, and they did not know him."). God in His sovereignty knew that the Jews would reject Christ and so John was not Elijah. When Christ comes the second time it would seem that the real Elijah will return, perhaps as one of the two witnesses of Revelation 11. Verse 2 speaks of the forerunner's purifying effect on the world. In ancient cities the launderers' guild had their shops downwind from the towns because of the smelly animal fats and urine (for uric acid) used in launderer's soap, making it a potent bleach. God would bring the sinful *chosen people* through the refining fires and bring forth people worthy of worshipping His great name. Sorcery is just one of the forbidden skills used to contact the spirit world. Deuteronomy forbids any contact with the spirit world and then concludes on the positive note that God would send another prophet like Moses to give people more information. Ultimately, this *other prophet* was/is Messiah. The first three sins are normally considered rather perverse and wicked (sorcery, adultery and lying under oath). Notice that not treating those around us fairly is in the same category. Oppressing the poor, widows, orphans and strangers is condemned in several of the Minor Prophets. Verse 6 abruptly changes from judgment to an explanation that God has promised (unconditionally) to eventually bless them.

LIFE STEP Discipline is not pleasant at the moment, but it yields eternal benefit, if we respond properly to God's direction.

FRIDAY 17

MALACHI 3:7-15

WHAT IS THE WRITER SAYING?

HOW CAN I APPLY THIS TO MY LIFE?

PRAY Jamaica – For churches to model compassion to the poor, who receive minimal exposure to the gospel.

Tithe means ten percent. The Israelites were required to give ten percent of all they earned each year as a *tax* for God's rule over them (the *theocracy*, which was for religious and governmental purposes). *Offerings* were above the tithe and were freewill. In failing to provide the *tax* and *love offerings*, they were snubbing God. The word for *nation* in verse 9 is the Hebrew word for Gentile nation (*goy*). The *storehouse* was part of the temple complex. The Old Testament economy had one theocratic capital, one temple, and one place of worship through giving. Since we live under a different system, there is no New Testament tithe (tax) mandated, nor a New Testament central *storehouse*. The Greek grammar of 1 Corinthians 16:2 speaks of regular but *private* (at home) storage of offerings from which discretionary giving can take place when needs arise. New Testament giving is to be done out of a heart of gratitude as God has blessed each one. In their spiritual dullness, these Israelites in Malachi's day had concluded that there was no profit in serving God and flagrantly rebelled against Him. Compare William Henley's famous Invictus: "Out of the night that surrounds me, black as the pit from pole to pole, I thank whatever Gods there be for my unconquerable soul. It matters not how straight the gate, how charged with punishments the scroll! I'm the master of my fate; I'm the captain of my soul!"

LIFE STEP Those of us who love the Lord and know better can calmly reply in the words of Dorthea Day: "Out of the light that dazzles me, bright as the noonday sun from pole to pole, I thank the God I know to be for Jesus the lover of my soul. It matters not how straight the gate, He cleared from punishment the scroll! Christ's the master of my fate; Christ is the captain of my soul!"

SATURDAY '17

MALACHI 3:16 - 4:6

WHAT IS THE WRITER SAYING?

HOW CAN I APPLY THIS TO MY LIFE?

Two types of people are listed in 3:16 18. Malachi watches as the angels bring a special book and the names of the righteous are written in the book for special care and blessing. Chapter 4 describes the nature of the coming judgment. It is the fiery *day of the Lord* (4:1). Sinners *get away with murder* for the time being, but all the while they are losing all of their moisture and one day they will go up in flames like a month-old Christmas tree. Verse 2 introduces the gracious Savior. Christ is spoken of as the *S-U-N* of Righteousness (The *SON* is the *SUN*). *Wings* refer to the rays of the sun. We know now that there is literally healing in the rays of the sun as the ultraviolet light kills germs and promotes the healing of wounds. Warmed by the rays of that life-giving orb, saints will skip through life like calves released on a spring day after a long, harsh, confining winter. Verse 3 explains why we don't have to envy the wicked. We should just consider their ends. The Israelites are told to remember the Law of Moses given on Mt. Horeb (Sinai) (4:4) and to look for Elijah, the forerunner of the Messiah (4:5 and 6). Both men made trips to Mt. Horeb (Exodus 19 and 1 Kings 19) and both appeared on the Mount of Transfiguration with Jesus before His crucifixion. Some feel that these two men are good candidates for the two witnesses of Revelation 11. Both had strange circumstances surrounding their departure from this life (Moses's body was buried by God Himself and Elijah went up in the fiery chariot). At least the two witnesses of Revelation 11 will function in the spirit and power of Moses and Elijah.

 Genesis tells how a curse fell on the whole human race. The last words of the Old Testament indicate that the curse is still there. The first book of the New Testament introduces Him who came to remove the curse!

Dr. Tom Davis

The fourth Gospel was penned by the Beloved Apostle John around A.D. 90 towards the end of his long life of ministry from the city of Ephesus on the west coast of modern Turkey. He was the only apostle to live a full life and certainly had deep reflections on all that he had experienced. One could wonder why God commissioned four biographies of His Son's earthly life. Actually, in light of the outburst of praise in John 21:25, the question is not, "Why so many?" but rather "Why so few!?!" Actually, God treats His Son as a fabulous diamond that when held up to the light at various angles produces different flashes of light from the fire within.

Matthew writes to Jews presenting Jesus of Nazareth as their prophesied Messiah, quoting many Old Testament passages in the process. As such, Matthew presents Jesus as the Lion of the Tribe of Judah, taking his genealogy back to Father Abraham. Mark writes to a Gentile Roman audience that knows so little about the Jews that he has to inform them that the Jordan is a river.

The Romans care little for Jewish customs but they do know a lot about slavery, servant-hood and obedience. As such, Mark presents Jesus as the perfect servant. No one cares about the background of a servant so Mark provides no genealogy for Jesus. But he is pictured as a busy man, "immediately" doing this or that as He bustles around doing the will of His Father in Heaven.

Luke writes for a Greek audience. They admired both the human intellect (Socrates, Plato, etc.) and the human body (The Olympics). As such, Luke presents Jesus as the greatest man who has ever lived. He takes Jesus' genealogy all the way back to Adam. Finally, John presents Jesus of Nazareth in His full-blown deity. Since God has always existed, there is no need for a genealogy of Jesus in John. In comparison with the other gospels, John has the following distinctives: twenty seven personal interviews, six Jewish holidays are mentioned, Christ is presented as greater than the Law, Temple, Shekinah and holidays, and the seven great "I AM" claims.

The purpose for the fourth Gospel is clearly stated by John in 20:30, 31 "And many other signs truly did Jesus in the presence of his disciples, which are not written in this book: but these are written, that ye might believe that Jesus is the Christ, the Son of God; and that believing ye might have life through his name."

The miracles recorded in the book are signs of Jesus' deity that should lead people to believe which results in the possession of real life. In fact, "sign" is the only word for miracle that John uses. He selects seven of the many miracles to illustrate the variety of Christ's power:

1. Water into Wine =
   Sensitivity to human frustrations
2. Nobleman's Son =
   Power over Distance
3. Lame Man =
   Power over Time
4. Feeding of the 5000 =
   Power over Quantity
5. Water Walking =
   Power over Nature
6. Blind man =
   Power over Human Misfortune
7. Raising of Lazarus =
   Power over Death

Belief is the response that John seeks as the word "believe" occurs ninety eight times as compared to only eight times in Matthew; thirteen times in Mark and nine times in Luke. John emphasizes three aspects of the life that belief brings. It is on-going pleasurable <u>consciousness</u> (self and other awareness); it derives pleasure from <u>conversation</u> (interaction) with other rational creatures; and by definition, possesses eternal <u>continuity</u> (never ends).

The following outline is provided by Dr. Merrill Tenney, whose commentary on John is highly recommended. It is based on the reaction of the Jewish authorities to the Person of Jesus Christ.

1. Consideration	1-4
2. Controversy	5-6
3. Conflict	7-11
4. Crisis	12
5. Conference	13-17
6. Consummation	18-20
7. Commission	21

SUNDAY '18

JOHN 1:1-8

WHAT IS THE WRITER SAYING?

HOW CAN I APPLY THIS TO MY LIFE?

PRAY Bosnia-Herzegovena – Pray that the tiny number of evangelical believers may grow in number and effectively build bridges across the ethnic divisions in this land.

John starts his account of the person of Christ in a style reminiscent of the first book of the Bible, "In the beginning God created the heavens and earth." "Beginning" does not imply a time before which God did not exist. It is referring to the beginning of human history. While some have argued that Jesus was the first being created, the point of verse one is the exact opposite. Furthermore, verse one argues that Jesus and God the Father are equal in essence. It is not accurate to translate the verse as though it was arguing that Jesus was a created spirit being (a god). Grammatically, without the article (the) modifying "God," the Greek language would allow the last phrase to be translated, *the Word was a god*. However, the word "God" appears many times in John. Half of the time it does not have the article but in no other passage is it translated *a god*. In fact, if the article was there, it would make an exclusive statement; *the Word was the (only) God*. This would deny the Father. Actually, without the article the Greek grammar is accentuating quality (Godness). The expanded translation then is: *And the Word was characterized by Godness* (He was equal with God!). *Logos* ("word") in Greek philosophy referred to the ultimate intelligence in the universe. Verse 3 describes the origin of the universe as an event (crisis), not the product of a process. Not only was Jesus equal with the Father, but He was also the engineer of the material universe. As a result, He possesses the key to life.

 LIFE STEP To be in vital connection with *The Logos* is to be plugged into the power source. He is God; He created us; He is the source of life; He is the true light. Wise men (like John the Baptist) still seek Him!

MONDAY '18

JOHN 1:9-13

WHAT IS THE WRITER SAYING?

v 13 Believers are born of God – of the will of God?

HOW CAN I APPLY THIS TO MY LIFE?

"World" (*cosmos*) refers to an *orderly system of thought and behavior*. It is a major concern of John, occurring seventy seven times. The opposite Greek word is *chaos* or *disorder*. We use both words in English. In the morning when we do our *cosmetics* we turn *chaos* into *cosmos*! This world system has been perverted by Satan. It therefore is spiritual darkness, as Satan is a "liar, and the father of it" (John 8:44). Satan's very name means *Adversary*. His person, philosophy and practice seek to spread deceit, confusion and darkness. Christ, on the other hand, comes to give light. It is ironic that Satan is also called "Lucifer" (Isaiah 14:12). "Lucifer" is a reference to the *bright and morning star*, Venus. It seems as though this is an attempt to counterfeit Christ's role as the "Dayspring" (Luke 1:78) and the "bright and morning star" (Revelation 22:16). Isaiah 9:2 also foresaw the day when "The people that walked in darkness have seen a great light: they that dwell in the land of the shadow of death, upon them hath the light shined." Coming to "His own" is the equivalent of saying *He came home* (cf. 16:32; 19:27). Since the world is triply blinded by the world, the flesh and the devil, the average earthling does not recognize or welcome home their Creator. But those who see with the eyes of faith and do welcome Him are given the "power" (*the delegated authority*, see 19:10) to be at home with the Family of God! The transaction involves a movement of the will. It is blinded by sin, so God has to overcome the blindness (v. 13). The individual then responds with a heart of belief, receiving what Christ offers.

LIFE STEP One of the underrated arguments for the validity of Christianity is the uniqueness and moral splendor of Jesus of Nazareth. No man could invent such a person! There would have to be a Jesus to create a Jesus – His is the *Greatest Story Ever Told!*

TUESDAY '18

JOHN 1:14-18

WHAT IS THE WRITER SAYING?

HOW CAN I APPLY THIS TO MY LIFE?

PRAY Hungary – For churches to mature in their giving and support of nationals involved in Christian work.

"Dwelt" (v. 14) is the root idea of *The Shekinah* (God dwelling with His people). "Beheld" means scrutinize. It has the same root as *theater*, where we scrutinize the arts. Jewish scholars had three terms for the *Manifest Presence of God with His People*. The first was *memra*, "The Word." The second was *shekinah*, "Dwelling." The third was *yekara*, "glory." John uses all three concepts to refer to Jesus Christ! "Only begotten" does not mean that Christ was born. It is a qualifying term. Isaac was the "only begotten" son of Abraham. He was not the only son but rather the *favorite* or *unique* son.

John the Apostle introduced John the Baptist as the *forerunner* of "the Word" back in verse 6. John the Baptist's ministry was to prepare the nation of Israel to receive Jesus. He proclaimed His eternality. He *came after*. Jesus was born after John and began his ministry after John, yet He was *before*, a clear declaration of Christ's pre-existence. He was from eternity past. John also describes the nature of Christ's ministry. His ministry is full of two Old Testament character qualities – grace (loving kindness) and truth. He provides *one gracious gift after another* (1:16). Jesus Christ is the One who declares or explains the Father to us. The Greek root form of the word being translated *declared* is the source of our word *exegete* (to explain or unfold divine mysteries). Jesus explained the truth of the Father to man (1:18).

 LIFE STEP God went to a lot of effort to introduce the world to His Son. Have you received God's gracious gift of salvation? If so, are you being a "light" in this sin-darkened world like Jesus and John were?

WEDNESDAY '18

JOHN 1:19-28

WHAT IS THE WRITER SAYING?

HOW CAN I APPLY THIS TO MY LIFE?

PRAY Bahrain – Bahrain has more social freedom than most other Arab states. Pray that there would be even more political and religious freedom to help spread the Gospel.

John 1:1-18 can be considered the *Theological Introduction to Jesus Christ*. Verse 19 begins the next section of John's presentation, a list of *witnesses* to the life of Christ. The word for "record" in verse 19 is the same Greek word translated "witness" in 1:7-8 and 15. It is the word *martureo*, from which we get our English word, *martyr*. John the Baptist was making waves. He was getting people's attention. The Jewish authorities sent a delegation to investigate who he was and what he was doing (vv.19, 24). John explained his ministry in verses 20-23. He told the religious examiners that he was not the Messiah, neither was he Elijah (Malachi 4:5), or the "Prophet" predicted to be greater than and coming to replace Moses in Deuteronomy 18:15. John simply referred to himself as "the voice" (see Isaiah 40:3). Notice that John the Baptist was increasingly terse with his questioners, answering in five words in verse 20, three words in verse 21a and only one word in 21b!

John informs us that the Jews (v. 19) who sent these men were from the sect known as the "Pharisees" (v. 24). The Pharisees were more conservative theologically than the Sadducees. The Pharisees were the *pastors* in the local synagogues and therefore would be more concerned about the *pastoral* nature of John's baptizing ministry. Notice that the author includes somewhat unnecessary details in verse 28. This is a mark of authenticity because writers who invent stories would not naturally include such details whereas an eyewitness just shares what he knows to have been the case. Bethabara means "the House of the Ford" and elsewhere is also called Bethany. Baptism by immersion would be the reason for baptizing in such a place with much water.

 LIFE STEP John the Baptist was a great promoter for his cousin Jesus. He is gone. Who takes his place today? Are we up to the task?

THURSDAY 18

JOHN 1:29-34

WHAT IS THE WRITER SAYING?

HOW CAN I APPLY THIS TO MY LIFE?

PRAY Pray for opportunities to witness to your unsaved friends and loved ones.

Another marker of authenticity in this account is the noting of days in which certain events occur (29, 35, 43 and 2:1). In verse 29 John announces that Jesus is the "Lamb of God, which taketh away the sin of the world." The Jewish people knew a lot about animal sacrifice. Adam and Eve had their fig leaves replaced by sacrificed animal skins. Abel brought a bloody sacrifice. God provided Abraham a ram to kill in place of his son, Isaac (Genesis 22:13). At the Exodus from Egypt God spared the children of Israel from the death angel by having them sacrifice a spotless lamb (Exodus 12:4-6; 1 Corinthians 5:7). Isaiah 53:10-12 anticipated that the Messiah would be a *trespass offering*. In Revelation 5:5-6, as we get ready for eternal life in heaven, we see Jesus as both a lion and a lamb,

in fact, a lamb "as it had been slain." Amazingly, three and one-half years after John's proclamation here in John 1, on the very afternoon that Jewish fathers were taking their Passover lambs to the temple to kill them for the Passover meal that night, Jesus the Lamb would be hanging on the cross!

In the Garden of Eden, God killed an animal for a man. At the Exodus, an animal died for a family. On the Day of Atonement, every year an animal died for the Nation of Israel, but on the cross, Jesus died for the sins of the entire world!

John explains that He knew who Jesus was because of the events that took place in His baptism. This implies that John had recently baptized Jesus, either the day before (v. 26) or this day.

LIFE STEP Jesus' own brothers and sisters did not believe His claim to be the Son of God, but his cousin John did. What made the difference? What kind of testimony are we to our brothers, sisters and cousins?

FRIDAY '18

JOHN 1:35-42

WHAT IS THE WRITER SAYING?

HOW CAN I APPLY THIS TO MY LIFE?

PRAY Panama – For youth ministry workers to commit their time, creativity, and love to Christ's use.

The first four chapters of John describe a period of consideration when seven different people or groups of people consider the claims of Christ. First is John the Baptist (Baptizer!). The second *consideration* involved the calling of the first disciples. "Again the next day" implies a repeat performance of the previous day's testimony. This time, two of John's disciples are so impressed that they leave John to follow Jesus. John does not try to stop them, nor is it the *forerunner's* job to join them. These first two disciples were probably Andrew (*Manly*) and John (*Jehovah is Gracious*), with Andrew bringing his brother Peter (*Rock*) to the Lord for the third. The two disciples call Jesus "Rabbi," a title of respect for a revered spiritual leader. John indicates his sensitivity to his primarily Gentile audience by translating this Hebrew word for them as "Master." "Where dwellest thou" (v. 38) means, *Can we come and talk with you?* The "tenth hour" would be 4:00 p.m. (John seems to use Jewish time throughout his Gospel until he gets to the Roman trials in chapter 19. Romans began daily time reckoning at midnight, the Jews at 6 a.m.). Custom would imply that the men spent the night with Jesus since it was too late in the day to travel elsewhere. Andrew is compelled to bring his brother to Christ. Simon Peter was named for Simeon, the unstable hothead who murdered innocent men in revenge for the rape of his sister Dinah (Genesis 49:5-7). "Cephas" is Aramaic for *rock*. Do you know Rock Johnson? Sure you do! (Peter son of John!).

LIFE STEP Meeting Jesus is life changing. John and Andrew were never the same. John the Baptist pointed them to the Lamb of God, and they followed. They immediately want to bring their friend and brother, Peter. Who are you pointing to Christ? Who are you following?

SATURDAY '18

JOHN 1:43-51

WHAT IS THE WRITER SAYING?

HOW CAN I APPLY THIS TO MY LIFE?

PRAY Mozambique – Pray that religious freedom might continue and that true Christian faith and love might be expressed throughout society.

In John 1:43-51 Jesus adds Philip (*Lover of Horses*) and Nathanael (*Gift of God*). Philip is from Bethsaida (*House of Fishing*), as are Andrew and Peter. Later, Bethsaida will be criticized for not repenting at the ministry of Jesus (Matthew 11:21).

Philip, like Andrew, found someone else to introduce to Christ, Nathanael. Nathanael, however, is not impressed with the news that Jesus is from Nazareth. Nazareth was small, had poor soil with no well, and housed a Roman garrison. This became the basis for the later accusation of Jesus' illegitimate birth.

The fig tree (v. 48) was a place of meditation and study. *Guile* is *supplanter*, the name for Jacob in Genesis 28. Perhaps Nathanael was meditating on that passage and Christ's knowledge of his thoughts convinced him of Jesus'

Messiahship and thus his declaration *Son of God, King of Israel*. Jesus is amazed that Nathanael so quickly turns from skepticism to belief. Greater evidences lay ahead for Nathanael as he would soon see Christ do the first of many miracles that demonstrated His deity. The reference to angels *ascending and descending* is another connection to Jacob (Jacob's Ladder).

Son of Man was a favorite title the Lord used of Himself. This is the first of eleven times the title occurs in the book of John and carries the idea of Christ's union with mankind through the incarnation. At His birth, He became fully man so that He might be able to offer Himself as a sacrifice for mankind. Jesus willingly laid aside the glories of heaven to become the ultimate servant and all-sufficient sacrifice (Mark 10:45).

 LIFE STEP When introduced to Christ, people react in different ways. Some, like Philip, are immediately sold-out. Others, like Nathanael, are skeptical and cautious. What a great example we see in Andrew and Philip, men who did not need the spotlight but quietly brought others to Christ.

JOHN 2:1-11

WHAT IS THE WRITER SAYING?

HOW CAN I APPLY THIS TO MY LIFE?

PRAY Costa Rica – For the growth and strengthening of Bible schools that train leadership.

The wedding at Cana of Galilee provided the third opportunity for considering the person of Christ. It is interesting that Nathanael was from the city of Cana. We are told that the wedding was on the "third" day, which would be Tuesday. This seems strange to us, but actually this was a popular day for Jewish weddings. Perhaps the reason why Mary feels compelled to do something about the wine shortage was because so many extra people had come to the wedding with her (Jesus and His disciples). Christ's response to Mary's request was not impolite. "Woman" was a proper title, similar to us saying, "Ma'am." Jesus protests that His hour (to reveal His Messiahship) had not yet come. The six large pots held water for washing hands. If only the guests knew where the wine came from! They held twenty to thirty gallons apiece. His creative act (bypassing both the growth stage of the grape and the proper aging of the wine) underscores God's ability to create with the appearance of age, whether it was an Adam and Eve who as one day-olds appeared as adults or a universe that seems to be billions of light years wide (old). Jesus came to bring the new wine of God's grace in a measure that exceeded man's need. This is the first of seven signs that John records striving to bring the reader to a place of *belief* in the deity of Jesus Christ. His power over natural processes was very convincing to those who knew and understood what had taken place.

LIFE STEP So far we have seen Jesus as the Word, God, Creator, Light, only begotten Son, Lamb of God, Son of God, Messiah, King of Israel and Son of Man. What title best speaks to me in my relationship with the One who even concerns Himself with trivial happiness and avoiding social blunders at a wedding?

JOHN 2:12-25

WHAT IS THE WRITER SAYING?

HOW CAN I APPLY THIS TO MY LIFE?

Cana was about eight miles from Jesus' hometown of Nazareth. Now He travels sixteen miles further to the more populated area of the northern edge of the Sea of Galilee. He goes "down" in elevation from the mountains of Cana (Galilee is already about six hundred feet below sea level). Capernaum is from the Hebrew *Kfar Nahum* for *Village of Nahum*. It is Peter's hometown and will be the center of His Galilean ministry for three of the next three and a half years. Verse 13 brings us to the half-year mark of His three-and-a-half-year ministry. It is three years from His crucifixion. They go "up" to Jerusalem in elevation. Jerusalem is about 2200 feet above sea level in the Judean mountains. Passover was one of the *Pilgrim Holidays* (along with Pentecost and Tabernacles). Every able-bodied Jewish person was expected to go to Jerusalem for these holidays. Due to the distances traveled, the pilgrims needed to buy animals for the ceremonies and change their foreign money. The businessmen had become unscrupulous in their dealings with their fellow Jews. Jesus charged them with turning worship into a moneymaking scheme. Jesus' zeal was for purity in the house of God! (See Psalm 69:9.) The Jewish leaders questioned His authority and demanded a sign of credentials. They didn't understand His sign but later His disciples were strengthened in their faith as they remembered His words (John 12:16). Verse 20 states that the Temple was forty-six years old at this time. Herod the Great began this beautification project in 20 B.C. so the year is now A.D. 26.

Jesus did other signs (2:23). It produced surface curiosity but not saving faith (2:24-25). Jesus knew their hearts and knew the quality of their belief and was not willing to *believe* in them.

LIFE STEP God is not interested in outward, vain, hypocritical worship, but in worship from the heart. He wants reality, not ritual; relationship, not ceremony. He expects this from worshipers and the worship leaders.

TUESDAY '19

JOHN 3:1-12

WHAT IS THE WRITER SAYING?

HOW CAN I APPLY THIS TO MY LIFE?

PRAY Pray that thousands will be reached with the Gospel of Jesus Christ in 2013 all across the world.

Christ's fourth encounter in chapter 2 was no low-key event. On His first trip to Jerusalem, He marches into the temple and runs out the moneychangers, instantly gaining the attention of the rulers of the Jews. The temple was to be a place of worship, not merchandise. In chapter 3, we meet one of these rulers, as Jesus has His fifth encounter with a ruler named Nicodemus. Nicodemus was a Jew and he came to Christ with intellectual needs. In the religious circles Nicodemus traveled in, he was a recognized authority (v. 10), yet he was spiritually blind. He was a Pharisee, a teacher (3:10), and part of the Sanhedrin. Jesus introduced Nicodemus to his need for rebirth. He initially understood this to be a physical rebirth, which would be impossible. Jesus helped him to understand that He spoke of a second birth into spiritual life (v. 6).

Jesus uses the wind (v. 8) to illustrate the ministry of God's Spirit to Nicodemus. Just like the wind, God's Spirit moves according to His sovereign will and His effect is unmistakable upon the hearts of mankind.

Nicodemus is only mentioned in the Gospel of John and only three times. In the three passages, it seems that John focuses on the progression of his spiritual life. Nicodemus appears first in chapter 3, but leaves with no apparent change. Then in John 7:50 we find him defending Jesus against charges made by the Sanhedrin. Last, we find him at the Crucifixion (John 19:38-39), with Joseph boldly and publicly standing as a disciple of Christ.

LIFE STEP Many who are brilliant and highly intellectual have a hard time grasping the simple truths of God's Word. Have you been born twice? To be alive is to have experienced physical birth. To be born again is to receive eternal life through placing your faith in Jesus Christ. You must be born again!

WEDNESDAY 19

JOHN 3:13-21

WHAT IS THE WRITER SAYING?

HOW CAN I APPLY THIS TO MY LIFE?

PRAY China – For the 44,000,000 members of unregistered house churches, persecuted by officials.

Nicodemus was not a novice. However, when Jesus taught using a simple earthly comparison between physical birth and spiritual birth, this great teacher could not grasp the simple truth. How would he ever understand heavenly things, which no one had seen (3:12-13)?

Jesus was trying to relate to Nicodemus in terms he could grasp. He uses the account from Numbers 21, which tells of a time in the history of Israel when they complained against Moses and God sent serpents among the people. Many were dying and God instructed Moses to make a bronze likeness of a serpent and raise it on a pole. Those who were bitten were to look upon the serpent and they would live. This required them to believe and look in faith. In the same way, at the cross, Jesus Christ would be raised up, and those who placed their faith in God's substitutionary sacrifice would be saved. Nicodemus eventually appeared to understand this (John 19:39).

Verse 16 shows the breadth (*world*); length (*gave*); depth (*not perish*) and height (*everlasting life*) of God's love. Christ has paid the price for the sin of all men of all time – past, present, and future (1 John 2:2). That means that the only issue left is whether men will believe and receive what has already been provided for them. This means that men go to hell, not because of their sins (plural), but because of the sin (singular) of unbelief. Once in hell, they then pay for their own sins (plural) having rejected Christ's gift of eternal life.

Again, John picks up the theme of light and darkness. Jesus came to bring light to those in darkness. Those who desire to know God are attracted to the light. Those whose deeds are evil reject the light and flee from it, not wanting to be exposed by it.

LIFE STEP Are you attracted to the things of God or do you avoid them? Those who are of the light love the light and want to be near it.

JOHN 3:22-30

WHAT IS THE WRITER SAYING?

HOW CAN I APPLY THIS TO MY LIFE?

John the Baptist was the first to consider and proclaim the claims of Christ. He was introduced as the first witness in chapter 1 and now John comes back to John the Baptist to note the humility of this great prophet. Verse 23 is a classic argument for baptism by immersion since it emphasizes that there was "much water" at Aenon (*Springs*). Beyond this, the root meaning of "baptize" is *to dip*. Finally, the Jewish ritual called "baptism" in Hebrews 6:2 was a cleansing bath in which the individual went completely under the water. Verse 24 indicates that the readers of John's Gospel would have access to other writings (such as Matthew) to know that John the Baptist eventually was thrown into prison. Some of John's disciples are jealous of Christ's increasing popularity. John corrects them, claiming that his role was merely that of a forerunner (Malachi 3-4). In ancient times, whenever a king went visiting, citizens of the cities would go out and fix up the roadway into the city. John the Baptist was with the Heavenly Department of Highways for The Royal visit! John was not the Bridegroom (main event) but as a friend of the bridegroom, he could rejoice to welcome his friend and enjoy his joy. In this marriage analogy, Old Testament saints (like John the Baptist) and Tribulation Saints will be the "friends of the bridegroom" while the Church is the bride of Christ.

We know from the book of Acts (19) that there were many disciples of John the Baptist at Ephesus. Since John the Apostle also spent time at Ephesus and those believers would be reading this gospel, it could be that he is emphasizing the fact that Jesus has superseded John the Baptist so they would have the proper respect for Jesus.

LIFE STEP An authentic ambassador of the King of Kings magnifies Christ and not himself. Whenever we serve the Lord, make sure He gets the credit!

FRIDAY 19

JOHN 3:31-36

WHAT IS THE WRITER SAYING?

HOW CAN I APPLY THIS TO MY LIFE?

PRAY Libya – Pray for freedom for believers to exercise their faith as Libyans move forward after four decades under Muammar Qaddafi.

These verses climax the testimony of Jesus' deity in chapters 1-3. Since Jesus came directly from heaven (v.31 "above"), His knowledge of ultimate truth is more likely than someone who is only from "the earth" (a reference to John the Baptist). The author complains that despite this superior origin, the men of that day did not believe Jesus (v. 32). The "no man" of verse 32 cannot be 100% since in verse 33 John goes on to say, *I believed*. John uses a formula to solemnly affirm the intensity of his belief ("set to his seal"). The analogy of indicating loyalty, devotion, belonging or belief in an individual by a seal also lies behind the "Mark ...of the Beast" which seals unbelievers in their allegiance to "The Lie" (Revelation 13:17 and 2 Thessalonians 2:11). John and anyone else who receives the testimony of Jesus are publicly affirming that they believe that God has told them the truth about Jesus. Believers are also *marked* with a new name as they enter eternal life in heaven (Revelation 2:17, 3:12, 14:1, 22:4).

It is hard to *prove* that anything is true. There is always an arrogant person who wants to argue that 1 + 1=11 (!). Atheists make the logical mistake of an *absolute negation: I have absolute knowledge that there is no being in the universe with absolute knowledge*. Since we are so limited, we can only expect to know the truth of the universe if a superior being comes from *out there* to *here* to tell us. John says that's what Jesus did. John concludes in verse 36 that, just as humans ignore the law of gravity to their own hurt, so is rejection of Jesus a foolish choice.

LIFE STEP Jesus made the Father real to the people of His day. Jesus is not here today but the Holy Spirit does the same for us. As we study Scripture, the Holy Spirit convinces us of the reality of both God the Father and God the Son.

SATURDAY 19

JOHN 4:1-15

WHAT IS THE WRITER SAYING?

HOW CAN I APPLY THIS TO MY LIFE?

PRAY Peru – For a softening of hearts among the 700,000 unusually resistant, university students.

The sixth encounter is with the Woman at the Well, a Samaritan with emotional needs. She will prove to be everything that Nicodemus was not! The rulers, in this case the conservative Pharisees, were concerned about Jesus' growing success and, unlike John the Baptist, were not happy. Unwilling to escalate the confrontation at this time, Jesus leaves the area of their concentration (Judea) and heads for safer, neutral ground in Galilee. Galilee was safer because ever since 930 B.C. the area was inhabited by non-religious Jews and then even Gentiles, starting in 722 B.C. Around 165 B.C. concerted effort was made by the religious authorities in Jerusalem to colonize the north (perhaps the reason for Jesus' family living in Nazareth) but it was still the *frontier* in Jesus' day. "Must" (4:4) is a moral necessity, not physical, as they could have done what religious Jews did when traveling north. They could have bypassed the area by crossing the Jordan River and traveling up the east bank. The sixth hour was high noon, normally too hot for the work of carrying water, but this woman avoided the other women of the city out of shame for her lifestyle. She has a smart mouth (v. 9), is argumentative (v. 12) and no doubt loud. She was accurate about the depth of Jacob's Well. Archaeologists have uncovered it and it is 138 feet to the water table! Jesus does the unexpected and asks the woman for a drink. Note that John finds it necessary to explain that socially Jews would normally not stoop to speak to a Samaritan, much less a woman. Jesus crosses both boundaries to reach this woman. Jesus uses a known item, *water*, to introduce this woman to the unknown, spiritual life.

 LIFE STEP To catch fish, you have to go where the fish are! Christ takes the road less traveled and is busy doing His Father's business. Jesus used things people knew and understood to unfold spiritual truth.

JOHN 4:16-30

WHAT IS THE WRITER SAYING?

HOW CAN I APPLY THIS TO MY LIFE?

Up until this point, the Samaritan woman has been proud and argumentative. Jesus responds to her graciously, obviously impressing her, since Jewish people of the day disdained the Samaritans as *half-breeds* and theological competitors. Racially, they were the product of the Assyrian foreign policy of population transfer to quell rebellion. The Israelites were moved out and Gentiles brought in. Verse 18 indicates that marriage is more than sexual relations. It requires both a marriage covenant and sexual relations. Christ's request to return with her husband would cause her to walk a mile in the noonday sun. Embarrassed and confused, the woman resorts to the tactic of changing the subject and launches into a *theological discussion*. She tries to bog the conversation down by introducing a point of contention between Jews and Samaritans – where they should worship. Worship comes from *worthship*, recognizing and appreciating the worth of God. The central issue was not where one was when worshipping God, but rather the heart with which they approached God. God desires a pure and true heart from those who would worship Him (Psalm 24:4). Jesus intercepts her and brings her back to the central issue, a vital heart relationship with the Creator. The disciples return, oblivious to the ministry that has been taking place, and are amazed that Jesus has crossed this cultural line. The Samaritan woman leaves her valuable water pot and rushes to the city to tell her fellow-citizens. She shrewdly words her question to make them want to come and see for themselves, in effect saying, *This couldn't be the Messiah, could it?*

LIFE STEP Jesus was more concerned for the spiritual needs of this woman than what people would think about Him talking to her. Is your stand for Christ muted by what you fear people will think of you?

JOHN 4:31-42

WHAT IS THE WRITER SAYING?

HOW CAN I APPLY THIS TO MY LIFE?

PRAY South Africa – For believers within the government to apply biblical principles in solving problems.

Upon returning, the disciples try to get Jesus to eat. He refers to the spiritual food He was already enjoying and confuses them in the shift from the physical to the spiritual realm. As the Samaritans were making their way down the road from the village to the well, Christ explained to His disciples that the harvest was not four months away, but that the fields were *white* unto harvest. We know that in Christ's day the Samaritans all wore white robes. Heads of grain would look white, but Jesus is probably referring to the white robes of the Samaritans coming toward Him! At a time like this, food should be the last thing on their minds. During the harvest, the reapers often are focused on the task of getting in the harvest to the neglect of meals. This is the case here. This is no time for eating; it is time to bring in the crop.

Jesus also shares an important ministry principle. Not everyone gets to do the harvesting. Some plant, some water, some cultivate, while others bring in the harvest. In the case of the disciples, they now had an opportunity to reap that which others had sown.

The final verses of this event (vv. 39-42) show us that the Samaritans first believed because of the woman's testimony. However, to the people of this culture, the testimony of a *woman* was inadequate. They would have to hear and see for themselves! Jesus did not share this condescending attitude toward women, as was evident from His dealings with her.

LIFE STEP Are you willing to set aside your comfort to minister for Christ? Whose needs are more important, yours or others? What part are you playing in God's harvest?

TUESDAY 20

JOHN 4:43-54

WHAT IS THE WRITER SAYING?

HOW CAN I APPLY THIS TO MY LIFE?

PRAY Equatorial Guinea – Pray that the 85% who claim Christianity – without having been born again – might hear and respond to the Gospel.

Jesus received opposition from the religious authorities in Judea. Now He predicts that He will also receive opposition in His home area (v. 44). Actually, this is based on a previous negative encounter mentioned in Luke 4 when His own fellow villagers tried to kill Him. Verse 45 seems to contradict this, but remember, back in Jerusalem Jesus already concluded that this excitement was untrustworthy (2:24).

Verse 46 introduces us to a nobleman with a great physical need. His son was sick and dying. Cana was about twenty miles from the man's home in Capernaum. Distance was no obstacle to Jesus' healing power. Jesus' first response to the nobleman seems rather harsh but is probably intended for the broader audience standing around. The Jews were always seeking a sign, especially ones that would directly benefit them, and were not interested in Christ's spiritual teachings. The nobleman was probably a Jew and possibly an important politician. The nobleman did not appeal to his position, nor did he defend himself in light of Jesus' charge, but rather in earnest faith again appealed to Him to save his dying son. The man asked Jesus to come to Capernaum, but Jesus sent him away with the simple statement, "Your son lives." The nobleman did not question, but returned the twenty miles home. When he learned of the hour of his son's healing, the nobleman believed, and in turn led his family to belief in Jesus.

 LIFE STEP Are you willing to take God at His word? How often have we seen God deliver only to then question it or explain it away? The miracles of Jesus demonstrated who He was, so that men might believe, not to draw attention or attract a crowd.

JOHN 5:1-9

WHAT IS THE WRITER SAYING?

HOW CAN I APPLY THIS TO MY LIFE?

In John 2:13 there is mention of the Passover. Now here in 5:1 another "feast of the Jews" is mentioned in which "Jesus went up to Jerusalem." After Passover there are two feasts in what we now call the *Week of Passover – Unleavened Bread*, which starts the day after the first Passover Meal, and *Firstfruits*, which occurs two days after the first Passover Meal. The next holiday, which is also the next *pilgrim holiday* (requiring all able-bodied Jews to go to Jerusalem to observe it), is Pentecost. This holiday comes fifty days after Passover and would be a good candidate for this unnamed holiday. It occurs in late May in our calendar. Pentecost is a celebration of the wheat harvest and also the giving of the Law of Moses on Mt. Sinai. Therefore Jewish people are celebrating the giving of physical food and spiritual food on this holiday. The sheep gate (v. 2) is near the Temple on the northern wall of the city. The pool mentioned was beautified by the five porches and was an attractive place to visit. "Bethesda" means *House of Lovingkindness*. The Jewish culture, as with most cultures, had various superstitions. One associated with this pool is mentioned here. This does not mean that John believed that the superstition was factual. How sad that many people cling to false hope built upon the traditions of men rather than the Word of God! In this case, Jesus takes the first step. The man doesn't even know who He is. Jesus heals him with no required action or response on his part. In this miracle, Jesus shows His power over time – the man had been lame for thirty-eight years!

LIFE STEP In the world many cling to false hope and false religion based upon myth and superstitions. We who know the truth are to be a light in the darkness for those who are lost.

JOHN 5:10-18

WHAT IS THE WRITER SAYING?

HOW CAN I APPLY THIS TO MY LIFE?

PRAY
Pray for some of the missionaries that your church supports.

The first four chapters of John demonstrate various people *considering* the deity of Jesus. In chapters 5-7 we enter the *Period of Controversy*.

The healing of the lame man occurred on the Sabbath. Jesus told the man to "take up thy bed" (v. 8) and he obeyed (vv. 9-10). "The Jews" (v. 10) is a reference to *the Jewish authorities* (since all the people in Jerusalem at that time would have been "Jews"). The observation that "it is not lawful for thee to carry thy bed" on the Sabbath is not accurate. Jesus would not have commanded a human to sin. This supposed *sin* was a violation of man-made rules, not what God originally said in the Law of Moses. In fact, eventually we will see that even Jesus using His powers to heal was considered to be a violation of the Sabbath in their eyes. In verse 14 Jesus speaks to the man again, ensuring that he would now know Jesus' identity. Jesus implies that in some cases, people do have physical problems as a direct result of their behavior. I wonder why the man felt it necessary to tell the authorities that Jesus healed him. Was he promoting Jesus' ministry or protecting himself? It is hard to imagine that Jesus' actions would incite the authorities to seek His death. Verse 18 explains another complaint. By calling God "My Father" (v. 17) (Greek *idion* as in idiosyncrasy) they felt (rightly!) that He was claiming deity. When dealing with people who claim that Jesus did not claim to be equal to God we should point out that in such cases as this, Jesus does not correct the conclusions of his accusers. Notice that Jesus will say, *My Father* or *Your Father*, but not *Our Father* in His discussions with the Pharisees!

LIFE STEP
Many today live their Christian lives under a cloud of do's and don'ts. The Pharisees missed Jesus because He did not fit their self-righteous mold. God wants us to follow Him from the heart not by a system of man-made religious regulation. The key is a relationship, not regulation.

JOHN 5:19-29

WHAT IS THE WRITER SAYING?

HOW CAN I APPLY THIS TO MY LIFE?

PRAY Argentina – Funding for students with a desire to study God's word at camps and Bible schools.

In today's passage, Christ builds on His claims to a special relationship with God, which the Pharisees correctly interpret as claims of equality with God. In verse 19, Jesus indicates that His works are led and empowered by His Father. Therefore, the authorities are not arguing with Him but with God. In verse 20, Jesus predicts that the Father will show even greater sign miracles in the future. Most of the Jewish authorities believed the Old Testament stories of resurrections (such as performed by Elijah and Elisha). Jesus says that the Father would perform resurrections through Him as well. His recent "resurrection" of the dead legs of the paralytic was a small picture of greater things to come. On the negative side, those who refuse the life-giving ministry of Jesus will face Him as judge. The authorities should have been aware of verses like Isaiah 48:11 "For mine own sake, even for mine own sake, will I do it: for how should my name be polluted? and I will not give my glory unto another."

Therefore, for Jesus to state that the Father will glorify Him was another claim of equality with the Father. Verse 24 nicely summarizes Jesus' theology at this point. The person who believes in the Father and the Son as deity and accepts their plan of salvation will avoid judgment and experience resurrection. In Scripture, when a numerical adjective is used with "day" or "hour" (such as "one day" or "one hour") we understand this to be a specific time designation. The unqualified "hour" of verse 25 is not *60 minutes* but rather a period in human history. There is coming a day when saved people will be resurrected (at the Rapture and also the Second Coming) and evil people will be resurrected (at the end of time).

 LIFE STEP The self-righteous man will move with greater vehemence against a righteous man than an immoral or irreligious man will. Brace yourself to patiently share the gospel with them as well.

SATURDAY 20

JOHN 5:30-47

WHAT IS THE WRITER SAYING?

HOW CAN I APPLY THIS TO MY LIFE?

PRAY For safety, salvation decisions, and consecration commitments during Christian winter camps.

In the on-going debate over Christ's claims, the Pharisees argue that a man cannot be his own character witness. Jesus agrees that if He alone bore witness of Himself, His witness would not be true (v. 31). By "true" He is referring to what is admissible as a legal defense, not just factually true. So, to satisfy their legal claims, Christ now brings five testifiers to the witness stand:
1) 5:30-31 – Himself.
2) 5:32-35 – John the Baptist.
3) 5:36 – His works.
4) 5:37-38 – His Father (three times: at His baptism, His transfiguration, and after His triumphal entry).
5) 5:39-48 – Scripture.

The religious leaders of the day thought themselves to be experts in the Scripture. They equated their strict observance of the Law of Moses with their salvation. Jesus plays on this respect for Moses by saying that Moses wrote of Him (v. 46). Genesis 3:15 is one such place. It points to the cross work of Jesus Christ where He dealt Satan the defeating blow that sealed his doom. In Deuteronomy 18:15 Moses says that God will send another prophet to replace him. Jewish and Christian commentators understand this to refer to the Messiah. Even in the face of overwhelming evidence, the unbelieving heart often is not softened, but grows even harder, like clay in the hot sun and not butter. Their confidence did not come from God's Word, but rather was self-generated as they compared themselves to one another.

LIFE STEP Self-justification is a terrible trait of humans. The writings of Moses should have brought the Jews to a place where they were humbly seeking a Savior. Yet they twisted his words and missed his highest thoughts. What might we be missing because of our focus on self?

SUNDAY 21

JOHN 6:1-14

WHAT IS THE WRITER SAYING?

HOW CAN I APPLY THIS TO MY LIFE?

PRAY Italy – For people to turn from the occult to Christ and for the city of Turin, a global center for Satanism, to be invaded by the power of the Gospel.

Chapter 6 jumps ahead in the story in space and time. Jesus has left Jerusalem and is back in the region of Galilee. Another Passover is approaching, meaning that we are at least ten months after chapter 5. In verse one John provides the Roman name for the Sea of Galilee, which honors one of the Caesars. The lake also goes by the Hebrew word *Chinnereth* meaning *harp* (referring to its shape) and *Gennesaret* meaning *Garden of Riches*. The feeding of the multitude was the fourth sign done by Jesus. Each sign was a demonstration of who He was, God the Son. John chose each one carefully to underscore an aspect of saving faith. John gives a tremendous picture of God's abundant supply for man's greatest need. Here bread was broken to meet man's physical need. In only a few verses Jesus will show that He is the true bread come down from heaven and that His sacrifice is more than sufficient to meet the needs of all humanity (John 6:35 and 1 John 2:2). In this Gospel we learn of some interesting details the other Gospels do not give: the nearness of the Passover feast, the testing of Philip (v. 5), and the type of bread used (barley was a coarse, cheap bread). When confronted with the need for food to feed the fainting masses, Philip (the accountant) calculates that it would take 66% of a man's annual salary to feed the crowd. He would know the local economy because this was his home area. Andrew (the visionary) finds a boy's lunch – and talks him out of it! This is the only miracle recorded in all four Gospels.

LIFE STEP Just as Jesus was not limited by physical circumstances, in the same way His sacrifice is sufficient to meet every spiritual hunger of mankind. Because He is God, His sacrifice is infinite and His gift of salvation is secure. Have you accepted the Bread of Life?

MONDAY 21

JOHN 6:15-21

WHAT IS THE WRITER SAYING?

HOW CAN I APPLY THIS TO MY LIFE?

PRAY Korea – For the unblocking of Christian radio broadcasts that reach into North Korea with the gospel.

The response offered by those who had been miraculously fed was not what Jesus intended, He wanted them to see Him as their Messiah, but they wanted to make Him their king. The miracles were proof of His deity, yet the people were only thinking of the physical. Several times in the various Gospel accounts Jesus tells someone <u>not</u> to advertise His miracles. This is because Jesus did not want people to follow Him just for the miracles. Unfortunately, many in His day saw His miraculous powers as a tool they could use to overthrow Rome and have an independent, prosperous Jewish kingdom. This seems to have been Judas' problem. It is true that he is called a "thief" (John 12:6), but his financial and political plans seem to have included Christ's popularity and powers. When Christ failed to use His powers to defend Himself in the Garden of Gethsemane, Judas realized that his plans had failed, he would not become a prince in the Jewish Kingdom and he, in fact, had sent Jesus to His death.

As He often did, Jesus came apart from the crowd to be alone on the mountain. The place was on the western bank of the Sea of Galilee near the city of Bethsaida (Luke 9:10). Jesus had sent the disciples on ahead and had possibly agreed to meet them near Bethsaida (Mark 6:45) on their way to Capernaum. He had remained to see the crowd off and then had gone up into the mountain to pray (Mark 6:46). The disciples had not expected to see Jesus coming to them walking on the sea. This fifth sign demonstrated His power over creation and the ability to transcend the physical limitations that hinder mankind. "With God all things are possible" (Mark 10:27).

LIFE STEP Many today seek after the miraculous and the spectacular. God's desire for man has not changed. It's that we might look to the Son and seeing with the eyes of faith, believe. What is your motivation in following God?

JOHN 6:22-34

WHAT IS THE WRITER SAYING?

HOW CAN I APPLY THIS TO MY LIFE?

PRAY Botswana – Pray for revival among believers in this predominately Christian and well governed country in southern Africa.

Today's passage shows a frantic crowd trying to locate Jesus by a process of elimination. The material evidence would bolster the fact that no ship carried Jesus away. If they could have thought outside of the box they would have figured out that He had walked away – on water! When they finally find Him, they ask "when" did you get here? (not how?) Jesus does not answer either question. Instead, He confronts them, exposing their motive for seeking Him – another free meal. Jesus instructs them to labor for *the meat that remains* (Consider the parallel concept of water that satisfies in John 4:14). The food is Christ Himself in a spiritual sense. Jesus' invitation to drink of the water of life and eat of the bread of life is similar to Isaiah 55:1-2, "Ho, every one that thirsteth, come ye to the waters, and he that hath no money; come ye, buy, and eat; yea, come, buy wine and milk without money and without price. Wherefore do ye spend money for that which is not bread? and your labour for that which satisfieth not? hearken diligently unto me, and eat ye that which is good, and let your soul delight itself in fatness."

Sealed in verse 27 is similar to our idea of something that is *certified*. The Father placed His certification upon the ministry of His Son.

The implication of verse 31 is *Feed two and a half million people for forty years like Moses did and then we'll consider your claims!* Jesus quickly corrects them stating that it was God, not Moses, who supplied the bread in the wilderness, and now the true bread from heaven was come down to them.

 LIFE STEP "Whose god is their belly (Philippians 3:19)." It is not a pretty picture when human existence is reduced to *gimme, gimme.* Let us not overlook true spiritual food in our lust for physical things.

JOHN 6:35-40

WHAT IS THE WRITER SAYING?

HOW CAN I APPLY THIS TO MY LIFE?

John 6:35 is the first of the seven great "I Am" statements in John. Most have a predicate nominative (in this case, "bread") to complete the sentence in the context, but all reflect the "I Am" of Exodus 3. This Hebrew verb form became the highest name for God among the Jews. It was the covenantal name for God we pronounce as Yahweh or Jehovah. ("Yahweh" attempts the Hebrew pronunciation and "Jehovah" comes into English by way of the European languages which alter the pronunciation of the Hebrew "Y" and "W" to "J" and "V"). We call this a "covenantal name" because it specifically was the name by which God wished to make Himself known to His Chosen People as their protector. Based on the Hebrew verb *to be*, it conveys both His eternality (past, present and future or the eternal present) and His self-sufficiency (I exist by my own power). So sacred is this name that Jewish people stopped pronouncing it in antiquity. We therefore do not really know how it was to be pronounced. In fact, in modern Hebrew they don't even use the present tense form of the verb *to be* because it sounds too much like "Yahweh." Whenever the word "Yahweh" appears in the text, a Jewish reader will say "adonai" instead. "Adonai" is a lesser name for God that is also the Hebrew word for *Mr.*, *Master*, and *Sir*. Perhaps you have seen Jewish friends who also show respect to God's name in English by writing *G-d* or *L-rd*.

In addition to drawing a connection with Jehovah's name, Jesus says that Jehovah sent Him to implement the power of His name in the saving of souls and resurrection to eternal life!

LIFE STEP The command in Exodus 20:7 "Thou shalt not take the name of the LORD thy God in vain" actually means *do not treat the name of God as common*. Therefore we should also be concerned with the misuse of God's name in our everyday speech.

THURSDAY 21

JOHN 6:41-51

WHAT IS THE WRITER SAYING?

HOW CAN I APPLY THIS TO MY LIFE?

PRAY Honduras – For God to provide the teaching staff and funding needed to keep Bible schools operating.

Jesus continues His extended conversation with the people of Galilee. They want Him to throw off the yoke of Rome and meet their physical needs. However, they are not interested in the spiritual aspects of His program. What do you think the *murmurers* thought when Jesus publicly revealed what they were thinking and saying? You would think that they would immediately repent at a display of such divine power.

Verse 42 is in the present tense, which might hint that Joseph is still alive at this point. Strangely he does not appear in Christ's public ministry and seems to have died before Christ's crucifixion (Mary is alone at the cross). Verse 44 explains the nature of the hardness and blindness of the unsaved human heart. Apart from the working of God to counteract the blindness, no one would come to Christ. Jesus states that the bread, which He was offering, was different from the manna, which their fathers had eaten in the wilderness (v. 49). Those who ate that bread were dead. He was offering Himself as the true Bread of Life, which brings eternal life. Elsewhere, Christ told His disciples that He spoke in parables to discourage the unbelievers (Matthew 13:13). In this passage, He uses a similar tactic, making His teaching sufficiently difficult to weed out the marginal disciples. They don't follow the analogy of eating His body (applying His sacrificial death to their own life) for (spiritual) nourishment. In light of the emphasis on salvation by believing and the many analogies that Christ uses in John, it should be clear that He is not referring to taking Communion as the basis of salvation or actually *eating* the body and blood of Christ. The entire passage speaks of a spiritual consuming and internalization of Him, the Word of God, by believing in Him.

LIFE STEP Those who have eaten the Bread of Heaven will never hunger again. It is only through the broken fellowship of unconfessed sin that the pangs of spiritual hunger return. Is your soul satisfied today?

FRIDAY 21

JOHN 6:52-59

WHAT IS THE WRITER SAYING?

HOW CAN I APPLY THIS TO MY LIFE?

Verse 59 indicates that this discussion did not take place in one session. It appears that it is a summary of His teachings over a period of time.

We can understand why they were confused and why some denominations have also confused Jesus' teaching. The literal words say in effect, *Eat my body and eat my blood for salvation*. To ancient ears, this would be repulsive as cannibalism. After centuries of such teaching, Christians don't think of cannibalism, but many denominations conclude that the communion bread and wine actually become the body and blood of Jesus based on this passage. What we have to ask is, "Did everyone who heard Jesus that day draw the same conclusion?" It is clear from Church History that the answer is "No." For starters, none of the Apostles in the Church Epistles repeat this kind of description of how communion (or salvation) works. Since cannibalism is condemned in the Law of Moses and Jesus taught that He came to fulfill, not destroy the Law of Moses, the careful listeners would have concluded that He was speaking metaphorically. One example of this is in 1 Chronicles 11:19. Three of David's brave warriors broke through the enemy lines to get David some water from a well in his hometown. David concludes that he could not drink this water because "... shall I drink the blood of these men that have put their lives in jeopardy?" Similarly, Ezekiel (3:1) and John (Revelation 10:9) were told to "eat" scrolls of written material. Everyone understands this to mean *read and internalize*. Likewise eating the body and blood of Christ is a spiritual concept not a literal activity. By accepting Jesus as savior we "eat" the salvation that He offers to satisfy our spiritual "hunger."

LIFE STEP Proper interpretation of Scripture is so important. Always check your ideas with other believers to make sure that you are not misunderstanding and going off in the wrong direction with an idea.

JOHN 6:60-71

WHAT IS THE WRITER SAYING?

6:1-14 feeding the multitude
27 labor for meat which endures
32 + 33 true bread from heaven
35 "I am the bread of life"
51 living bread from heaven giving His bread / His flesh

HOW CAN I APPLY THIS TO MY LIFE? that He gives for the world
53-56 eat the bread + drink his blood to have life
63 the spirit quickeneth

spiritual eating, not physical

In Matthew 13 Jesus says that He teaches using parables for two reasons: (1) so believers could understand abstract spiritual truths through the concrete illustrations in parables and, (2) so unbelievers would be confused and not understand what He was saying. In this passage He uses a similar tactic, making His teaching sufficiently difficult to weed out the marginal disciples. They don't follow the analogy of eating His body (absorbing His teachings) for (spiritual) nourishment. Verse 62 implies that if they struggle with the eating concept they will also be offended at His death, burial, resurrection and ascension. Verse 63 makes it clear that He is speaking of spiritual eating, not physical. As they puzzle over the offensive cannibalistic thought some "disciples" begin to doubt Him. The word "disciple" means

follower. It implies that the one following appreciates, believes in and will obey the one he follows. However, verse 66 makes it clear that even *discipleship* does not guarantee that a person is a *true* believer. That they turn back from their discipleship does not mean that they lost their salvation but that they never possessed it to begin with. As some drift away, Jesus challenges the twelve original disciples. Spokesman Peter eloquently professes their trust in Him. He uses a perfect tense of the verb (a present condition based on a previous act) saying: *We have been and are currently believing that You are the Holy One of God* (v. 69). It is interesting that elsewhere a demon makes the same identification (Mark 1:24) because Jesus responds by saying in effect, Y*es, but one of you has sold out to Satan.*

 LIFE STEP To whom indeed shall we go? Everything else in life pales in significance. If my wealth is lost, nothing is lost. If my health is lost, much is lost. If my soul is lost, all is lost. How much do we leave when we die? All of it!

SUNDAY 22

JOHN 7:1-13

WHAT IS THE WRITER SAYING?

HOW CAN I APPLY THIS TO MY LIFE?

PRAY Pakistan – Pray for the calling of more intercessors, advocates and missionaries for these people in the very heart of the unevangelized world.

John starts today's account by explaining that Jesus could not safely travel openly in Judah. Judah was the stronghold of the Jewish authorities. They had less influence in Galilee due to the diluting presence of Gentiles in the area (the Roman authorities being sympathetic to the desires of the local Gentiles). Unfortunately, having Jesus in their home area did not please his brothers. They did not believe His claims and therefore He was an embarrassment to them. Try to imagine the dynamic of growing up in a large household where the oldest child never does anything wrong! His brothers chide Him for not dramatically traveling to Jerusalem and facing down His critics. He logically points out that every significant human event must be timed properly. *Armchair quarterbacks* always know the right move (v. 6) but Jesus was waiting for the right moment. The next holiday mentioned in John is the Passover on which He was crucified, so we are now six months from His death in this passage.

The Feast of Tabernacles was a pilgrim holiday in which most Jews traveled to Jerusalem for the celebration. It was the fall *harvest home* festival, much like our Thanksgiving. They thanked the Lord for the good harvest past and prayed for the fall rains to start the agricultural cycle over again. They made tabernacles (booths) to take their family meals in as a reminder of God's protection for the forty years in the wilderness (see Leviticus 23:42). The celebration lasted for eight days, which gave visitors from the outlying regions a long time to socialize. Jesus quietly enters Jerusalem after the celebration had begun (v. 10). The climate in Jerusalem is volatile (vv.11-13). The authorities were looking for Him; men were discussing Him and taking sides. Notice again that since all of the people were Jewish, "the Jews" in verse 13 refers to the authorities.

 LIFE STEP Christ divides. He divides family members. He divides neighbors. He divides friends. What side of the divide will we stand on?

190

MONDAY 22

JOHN 7:14-24

WHAT IS THE WRITER SAYING?

HOW CAN I APPLY THIS TO MY LIFE?

PRAY Nigeria – For the Lord's guidance and direction in the training and follow-up of new converts that are won to Christ through evangelism.

Jerusalem was a city of about fifty thousand people in Christ's day, but for the festivals it would swell to 250,000 people. It would have been chaotic. Jesus waits until the mid-point of the week, the time of highest attendance, to stir the pot. He went to the center of attention, the Temple, to teach. I wonder what his brothers thought and said! The Jewish authorities were amazed at His words. They could not understand how one with no formal training could teach with such eloquence, logic and power. Christ explained that His wisdom was from above, given to Him by His Father. God requires man to believe, to take God at His word by faith. Verse 17 is such an appeal, *Take me at my word and see the truth of what I am teaching.* Too often men look to one another instead of looking to God for truth. Jesus reveals the murderous intents of His enemies (v. 19) that only a few would recognize as accurate. It must have been unnerving for them to hear that Christ knew their hearts.

The *one work* (v. 21) is a reference to the healing of the lame man at the pool of Bethesda near the Temple (John 5:1-15). Earlier the Jewish authorities had condemned Him for violating their Sabbath laws. Jesus picks up on their discontent and reveals the hypocrisy of it. If the Law of Moses allowed circumcision on the Sabbath, why couldn't they allow healing on the Sabbath? Judging by appearance (v. 24) was looking only at the letter of the Law and not the Spirit behind it. The Jewish authorities had reduced their worship of God to a legal code that must be followed rigidly. God was looking for heart obedience based in a relationship with Him.

LIFE STEP What is the basis of your faith – ritual or relationship? Those who heard the Son of God speak were often too stuck in their ritualistic mindset to hear what He was really saying.

TUESDAY 22

JOHN 7:25-29

WHAT IS THE WRITER SAYING?

HOW CAN I APPLY THIS TO MY LIFE?

PRAY Cuba – For the persecuted Christians to be encouraged and continue their service for the Lord.

Many of those who had made the pilgrimage to Jerusalem were not familiar with Jesus, but were able to connect Him with the whispering (v. 25). Others concluded that because the authorities did not immediately stop Jesus, they must be pondering His identity and perhaps concluding that He indeed was the long-awaited Messiah (v. 26). In rebuttal, others argued that Jesus could not be their Messiah *because* they knew where He came from (v. 27). This statement was based on a current Jewish misconception that the Messiah would burst on the scene seemingly out of nowhere. This is contradicted by Genesis 49:10 which teaches that the Messiah would come from the Tribe of Judah, by 2 Samuel 7:12 which says He would come from the line of David and Micah 5:2 which says He would be born in Bethlehem. Years earlier the religious rulers told Herod that as well (Matthew 2:5).

For the second time in chapter 7 Jesus announces publicly what people are discussing privately. He explains that while they may know Him and where He came from, they do not know the Father who had sent Him. Throughout the Gospel of John Jesus repeats certain concepts. "Belief" is a major emphasis. "Resurrection," "life," "eating to sustain life," "drinking to sustain life" and "eternal life" are repeated themes. Another is the emphasis on "knowing God the Father." All Jews in that day, regardless of their particular party, would say, "We want to know God the Father." Some might even say, "We know God the Father." Jesus tells them all, "You can only know God the Father by knowing Me. If you do not know Me you will never know God the Father." Jesus' mission was to make God the Father *real* to mankind.

There is a great difference between hearing God's Word and doing something about it. Are we responding to the teachings of Jesus?

WEDNESDAY 22

JOHN 7:30-39

WHAT IS THE WRITER SAYING?

HOW CAN I APPLY THIS TO MY LIFE?

PRAY Taiwan – For God to break this people's bondage to materialism and its devotion to Buddhism.

Many who heard His words at the Feast of Tabernacles were convinced that He was their Messiah and believed (v. 31). The Jewish leaders only increased in the hardness of their hearts and their rejection (v. 30). Finally the Jewish authorities decided they had to act. The "chief priests" (v. 32) were from the party of the Sadducees. They controlled the Temple. The Pharisees were the pastors of the people and controlled the synagogue system. They normally did not get along, but now they joined hands against Jesus. Jesus predicts His imminent death and departure to heaven (at the next Passover six months ahead). His words went right over their heads (v. 36). Interestingly, they did wonder if He intended to take His gospel to the Gentiles (v. 35)! During the Feast of Tabernacles, every day the High Priest would lead a procession from the Pool of Siloam with water in a gold pitcher to pour out at the temple. They were thanking God for the rains that gave the good harvest and they were praying for the rains to come again for the next harvest. During the procession they would quote Isaiah 12:1-4, "And in that day thou shalt say, O LORD, I will praise thee: though thou wast angry with me, thine anger is turned away, and thou comfortedst me. Behold, God *is* my salvation; I will trust, and not be afraid: for the LORD JEHOVAH *is* my strength and *my* song; he also is become my salvation. Therefore with joy shall ye draw water out of the wells of salvation. And in that day shall ye say, Praise the LORD, call upon his name, declare his doings among the people, make mention that his name is exalted." With this as a backdrop, Jesus stands on the eighth day and calls out to the spiritually thirsty crowds (v. 37). Jesus proclaimed that He was the source of true satisfaction and that those who find this satisfaction would become a source of refreshment to all (v. 38).

LIFE STEP John says that the "water" is the "Holy Spirit" (v. 39). Will we allow the Holy Spirit to refresh and empower us today?

THURSDAY 22

JOHN 7:40-53

WHAT IS THE WRITER SAYING?

HOW CAN I APPLY THIS TO MY LIFE?

PRAY Romania – For trained leadership in a land where the average pastor oversees five churches.

The opening verses of this section show the range of opinions about Jesus that swirled around the Jerusalem streets. Some said He was *the Prophet* (see Deuteronomy 18:15-18), while others (v.42) said He was *the Christ* (Messiah), and yet others were sure that He could not be the Messiah, because Jesus came from Galilee and the Messiah was to come from Bethlehem. Their statements show both their lack of knowledge concerning Jesus and their impulsiveness, for in verse 44 they are ready to seize Him. Their inability to lay hold on Him shows that everything was moving forward on God's timetable, not man's. If "never man spoke like this man" then apparently the officers were afraid that He was divine (v. 46)!

In typical Pharisaic fashion, they upbraided the officers for being deceived by Jesus' words. Their *logic* in verse 48 is an invalid ad hominem argument. Instead of dealing with the issues they deal with personalities. Their statement says little about their knowledge, but much about the hardness of their hearts. "This people" (v. 49) is also insulting. It is a put-down of the common man. The claim that none of the Pharisees were believing in Jesus (v. 48) begins to lose its weight as Nicodemus speaks. The first time John introduced Nicodemus was in chapter 3. There, he came in the darkness to interview Jesus having seen the miracles He did. Now, he defends Jesus' right to a fair hearing. The response of the Pharisees (v. 52) "Art thou also of Galilee?" was an insult and an erroneous one at that, seeing that the prophet Jonah was from Galilee (see 2 Kings 14:25) as was Nahum (Capernaum means "Village of Nahum"). Verse 53 ends the story with a draw.

 LIFE STEP Our words always reveal the attitudes of our hearts. James said it best when he asked if the same fountain could bring forth both fresh and bitter water. What are your words telling about the condition of your heart?

JOHN 8:1-11

WHAT IS THE WRITER SAYING?

HOW CAN I APPLY THIS TO MY LIFE?

PRAY Bulgaria – Pray for the swift and accurate completion of the new translation of the Bulgarian Bible.

The episode in chapter 8 is designed to entrap Jesus and discredit him. The scene begins on the Mount of Olives where He is already ministering to a constant stream of people (v. 2: "came" actually means "were coming," indicating *constantly*). The Pharisees show up with a woman taken in the very act of adultery. (Where was the man?) The tense of the verb *say* (v. 4) indicates that they were *repeatedly saying.* Their statement about the Mosaic Law was accurate although God in His grace did not always insist on capital punishment, such as in the case of King David. They were hoping to either accuse Him of contradicting Moses or of contradicting Roman law, which did not allow the Jews to inflict capital punishment. It seems that Jesus was embarrassed by the crassness of their treatment of the woman (v. 6). He brilliantly avoids the trap by putting it back on them to fulfill the Law, if they are worthy. John uses an unusual word for "wrote" in verse 8, which means "to write down a record" as in an official court document. Perhaps Jesus recorded their secret sins as they then began to disappear. Christ succeeded in turning another challenge back on His interrogators when questioned about the tribute money [("Render therefore unto Caesar the things which are Caesar's; and unto God the things that are God's." (Matthew 22:21).] In neither case did He really answer their question, but rather He exposed their ulterior motives for asking the question. Out of gratitude for His gracious treatment, the woman awaited His direction. It is established that not one of the men stayed to pursue the matter. Jesus does not condone the woman's sin, but releases her with the admonition to cease her life of immorality.

LIFE STEP We are to hate the sin, but love the sinner. Jesus associated with the dregs of society. They were the ones who needed the *doctor.* He did not water down His demands, however. Sinners were forgiven, but expected to repent and forsake their sin.

SATURDAY 22

JOHN 8:12-20

WHAT IS THE WRITER SAYING?

HOW CAN I APPLY THIS TO MY LIFE?

PRAY Finland – For the hopelessness that pervades society to be replaced by the joy of salvation.

Jesus is still in Jerusalem at the Feast of Tabernacles. John again picks up the theme of light and darkness. This is the second of the seven great "I am" statements of Jesus that John records. The priests in the temple would light the Court of Women for dancing and singing, making large lamps and using worn out priestly linen garments as wicks. In the light of these festive hanging bonfires, Jesus made the analogy to His spiritual illumination. The Shekinah Glory had lighted the way of redemption for the children of Israel from Egyptian bondage and through the forty years of wilderness wanderings. That same light is now available for daily guidance in righteousness. Soon, at the Feast of Pentecost, it would descend from heaven and enter individual believers in the form of the indwelling Holy Spirit. Jesus' testimony was valid because He knew the answers to the big questions of life: Who Am I? Where did I come from? Where am I going? The Pharisees could not answer those questions. Christ's second witness of validity (satisfying the demands of the Law for two witnesses in a court of law) was the testimony of His own Father, who not only empowered Him for His miraculous works but also spoke from heaven on three different occasions stating His approval of His Son (at His baptism, the Transfiguration, and after the Triumphal Entry). John gives an explanatory note in verse 20 that these events took place by the treasury which was in the Court of the Women, the very place where the lamps were set up for the week of Tabernacles.

 LIFE STEP It is stunning to see the hardness of the human heart. The Pharisees were intelligent men. Though they argued vehemently with the Lord, they must have felt the power of His words. They never denied the reality of His miracles. Yet in the face of such obvious power, they persisted in their opposition.

JOHN 8:21-30

WHAT IS THE WRITER SAYING?

HOW CAN I APPLY THIS TO MY LIFE?

PRAY Pray for the elderly in your church and those who are shut-ins.

This is the second time that Jesus mentioned that He was going away and that where He was going they could not go (because they weren't righteous and wouldn't be welcomed into heaven). The first time they wondered if He was planning to leave the country to live among the Jews in the area outside of Palestine (John 7:35). Now they wonder if He is planning to commit suicide (John 8:22). In 8:24, Jesus literally says, "If ye believe not that **I Am** [no 'he'! The same in v. 28], ye shall die in your sins." This is an allusion to the name *Jehovah* from Exodus 3 (although they and many translators assumed He meant, *I am he*). Jesus is exasperated with their insolence, and rightly so, since He clearly claimed to be the Messiah sent from heaven with the signs to verify

the claim. *Lifted up* normally means *glorified*, but here, as in chapter 3, it refers to His crucifixion. Christ predicts His own death and specifies death by crucifixion so that when it happens, the people can remember His prediction and know that He was telling the truth.

Twice in this section Jesus tells these proud religious leaders that they will die in their sins. The first time (vv. 21, 22) they ignored His statement and focused on His own departure. The second time (vv. 24, 25) they ignored His statement and focused on His identity. He replies that "He" sent me (v. 26) and the religious authorities don't understand that He is referring to God the Father (v. 27). Amazingly, while the trained theologians get further confused, some of the common folk believe!

LIFE STEP The prophecies in the Old Testament about the coming of Messiah and the teachings of Jesus seem so clear to us living after the fact. How many teachings of our duties during the Church Age will seem equally clear *after* the return of Christ? We need to be diligent students of the Word so we are not embarrassed.

MONDAY 23

JOHN 8:31-38

WHAT IS THE WRITER SAYING?

HOW CAN I APPLY THIS TO MY LIFE?

PRAY Lithuania – Pray for the good unity between different Christian groups and denominations, unusual for a former Soviet state, to continue.

Salvation is solely by faith, not by works. However, works are a fruit, an indication that a person is saved. A human cannot please God or consistently follow God in his own power. But, if a person places faith in Christ, then the indwelling Holy Spirit (the "water" of 7:38) generates faithful behavior. Therefore true believers will automatically demonstrate their genuineness by their continuation in the faith. It is the unsaved pretenders who do not have the inner energy to persevere in their proclaimed faith. In cases where professing believers fall away, fortunately we do not decide their fate. God knows what is happening within. If they are children of His, He will bring them back through discipline or even take them home prematurely (Hebrews 12:7; 1 Corinthians 11:30). If not, they will continue to slide away from their initial interest in the things of God. In 8:31-32 Jesus hits the themes that John started the book with: the Logos of God and ultimate truth. Verse 32 mentions three highly prized commodities: Knowledge, Truth and Freedom. His Jewish audience bristled in their pride of being "Abraham's Seed." Their claim of never being enslaved is strange in light of four hundred years in Egypt and their then current domination by Rome ever since 63 B.C. (8:33)! The discussion gets heated as Jesus points out that their Father is really Satan, as demonstrated by their murderous intent (vs. 38, 44). In verse 37 Jesus says, "I know that ye are Abraham's seed; but ...." What He means is, *not all those who are "Abraham's seed" have the "faith of Abraham."* A person can be an unsaved, unrighteous descendent of Abraham.

LIFE STEP Our society honors education and *academic freedom*. The secular mind cherishes, "You shall know the truth and the truth shall set you free" until it discovers that the same individual who said that also said, "I am the way, the truth and the life, no man comes unto the Father but by me!"

TUESDAY 23

JOHN 8:39-47

WHAT IS THE WRITER SAYING?

HOW CAN I APPLY THIS TO MY LIFE?

PRAY Ukraine – For God to give youth a passion to live for Him and reach their land.

The Jewish authorities did not understand Jesus' argument in verse 37 that being "Abraham's seed" does not guarantee godliness. They apparently missed His implication in verse 38 that their father was Satan. When they attempt to claim Abraham as their father in verse 39, Jesus exhorts them to act like it! Their "father" Abraham would never act the way they were (v. 40). Verse 41 comes out of the blue and might be a jab at the rumors surrounding Christ's virgin conception and birth (see v. 48). In 6:66 we noted that even *discipleship* does not guarantee that a person is a true believer. We see this as some drift away from Christ. In today's passage, Jesus shows that true discipleship depends on having the right Father. Jesus refers to *your father* three times (vv. 38, 41, and 44). The Jewish authorities claimed to be the sons of Abraham in verse 39, but Jesus shows this to be false. They were of Abraham's physical seed. This is true. However, Abraham is not their spiritual father. The Jewish authorities also claimed to be sons of God in verse 41. Again, Jesus shows this to be false by showing that if you love the parent, you will not hate the son, which they were doing. Lastly, Jesus says they are sons of the devil (v. 44), the father of lies, for they were knowingly doing his works as seen in verses 38, 41, and 44.

Jesus substantiates His claim to be speaking the truth on the premise that no one could charge Him with sin. His enemies often debated whether Jesus was a sinner (John 9:24; 18:38; 19:4, 6). Christ answers His own question of why the Jewish authorities would not believe Him. They have rejected Him because of their relationship to the devil.

LIFE STEP There are many who claim to be disciples of Christ, but this does not mean that they are! The only way for a person to be a true disciple is to first have the right lineage. To whom do you trace your lineage? If it is to anyone but God the Father, then you are not a disciple of Christ.

WEDNESDAY 23

JOHN 8:48-59

WHAT IS THE WRITER SAYING?

HOW CAN I APPLY THIS TO MY LIFE?

PRAY Slovakia – For Slovakian and Hungarian believers to overcome cultural animosities and embrace unity in Christ.

To call Jesus a Samaritan was the equivalent of calling Him a religious fraud. The authorities begin hurling all kinds of abuse at Him, even to the point of saying He was demon possessed! So far they have slurred Him morally (v. 41), racially (v. 48a) and religiously (v. 48b). In verse 55, Jesus says that these *Sons of Abraham* had not come *to know* the heavenly Father (this word for *know* means *to come to know by experience*) while He *knew* the Father (a different word for *know* which means *to know inherently*). Jesus' words in verse 51 do not miss their target, as the Jewish authorities clearly understand the implication of *shall never see death*. They fume over the fact that these statements would clearly make Him superior to Abraham and the prophets! "Who do you think you are?" would be how we would

say it today (v. 53). We can almost feel the indignation coming from the crowd! Jesus understands their frame of mind, but makes it clear He is not attempting to glorify Himself, but simply carry out the will of His Father.

Your father Abraham (v. 56) is stated in the ancestral sense. What he *rejoiced to see* was the promise of future salvation through his descendant. How much Abraham understood is not known. The Jewish authorities again are stuck in the present because they do not recognize the deity and therefore, the eternality of Christ. That Jesus would have first-hand knowledge of Abraham is beyond their comprehension. The discussion comes to an explosive climax with Christ's clearest "I Am" (Jehovah) claim in verse 58! This time He clearly is saying just "I Am" (not, "I am he").

 LIFE STEP How do you respond when those who do not agree with you, challenge the basis of your claim to have a relationship to God? We can imagine in this event in Christ's life that His accusers were livid, while He remained calm and confident (see Philippians 1:28).

THURSDAY 23

JOHN 9:1-12

WHAT IS THE WRITER SAYING?

HOW CAN I APPLY THIS TO MY LIFE?

PRAY Eritrea – For Christians to be fervent for Jesus and make a significant impact on their nation and beyond.

John 9 is the fascinating story of the healing on the Sabbath of the man born blind (the second Sabbath healing in John that infuriated the religious establishment). This is the only recorded miracle of one defective from birth. A number of Christ's miracles involved the healing of the blind in fulfillment of Messianic passages such as Isaiah 35:5. In this type of healing the person goes from "darkness" into "light," as illustrated in John 8:12. "Darkness" speaks of danger, decay and death. "Light" speaks of safety, growth and life. The ultimate is the "light of life" (8:12)!

The event begins with a philosophical discussion among the disciples as to why the man was born blind. In verse 34, the Pharisees will voice one popular opinion. As far back as the book of Job, we find that those who suffered were considered to be under God's judgment for their sins. Christ, however, states that it was for this very moment that he had been born blind, that the Father might be glorified. Christ makes clay, anoints the man's eyes, and tells him to wash in the pool of Siloam (*sent*). The clay encouraged the man to display faith. For a person who could not see objects, the weight of the clay on his eyes made Jesus' touch memorable as he traveled to his destiny.

Throughout his Gospel, John has highlighted specific miracles (signs) to show that Jesus is God and to bring his readers to the point of believing in Him. Jesus had previously stated before the crowd in the temple that He is the *light of the world* (see John 8:12; 9:5). Now He illustrates this truth by bringing one born in both physical and spiritual darkness into the light.

LIFE STEP We are all born blind. God's Word peels back the blindness until we stand in the dazzling light of truth and respond in faith receiving spiritual sight and a new way of life!

JOHN 9:13-23

WHAT IS THE WRITER SAYING?

HOW CAN I APPLY THIS TO MY LIFE?

PRAY Philippines – For seminary graduates willing to work among the rural poor.

This portion of John's Gospel shows the tragedy of following man's traditions rather than walking with God. Clearly there were no sustained doubts from anyone present that a great miracle had occurred, but it was against the Pharisaic Code to knead clay on the Sabbath (it was considered *work*) and therefore, they labeled Jesus a sinner (v.16). Previously, when Jesus had healed the lame man at the Pool of Bethesda, the religious authorities had taken issue with the man because he had taken up his bed and walked, just as Jesus had told him (5:10). The authorities were so blind that they could look right past a great miracle and only see a technical violation of their tradition. Here in this passage the very same thing is again taking place.

The exchange between the Pharisees and the blind man is amazing! The blind man's opinion of the identity of Jesus goes from *the man* (v. 11) to *prophet* (v. 17) to *Lord, I believe* (v. 38)! The response of the man's parents is sad. How could they not be overjoyed at the healing of their son? Yet their fear of the Jewish authorities caused them to shrink back from a great opportunity to embrace Jesus as the Christ. This is a great illustration of the truth taught in Proverbs 29:25, "The fear of man bringeth a snare." In that day, to be "put out of the synagogue" would result in total isolation from all Jewish friends, neighbors and family. The Pharisees in the synagogue controlled birth certificates, marriage licenses, divorce papers and burial in Jewish cemeteries.

LIFE STEP The Pharisees' greatest deterrent to seeing Jesus as the Christ was their zeal for their traditions. What best describes your spiritual walk – on-going fellowship with the person of Jesus Christ or mechanical obedience to a list of religious ceremonies?

JOHN 9:24-34

WHAT IS THE WRITER SAYING?

HOW CAN I APPLY THIS TO MY LIFE?

The blind man's parents were not cooperating so, as they had suggested, the Pharisees go back to the man himself. His response to their biased and intense question is stunning for its power and logic (v. 25). Christians who try to prove their faith to skeptics must use a binary argument. The first agent is the Word of God itself. Its teachings are "light," "truth," and "power." Verse 25 contains the second agent of our ultimate proof of God's existence and concern for humans. The second agent is the miracle the Word of God produces in our own life: "Whereas I was blind, now I see!"

The Pharisees press for more details. The formerly blind man is getting annoyed. The only possible reason for his annoyance is that they were ignoring the obvious conclusion. He may have been blind from birth but he wasn't dull – with quick wit he deflects their interrogation (vv. 27, 30).

This passage shows a profound truth. Often the simple must instruct those who claim to be learned. The blind man holds to a simple faith, "I was blind, now I see." He knows that God's power had been demonstrated through his infirmity and cannot but believe in the One who made him whole. The Jewish authorities call Jesus a *sinner* because they placed their Sabbath regulations above the spirit of the Law. When one was born blind, the common belief was that the family was being judged for their sin. The disciples certainly thought this way (John 9:2). When the man refused to call Jesus a sinner (John 9:24), they turned on him and claimed he had been in sin since his birth (v. 34). *Cast him out* means they kicked him out of the synagogue, the local assembly of the Jews, similar to our churches.

LIFE STEP Great darkness surrounds those who trust in their religion and not Christ. Only by coming to the Savior will they ever know real light.

SUNDAY 24

JOHN 9:35-41

WHAT IS THE WRITER SAYING?

HOW CAN I APPLY THIS TO MY LIFE?

PRAY Afghanistan – Pray that the people of Afghanistan may experience genuine freedom and an improved quality of life.

After the Pharisees excommunicate the blind man in disgust, Jesus meets with Him again. The blind man does not recognize Him at first (The man had never seen Jesus!), but imagine the slow dawning as he began to place the familiar voice!

Jesus asks the man if he believes on the Son of God. He does not say *Messiah* even though that is the natural connection between the healing of the blind man and His ministry (as predicted in Isaiah 35). Nor does He ask the man if he believes that he needs his sins forgiven. Nor if Jesus would die, be buried and rise again to be able to forgive sins. We can conclude that the man's common knowledge certainly included a concept of his own sinfulness, both from personal experience and his Jewish culture. It is also reasonable to assume that he understood the shedding of blood as a remedy for sin. But, could he at this point in his life project that God would take on human flesh to die as the sin bearer?

If he knew Old Testament scriptures perhaps yes; but as an unschooled blind man, probably not. Therefore, Christ's question to him was simply, *Will you accept with a heart of belief that which has been revealed to you?* Jesus' power as God in the flesh ("the Son of God") had been revealed in his healing. Jesus asks, *Do you believe it to be true?* The man says *yes*!

Obviously, the Pharisees are still hovering about this man (v. 40) and feel the weight of Jesus' statement about the blind receiving sight and the seeing being blind. Because they were not willing to admit their sin (blindness) and need for healing (salvation), they would remain in their blind state!

 LIFE STEP Baby steps. All Christ asks for are baby steps. Then He takes control that we might toddle, walk, run and become marathoners spiritually!

MONDAY 24

JOHN 10:1-13

WHAT IS THE WRITER SAYING?

Good shepherd — gave His life
Great Shepherd — guides His followers
Chief shepherd — will reign & reward

HOW CAN I APPLY THIS TO MY LIFE?

PRAY Kenya – For church leaders to have wisdom and boldness when speaking out against sin.

In verses 1-5 Jesus views Himself as the "shepherd." The sheepfold in a village protected the sheep at night from thieves and wild animals. It had walls, a door and even a guard (v. 3). In some cases it was a community structure used by many shepherds so the sheep would have to respond to the voice of their shepherd to leave in the morning. Christ is the *Good Shepherd* because He gives His life for the sheep (v. 11, Psalm 22). For us, that is His *past* ministry. He is the *Great* Shepherd because He presently guides the sheep all the way to glory (Hebrews 13:20; Psalm 23). He is also the *Chief* Shepherd of the sheep and in the future will return to reward all the *under shepherds* or pastors (1 Peter 5:4; Psalm 24).

In verses 7-13 He changes the analogy and refers to Himself as the *door* to the sheep. In some cases, particularly when traveling in the fields for days at a time, a shepherd literally was the door of the sheepfold as he lay down in the doorway of the stone enclosure. Sometimes these were topped with brambles as a form of *barbed wire*. The enclosure had only one entrance. Anyone getting to the sheep had to come through the shepherd first. Today many would like us to believe that there are many roads that lead to God. The message of the cross is very exclusive. There is one door (v. 7), one way (John 14:6), one God and mediator (1 Timothy 2:5).

The Pharisees were spiritual thieves, robbers, or at best, hirelings (vv. 8, 12). Perhaps Jesus had in mind the words of the prophet Zechariah as He made these statements (Zechariah 11:4-9, 17).

LIFE STEP Christ is the only door into the security of the sheepfold. There is no other way of salvation than through the sacrifice of Jesus Christ. One of our great comforts as believers is the knowledge that the Great Shepherd has placed us into the fold.

TUESDAY 24

JOHN 10:14-21

WHAT IS THE WRITER SAYING?

HOW CAN I APPLY THIS TO MY LIFE?

PRAY India – Protection and boldness for believers facing persecution by Hindu extremists.

Verse 14 is an interesting look at how language works. The word "sheep" does not appear in the verse in the Greek but is obviously what is being talked about since "sheep" does occur in verse 13 and "shepherd" in verse 14.

The Good Shepherd has a special relationship to His sheep. This is seen by the nature of the relationship. The shepherd is not a hired hand but rather the owner of the sheep (my sheep), and the relationship is reciprocal (know and known). Think about the logic of verses 14-15. Jesus says, ① I know my sheep, ② My sheep know me, ③ The Father knows me, ④ I know the Father and ⑤ I give My life for the sheep. How does the fifth statement fit logically with the first four? Answer, *if you want to know the Father you have to accept the death of the Son for you!*

The Father loves the Son because of His willing obedience. *Other sheep* (10:16) refers to Gentiles who would believe and be joined with the Jewish believers (this fold) into one body (see Ephesians 2:13-16). This means that today in the Church, Jewish believers and Gentile believers are merged into one entity. However, it does not mean that the Church replaces Israel in human history. Israel has a future as a redeemed people alongside the Church in the future. Verses 17 and 18 teach that Jesus was in total control throughout the events leading to His crucifixion. No one took His life from Him but rather, He willingly offered Himself as our substitutionary sacrifice. A worthy shepherd would sacrifice himself to save his sheep and Jesus proved He was our Good Shepherd at Calvary.

 LIFE STEP Believers are in a spiritual war zone. The battle has already been decided, yet it still rages. To bring men to Himself, Jesus endured much suffering and abuse. How willing are you to stand for Him?

WEDNESDAY 24

JOHN 10:22-30

WHAT IS THE WRITER SAYING?

HOW CAN I APPLY THIS TO MY LIFE?

PRAY Pray for the faithfulness of those who evangelize and minister to those in your local prisons.

John 10 contains two great discourses on Christ as a Shepherd. The second one (10:22-42) is His last public teaching before His death.

John indicates (v. 22) that this confrontation takes place during the time of the Feast of Dedication. In Hebrew this feast is called Hanukkah. It was a celebration of the rededication of the temple by Judas Maccabeus in 164 B.C. after its desecration in 167 B.C. by Antiochus Epiphanes.

Verse 22 informs us that it was "winter." This is true physically, politically and spiritually. Hanukkah comes in December. Jerusalem is 2200 feet above sea level and therefore, it is cold in Jerusalem in December. There can even be snow at times. Politically it was winter. Hanukkah celebrates a great Jewish military victory that led to one hundred years of relative freedom (164-63 B.C.) but for over ninety years now the Jews had

been under the control of pagan Rome. Spiritually it was winter. The Pharisees and Sadducees controlled the Jewish culture with their misunderstandings of theology and for the previous three years the bulk of the nation had been ignoring Jesus' call to national repentance. They continue to resist Jesus' claims in this section (vv. 24-26).

Hanukkah was celebrated by lighting candles every night for eight nights. Each night one more candle was added until on the final night all eight major candles were lit plus a *servant* candle. This candelabra (hanukkiah in Hebrew) had to be on an outside windowsill. Having just walked into Jerusalem viewing these lights, Jesus proclaims the greatest shaft of light this sin-darkened world has ever seen: "I and my Father are one." (!) This section concludes with a powerful declaration of the security of our salvation (vv. 27-30).

 LIFE STEP Christ's attributes are the basis of the security of our salvation. He suffered to purchase our redemption and He actively keeps believers from eternal harm.

THURSDAY 24

JOHN 10:31-42

WHAT IS THE WRITER SAYING?

HOW CAN I APPLY THIS TO MY LIFE?

PRAY

Brazil – For many to accept Christ through the ministry of Christian concerts and musical dramas.

If anyone ever doubted whether Jesus claimed to be God, He put the question to rest as He plainly says, "I and my Father are one!" (v. 30).

Jesus was not just saying that He and the Father were *unified* in purpose. As we see from the Jewish authorities' response, He was claiming equality with God. In fact, that is the accusation leveled at Him at His trials which led to His crucifixion and He never corrected their thinking to the contrary.

The Jewish authorities understood perfectly that by making such a statement Jesus claimed to be God. In response, they lashed out stating that His claim was blasphemy! Yet Jesus used the Scripture to silence their complaint. In the passage He quoted (Psalm 82:6), the psalmist used the common Hebrew word for God, *Elohim*, to identify key men who spoke for God. How much more should the incarnate Son Himself be free to speak of His oneness in nature with the Father!

Once again, Jesus was willing to let His works speak for Him (vv. 37-38). If they could not believe His words, they only needed to examine His works to see that He did all that the Prophets had said that Messiah would do when He came (see Isaiah 35:4-6).

As so many times before, the Jewish authorities wanted to grab Him, but He eluded their grasp. Each time we are reminded that Jesus was in complete control of every situation (v. 39).

Withdrawing to the Jordan River, His ministry now comes full circle to where it all began (John 1:28 ff.). Though most of the religious leadership had rejected Him, yet many sought Him and believed upon Him there.

LIFE STEP We have come full circle in John. Chapter one began with John the Baptist and chapter 10 ends with John the Baptist. What was so great about John? He believed and obeyed. Can this be said of us?

JOHN 11:1-13

WHAT IS THE WRITER SAYING?

HOW CAN I APPLY THIS TO MY LIFE?

Chapter 11 contains the last and greatest of Jesus' sign miracles prior to His own resurrection. Bethany ("house of dates") was a small village on the backside of the Mt. of Olives, about one and a half miles from Jerusalem. It would be a convenient retreat for Christ from the crowded city. It was from here that He began His Triumphal Entry into Jerusalem on Palm Sunday (down the Mt. of Olives, to the Kidron Valley, up through the Eastern Gate into the Temple) reversing the route of the Shekinah Glory of God as it had left the Temple in 591 B.C. (five years before it was destroyed). Lazarus (*whom God aids!*) is not as well known as his two sisters, Mary (*rebellion*) and Martha (*lady*). Verse 2 refers to the event in John 12:1-5. Verse 5 mentions Martha first. She was also the one who hustled to make Him a nice meal in Luke 10:38-40. On hearing the news of his friend's sickness, Christ explains that this episode is designed to glorify the Son.

He means not just in the miracle, but also in the aftermath, for this miracle causes the final confrontation leading to His crucifixion. Verse 9 poetically relates that as long as you are walking in the center of God's will, no harm can befall you.

Throughout his Gospel, John has highlighted many miracles done by Jesus, but draws particular attention to seven that he identifies as signs, each underscoring some aspect of what it means to believe. This final sign points to the newness of life that awaits those who have trusted Christ as Savior.

LIFE STEP Christ taught the masses but was focused on individuals. He poured His life into individuals who then turned the world upside down when He was gone.

SATURDAY 24

JOHN 11:14-29

WHAT IS THE WRITER SAYING?

HOW CAN I APPLY THIS TO MY LIFE?

Verse 14 is also a miracle in that He knew what took place over sixty miles away. *Didymus* means *twin* (as does Thomas), perhaps the twin brother of Matthew because they are frequently mentioned together. Verse 6 tells us that He waited two days and verse 17 that Lazarus had been dead four days (The Jews believed that the soul did not leave for heaven until three days had passed). It is a two-three day journey from Galilee to Jerusalem. Christ purposely waits until the fourth day to increase the drama and impact of this His crowning sign miracle. The contrast in the personalities of Mary and Martha make an interesting study (John 12 and Luke 10). Luke 10 is the famous *Martha/ Mary Syndrome* where Martha is busy preparing a meal for the Lord and rebukes Him for allowing Mary to sit and listen to Him while she did all the work. Martha is told that Mary had chosen the better part – sitting at the feet of Jesus! Here in John, Martha is active, running out to meet Jesus while Mary passively mourns in the house. Martha aggressively announces her hurt in losing "<u>my</u> brother" (Greek emphasis) whereas Mary tenderly mourns "my <u>brother</u>" (Greek emphasis, v. 32). Martha is vocal and Mary is tearful. Christ and Martha have a rational discussion about the resurrection whereas Mary just falls at Christ's feet and worships. That Martha called Jesus *The Teacher* ("Master") is interesting because the Pharisees would not teach women, but Jesus did (v. 28).

LIFE STEP God always deals with us as individuals. Martha needed instruction, while Mary needed to be comforted. Ask God to help you meet people where they are. What a blessing it is to know that those who believe in Jesus will live even if they die!

JOHN 11:30-37

WHAT IS THE WRITER SAYING?

HOW CAN I APPLY THIS TO MY LIFE?

PRAY Pray for those that work with the youth of your church to have love, wisdom, and perseverance.

This passage is filled with emotion. Martha goes to fetch Mary having had a few moments with Christ outside the village. She calls her sister unobtrusively. The Jews, who had stayed with Mary consoling her and had not followed Martha when she went out to meet Jesus, followed Mary as she rises to go. They thought she was going to the tomb to weep, and they wished to share in this activity as an encouragement to her. Mary's words were almost identical to Martha's and as such were a firm conviction that Christ's power could have saved Lazarus from death. Jesus' response in verse 33 is a display of anger at Satan for the heartache he has brought to mankind. *Groaned* is used of the snorting of a warhorse. Death, to Christ, was not an impassable barrier, but a call to battle! The *wept* of verse 35 was a quiet, dignified weeping, not the raucous uncontrolled weeping that was the style of the hired mourners in that day. Jesus' sorrow was a good testimony to the observing Jewish authorities. Some even speculated that if He had been there earlier, He could have healed Lazarus just as He had power over the blind. No one was expecting a resurrection! But then, Jesus exceeds all that we ask or think, doesn't He?

LIFE STEP Jesus knew that He would soon resurrect Lazarus and solve their problem but He still entered into the sorrow of the human tragedy. We know how our story ends but still need to show compassion to those going through the deep waters of sickness, death and loss.

MONDAY 25

JOHN 11:38-44

WHAT IS THE WRITER SAYING?

HOW CAN I APPLY THIS TO MY LIFE?

PRAY Austria – For missionaries not to be discouraged with all the obstacles they encounter.

At the tomb, Christ orders the stone removed. Martha, the aggressive sister, warns of the certain decay. Jesus reminds Martha of His previous statement to her. He offers a thanksgiving prayer before the miracle. In the prayer He even discusses His motivation for the prayer with His Father. Since the Father knows all, even this revelation was for our instruction, not the Father's! Lazarus, upon hearing the voice of the all-powerful One, responds and comes forth! Would it be too much to suggest that Christ had to specify "Lazarus, come forth," lest the whole cemetery empty out!?!

The main miracle is the coming back to life of one certainly dead and departed. However, other miracles are present as well. Back in verse 4 Jesus predicted the conclusion of the matter. In verse 14 He knew without being told that Lazarus had died. Even verse 44 implies some sort of miracle because normally the dead were wrapped so tightly they would not have been able to walk under their own power. Did Lazarus float out? The other item we often overlook is Lazarus' thoughts on this matter. Was he happy to be alive again? (I'm guessing No!). The poor man had been enjoying paradise and now had to re-enter this world of sorrow and pain and then consider the prospect of dying again. Not only that, but shortly he will find out that the Jewish authorities want to kill him. Most importantly however, note that Lazarus does not describe his experiences in paradise and no one tries to make him speak of those private matters. It is a shame that modern writers feel a need to speak of things that the Scriptures purposely leave silent.

LIFE STEP Many Christians are like Lazarus as he comes out of the tomb… alive in Christ, but still bound by the grave clothes of the world. They cannot work for their hands are bound, nor witness because their mouths are bound. Christ wants us to be free – free to move, serve and testify.

JOHN 11:45-57

WHAT IS THE WRITER SAYING?

HOW CAN I APPLY THIS TO MY LIFE?

PRAY Paraguay – For God to call laborers to the more than 400 interior villages that remain unreached.

When Jesus gives the command to loose Lazarus, it would appear that the miracle is finished. There is more though! In verse 45, we see that because of Jesus' prayer, many believed! Sadly, though, some merely went to report the incident, their hearts hardened to the truth. The religious authorities were not happy campers! The *place* they were afraid of losing was the temple. Caiaphas offers what he believes is the expedient thing to do – to sacrifice one man for the good of the whole nation. Caiaphas, being the High Priest, is speaking prophetically (v. 51), yet he himself does not have God's will in mind but rather the removal of a nuisance for the good of the whole. Earlier, Jesus had told them they were of the devil and would do his works ("a murderer from the beginning," John 8:44). Here we see them plotting that very thing. Ironically, despite the sacrifice of that one man, the nation still perished in A.D. 70. Caiaphas was High Priest from A.D. 18-36. In 2002 his tomb and his highly decorated stone burial box (called an ossuary) were found in Jerusalem.

Verse 52 speaks of the scope of Christ's sacrifice, sufficient not only for the nation of Israel but for the Gentile also. This day marked the beginning of the Jewish authorities' open plans to kill Jesus. Verse 55 is an amazing backdrop. The Passover was at hand! Jesus was soon to be the ultimate Passover lamb. The blood He would shed would be a once-for-all sacrifice that would serve not as a covering for sin but as the satisfaction of God's righteous demands (1 John 2:2) and the basis of cleansing from their sin, to those who believe (Hebrews 10:10-14).

 LIFE STEP The substitutionary sacrifice of Jesus Christ at the Cross is the basis for our forgiveness. This forgiveness is made available to every man yet is only known by those who believe and place their faith in Christ. What a tragedy to know of God's grace and yet not receive it.

WEDNESDAY 25

JOHN 12:1-11

WHAT IS THE WRITER SAYING?

HOW CAN I APPLY THIS TO MY LIFE?

PRAY Nigeria – For the staggering growth of the church to continue and for the body to become mature.

We are now six days before the crucifixion. John 12:12 places the triumphal entry (Palm Sunday) on the following day which means that this supper was at the end of the Sabbath on Saturday night, assuming a Friday crucifixion. It has been no more than three months since Lazarus was raised (from the Hanukkah of John 10 to Passover is about one hundred days). Martha is still active and Mary worshipping! This was apparently a special meal as the Greek says they reclined at the table. Only the wealthy regularly ate this way. The poor would only do so at special meals like Passover. In the reclining position, it was easy for Mary to reach the Lord's feet. Normally a servant would wash the feet. It was also unusual for a woman to let her hair down in public. These acts of humility are impressive. The value of the perfume is overwhelming. Three hundred pence (*denarii*) represents about a year's wages for a common laborer. The spikenard (nard) was expensive because the closest that it was grown and processed was northern India. The mean-spiritedness of Judas is depressing. It is hard to imagine why he thought he had the right to question Mary's actions. The Lord graciously protects Mary and turns Judas' complaint back on him. If he was so interested in the poor, he could make that his personal ministry for the rest of his life! John explains from his own hindsight that Judas was insincere, although no one suspected him at the time. In verse 10 we see that sinful intent is multiplying. Whereas they started with plans to kill one man "for the sake of the nation," they have now added a second. Before the story is done, it will include many others!

 LIFE STEP Martha, Lazarus and Mary. Service, Fellowship and Worship. All are necessary, but Worship is the starting point.

THURSDAY 25

JOHN 12:12-19

WHAT IS THE WRITER SAYING?

HOW CAN I APPLY THIS TO MY LIFE?

This section, often referred to as the Triumphal Entry, is common to all four Gospels. People in the crowd coming to Jerusalem to celebrate the Passover began to continually call out (the verb is in an imperfect tense) to Jesus as He enters the city. These Jews enthusiastically proclaiming Christ's Messiahship were probably from Galilee. They had seen more of Jesus' miracles, heard more of His teaching and were not greatly influenced by the religious authorities in Jerusalem.

The palm branch was a symbol of happiness in both the Roman and Jewish culture. It is used to this day in the Feast of Tabernacles celebration (it is called the *lulav*). *Hosanna* is a transliteration of the Hebrew or Aramaic meaning, *please save*. Both this phrase and *he who comes* are found in Psalm 118:25-26. The crowd obviously has these messianic ideas in mind as they greet Jesus. Jesus riding on a donkey's colt is a direct fulfillment of Zechariah 9:9, "Rejoice greatly, O daughter of Zion; shout, O daughter of Jerusalem: behold, thy King cometh unto thee: he is just, and having salvation; lowly, and riding upon an ass, and upon a colt the foal of an ass."

Unlike the pomp and circumstance usually associated with the coming of a king, Jesus' entrance is humble. Nonetheless, the Pharisees are greatly agitated and are stirring one another up as a result of their perceived ineffectiveness at squashing His popularity with the people.

John editorializes the event (v. 16), showing the disciples lack of understanding about what was happening as the events unfold. Later, after the Lord's Resurrection, they were able to put the events together.

LIFE STEP The fulfillment of Scripture is a common theme in the Gospels. God's Word will not fail. The things written concerning Jesus will all be completely fulfilled. If all these predictions of His First Coming were fulfilled, what about the predictions about His Second Coming? Are you ready for His promised return?

JOHN 12:20-26

WHAT IS THE WRITER SAYING?

HOW CAN I APPLY THIS TO MY LIFE?

PRAY Thailand – For courage to accept Christ in a land where patriotism and Buddhism are seen as one entity.

Throughout the book it is clear that John is writing both to a Jewish and Gentile audience. The mention of the Greeks (vv. 20-22) is important in that Jesus' death was for the sins of all of mankind, not just the Jews.

The Greeks (v. 20) were *God Fearers* – Gentiles who were impressed with Judaism but didn't want to be circumcised. They came to Philip since he had a Greek name (*lover of horses*) and was from a Greek area (the northeastern Galilee region). It appears that the further removed a person was from the Jewish authorities in Jerusalem the more likely they were to consider the claims of Christ. It is touching to see the way Philip goes to Andrew for advice.

You will notice that no more mention is made of the Greeks' request, but Jesus uses it as an opportunity to predict His imminent death, "The Hour" towards which the entire story has been moving. Significant, is it not, that Gentiles trigger this announcement as through His death we are elevated to equality with Jews in the family of God! Verse 24 applies *the law of the harvest* to the spiritual realm. Verse 25 is a paradox. Those who wish to save their life, living for their own selfish ends, will destroy (present tense) that to which they desperately cling. Those who hate their lives (by comparison), gain (future tense) that which is true life indeed.

LIFE STEP We fear death because it makes no sense to us that out of death and decay can come another life. Nature encourages us, whether it be the *dead* grain of wheat or the stunning metamorphosis of the lowly caterpillar into a mass of jellied protein and then the stunning butterfly!

JOHN 12:27-43

WHAT IS THE WRITER SAYING?

HOW CAN I APPLY THIS TO MY LIFE?

Jesus shows His first concern over His impending sin-bearing. He is not expressing intent to reconsider. He is simply vocalizing for our benefit the horror of an infinitely perfect being taking on the guilt and sin of mankind. He submits by requesting that the Father be glorified through this incredible demonstration of selfless love. The Father thunders His approval from heaven (v. 28). Jesus confirms that once again God has said or done something to verify Jesus' person and ministry to humans.

Lifted up (v. 32) normally means *exalted*. The cross is a triumph, not a defeat! It was here that the serpent received its head wound (Genesis 3) and the prince of this world system was cast out (v. 31)! Likewise, on the cross when Jesus says, "It is finished," His words are not a sigh of resignation but a triumphant cry of success.

The crowd is puzzled by the apparent contradiction between His obvious power and His prediction of imminent death. "Son of Man" was Christ's favorite title for Himself (see Daniel 7). It speaks of His identification with mankind as a man. Verse 36 announces Christ's withdrawal from the public. In chapters 13-17 He limits His ministry just to the twelve disciples. Verse 37 announces the reason for going private. Those who reject the deity of Christ do so claiming that nowhere in Scripture is Jesus referred to by the name "Jehovah." John 12:41 is one place in Scripture where there is a direct connection between Jesus and the name Jehovah. In Isaiah 6:1, it is Jehovah high and lifted up that Isaiah views but John tells us that the prophet was beholding the glory of Jesus!

LIFE STEP The people of Christ's day completely missed the predictions of Messiah's death (Psalms 16, 22; Isaiah 53). Christ <u>expected</u> them to know these *hard* passages! What hard passages does Christ expect us to understand and believe?

JOHN 12:44-50

WHAT IS THE WRITER SAYING?

HOW CAN I APPLY THIS TO MY LIFE?

PRAY Pray for the peace of Jerusalem (Psalm 122:6).

The final paragraph in John 12 is a summary statement of Jesus' message and mission. It wraps up chapters 1-12 before John takes us into the private conversation Jesus had with His disciples the very night that He was betrayed – the night before He died. This private conversation will go from chapter 13 through 17. Let's review the outline of John to see where we are in the flow of the book:

1-4 – Consideration (seven encounters with seekers)

5-6 – Controversy (seven eye-witnesses to Jesus' divine powers)

7-11 – Conflict (seventh pre-death miracle in John)

12 – Crisis (seven days before His death)

13-17 – Conference (seven lectures from Christ to His eleven remaining disciples)

18-20 – Consummation (His trials and crucifixion)

21 – Conclusion (His resurrection and ascension)

Jesus sums it up: See Me, See the Father; Believe on Me, you'll also Believe on the Father; Choose Me, Choose Light; Reject Me, Remain in Darkness; Accept My Word, Be Granted Eternal Life; Reject My Word, My Word will Reject You.

Those who reject Jesus Christ will only have themselves to blame ultimately. Jesus makes it clear that those who hear and reject the Gospel will be judged by the very Word of God from which they have turned away (vv. 47-50). This is affirmed in Romans 1 where Paul concludes that no man will have an excuse. In the final judgment every human will agree that he/she deserves the punishment they receive.

LIFE STEP Are you "walking in the light?" How does that make your life experience different from an unsaved person's? Could you share the difference with an unsaved person?

JOHN 13:1-11

WHAT IS THE WRITER SAYING?

HOW CAN I APPLY THIS TO MY LIFE?

PRAY
Canada – Pray for churches to hold fast to biblical truth, ethical integrity, and evangelical zeal.

Chapters 13-17 contain seven lectures designed to prepare the disciples to carry on Christ's work in His absence. Seven times in these chapters He says, *These things have I spoken unto you.* In four of these, we are given the purpose for His teachings:
1) For their joy (15:11)
2) For their confidence (16:1)
3) For their memory (16:4)
4) And for their peace (16:33)
Chapter 13 contains the account of the Last Supper. Verse 1 states that Christ loved His disciples *to the uttermost* (fullness of His love). He leaves them with an example of humility to follow. Prior to chapter 12, four times Jesus stated that His hour had not yet come. Now it had come. *Hour* is a reference to the whole series of events leading up to and including His death, burial, and resurrection.

In the exchange between Peter and Jesus (vv. 6-11) much more than dirty feet are being discussed. Peter's initial refusal quickly becomes an overreaction as he requests a complete cleansing. The reply of Jesus (v.10) is a reference to salvation. *He that is washed,* (saved) needs only to wash his feet (confession of daily sins for unbroken fellowship). The statement that they are *not all clean* is a reference to the unbelief of Judas.

LIFE STEP Peter always tries to control the situation. In his befuddlement, (probably because he was seated where the assigned foot washer would sit) he first rejects the washing then requests a whole bath. Consistent with 1 John 1:9, Christ strikes the balance. Believers are bathed in the blood of Christ for salvation and kept in fellowship by the confession of daily sin.

TUESDAY 26

JOHN 13:12-20

WHAT IS THE WRITER SAYING?

HOW CAN I APPLY THIS TO MY LIFE?

PRAY Ethiopia – Pray that Ethiopia which has remained a bastion of Christianity, withstanding Islamic advances for centuries will continue to do so.

Jesus has just washed the disciples' feet. This was a task performed by the servant of a household. In the absence of any subordinate, no one was jumping to be the one to carry out this task. Jesus takes on the role of servant to the group and performs this menial task.

Returning to His place at the table, He now explains the importance of this act to His disciples. His preeminence among them was never an issue (v. 13). The terms they addressed Him by were terms of respect and honor. If their teacher, the Lord, was not too good to serve them by washing their feet, they also were not too good to serve one another. The example (v. 15) He left them was not of washing feet but rather of service. Blessing (v.17) is found not in the knowledge of what pleases God, but in doing those things that please Him. Verse 18 is a fulfillment of verse 19. Jesus was going to tell His disciples plainly of His betrayal before it occurred, so when it happened, their faith would not be shaken but rather strengthened. The cross was not a mistake but part of God's plan. The betrayal was a necessary element on the road to Calvary. In verse 18 Christ quotes Psalm 41:9 describing the treachery of Judas in betraying Him. "Lifted up his heel" is a *donkey kick* to the head. (Particularly ironic as Christ washed that very heel!) Verse 20 shows the connection between the Lord and His servants. Those who minister unto the servants of God are ministering to the Lord. Verse 1 began this section stating that Christ loved His disciples *unto the end (end of His ability to love)*. He leaves them with an example of humility to follow. Christ still enlists men and women to join *The Order of the Towel*!

LIFE STEP Service is not glamorous, but it is Christ-like. Jesus used this opportunity to demonstrate vividly that to humble one's self to serve others was not above Him, and should not be too much to ask of us!

WEDNESDAY 26

JOHN 13:21-30

WHAT IS THE WRITER SAYING?

HOW CAN I APPLY THIS TO MY LIFE?

PRAY Macedonia – Pray for the evangelical church in Macedonia, that they may continue to share the Gospel across ethnic and national boundaries.

Knowledge of an event, even the knowledge that it will turn out all right in the end, does not take away the sting of a betrayal. As Jesus announces the imminent fulfillment of a prophecy given almost one thousand years earlier (v. 18, Psalm 41:9), He experienced emotional distress. This is one of the markers of His true humanity – He displayed real human emotions (He was not just a spirit being pretending to be a human). The word "troubled" was used back in John 5:7 referring to disturbed water and in John 11:33 to speak of Jesus' sadness at the death of Lazarus. In John 14:1 He will tell the disciples, "Let not your heart be troubled."

Peter persuades John (the disciple whom Jesus loved, v. 23) to ask Jesus who His betrayer would be. Jesus plainly identifies Judas, however many of the disciples are still oblivious to his treachery (v. 29). It is sobering to think that the twelve men could spend three and a half years together and never suspect that Judas had ulterior motives! There are hints at the seating arrangement at this Passover Meal. John is able to lean back to ask Jesus a question. He would be reclining on the floor at the low table in front of Jesus. Jesus dips in the common pot with Judas who would be behind him. Peter is at a distance and has to "beckon" (gesture) to communicate with John. In this set-up, Jesus is in the position of the host of the meal. John is in a favored seat, the right hand as a bodyguard. Judas is in the slot for the guest of honor. (So considered because it was the left hand side and also exposed the back of the host indicating trust). The "sop" was a choice piece of meat fed by the host with his own fingers to a guest he wished to honor. The very night he betrayed Jesus, Jesus was telling Judas, *It's not too late. I know what you are planning to do and I still love you.*

LIFE STEP Do we have any Judas-like tendencies? Do we use Church for any ulterior motives? If a respected church member falls away, can we keep our eyes on Jesus instead of the shocking failure?

THURSDAY 26

JOHN 13:31-38

WHAT IS THE WRITER SAYING?

HOW CAN I APPLY THIS TO MY LIFE?

PRAY United Kingdom – For many teens to be saved through Christian camping and outreach events.

It must have been a relief for Christ to have Judas gone (v. 31)! Judas' absence would give Jesus a more intimate time with His true disciples as He shared His final thoughts before death. In the next major section of John (13:31–14:31), Christ in effect tells his disciples, *Brace yourselves, I'm leaving!* He affectionately calls them "Little children" (v. 33) and certainly they would so behave in the next seventy-two hours! Jesus tells them that in His absence, love for one another would be the glue to hold them together, individually and corporately.

Peter ignores the Lord's challenge to love the brethren and goes back to His statement in verse 33, "Whither I go, ye cannot come." When Christ said that to the religious authorities (7:34, 8:21) He implied "never" (since they refused to repent and believe). In verse 36 He

softens the statement for the disciples indicating that their separation would be temporary, not permanent. Peter gets the drift and protests his intent to lay down his life as well. Christ calls his bluff and states the reality – at the crisis time no one will stand with Him. He will go through the Valley of the Shadow of Death alone. Peter's denial is recorded in all four Gospels. In this first private discussion after Judas' departure, Christ is asked four questions by the puzzled and increasingly alarmed disciples:

1. Peter: Where are you going? (13:36) Answer: Somewhere you can't.
2. Thomas: How can we get there? (14:5) Answer: Through Me!
3. Philip: Can we take a peek? (14:8) Answer: Look at Me!
4. Judas: Why the change in the program? (14:22) Answer: Belief required.

LIFE STEP How do you say goodbye? What final words can you leave behind to strengthen your loved ones in your absence? Love for the brethren was Christ's choice!

FRIDAY 26

JOHN 14:1-6

WHAT IS THE WRITER SAYING?

HOW CAN I APPLY THIS TO MY LIFE?

PRAY South Africa – For loving outreach by those in youth ministry to a very vulnerable generation.

Christ gives the alarmed disciples something to look forward to and hang their hopes on. We have seen the verb "troubled" (stirred up) several times in John. Christ does not want His disciples to be in emotional or theological turmoil. Belief is the key. It is interesting that He begins with "ye believe in God." This implies that prior to meeting Jesus, these eleven men already had a vital relationship with God the Father. Now they are to extend that same trust to the Son. *Mansions* is from the Greek root *meno*, meaning *to abide*. It is not referring to palatial country estates but rather *dwelling places* (rooms in a father's house for the children). The only other time this word occurs in scripture is in 14:23 where it refers to our heart as Christ's home!

Christ promises to return for the disciples. Theologically, this is a unique proposition since up to this point in their understanding of Scripture, the coming of Christ was for the sake of establishing a kingdom on the earth, not taking saints back to heaven. The analogy comes from Jewish wedding customs. After the engagement the groom had to prepare a home for his bride before the wedding could take place. At the rapture, believers will be taken to this new home to spend the seven years of the tribulation period in seclusion with the Bridegroom. Then we will return with Christ to help establish His Kingdom in the same arena where He was originally rejected (Revelation 19).

Verse 6 contains the sixth of Christ's great "I am" statements. Jesus, being one with the Father, was of the same essence as the Father. To know Him was equal to knowing the Father. Those who know Jesus know the way home.

 LIFE STEP Believers are warned of persecution and even prepared for martyrdom. Our blessed hope, however, is to one day be delivered from this world and taken home!

SATURDAY 26

JOHN 14:7-14

WHAT IS THE WRITER SAYING?

HOW CAN I APPLY THIS TO MY LIFE?

PRAY Dominican Republic – For God to send workers to the more than 3,500 villages that have no Gospel witness.

Jesus again repeats His teaching that to know Jesus is to know the Father and vice versa. Philip is not satisfied. He had a *show me* personality. In response to Philip's request to see the Father, Christ offers His own life as an open book about the Father. He points to His works as manifestations of the Father's power. He then goes on to make an utterly astounding statement. The disciples would do greater works than what Christ had done. Greater works than the Messiah Himself! It is true that the disciples did many miracles in the book of Acts, including raising the dead, but the emphasis here is on spiritual service. Christ was localized. He could only minister to so many people per day. But when He leaves and sends the Holy Spirit, the Holy Spirit will be universal. He will work through many human bodies at once, not just the one body of the Messiah.

What work is greater than seeing a dead body come back to life? Answer: Seeing souls dead in sin, shackled by Satan freed and resurrected to newness of life! As part of this process, Christ reminds them of their power in prayer. This was not to be a *magic wand* that would give them anything they longed after. Jesus had "nowhere to lay His head" (Luke 9:58). There is no evidence that any of the eleven disciples became wealthy from their ministry. Therefore, we should be suspicious of modern preachers who imply that God wants us *healthy and wealthy* based on such prayer promises. This prayer promise was for the sake of ministering in the spiritual realm, not the physical. It is qualified by the concept that when we pray, we must consider the Lord's will because that is the type of prayer that will receive a positive response (1 John 5:14-15).

V. 13 + 14

 LIFE STEP We are a power-conscious society. Real displays of power are there for the viewing in the spiritual realm as we claim Christ's power over the world, the flesh and the devil.

JOHN 14:15-24

WHAT IS THE WRITER SAYING?

HOW CAN I APPLY THIS TO MY LIFE?

In light of His soon departure, Christ tells His disciples that He will ask the Father to send another Comforter. There are two words for *another* in Greek. *Heteros* is *another of a different kind*, such as the false gospel that was no gospel at all in Galatians 1, or our word *heterosexual*. The other, which is used here, is *allos*, which means *another of the same kind*. Both Jesus and the Holy Spirit are *comforters*.

In 1 John 2:1, the term being translated *comforter* is used of Christ and translated *advocate*. When we slip into sin, Jesus Christ is our advocate with the Father. The Greek term is *paraklete*, a compound word composed of *para* (alongside; parallel) + *kaleo* (to call): *one called alongside to help in time of need*. It was used as a legal term – aid, counsel, or intercessor. Even our English word *comfort* helps us appreciate the Holy Spirit's ministry. It too is a compound word, *com* (with) and *fort* (strength). He doesn't just comfort us when we get hurt but strengthens us before we go out into battle! In Romans 8:37, Paul says that we are "more than conquerors" in Christ Jesus. Not just conquerors but <u>more</u> than conquerors! "More" is *hyper* (know anyone who is hyper?!?) In Latin it is *super*. Super men, super women, super heroes through the indwelling Holy Spirit! Just fifty-two days later, in the Upper Room on Pentecost (the celebration of the wheat harvest and anniversary of the giving of the Law) little tongues of fire – miniature Shekinah glories – would settle on the heads of each of these men as they received this empowerment.

Verses 15 and 24 are like the bookends of this section. The life of the true believer is characterized by obedience to the commandments of God.

 LIFE STEP The function of the Spirit is to make the reality of God convincing to all men in the same way that Jesus did to His disciples.

JOHN 14:25-31

WHAT IS THE WRITER SAYING?

HOW CAN I APPLY THIS TO MY LIFE?

One of the ministries of the Holy Spirit was temporary and limited to the disciples resulting in the book we hold in our hands almost two thousand years later, the Bible. He would cause the disciples to remember all that Christ said even though they didn't understand much of it at the time it was spoken. He would guide them as they penned the New Testament. He emphatically states that My (kind of) peace (not the world's peace) He would leave with them (v. 27). Christ wants the disciples to be happy for His imminent reunion with the Father. He also implies that He has to go away for this special gift of the Holy Spirit to come. It is clear that the ministry of the Holy Spirit is different after the Cross than before. The event that makes the difference is the crosswork of Christ. The actual payment for the sin of mankind gave the Spirit of God greater influence in the lives of men than what was normally experienced by the Old Testament saints. This could be one of the reasons why we see so many of the Old Testament saints falling into gross sin (such as David and Solomon) while most heroes of the New Testament stayed faithful to the Lord. Christ knew that the disciples were in a state of shock but He informs them of these things now so when they happen the disciples will have further proof that He was right and indeed is the Messiah. The *prince of this world* (v. 30) is a reference to Satan, whom soon would throw everything he had at the Son of God. In unwavering obedience and submission to the will of the heavenly Father, Jesus Christ walked full face into the adversary's fury.

 LIFE STEP It is sometimes tempting to say that God is not doing anything special in my life. I want to see some power! But when you look at the sweep of human history and see the impact the Bible has had on human culture, now there's a demonstration of incredible power!

JOHN 15:1-11

WHAT IS THE WRITER SAYING?

HOW CAN I APPLY THIS TO MY LIFE?

PRAY Angola – Pray for churches to develop a unity in Christ that transcends tribal loyalty and politics.

As Christ and the disciples make their way out of the city to the Garden of Gethsemane (*olive oil press*), He uses an agricultural analogy to describe the relationship of Himself to the believer (15:1-11). The grape vine was a powerful symbol in Israel, like our *bald eagle*. Herod had placed a massive golden grapevine on the façade of the Temple. Isaiah chapter 5 also uses the vineyard analogy with the following symbolism:

My loved one	=	God the Father
Vineyard	=	Israel
Fertile Hillside	=	Promised Land
Stones Removed	=	Canaanites
Vines	=	Individual Israelites
Watchtower	=	Protection
Winepress	=	Law
Grapes	=	Fruit of the Spirit
Bad Fruit	=	Sin ("Stench" in Hebrew!)

Notice the principles of the Master Husbandman's "Viticulture:"

Right Stock – Jesus	=	True (Genuine) Vine
Right Expert – Father	=	Husbandman
Right Culture – Productive Christians	=	Fruitful vines
Right Contact – Christ + Believers	=	Fellowship
Right Fruit – Believers' Works	=	Abundant Harvest

The vinedresser works with the branches of the vine to maximize their fruit bearing. The branches that are burned (v. 6) can picture the following things: 1) unproductive Christians taken home to heaven prematurely, 2) dead wood in a believer's life (not the whole person), 3) those, like Judas, who professed to be followers of Jesus Christ but did not continue in faith, demonstrating that they were not genuine branches.

LIFE STEP Notice the progression of what Christ expects from His vines (15:2, 5): "fruit"; "more fruit"; and "much fruit"! Where are we in this process?

JOHN 15:12-27

WHAT IS THE WRITER SAYING?

HOW CAN I APPLY THIS TO MY LIFE?

Verse 13 is a dramatic principle, but should be easy to follow since Christ actually went one better by dying for His enemies! In the new set of circumstances, believers are not lowly servants but rather *friends* of Christ. This gives us great authority, privilege and responsibility. It is significant that the Church Age began on Pentecost, the anniversary of the giving of the Law. The great transition from the Age of Law to the Age of Grace begins on the same anniversary in the calendar. On that day, the disciples went from being children under the babysitting of the Law (Galatians 4) to adult sons in the Family of God! In their day, students chose the rabbi they wanted to study under. Christ says that He reversed the process, choosing them (v. 16). He chose them to be fruit bearers. The authority they have in prayer is to fulfill that commission.

John 15:18-27 discusses their relationship to the world. There is a chain of *guilt by association*. The world hates the Father therefore it also hates the one sent from the Father (the Son). Since it hates the Son, it also hates those associated with the Son. It also resents that the Son has chosen them out from the world (v. 19). The words of Jesus condemn the earthdwellers (v. 22). The works of Jesus do as well (v. 24). The Pharisees looked pretty good from the outside. It was only in the presence of Christ's words and works that they were exposed for what they were: whited sepulchres filled with dead men's bones. Verse 26 returns to the coming of the Comforter who will energize the disciples in their relationship to the world (as that of light, witness and testifier). Notice that His job is to magnify Christ, not Himself. Likewise, as we witness of Christ we are to magnify Him, not ourselves.

LIFE STEP We are free—free to choose to show our gratitude to our Savior by working for Him and His glory!

THURSDAY 27

JOHN 16:1-11

WHAT IS THE WRITER SAYING?

HOW CAN I APPLY THIS TO MY LIFE?

PRAY Pray for the salvation and protection of those serving in the military around the world.

In John 16:1-11 Christ discusses the relationship of believers to the Holy Spirit. The parents of the blind man in chapter 9 were afraid of being excommunicated from the synagogue. In chapter 12 we find out that some of the Pharisees did believe in Jesus but they were afraid to lose their position of prominence in society. Being put out of the synagogue was a serious event for a Jewish person. The Pharisees controlled the synagogue system (while the Sadducees controlled the Temple). Birth certificates, marriage certificates, bills of divorcement, and burial rights were all controlled by the synagogue. All of Jewish life and society centered around the synagogue. Jesus warns them of their own excommunication so they are not caught off guard when it happens. By warning them ahead of time He wants to inoculate them from despair leading to apostasy. The Apostle Paul is a good example of verse 2. Christ says it will be *profitable* to them for Him to leave (v. 7). This is the same word used by Caiaphas when he said that it was "expedient" for one man to die to save their position! The Old Testament does not say much about the Holy Spirit's ministry of conviction. Now we are informed of three areas in verse 8 which are explained in 9-11: "sin" (of unbelief, v. 9), "righteousness" (now that my example is no longer in front of their eyes, v. 10) and "judgment" (since Satan's and sinners' judgment is sealed, v. 11). Here are the special relationships and ministries of the Holy Spirit:

Spirit & World: Convict   (8)
Spirit & Disciples: Guide   (13)
Spirit & Christ: Glorify   (14)

LIFE STEP Satan is a defeated foe. He still roars and is dangerous in his death throes, but we can claim the victory in the power of the Spirit. The fear of man is a snare. Let us not be concerned about our appearance in man's eyes, but rather, let us serve Christ in obedience.

FRIDAY 27

JOHN 16:12-22

WHAT IS THE WRITER SAYING?

HOW CAN I APPLY THIS TO MY LIFE?

PRAY Iran – Pray that the number of Muslim-background people who have recently been coming to Jesus in rapidly increasing numbers will continue.

Jesus now turns to the Holy Spirit's teaching ministry. Beginning in John 14:26, Jesus pre-authenticates the whole of the New Testament writings. "Bring all things to your remembrance" (John 14:26) speaks of the Gospels. "Guide you into all truth" (v. 13) anticipates the Epistles. These letters gave the early church the direction and instruction it so desperately needed. "Shew you things to come" (v.13) refers to the book of Revelation. Today, we have the Scripture in totality. There is no need for new revelation. However, the Spirit of God still guides believers in understanding God's revealed Word found only in the Bible. "He shall glorify me" (v. 14); the ministry of the Holy Spirit is never to bring attention (glory) to Himself, but to bring glory to Christ.

Verse 16 is puzzling to the disciples since they had not comprehended the death, burial and <u>immediate</u> resurrection of Christ. Within twenty-four hours, He would be gone, but within another forty eight hours He would be with them again in His resurrected body (v. 16)! He does not spell it out to them, but further illustrates the significance of their mood swings over the next seventy-two hours. Their despair will be bitter as they hear the religious authorities mocking and rejoicing at His demise. The tables will abruptly turn, however. Imagine the demonic parties that came to a crashing halt when the news was screeched, "He's Alive"! Picture the white knuckles in the Temple Court. Visualize the sleepless nights in Pilate's palace. And think of the unalloyed joy that transformed this gloomy little band of cowards into a force that turned the Roman world upside down! Verse 22 predicts their joy at the other end of these events.

 LIFE STEP It is hard to think that anything could be better than having Jesus living with you in the flesh. In the plan of God, the indwelling Holy Spirit and His Written Word (which He has honored above His name) gives us a richer relationship with the Godhead!

SATURDAY 27

JOHN 16:23-33

WHAT IS THE WRITER SAYING?

HOW CAN I APPLY THIS TO MY LIFE?

PRAY Bulgaria – For believers to have the wisdom and discernment to avoid doctrinal error.

The Resurrection of Christ institutes a new doctrine of prayer. The disciples used to ask (*request between equals*) Christ directly for help. Now in His absence they will ask (*request from subordinate to superior*) the Father through (in the name of) the Son.

John 16:23-33 Christ mentions the pattern of prayer that is followed during the Church Age. We ask the Father in the name (authority) of the Son. This does not mean that it is out of the question to pray to Jesus or the Holy Spirit but that the normal pattern is to pray to the Father in the authority of the Son empowered by the Spirit. Jesus indicates that as the ministry of the Holy Spirit enlightens their thinking, they will understand spiritual truths plainly (v. 25). Three different Greek prepositions describe Christ's relationship to the Father in this section: v.27, "out from" (*para*: indicates authority or commission); v. 28, "came forth from" (*ek*: source); v. 30, "from" (*apo*: separation from the Father).

The disciples seem uncomfortable with the conversation and seek to end it by saying *yes, now we understand* (v. 29). Jesus is skeptical (v. 31), knowing that in a few hours the sheep would scatter (Zechariah 13:7). Even with that depressing acknowledgment, Christ leaves an example for us to follow in our lonely times as He rightly observes that the Father will be with Him. (This sets the stage for the horror of the three-hour period when even this was not true as He bore the sin of the entire world on His back and was temporarily abandoned by His own Father.)

"Overcome" (v. 33) is the same as "conquerors" in "we are more than conquerors" (Romans 8:37).

 LIFE STEP Christ's appreciation for His relationship with His Father should cause us to cultivate our own relationship with the Father. Otherwise it could be embarrassing arriving in heaven and not feeling as though we really know the Father!

SUNDAY 28

JOHN 17:1-13

WHAT IS THE WRITER SAYING?

HOW CAN I APPLY THIS TO MY LIFE?

PRAY Netherlands – Pray that spiritual depth, lasting discipleship, and effective outreach might be strengthened.

John 17 is the real *Lord's Prayer*, His *High-Priestly Prayer of Intercession*. (Matthew 6 is better called The *Disciples' Prayer*). The structure of John 17 is very interesting. The *bull's eye* is *eternal life* with the following three sections, forming three concentric circles, each section broader in scope than the former.
1) Verses 1-5 have two commands: *glorify thy Son* (that is, His authority as the Son to give eternal life due to His work on earth) and *glorify thou me* (that is, return my person to its pre-incarnate glory with the Father).
2) Verses 6-19 have two more commands: *Keep them* (that is, protect my disciples from evil) and *sanctify them* (that is, set them apart for the continuation of my work on earth).

3) Verses 20-26 contain two requests: *I ask* (v. 20) is a request for unity among all believers and *I desire* (v. 24) is a request to unite all believers with their Savior in glory. *Eternal Life* (v. 2) is defined, not as endless existence (although it is that!) but as a living contact with God. *Know* is in the present tense, which means that even in heaven the contact and growth is ongoing throughout all eternity! (*Know* means more than just imparted knowledge.) The *life* now enjoyed by the disciples is revealed in this prayer as enlightenment (v. 8), preservation (except Judas whose betrayal was predicted, Psalm 41:9, vv. 11-12) and joy (v. 13). Tomorrow we will add employment (v. 18), sanctification (v. 19), unity (v. 23) and fellowship (v. 24).

LIFE STEP Eternal life is not luxurious idleness, but purposeful labor for the Creator, both now and for eternity! What activities can we add to our schedule today that would result in a "Well done good and faithful servant" when we arrive on heaven's shore?

JOHN 17:14-26

WHAT IS THE WRITER SAYING?

HOW CAN I APPLY THIS TO MY LIFE?

The "Life" (v. 3) now enjoyed by the disciples is further revealed in this prayer as: 1) joy (v. 13), 2) employment (v. 18 *So send I you!*), 3) sanctification (*to set apart for God's use*)(v. 19), and 4) unity of common belief, worship and service (17:23), which is not the same as *Unanimity of Mind* (such as Programmed Computers); *Uniformity of Practice* (such as Robots); nor *Union of Organization* (such as a Bureaucratic Monstrosity) and finally, 5) fellowship (v. 24) now and for eternity!

In verse 17 note the close association between sanctification and revealed truth. Verse 18 likens our mission to Christ's. We take up where He left off. Back in 10:16, Jesus talks about the "other sheep …which are not of this fold," referring to the Gentiles that would come to Him as a result of His death on the Cross. Now He specifically prays for them (us!) in 17:20. With these eleven disciples there begins a long chain that reaches down the corridors of time to the twenty-first century, which has resulted in my salvation! There is much work to be done, but Christ looks forward to that grand day when labor is over and we can all meet in the Father's house. Jesus is anxious to introduce us to His Father! His Father is a very prominent theme in John, occurring over 120 times. "Holy Father" only occurs once in the Bible, in 17:11. The unity of the disciples was important for the evangelistic outreach of the early Church. 17:23 says that their unity will be a signal to the world that Jesus was the Messiah. Humanly speaking, it is only because of the united testimony of the transformed disciples that the Church was founded.

LIFE STEP What can a watching world conclude by the relationship of believers in your town? Are you a promoter of unity or are you weakening the local Christian witness by sowing discord?

JOHN 18:1-14

WHAT IS THE WRITER SAYING?

HOW CAN I APPLY THIS TO MY LIFE?

We now enter the fifth major section of John, the Period of Consummation (18-20). Back in 14:31, Jesus announced that they would leave the upper room and head for the Garden of Gethsemane. Here in 18:1, they are just arriving at the garden. Apparently chapters 15-17 were spoken en route or they stopped at another private location for these lectures. The other Gospel accounts speak of Him praying in the garden, although here in John He has already prayed an extensive prayer. It could be that the prayer of John 17 was spoken in the hearing of the disciples <u>for their benefit</u> whereas the other Gospels mention the private agonizing that He did in the garden in private with only a few of the details known by the disciples (because they were asleep!). The Kidron was a steep valley between Jerusalem (The Temple Mount) and the Mt. of Olives. A stream runs through it all the way down to the Dead Sea 17 miles to the east. Today it provides a strip of green lushness in an otherwise bleak wilderness.

The band (*cohort*) of men that Judas brought would number 300-600 soldiers. Christ responds with the name of Jehovah, "I Am (he)." This display of raw power is a reminder that Jesus did not have His life taken from Him, but that He laid it down willingly. The prediction that verse 9 fulfills was only minutes old, having been prayed in 17:12! Peter (!) tries to make it happen. Only problem, he doesn't know what "it" is! Jesus stops Him from any further embarrassment and announces His intentions to go with the men. He is taken to Annas, the real power behind the current High Priest Caiaphas who had been deposed by the Romans earlier for political reasons.

LIFE STEP Only the hardness of the human heart, blindness of sin and trickery of Satan could have produced this type of foolishness! How faithful are you to study God's Word that you might know truth from error?

JOHN 18:15-27

WHAT IS THE WRITER SAYING?

HOW CAN I APPLY THIS TO MY LIFE?

"Another disciple" was John who doesn't mention his name out of humility, but is the best candidate, especially as he seems to have come from a wealthy family who would move in such circles. Only two of the twelve have stayed with Jesus, nine have scattered already. The dignity of Jesus is in stark contrast to the seething anger of these men. Not only is His first response logically accurate, but His rebuke to the one who struck Him is also eminently reasonable. It also includes a legal term, "bear witness" which contains an implied request for a fair trial. The legality of these *court* procedures is suspect, but then such niceties are difficult to observe when you've already tried and executed the man in your heart! As Isaiah 53 predicts, the suffering servant will be the victim of a judicial murder. Interwoven with Jesus' questioning is the drama of Peter's denials in the courtyard. Comparing the other gospels, some have complained that there is a discrepancy on the identity of his questioners. We need to realize that *selective reporting* is not the equivalent of *error* or *deception*. Many people around the fire could have chimed in questioning Peter. Each author reports the questioner that caught his attention in the retelling of the events of that fateful night. The bottom line is that Peter denied the Lord three times, just as Christ predicted just hours before. In the parallel account in Mark, Peter uses a typical legal formula to deny knowledge of Christ, "I know not, neither understand I what thou sayest." He then calls curses down on himself if he were lying. As Jesus is transferred to His next interview, the cock crows and eyes meet, bringing instant shame and regret to Peter that is only relieved after his interchange with Jesus in chapter 21.

LIFE STEP When the heat was on, most of the disciples scattered. How will you fare if persecution comes to you? Jesus remained calm under the pressure of examination. His strength is available to us as we stand for Him!

THURSDAY 28

JOHN 18:28-40

WHAT IS THE WRITER SAYING?

HOW CAN I APPLY THIS TO MY LIFE?

PRAY Belarus – Pray for renewal and reformation within the Russian Orthodox Church.

Jesus endured a total of six interviews. Three were Jewish, three were Roman. He met with Annas, Caiaphas and then the entire Jewish Supreme Court (Sanhedrin), which numbered seventy men plus the presiding High Priest. The Jewish portion took place through the night (in violation of Jewish law). The "cock crow" was a Roman watch in the night, 3:00 a.m. Mark 15:1 indicates that the Sanhedrin finalized their official ruling very early in the morning (perhaps in a vain attempt at legality since a man was not to be sentenced the day he was tried). Since they did not have the right of execution under Roman Law, He had to be taken to a Roman Court. He met with Pilate, then Herod Antipas (since Jesus lived in his territory) and finally was condemned to die in a second interview with Pilate. The "Hall of Judgment" was probably the Fortress of Antonia that overlooked the Temple Mount area and housed soldiers for riot control. The Jewish authorities were not willing to defile themselves (!) by entering a Gentile living area. There was no love lost between Pilate and the Jews, as is felt in the sullen words exchanged (Pilate had already offended the Jews by bringing Roman standards with pagan images on them into the holy city). The Jewish form of execution was stoning. God in His sovereignty works it out that Christ be crucified the Roman way in fulfillment of Old Testament prophecy (v. 32 see Deuteronomy. 21:22; Psalm 16; 22). "What is Truth" (v. 38) is answered in the form of the very one standing in front of him! Barabbas (v. 40) is Aramaic for *son of the father*. He goes free and "The Son of The Father" is crucified!

 LIFE STEP The world seeks truth. Pilate is amused by the Jewish authorities' fear of the meek man in front of him and the philosophical turn of the conversation. If only he had paid closer attention!

JOHN 19:1-11

WHAT IS THE WRITER SAYING?

HOW CAN I APPLY THIS TO MY LIFE?

PRAY Nicaragua – God's guidance for pastors counseling the many devastated by death, poverty, and divorce.

Pilate was Roman Governor of Judea from A.D. 26-36. He had a history of stormy relationships with the Jews that displeased his Roman superiors. He was anxious to avoid having another bad report sent back to Rome. The crucifixion of Christ is variously dated from A.D.29 to 33. In any case, Pilate would have been in Judea for a number of years and would have several years thereafter to consider the error of condemning an innocent man. Despite his care here, he eventually is recalled by Rome for misadministration in another matter. Pilate was not willing to execute an innocent man and flogged Jesus to satisfy inherent bloodlust and perhaps arouse pity to let Jesus go. He also allowed his soldiers to take out their frustrations on the Jews by mocking their "king." The Romans played a game called "The Game of the Kings" to while away time. The climax involved mocking an innocent by-stander, which might be the cultural background to their mockery of Jesus.

The original charge brought against Jesus before Pilate was treason (18:33) since the Sanhedrin thought that would be easier than explaining the real charge of "blasphemy," which now slips out in their anger (19:7), further confusing the issue. Jesus maintains a dignified silence (v. 9), fulfilling Isaiah 53:7. Jesus minimizes Pilate's role in His execution, placing the burden on the theocratic representative of the chosen people, Caiaphas (v. 11).

LIFE STEP Pilate was in over his head, both in Judea and in this trial. You might lose (in this life) if you live by principle. You will always lose if you don't.

JOHN 19:12-22

WHAT IS THE WRITER SAYING?

HOW CAN I APPLY THIS TO MY LIFE?

PRAY Costa Rica – Pray for the Holy Spirit to break the bonds of materialism, apathy, and ritualism.

So blinded are the Jewish authorities by their hatred of Jesus of Nazareth (a fellow Jew!) that they defend the pagan emperor that they otherwise would resent (an unclean Gentile! v. 12). This alarmed Pilate so he called the sixth and final trial. "The Pavement" refers to the stones lining the floor of the judgment hall. In the language of the Jews, it was called the hill ("Gabbatha") as Pilate sat elevated in his judgment seat.

Pilate skillfully baits his enemies into professing a heresy of their own: "We have no king but Caesar" (v. 15). At 9:00 a.m. the decision is made (vv. 14, 16).

The point of Roman crucifixion was two-fold. First was the agony of the event, designed to discourage rebellion. The other was the total humiliation from the cruelty of carrying your own instrument of death (like digging your own grave) to the shame of public nakedness to the prying eyes and scorn of those who pass by reading the published charges. Pilate further insulted the Jewish authorities by having "The King of the Jews" placarded between two common thieves! Golgotha "skull" has been identified as a rocky outcropping just north of the current (Turkish) walls of Jerusalem, called "Gordon's Calvary." It is a nice visualization of what the site might have looked like, but probably the real site was at The Church of the Holy Sepulchre, which is inside the Turkish Walls today but was just outside to the northwest in Christ's day. John does not detail the horrors of the crucifixion. Archaeologists have uncovered skeletons with the spikes going through the wrists and heel bones. Death came through a combination of blood loss, shock and suffocation.

LIFE STEP We are physical beings. It is natural to concentrate on the physical horrors of crucifixion. Don't forget the spiritual ramifications of the humiliation, selfless love, sin bearing and the spiritual death that were also involved.

JOHN 19:23-30

WHAT IS THE WRITER SAYING?

HOW CAN I APPLY THIS TO MY LIFE?

PRAY Romania – Funding and godly staff for the expansion and establishment of Bible schools and seminaries.

Psalm 22:18 and 69:21 are being fulfilled with the parting of Jesus' garments and the drinking of vinegar. You would have to stay up many nights inventing *fulfillments* of such passages in a fictitious story. God's sovereignty is evident, even down to the number of soldiers (four) present at His crucifixion (v. 24) and their casting of lots (some sort of random numbering device like dice) for His tunic.

Also present are His mother, her sister (while the passage could be read to understand her name was Mary also, this would seem highly unlikely), two other devoted women, and John. While John does not record Jesus' prayer for His executioners (Luke 23:34) or His pardon of the repentant thief (Luke 23:43), he does record His words to His mother and the *disciple He loved*. His concern for His mother is touching. *Woman* was not a disrespectful way to address one's mother in that culture (as also in John 2:4). "Behold thy son" was instructive to Mary as He commends her to the care of John, *whom He loved*. The care of a widow was the responsibility of the oldest son. Jesus entrusts his mother to the care of John, rather than His unbelieving brothers (7:5).

Jesus takes a drink to clear His throat for His final triumphant declaration (vv. 29-30). Notice that He controlled His life to the very end and at the proper time He dismissed His spirit from His body (see John 10:18) after the victorious statement, "It (the provision for the salvation of mankind) is finished!"

 LIFE STEP Jesus' love and concern for others was evident to the end. Even on the cross, His thoughts were for the needs of those with Him. Lord, help us to see with your eyes!

JOHN 19:31-42

WHAT IS THE WRITER SAYING?

HOW CAN I APPLY THIS TO MY LIFE?

Despite suggestions for a Wednesday or Thursday crucifixion, Friday still is probable. All the biblical data can be explained to fit with a Friday crucifixion and it has the respectability of tradition behind it. (Lest we be too skeptical of *tradition*, let's remember that we also worship on Sunday for the same reason. Sunday worship can be illustrated, but not commanded from Scripture!) This particular Sabbath was a *high day* because it occurred during Passover (either the first full day of Passover or the first day of the seven-day Feast of Unleavened Bread). It is possible that Christ celebrated the Passover with his disciples Thursday night according to one religious calendar (Essene) and then was crucified the very afternoon that Jewish fathers were butchering their lambs for the Passover meal Friday night according to the other calendar (Pharisaic).

John injects strong emotion in verses 35-37, identifying himself as an eyewitness (*the disciple* of v. 26) of the proof of Christ's death (*water* is the plasma that separates from the red blood cells once the heart stops) and His fulfillment of yet more specific Old Testament prophecies (Exodus 12:46; Zechariah 12:10). Two influential men procure the body, allowing it to suffer no more indignities. Nicodemus supplies a large amount of spices, such as would be used in a royal burial (2 Chronicles 16:14).

LIFE STEP Not many mighty, not many noble are called into the family of God. Queen Victoria once praised the Lord for the letter "m" as it saved her from *not any*!

JOHN 20:1-10

WHAT IS THE WRITER SAYING?

HOW CAN I APPLY THIS TO MY LIFE?

Another argument for a Friday crucifixion is that the women were coming on Sunday to further adorn the body for burial, something that should be done as soon as possible, in this case, the Sabbath day intervening.

It is interesting that John records Mary Magdalene as the first eyewitness of the empty tomb (although she doesn't realize that Christ is alive until v.16). She was a devoted follower of Jesus ever since He cast seven demons out of her (Luke 8). Actually, if John was making this story up he would have chosen a more respectable first witness since in that day women were not allowed to testify in a court of law.

John was younger and faster than Peter but not as bold, and it was Peter who entered the tomb first to inspect the proof of Jesus' resurrection, the empty tomb, and the abandoned grave clothes. That point in human history is the launch pad of the church, the event that turned cowards into dynamic, fearless testifiers of the risen Lord!

The *ironic tragedy* of the life of Christ which is resolved in the resurrection is this: "Although virtuous, He suffered all possible indignities; majestic, He died in disgrace; powerful, He expired in weakness. He claimed to possess the water of Life but died thirsty; to be The Light of the World, but died in darkness; to be The Good Shepherd, but died in the fangs of wolves; to be the Truth, but was executed as an imposter; to be Life itself, but He died quicker than the average crucifixion victim. The greatest example of righteousness the world had ever seen became a helpless victim of evil!" (Merrill Tenney, John, p. 52.)

LIFE STEP The resurrection of Jesus Christ was a powerful demonstration of victory won over sin and death. Those who know Christ as Savior will experience this newness of life.

WEDNESDAY 29

JOHN 20:11-18

WHAT IS THE WRITER SAYING?

Handwritten notes:
READ Gen 37-50
Lauren's cousin
Neill - praise
Robin's surgery
Shay

HOW CAN I APPLY THIS TO MY LIFE?

PRAY Cayman Islands – For the wealth of the island to be used to extend the Gospel.

John explained in verse 9 that no one expected Christ to rise immediately from the dead. It wasn't until after the resurrection that they began to understand it from Scripture (such as Psalm 16:10, "Thou wilt not suffer thine holy one to see corruption.").

Mary missed Peter and John on the way back to the tomb and didn't receive any encouragement from their newfound conviction. She was sobbing broken heartedly (literally, *wailing* as in 11:33) when she decides to look inside. She sees the angels and talks with them, but nothing is registering. She must have thought it perfectly natural for two men to be sitting in a tomb! As she turns, she notices another man and launches into a fresh attempt to locate the body of her Lord. The inability of Mary and others (like the two disciples on the road to Emmaus) to recognize the Lord at first argues strongly against the theory that the resurrection is a myth of wishful thinking. Finally, through the blur of her tears, noting the urgency in the familiar voice, she finally realizes that she is talking to her Lord! Two natural acts followed: first, use of the familiar name, *Master* (Rabboni, *My Teacher*, normally used in prayer to God Himself) and then a grip that hinted she would never let go. Jesus did not want Mary to cling to Him because she needed to make the transition from reliance on Him to reliance on the Holy Spirit.

LIFE STEP

Those forgiven much, love much. Jesus of Nazareth meant the world to Mary Magdalene, physically, spiritually, and emotionally. The day He died; all her lights went out. Now, after forty-eight hours of weeping, her nightmare is over! What an explosion of joy.

JOHN 20:19-31

WHAT IS THE WRITER SAYING?

HOW CAN I APPLY THIS TO MY LIFE?

The word of Christ's resurrection must have spread like wildfire through both the ranks of the disciples and the Sanhedrin. Matthew records the attempts of the religious authorities to silence the *rumor* of the resurrection with hush money.

John does not tell us how many people were gathered with the disciples. They were afraid of the Jewish authorities, but imagine how they must have been dissecting every little detail that Mary, Peter, and John could provide. Suddenly, without a door opening, Christ is standing there in their midst! (Item #1: Glorified bodies can pass through solids!) He could have said a million different things but He settles on a routine *Hello* (*shalom aleichim*). The routine greeting of peace also allayed their fears, both of the sudden appearance and concern about the cowardly behavior less than seventy-two hours earlier. His next comment concerned their commission, which requires empowerment (v. 22) symbolized by His breath (creative power) and actualized at Pentecost.

Since only God can forgive sin, verse 23 is talking about the results of the disciples' preaching ministry. Some will respond, be saved and as a result, have their sins forgiven by God. Thomas (*the Twin*) was not there and will forever be known as *Doubting Thomas* by his comments. Before we are too hard on poor old Thomas, let's remember that the very proof that he requested had already been provided for those who were there that night (v. 20). Those who believe having not seen the resurrected Lord (like us) are commended for their belief (v. 29). Thomas' testimony is the fitting conclusion to John's thesis, and John says so in verses 30 and 31.

 LIFE STEP We would like Jesus to be physically here, but the power of the Word and the internal confirmation of the Spirit are sufficient for us today.

FRIDAY 29

JOHN 21:1-14

WHAT IS THE WRITER SAYING?

HOW CAN I APPLY THIS TO MY LIFE?

PRAY Madagascar – Revival as well as biblical teaching and leadership are urgently needed in the churches of this proverty stricken ilsand nation.

John 21 is the final section of our outline: the commission. Having established the believability of the life and message of Jesus Christ, John now tells us how this message was spread throughout the world.

Seven of the eleven disciples gather together in their home territory of Galilee. That Christ would appear to them on their familiar home ground negated any lingering sense they might have had that, perhaps, what they experienced in Jerusalem was a product of their confusion and fear in a hostile environment. Once again, Christ appears to people who should have recognized Him, but they do not. His question implies that He knows they didn't catch any fish. Now that it was daylight, the fish would be able to see and avoid the nets. They nevertheless obey the voice of the stranger on the shore with startling results. Christ had called them to the ministry with a similar miracle three years earlier (Luke 5).

Propriety (not necessarily modesty) called for Peter to be properly dressed to greet his Lord, despite the fact that it would be harder to swim thus attired. The Lord had already procured some fish (small sardines), which are cooking on the breakfast fire, a considerate gesture for men who had worked all night. We can only imagine the rush of memories, as Christ broke the bread and fish and fed them once again from His own hands. It left an indelible mark on Peter as he refers to it in Acts 10. This meal is a not-so-subtle reminder that He can provide for all of their needs. Just as a miraculous draught of fish initially convinced them to leave all and follow Him (Luke 5), they are to do so once again.

LIFE STEP Hard work is therapeutic. It is proper to be busy as long as we are sensitive to the Lord's direction in our life when higher business calls.

JOHN 21:15-25

WHAT IS THE WRITER SAYING?

HOW CAN I APPLY THIS TO MY LIFE?

PRAY Uganda – For new missionaries to adapt quickly, live the Word, and persevere amidst opposition.

It is not clear what Peter's love is being compared to. More than he loves his fishing equipment? More than he loves his brethren? More than their love for Christ? At any rate, Peter had publicly denied the Lord three times after protesting greater love than the rest. 1 Corinthians 15:5 indicates that the day of the resurrection Christ met with Peter privately where presumably appropriate apologies were given and accepted. Now Christ gives Peter three chances to publicly affirm his chastened love for the Lord in front of the other disciples. Peter is not confident enough to tell the Lord that he "agapes" Him (self-sacrificing love – love given with no thought of a return) but "phileo" is strong enough (brotherly love as in Philadelphia, The *City of Brotherly Love*). Christ probes the deepest in the third question by using "phileo" saying, "Okay, you can't say 'agape,' but do you <u>really</u> 'phileo' me?" Both "lambs" and "sheep" are mentioned representing all kinds of believers in different stages of development. Two aspects of "shepherding" are mentioned by the master shepherd: feeding the flock and caring for all their needs. After giving Peter (and by extension all believers) His commission, he predicts Peter's death by martyrdom. This is not designed to cause anxiety but perhaps part of the healing process as Peter is told he will one day actually do what he was afraid to do previously – lay down his life for the Lord. By tradition, he was crucified upside down at his own request because he didn't feel worth to die exactly as his Lord did! John asserts that this is an eyewitness account of the Greatest Story Ever Told. His years of service, communion and reflection have made him quite the wordsmith as well. He closes his gospel with a precious tribute to the grandeur of the Greatest Man Who Has Ever Lived!

LIFE STEP God is so gracious. Not only does He forgive our sins, He also uses us in His work, giving us reward for what He plans, energizes and executes through our lives!

ROMANS

BIBLE BOOK INTRODUCTION

Dr. Marshall Wicks

At the time of writing Paul has not yet visited the church at Rome. This is an important fact to keep in mind. In many of his letters Paul writes to shore up the things he has already told the church or to address some practical or theological problem that has arisen since his last visit. This would lead us to believe that Paul is writing from a much broader perspective. He wants to be sure that this church have the same basic understanding of salvation that he has taught elsewhere.

This book is therefore more theoretical in nature and assumes that the church needs to have a thorough presentation of the materials that Paul usually would have taught when he first came to a city. Because of this, the occasion of writing is not as important as it usually is in interpretation. Paul is not addressing any particular problem, but rather, is giving a general account of his doctrine of salvation. This, of all Paul's writings, is the most systematic and detailed. In it he explains in the most logical terms possible his understanding of the gospel. It is very possible that this writing represents Paul's usual manner of presenting the gospel when he first came to a new city.

One also needs to keep in mind that Paul is not teaching a new gospel. Paul documents all of his primary assertions via the Old Testament. This gospel may have new teaching aids but it is still the unchanged gospel constantly preached throughout the Scriptures.

According to Romans 15:22-26, Paul writes this letter from Corinth just prior to heading to Jerusalem with the gift that he collected in Greece and Macedonia. This would be at the end of his third missionary journey. His purposes for writing were 1) to gain support for the evangelizing of Spain, 2) to clarify the doctrine of salvation to a church he had not founded, and 3) to be an encouragement to all the believers in Rome.

The theme of the book is God's righteousness and how that righteousness can be transferred to sinful mankind. The key verses are Romans 1:16-17 "For I am not ashamed of the gospel of Christ: for it is the power of God unto salvation to every one that believeth; to the Jew first, and also to the Greek. For therein is the righteousness of God revealed from faith to faith: as it is written, 'The just shall live by faith'." Here is the outline that we will follow in our presentation of this epistle:

Romans: God's Righteousness

Introduction: 1:1-17

I. Justification: The Imputation of God's Righteousness (1:18–4)

   a. The need for imputed righteousness (1:18–3:20)
   b. The provision of imputed righteousness (3:21-26)
   c. The explanation of imputed righteousness (3:27-31)
   d. The example of imputed righteousness (4:1-25)

II. Sanctification: The Process of God's Righteousness (5–8)

    a. The basis of sanctification (5:1-21)
    b. The nature of sanctification (6)
    c. The freedom of sanctification (7:1-25)
    d. The power of sanctification (8:1-39)

III. Vindication: The Defense of God's Righteousness (9–11)

    a. Election is a matter of divine choice (9:1-29)
    b. Rejection is a matter of human choice (9:30–10:21)
    c. Rejection is not necessarily terminal (11:1 33)

IV. Application: The Practice of God's Righteousness (12:1–15:13)

    a. The believer and his God (12:1-2)
    b. The believer and the church (12:3-13)
    c. The believer and the lost (12:14-21)
    d. The believer and the government (13:1-7)
    e. The believer and his possessions (13:8-13)
    f. The believer and his decisions (14:1–15:13)

Conclusion: 15:14–16:27

ROMANS 1:1-7

WHAT IS THE WRITER SAYING?

HOW CAN I APPLY THIS TO MY LIFE?

PRAY Slovakia – For the church planting to be successful in bringing the Good News to many unbelievers.

Paul invariably uses his introduction to cover more than the usual, "Hello, how are you? I'm fine," etc. He uses it to set the theme and the tone for the rest of the letter. In this case his introduction serves three important functions: it is a standard salutation and greeting, it describes Paul's relationship to the Roman church, and it states the theme of the epistle.

Verses 1-7 are the salutation. This is the commonly used format for addressing a letter. Verse one identifies the author. Paul describes himself as a "bondservant," which literally means *slave*, and a slave has but one primary purpose in life: to serve his master. As a slave, Paul has been given a task by his master. That task is to be an apostle. An apostle is an appointed substitute who spoke with the full authority of the one who had appointed him. According to verse 5, Paul's position was given to him for a purpose, namely, evangelism, specifically to evangelize the Gentiles.

In verse 6 we see God's sovereignty. Paul was called to both salvation and vocation. He was called first to be a saint and then an apostle! In like manner we too are called as "saints," that is, *holy ones*. The word translated "holy" in the Bible basically means *separate* or *distinct*. God expects his children to live a different kind of life from the world, not just different in external matters but different all the way to the very core. This is a different kind of life from start to finish. It is no longer we living but it is Jesus living through us.

LIFE STEP The progression established in this passage is important. Paul was first called to be a servant and then to serve in the capacity of apostle. Christ humbled Himself and then God highly exalted Him. Look for a place to serve and God will provide the opportunities to excel.

ROMANS 1:8-17

WHAT IS THE WRITER SAYING?

HOW CAN I APPLY THIS TO MY LIFE?

PRAY Ecuador – For an end to anti-missionary propaganda from anthropologists, traders, jungle exploiters, and those with a political agenda.

How the church at Rome started cannot be determined with any certainty. From verse 8 it is clear that Paul has some knowledge about this church – he has heard of them perhaps by word of mouth. In verses 9 10 we see a little of Paul's prayer life. His prayers for these believers are both regular and specific. His greatest desire was to come to them. He longs to see these people, many of whom he has never met before. Why? To minister to them and to be ministered to by them. Paul always viewed the ministry as a two-way street. Notice the obligation that Paul feels in verse 14. Why are we under obligation? Because we will spend an eternity in heaven, but the lost an eternity in hell!

Verses 16-17 state the theme of the epistle. The word "gospel" means *the good news* and is defined in 1 Corinthians 15 as "that Christ died for our sins according to the Scriptures, and that he was buried, and that he rose again the third day according to the Scriptures." This gospel is the "the power of God." This means that the gospel alone is God's chosen means to save men. It is the ultimate display of power in the universe. "From faith to faith" clarifies that salvation starts by faith, ends by faith and is by faith all the way through. Every aspect of salvation is by faith. Habakkuk 2:4b is quoted by Paul to support his "from faith to faith" claim. The verse in its Old Testament context is saying that the man who is truly righteous will live a life controlled by his faith, namely, faithfully. He lives according to the Word of God as he knows it. The verse does not talk about becoming a righteous man, but about what make a righteous man tick. Faith is the mainspring and the only spring for true righteous living. Any other so-called righteousness does not count with God.

 LIFE STEP Faith is the key to pleasing God, not works. Any system that involves following rules and regulations in order to impress God will always fail because we cannot do anything to impress God.

TUESDAY 30

ROMANS 1:18-32

WHAT IS THE WRITER SAYING?

HOW CAN I APPLY THIS TO MY LIFE?

PRAY Portugal – For the churches to raise up full–time workers of the Gospel.

In 1:18–3:20 it is Paul's purpose to demonstrate that all mankind stands in need of God's imputed righteousness in order to protect them from God's wrath. "Imputed" means that God *gives it* to us, not that we somehow conjure it up through our own efforts. Paul views mankind in two categories, those who have received special revelation (Scripture) and those who have not. He then sets out to prove three facts. Fact 1: those who have never heard are still without excuse and therefore under God's wrath (1:18 32). Fact 2: those who have received God's Word are unable to keep it and are therefore under God's wrath (2:1–3:8). Fact 3: if those with and those without are equally under God's wrath, it follows that all men, without exception, must be guilty before God. (3:9 20). In 1:18 23 we are told that God's righteous nature forces Him to condemn all men from heaven, because they have suppressed the truth within them, the image of God (v. 19), and the truth in nature (v. 20). Therefore, they have no defense. "They became fools" because they preferred their own wisdom to God's; what could be more foolish? They stopped worshipping God and replaced Him with gods of their own invention (pagan worship) and even themselves (evolutionary humanism).

In verses 24 32 we see God's threefold response to man's guilt. First they fall into heterosexual immorality (vv. 24-25), then homosexual immorality (vv. 26-27) and then finally immoral exploitation (vv. 28-32).

A quick walk through history will verify these facts. Successful cultures have always started with strong family values. As those values erode so does the vitality of a nation. Only a commitment to God's truth can keep a family or a nation from the slide described in these verses. When we lose contact with God's truth, we commit intellectual and moral suicide.

 LIFE STEP
Paul's purpose in these verses has been to establish the *without excuse-ness* of those who possess no written revelation whatsoever.
Man's problem has never been a lack of truth; it has forever been the willful rejection of the truth God does supply.

ROMANS 2:1-16

WHAT IS THE WRITER SAYING?

HOW CAN I APPLY THIS TO MY LIFE?

Today's passage discusses the fact that knowledge of the law by itself generally produces legalism. The one who *passes judgment* is the one who considers himself knowledgeable on the Law of Moses – religious leaders, teachers, etc. Such a person is no more able to keep the law than the worst sinner. To judge others concerning things that we ourselves do is hypocritical. That is exactly why Jesus condemns the Pharisees in the Gospels. The one who violates any part of the Law violates the whole and is therefore guilty before God (James 2:10). Since no mere human can keep every part of the law, all stand guilty of all infractions.

From verse 9 we see that *judgment* (not salvation) is always based on works, "man that doeth evil." This means that there is no advantage to having the Law if one doesn't keep the law. Those without Law are judged by one standard and those with the law are judged by another. There is no partiality with God – positive or negative. Both God's rewards and God's judgments play no favorites. Time, place, or race does not matter. With respect to judgment it is not how much truth a person knows, but how much truth he lives.

The "work of the law written in their hearts" applies to all men because all are created in the image of God and have some innate knowledge of right and wrong, thus the "conscience also bearing witness" to those who have no law. It is a guide in matters of morality. It is not perfect, but it is sufficient to condemn mankind. It is only a tool for judging, not a tool for justifying. All law, including the conscience, is works-based and ultimately can only condemn.

 Judgment is based on works. Justification is based on faith. The two are mutually exclusive and therefore one must exit the works system before entering the faith system. Works are a product of salvation, not a means to it.

THURSDAY 30

ROMANS 2:17-29

WHAT IS THE WRITER SAYING?

HOW CAN I APPLY THIS TO MY LIFE?

Paul has just stated that it is the *doers of the law* who shall be blessed; however, he now clarifies that doing the law is impossible. Paul shows that even teachers of the law break the law. He first mentions stealing. Do we keep track of the small things we *borrow*? What about another person's time? Or pen ink? Or shampoo? Next is the commandment regarding adultery. Jesus said in Matthew 5:27-28, "You have heard that it was said… 'You shall not commit adultery,' but I say to you that whoever looks at a woman to lust for her has already committed adultery with her in his heart." The third is idolatry. "Dost thou commit sacrilege" refers to offering the proper respect due to God. Could anyone say that they had not missed a ¼ cent of the tithe?

Paul next turns to circumcision. This is even more devastating. What man needs is a circumcision "of the heart." See Deuteronomy 10:16; 30:6 and Jeremiah 4:4. Think about it. What would be the consequence of actually going into a person's chest cavity and cutting off a piece of their heart? It would kill them. This kind of circumcision is humanly impossible.

We must come to the conclusion that salvation is humanly impossible. If righteousness must begin at the heart and work its way out, a person must be righteous in order to be circumcised, and that is impossible. If it cannot begin at the skin and work its way in, there is no way that anyone can accomplish it. Actually, verse 27 argues that those who have circumcision but fail to keep the law (which is true for all men) are in worse condition than those who are not circumcised.

 LIFE STEP This ought to be depressing to everyone who ever thought that they could do something in order to merit salvation. Salvation cannot be earned. It is only available by faith. Any road to salvation that includes any human requirement other than faith is a broad road that leads to destruction.

ROMANS 3:1-8

WHAT IS THE WRITER SAYING?

HOW CAN I APPLY THIS TO MY LIFE?

PRAY For Local Church Ministries missionaries as they prepare for International Teens Involved competitions and summer camp ministry.

Paul in these verses anticipates and answers the objection that he is in some way criticizing the Law. Paul argues that it is a great benefit to have the Law of Moses. It is not evil just because it brings greater judgment. Greater opportunity always brings greater responsibility. Paul argues that it is greatly desirable. We should desire to have God's law, but realize that the mere possession of it or outward conformity to it is not sufficient. It is the misunderstanding of the purpose of the law that causes it to become a judge rather than a protector. If we choose to use a chainsaw to brush our teeth, we should not blame the saw when we end up toothless. However, this misuse of the law will not nullify the faithfulness of God. Believing the chainsaw is a toothbrush does not make it one. Because we do not believe something, that does not affect whether it is true or not. It is God's truth that governs the universe, not what men do or do not believe.

When Paul suggests in parenthesis that he "speaks as a man," he is simply saying that he is using a human illustration. When he asks, "Why am I also judged as a sinner," he is anticipating the human argument that if God is glorified by my sinning, why shouldn't I just keep on sinning. Just because we cannot keep the law does not mean that it is acceptable to break the law carelessly. This is an argument that people still use today to reject or abuse the privilege of eternal security. It is as wrong today as it was in Paul's day. The Law was never meant to make a man righteous; but that does not mean it is useless. Remember, the chainsaw is a very useful tool when it is used to cut down trees.

LIFE STEP Possession of written revelation from God, even though it is good to have, only makes us guiltier before God. True, it is our only hope, but *without our response in faith* it can only increase our condemnation.

SATURDAY 30

ROMANS 3:9-20

WHAT IS THE WRITER SAYING?

HOW CAN I APPLY THIS TO MY LIFE?

Paul wraps up this section with a sweeping overview of man's universal need for justification. He offers as his final and most powerful proof the actual words of Scripture. Verses 10 12 emphasize the extent of man's sin. Verses 13 18 emphasize the specific character of man's sin. The final two verses (vv.19-20) form a conclusion to the whole section. Paul's statement in verse 9 is the thesis, which verses 10-17 verify. It is his contention that all men, whether they have Scripture or whether they have never had an opportunity to even hear the name of Jesus, stand equally condemned under the eternal weight of sin. They are absolutely without hope from the human perspective.

The generic description of "sinner," because it can be applied to all people, can very easily lose its sting. For that reason Paul begins to give a list of some of our specific sins, not a very flattering list by any standard. It is clearly the intention of the apostle to make us squirm. Not only are we sinners, but we commit horrible sins.

According to verses 19 20, the law is only valuable as a means to diagnose sin. It has no power to cure it. The law is a tool that has a very specific purpose. As long as we use it for the purpose for which it was intended we will be all right. But, when we try to use it as a way to merit righteousness we not only insult the law, we jeopardize our own spiritual wellbeing. Thus it is with the law; it shows us why we are going to hell, but it does not provide any way of escaping hell.

LIFE STEP By this time any first-time reader of the Book of Romans should feel pretty bleak about their situation. It's hopeless. That's the great thing about this salvation that we share; it was never designed for the righteous. It is designed for sinners. Blessed are the poor in spirit.

SUNDAY 31

ROMANS 3:21-31

WHAT IS THE WRITER SAYING?

HOW CAN I APPLY THIS TO MY LIFE?

PRAY Indonesia – For the unity and continued growth of churches in the midst of intense persecution.

If the book stopped at verse 20, we would have to conclude that salvation was impossible since no one could attain God's standard of righteousness. But that is exactly Paul's point. God's righteous standard cannot be attained by human effort with or without the law; it must be given to us by God. According to verse 21 it is "apart from the law," that is, apart from any system of good works designed to earn favor with God. It is "being witnessed" by the law and the prophets in that the gospel has never changed. It is "through faith." Faith and works are mutually exclusive. Paul moves next to a discussion of the relationship of law and faith. They are now and forever mutually exclusive. If faith is present, works are excluded; if works are present, faith is excluded. No combination of the two is possible. According to verse 27, faith excludes boasting. No one is saved because of any natural righteousness he may possess. God saves: therefore, only God can boast. Why is this so? Because it is a *gift*. One cannot earn a gift, for then it would be wages. A gift is a giving by one person to another because of love.

Verse 29 says that God is the God of the Gentiles also. Since God has always been the God of all men (Gentiles included), law (a Jewish institution) cannot be the answer to man's problem. Law or *Jewish-ness* cannot be required since Gentiles who are not circumcised are being saved. Thus neither law nor circumcision is essential to salvation. Does this nullify the law (verse 31)? No, this does not mean that the law is useless; nor is it neutralized. Its teachings are still valid. However, it was never designed to produce a righteous man.

LIFE STEP Law and faith, while mutually exclusive, are not contradictory. They have separate functions within the plan of God. Problems only occur when we attempt to use one to do a job that requires the other.

ROMANS 4:1-12

WHAT IS THE WRITER SAYING?

HOW CAN I APPLY THIS TO MY LIFE?

Paul now compares his teaching with the most appropriate of Old Testament examples. Was Abraham saved because of his righteous deeds or was his righteousness the *imputed righteousness* that God graciously gives to those who believe? Chapter 4:1-8 asks the question whether Abraham's righteousness was by good works. 4:9-12 asks whether his righteousness was by circumcision.

The *good works* question revolves around the issue of compensation. If Abraham's justification was by good works, then it was earned and Abraham clearly has something to boast about. According to verse 4, wages are the rightly expected compensation for services performed, but Paul has argued that righteousness is decided independent of what is deserved. What, then, does the Old Testament teach about Abraham's righteousness? Paul quotes Genesis 15:6 in support of his argument. Clearly Abraham's righteousness was given by God on the basis of *believing* and therefore could not have been by good works. Remember, the key to his argument is that anything that is earned cannot also be "imputed" (*given*).

Regarding the second question, namely, whether Abraham's justification was by circumcision (4:9-12), Paul points out that the Old Testament is very clear. Abraham was justified (Genesis 15:6) before he went through the ritual of circumcision (Genesis 17:10ff). Circumcision was a sign of the covenant, not a source of it. Abraham was not justified because he was circumcised; he was circumcised because he was justified. Circumcision, like the law, had a purpose, but that purpose was not related to justification.

LIFE STEP Our human nature always tries to make forgiveness more difficult than it is. Don't require of yourself or of others any additional "good" in order to be forgiven of sin. To acknowledge guilt and accept forgiveness is more than just sufficient; it is mandatory.

TUESDAY 31

ROMANS 4:13-25

WHAT IS THE WRITER SAYING?

HOW CAN I APPLY THIS TO MY LIFE?

PRAY

Pray for those in your church who have lost a loved one this year.

The proper explanation of Abraham's justification is found in verses 13-22. It was first of all "by (*in accordance with*) grace." Only faith allows grace to be grace (*unmerited*). If it is by any other means it becomes merited. Only salvation by faith alone allows a correct definition of grace. It was also by faith in order that the promise might be certain. There can be no certainty where conditions must be met. Only a one-party covenant (*promise*) can assure that something will occur.

This promise is made to those who are of the faith of Abraham. It is not a physical relationship to Abraham that matters. If it were, then circumcision would matter. It is those who are like Abraham spiritually who are blessed.

When Paul writes, in verse 22, that "it was imputed" to Abraham, he speaks of a one-sided transfer to his account. Abraham possessed no righteousness of his own, but God, based on His own character and not Abraham's, filled Abraham's account to the brim. God did this not only "for his sake alone," but also as an example of what pleasing God is all about. It is not we doing for God, but God doing for us. Jesus was "delivered for our offenses." The things He suffered He suffered because of our sin. He paid our price. He was "raised again for our justification." His resurrection contains the power to live the way a justified person should. God's righteousness has more to it than a justified position before Him; it also involves justified living. God's righteousness is "from faith to faith." This means that the one who has been declared righteous by faith will also live righteously by faith.

LIFE STEP

Sanctification (living the daily Christian life successfully) is as much a gift of God as is salvation. To be declared righteous ought to produce a desire to live righteously. If justification is not by law, then can sanctification be by the law? Paul resoundingly answers, NO!

ROMANS 5:1-11

WHAT IS THE WRITER SAYING?

HOW CAN I APPLY THIS TO MY LIFE?

PRAY Hungary – For summer outreach and camping ministries as they evangelize and disciple youth.

Chapter 5 contains two distinct parts. Verses 1 11 speak of our new perspective on life. We have been reconciled and have a totally rearranged outlook—we are at peace with God! All fear is removed. Paul chooses to give a concrete example of what this new way of living is like. When we were lost, tribulations were major causes of depression. Today, in our new life, they are a cause to rejoice. We have a constant assurance that all events in our lives are designed by a gracious and loving God who died for us while we were unlovable. We are now at "peace with God." Prior to salvation we were at enmity with God and God's wrath was out to get us. Now all that has changed. We may not understand the why of each circumstance, but we now know that it is our Friend who is working all things out for us. Beyond this we now "glory (*exult*)

in tribulations." If God is for us, then so-called troubles must be good gifts from a good God.

In verse 6 Paul points out that, while we were "yet without strength (helpless)," Christ died for us. There was nothing in it for God. No ulterior motives. In verse 8 it is "while we were yet sinners." To be helpless means that we are unable to improve our condition, to be sinners means that we are constantly placing ourselves in greater and greater jeopardy. Verse 10 is the ultimate irony. Not only are we helpless sinners, we are also his enemies. Think about it, if we were all those things when he saved us, will He not do so much more for us (sanctification) now that we are His friends? How could such a God ever leave us captive to the power of sin?

LIFE STEP If God is for us, what or who can stand against us? Sure, man may mean it for evil, but we can have an unwavering confidence that God has always and will always mean it for good. Cheer up, not because it cannot get any worse (man's lame word of encouragement!) but because our Helper cannot be any better.

THURSDAY 31

ROMANS 5:12-21

WHAT IS THE WRITER SAYING?

HOW CAN I APPLY THIS TO MY LIFE?

PRAY Panama – Increased educational opportunities for those in or considering full-time ministry.

We are being sanctified because of the new relationship that exists between us and God. Paul's comparison of the *sin nature* and the *righteous nature* helps to clarify how this new life operates. We became sinners when the head of the human race, Adam, acted sinfully. We may become righteous because our spiritual head, Christ, has acted righteously. All are sinners in Adam and, given the opportunity, we will sin. Even before there was a Mosaic Law, sin was in the world (v. 13); therefore, even without the Mosaic Law right and wrong exist. And, since "sin is not imputed when there is no law," even before the Law of Moses was given, there must have been some kind of law. Where there is no law, there can be no execution of judgment. However, "death reigned from Adam to Moses." Furthermore, it reigned over those who did not sin willfully ("after the similitude of Adam's transgression"). Therefore the problem has always been a who-we-are problem not a what-we-do problem. Therefore, the solution must change who we are. We need a substitute for us! And that is exactly what Jesus did. He replaced us in death and He wants to replace us in life. The life that we now live is Christ living in us (Galatians 2:20).

The penalty is earned but the gift of eternal life is absolutely free. If Adam's single sin was sufficient to make all men sinners, Christ's single act is sufficient to make all men righteous. And just as being in Adam makes us act sinfully, so being in Christ is able to produce *justified living* on a day-to-day basis.

LIFE STEP All systems that include "wages" must result in condemnation. If we are saved by faith, then it is only possible for us to be sanctified by faith. The law may be compared to a yardstick. It can tell you where you need to cut a board but it cannot cut it for you. God promised to do that.

FRIDAY 31

ROMANS 6:1-12

WHAT IS THE WRITER SAYING?

HOW CAN I APPLY THIS TO MY LIFE?

PRAY Turkey – Is the least evangelized country in the world. Pray that God would send forth laborers into the harvest.

Paul opens today with a question. If our great need allowed God's grace to abound all the more (5:20), shouldn't we sin to give God more opportunities to be gracious? Paul argues that since we have left the classification of *sinners*, we ought to now live out our new life as *saints*.

Verses 4 7 are an analogy to help us understand this freedom from sin. To be *baptized into Christ* is to be identified with Him. Because we are identified with Christ, we are "buried with him" – what we were, *sinners*, is done away with. We now need to start living our new position. We are now united with His living. We have become a part of his family; we are partakers of His nature. Thus, we now live in "newness of life." The "old man" is we before we were saved. The "body of sin" refers to that person we used to be, dominated by sin. We no longer have to be "slaves of sin." We used to be unable not to sin. Sin controlled every area of our lives. We were its slaves. We are now free.

Verses 8 11 give a second analogy to help us understand our new life. This second analogy is the death of Christ. He was resurrected *never to die again*. Therefore our new life is a permanent life. Death is caused by sin but we are no longer legally considered to be in the category of *sinners*. Since Christ conquered death, it no longer has dominion over Him, and since we are in Christ, sin has lost its power over us. Its power rested in its ability to kill us, but that price has been paid. It has no real power anymore. Paul writes that we are to "reckon" (or *consider* – a faith word) ourselves dead to sin and alive unto God. Since sin has lost its authority, we need to stop surrendering authority to it. By faith we need to start living what we are by faith in God. We must become what we are destined to be.

LIFE STEP True spiritual growth must be produced by the Spirit of God from within. It cannot come from what we do, but must come from who we are. Transformation must begin on the inside and work its way out.

SATURDAY 31

ROMANS 6:13-23

WHAT IS THE WRITER SAYING?

HOW CAN I APPLY THIS TO MY LIFE?

PRAY Australia – Pray for churches to understand the 'post-modern' society in Australia and reach out to generations who increasingly see God as irrelevant.

Verses 12 14 are a statement of our new position. Sin will continue to dominate us if we do not stop yielding ourselves to it. We must make ourselves available to *be* good. We have left Adam's line and are joined to Christ's. Each day, each hour, each minute we need to be consciously presenting ourselves to God for transformation. Sin only rules us so long as we allow it to.

Verse 15a gives a second wrong conclusion. Paul's answer is contained in verse 16: the principle of irresistible servanthood! We will serve the one to whom we yield ourselves. If we don't yield to God, we will serve sin. Our responsibility is to reckon and to yield. If we do that, the new nature will do all the rest.

Paul's bold statement in verse 20 that we used to be "free from righteousness" (or better "free in regard to righteousness") should not go unnoticed. Sin's slaves are unable to live righteously because they are free from the power of righteous living. If we are sin's slaves, we cannot serve righteousness. Now that we are in Christ we need to submit ourselves to Him with the same kind of loyalty with which we served sin. In fact, it ought to be much greater loyalty, for the end of the story is life everlasting. According to verse 23, sin has wages and God has a gift. Wages are those things that a person deserves. People die because they deserve to do so. Righteousness is a gift. A gift cannot be earned; otherwise, it is no longer a gift. Therein is the crucial difference between being a slave to sin and a slave to righteousness. The former is a works-based system and the latter is a grace-through-faith system.

LIFE STEP Before salvation we were all locked into a works system that was only capable of producing frustration and death. Now that we are saved, the only way to true sanctification is the path marked by grace through faith.

ROMANS 7:1-13

WHAT IS THE WRITER SAYING?

HOW CAN I APPLY THIS TO MY LIFE?

PRAY Namibia – Pray for a biblical faith to be restored throughout Namibia's many churches.

In chapter 7 Paul speaks of the freedom of sanctification. Works-based sanctification produces bondage to a set of "do's and don'ts," while a faith-based sanctification produces freedom. He uses marriage to illustrate how law and grace are mutually exclusive. We are only enslaved to the law as long as both parties are alive. The law is forever; therefore, it is we who must die to alter the legal situation. To be "married" to the Spirit one must first be dead to the law. To try to marry a new bride while the first is still alive is adultery. Only by dying to the law can we ever hope to live by the power of the Spirit.

In verse 6 he speaks of the "newness of the Spirit" and the "oldness of the letter." The new man lives by the Spirit just as the old man dies by the law. Before salvation we were trapped in some form of works system. Under that system we were always coming short of the glory of God and thereby bringing condemnation to ourselves. That is all behind us. We now stand justified by grace through faith and are enabled by God to live righteously by the power of God's Spirit. The Law was never meant to make people righteous. Sin uses the law to destroy us. Law was originally given to confirm life (in the garden), but once sin entered, law became a judge and condemner of all. The power to destroy is with the law. Sin needs law in order to produce death. Sin deceived us into thinking that we could be righteous in and of ourselves. It convinced us that if we would just try a little harder, we could be like God. And for a while it even seemed to be working. Paul says he was seemingly alive before the law, but alas, this was only blissful ignorance, he simply did not know the jeopardy he was in. The law is holy. The law is not the problem—we are!

LIFE STEP Sanctification by works is so tempting. It puts righteousness so close that we can taste it. Unfortunately, that is as close as we will ever get if we are striving through our own efforts to please God.

ROMANS 7:14-25

WHAT IS THE WRITER SAYING?

HOW CAN I APPLY THIS TO MY LIFE?

Verse 13 introduces a second wrong conclusion. If it is the law that empowers sin, then clearly the law is responsible for my problems. It is the law's fault, not mine. Paul's answer to this covers the rest of the chapter. He chooses to use an illustration taken from his own life. Paul speaks of his struggle as a young Christian to use the law as a means for sanctification. When Paul says that he is "carnal, sold under sin," he is talking of the sin nature. The problem with law is that one has to be holy to benefit from it (Adam), but Paul was a slave of the sin nature. Law, as a means to righteousness, can only benefit those who are capable of keeping it. Paul coveted even though he knew it was wrong.

When Paul speaks of the "sin that dwelleth in me," he is making reference to the sin nature. Salvation does not eradicate the principle of sin that exists in every man, woman, and child. It simply declares us righteous; it does not immediately make us righteous. The "law of my mind" is that which I know to be right or wrong, or pure knowledge. The "law of sin" refers to the influence of the sin nature on this *knowledge*. Knowing right is insufficient to produce doing right.

Fortunately, there is a greater power, a by-grace-through-faith sanctification. Thanks be to Christ Who has delivered us from this body of death. Notice that Paul does not include any requirements at all. He just says thanks. Why? Because the power of sanctification is resident within our salvation. It is not an addition that is acquired later. Those who are saved will be sanctified!

LIFE STEP So often we hear the phrase, "struggling in our Christian walk." The power to walk in newness of life is available to all who are willing to leave their old "by the works of the law" system and join God's "apart from the works of the law" salvation. The choice is ours: burden or freedom.

ROMANS 8:1-11

WHAT IS THE WRITER SAYING?

HOW CAN I APPLY THIS TO MY LIFE?

PRAY Rwanda – Pray for a revival to break out, one that places tribalism and revenge at the foot of the cross and is characterized by repentance and reconciliation.

Chapter 8 addresses the power of sanctification. How do we overcome the "law of sin" that rages in our flesh? To that question Paul now turns. Salvation is "from faith to faith." If the law could not save, neither can it sanctify! Sanctification must be by faith in Jesus Christ. Condemnation is no longer a possibility. Love reigns and the Spirit empowers.

Verses 5 8 tell us about the work of the indwelling Spirit. He changes our mindset so that our inner man is able to serve God. Being "carnally minded" speaks of a person who is controlled by the flesh. Every attempt to do good by the flesh draws us into a carnal system and all "carnal" systems lead to death. For the unjustified the death is absolute. For the justified it is death to any possibility of living a godly life. Those who try to use rules and regulations to please God are actually fighting against Him.

Only by this work of the Holy Spirit in our lives can our bodies experience life, that is, behave righteously. The argument is subtle but convincing. According to verse 9, all those who are saved are indwelt by the Spirit. Anyone who does not have the Spirit cannot claim to be saved. Therefore, all who are saved have an equal opportunity to live righteously. Verse 10 argues that all those who are by faith the children of God are still dead with respect to the law in their bodies. Justification was not accomplished by good works; therefore, the flesh has not been changed to acquire this salvation. Salvation was accomplished in spite of the flesh. If, therefore, justification was a matter of the Spirit, it only follows that sanctification must be a matter of the human spirit/Holy Spirit connection. True righteousness begins at the spirit and works its way out.

LIFE STEP To be dead to sin is a matter of the heart. Until we consider ourselves dead, that is, realize that we are incapable of pleasing God by our own efforts; we can never experience the freedom of true Christ-like living.

ROMANS 8:12-25

WHAT IS THE WRITER SAYING?

HOW CAN I APPLY THIS TO MY LIFE?

Today, Paul summarizes the basic principles of Spirit-empowered sanctification. It must not be viewed as an option; it is an obligation. We are debtors. Human effort (the flesh) had no part in our salvation and therefore should be given no privileges in our sanctification. We owe the flesh nothing, and the Spirit everything. We are sons of God. And sons grow up to be like their parents, not by any effort of their own but by reason of the fact that they are sons. Sonship guarantees likeness.

The Spirit of God "bears witness with our spirit" in that He is now related to us. We are family. We think alike. We look alike. We are kindred spirits. This "bearing witness" is not some voice that we hear in our minds; it is an observation based on the new attitudes and behaviors that we see at work in our lives. The presence of the Holy Spirit and the change in our spirit give mutual expression to the fact that we are saved.

For the rest of this chapter Paul extols the superiority of the indwelling Spirit as a means to sanctification. First he suggests that such an approach is superior in troubles. Even the whole of creation is *troubled* and is clearly out of sync with the perfection that is God's. Everywhere we look we can see examples of the effects of sin on the environment and the inhabitants of this planet. The outward effects of sin continue to wreak havoc on us personally and on the environment in which we live, but the inner man is constantly renewed by our new perspective. If we had total salvation here, we could no longer have faith because faith is the "substance (*conviction*) of things hoped for, the evidence of things not seen" (Hebrews 11:1). A faith-based sanctification is one of hope that will always supersede an outward (works-based) one.

LIFE STEP Outward circumstance will always conspire and defeat a purely outward righteousness. Only a by-faith, Spirit-powered righteousness can enable the child of God to overcome the world.

ROMANS 8:26-39

WHAT IS THE WRITER SAYING?

HOW CAN I APPLY THIS TO MY LIFE?

PRAY France – For missionaries to integrate well into French culture and to persevere amidst slow results.

Paul's second argument for the superiority of a Spirit-empowered sanctification is that it is superior in prayer. The Spirit has two clear advantages: immediate access to the Father and comprehensive knowledge of His will for our lives. Since we have this Advocate who knows God's will, He can direct, redirect, and initiate our prayer life. His "groanings" indicate that He is able to express all that I am incapable of expressing; they come from His knowledge of my pain.

The sequence of terms in verse 28 is designed to show the Spirit's participation in every part of our pilgrimage. To "foreknow" means *to love beforehand* (see Amos 3:2). To "predestine" means *to set on a path toward salvation*. "Calling" is God's work in drawing us toward Him for the purpose of saving us. "Justification" means *to declare righteous*, and speaks of the transaction at the point of salvation. "Glorification" speaks of our final sinless perfection in God's perfect new heavens and new earth. If any one of these is true, they all are true. Because each step is supervised by the Spirit, there can be no *casualties*. If any part of the process were left to human effort or human works, the end could not be guaranteed.

Finally, Paul argues that the Spirit is superior in love. Not only does He give us security in our legal standing before Him (vv. 31-34), but He also gives us security in our daily walk (vv. 35-39).

How can we ever be sure that God loves us if He allows so many trials to enter our lives? That assurance can only come from a Spirit-inspired, faith-driven salvation. Paul concludes the chapter with a resounding tribute to the faithfulness and power of God. All that transpires in our lives is an expression of God's grace and love, even if we can't fully understand everything at the time.

LIFE STEP We can *exult in tribulations* because every event that comes into our lives is orchestrated by the God who loved us and gave Himself for us.

ROMANS 9:1-16

WHAT IS THE WRITER SAYING?

HOW CAN I APPLY THIS TO MY LIFE?

PRAY Chile – For the perseverance of Chilean saints as only 38% attend church regularly.

Chapter 9 opens a new section in which Paul explains how Israel could appear to fall from God's favor. Didn't God judge Israel for failing to keep the law? Paul's argument is that God allowed this to happen to Israel because of his grace and love for Israel and all of mankind. All things work together for good, even those things we consider to be punishments. Even hardening is an act of grace and love. We should not judge God's motives based on a narrow view of history. God works with eternity in perspective.

Paul affirms in this chapter that all decisions are a part of the divine plan. God's promises did not fail because God never promised to save every Israelite (9:6 9). His promises have never been a matter of human relationships (an analogy of human "works"). Only Isaac was chosen and not Ishmael. And so it has been throughout human history. There is no physical or racial characteristic that makes one person more likely to be saved than another. Secondly, Paul points out that God only promised to save certain Israelites (9:10 13). Even among the descendants of Isaac, only some were chosen. The twins were as yet unborn when the plan was already set. God's plan is not limited by human weakness. It is impossible to determine a person's spiritual situation based on his physical situation. God desires that all men be saved. Even when he hardens, he does so for spiritual reasons. So it was with Pharaoh. God hardened him only after Pharaoh had hardened himself against God. While human logic would suggest that the act of having mercy on one, excludes the other, theology does not. Men reject God. God does not reject men for He has reconciled the whole world to Himself.

 LIFE STEP If we trust God with our personal lives, we should have no trouble trusting Him with the lives of every man, woman, and child on Planet Earth. He has a plan for them, too. And that plan might include sending you to share the love of God with them!

ROMANS 9:17-33

WHAT IS THE WRITER SAYING?

HOW CAN I APPLY THIS TO MY LIFE?

PRAY Pray for those who teach in your church to be faithful to the word, enthusiastic in their presentation, and compassionate toward the lost.

Paul bristles just a little in today's passage. He will tolerate legitimate questions that arise within any theological discussion, but he will not tolerate any question that sarcastically challenges God's good name. In verses 19-23 he argues that God's plan is never biased. He says, *Hold it right here! Perhaps you are thinking that God might be unfair. Where is your faith? Such a thought is unworthy of an answer. Can we, sinful as we are, question God about His integrity? End of discussion... Worthy is the Lamb!* Beginning at verse 25 Paul suggests that Scriptures have always clearly taught these facts. Here we see a variety of quotes taken from the Old Testament showing that Israel's present situation was always a part of God's plan and it should not have surprised us. In verses 27-29 Paul gives us the bottom line – anything we have, we owe to Him.

I have life only because He is gracious. We deserve hell; He gives us heaven. We cannot question or criticize such an awesome God. The whole discussion of God's sovereignty versus man's responsibility must ultimately boil down to a matter of character, God's character. Either we will trust God with the destiny of all human souls or we won't. But remember, if you cannot trust God, who can you trust? He willingly offers everything He has to sinful humans, not because He has to but because He wants to.

Beginning at verse 30, Paul starts a second major thought: rejection is a matter of human choice (9:30–10:21). First, he speaks of the fact of Israelite rejection (9:30 33). They stumbled because they rejected grace. They could not and would not accept a not-by-works-of-the-law salvation.

 LIFE STEP What we control is no longer a matter of faith. If I built the chair, I know whether it will or will not hold me. God built salvation. We simply sit in it. We know it will hold us because of faith in God's craftsmanship and nothing else.

ROMANS 10:1-13

WHAT IS THE WRITER SAYING?

HOW CAN I APPLY THIS TO MY LIFE?

PRAY Malawi – Praise! The gospel has penetrated nearly every section of society, and some places have seen local revivals in this landlocked central african nation.

Paul gives three basic reasons why the nation of Israel missed out on God's blessing. He says in verses 1 5 that they had a misdirected zeal. That is, they chose works and accepted law over grace. Therefore, their zeal could only produce frustration. Although they sought this man-made righteousness with great intensity, they were doomed to failure since their resources were totally inadequate. The harder they tried the more lost they became. Great knowledge of the law only serves to increase one's accountability without improving his condition. Their final condition after so much effort was actually worse than what it was in the beginning.

Furthermore, according to verses 6-9, they misunderstood the task. They wanted to do something great, to attain some great objective. We do not attain God's righteousness by effort or drag ourselves out of hell by works. Faith is always as near as my heart. In fact, it is too near for many. Only those who are willing to humbly accept (the poor in heart) will ever experience the thrill of an apart-from-the-law righteousness. There is no task that we could ever hope to perform that would make us worthy of so great a salvation. What cannot be bought is freely given.

The third reason that Israel missed out on God's promises is that they were mistaken about their condition. They did not understand that they were without excuse. They are without excuse first of all because the plan is simple (vv. 10-13). What could be simpler? Whosoever calls upon the name of the Lord shall be saved. Everybody is a 'whosoever.' It doesn't matter where you live, or what you do. It doesn't matter how old you are or what language you speak. 'Whosoever' means me and it means you.

LIFE STEP

Never abuse God's grace by trying to pay for His mercy. It could never be afforded at any price. Gratitude is all that God requests. His gift of absolute righteousness is simply that and only that – a gift.

ROMANS 10:14-21

WHAT IS THE WRITER SAYING?

HOW CAN I APPLY THIS TO MY LIFE?

PRAY Ukraine – For the teachers, textbooks, buildings and scholarships essential for leadership training.

In today's passage Paul continues his assertion that God's plan for saving men was not only for Israel, but is also universally available (vv. 14-21). This by-faith-and-apart-from-the-works-of-the-law salvation has never been hidden. God has always had preachers, the prophets in the Old Testament and the apostles in the New. Israel has had every opportunity imaginable to hear the message. Paul makes this abundantly clear in verses 15-17. He also makes it abundantly clear that this gospel message is indispensible to the plan. Faith comes by hearing and hearing by the Word of God. Paul could not make this any clearer. Where there is no faith there is no salvation, where there is no hearing there is no faith, and where there is no gospel there is no hearing. Therefore, where there is no gospel there is no salvation. We as believers must recognize our indebtedness, not to God (because His salvation is a gift, not a debt) but to the lost around us (Romans 1:14) and share with all mankind the only hope that exists in this messed up world. The gospel is the power of God unto salvation.

Furthermore, in verses 18-21 Paul argues that others with less opportunity accepted this gospel. This message has gone to the ends of the world. While Israel was turning a deaf ear to the law-free gospel, those who were not called his people (Gentiles) gladly received the message and were gloriously saved. How could Israel ever suggest that they did not know when those who had much more limited opportunity had accepted the gospel with open arms?

LIFE STEP God's arms are always open wide. He calls night and day. There is no speech where His words are not heard. And yet men stubbornly resist His simple plan. Salvation is free. Salvation is now. Salvation is ours. All we have to do is to accept it!

ROMANS 11:1-12

WHAT IS THE WRITER SAYING?

HOW CAN I APPLY THIS TO MY LIFE?

Chapter 11 contains Paul's final argument concerning Israel's present situation: rejection is not necessarily terminal. In Verses 1-10 he suggests that it is not total. Why? Because many Israelites are still being saved. In verse one Paul indicates that he himself is an example. In verses 2-4 he points out that there is always a chosen few and in verses 5-10 he states that only some have been rejected and hardened. Israel's national rejection was not a denial of individual Jewish people's salvation, but a termination of the Law-based, sacrificial worship system. In all of this, however, the theme of God's grace is emphasized. What could not be obtained by good works, or by following the law, or by national origin is freely obtained by those who willingly accept it.

Verses 5-6 are critical to understanding Paul's understanding of salvation. Grace and works are mutually exclusive. What is according to grace cannot include any human works as a part of that system of righteousness. Conversely, any system of works that includes grace is not a true works system. In other words, one cannot suppose that man is required to do what he can, and God's grace will cover the rest. A partly-by-works salvation or sanctification is just as deadly as a totally-by-works version. Israel was never given a law system of salvation but a Law system of worship. They were not rejected because of their failure to keep the Law. They were rejected because of their lack of faith. The just have always lived by faith and always will live by faith because without faith it is impossible to please God.

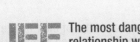

LIFE STEP The most dangerous trap for believers is to base one's relationship with God on behavior. True, bad behavior generally indicates a poor relationship. However, it is faith that empowers the relationship, behavior only attests to it.

ROMANS 11:13-24

WHAT IS THE WRITER SAYING?

Jordan – tech. competition   Larissa

Jasmine – knee replacement May 24
       road test the day of TI

Lauren – CDE competition – fri.

HOW CAN I APPLY THIS TO MY LIFE?

PRAY El Salvador – For sound, Bible-believing churches to be planted among the Amerindian people.

The argument begun in verse 11 is crucial. Israel's rejection is not permanent. Notice why they were rejected! It was not to destroy *them* but for the benefit of *others*. If their rejection has produced the Church Age (a new worship system, not a new salvation system), what awesome enhancement will their reinstatement produce? The promises of God were never jeopardized by the waywardness of His nation. In fact, God's promises to bring His blessings to the Gentiles have been accomplished by that very rejection. Does this then suggest that God's promises have been transferred? Not so. They are still to be fulfilled and at that time the full blessings of God will be poured out upon both Gentile and Israel alike. God's promises are as sure today as ever, they have just taken a turn that Israel never expected. In effect, all things have worked together for the best in this matter.

Verses 17 24 teach a lesson that we all should learn from this temporary rejection! Don't play games with God! He has less reason to keep the wild branch than He did the cultivated one. God cultivated Israel for the future kingdom that He will establish at some future date. Because of Israel's unbelief the present Gentile-friendly system of worship, namely, the church, was temporarily grafted into that pre-existing root. If we despise the gracious gift we have received by acting like we have earned or deserve it, then God can easily reinstate Israel as His people to the root that is naturally theirs. They stumbled at the rock of grace. Let us not make the same mistake.

LIFE STEP God's rejection of Israel has never been a matter of their failure to live up to His standards. It has always been based on their failure to accept that which is and can only be free. Don't choose works over grace. It is a fatal mistake.

ROMANS 11:25-36

WHAT IS THE WRITER SAYING?

HOW CAN I APPLY THIS TO MY LIFE?

Verses 25 32 speak of the future that God still plans for Israel! Rejection is not forever. God will bring the nation of Israel back into fellowship. He will reestablish them as His worship leaders once again. That is the great thing about God. Anyone who wants to fellowship with Him can. There are no cliques with God. Faith is not an exclusive club. The day will come when once again His people who are called by His name will gaze with remorse on Him whom they pierced. In faith they will throw themselves on the tender mercies of their God and He will save them, not because of who they are but because of who He is. What a day that will be! As Gentiles we should long for that day also, because if their setting aside was for our benefit, how much more will their restoration bring light to the nations?

Paul wraps up this section in verses 33-36 with a doxology. What a conclusion! Paul throws his hands into the air and cries out in spontaneous awe and worship. Why? Because God is so great that we can only scratch the surface of the understanding His grace. It is too awesome for any mortal mind to comprehend. We simply follow along as far as Paul has taken us and by faith trust God for the rest. There are no secrets. There are no hidden costs. This is simply one absolutely free gift from a gracious God: bought, sealed and delivered. It's universally available and it's unfailingly effective. That we cannot understand everything about how it works should not frustrate us; it should cause us to cry out in praise that we serve such a magnificent God.

LIFE STEP What we take for granted we treat as common. We must never do that with our salvation. It is a treasure that defies description and an opportunity without parallel. We ought simply to bask in the wonder of it all. Paul did.

FRIDAY 33

ROMANS 12:1-8

WHAT IS THE WRITER SAYING?

Rom. 8:6-8   Gifts

prophesy
ministry - service
- teaching
exhortation
giving
ruling
showing mercy

Eph. 4:11 -
apostles
prophets
evangelist
pastor
teacher

HOW CAN I APPLY THIS TO MY LIFE?

PRAY Kenya – For the 500 Kenyans working as missionaries within sub-cultures and in other countries.

Beginning in chapter 12 Paul describes the standard growth patterns of a maturing believer. These are the things that accompany salvation. Paul arranges his material so that each section addresses a different relationship that the believer must function within: the believer and his God (12:1-2); the church (12:3 13); the lost (12:14 21); his government (13:1 7); his possessions (13:8 13); and his decisions (14:1–15:13). These areas are synthetic in character; that is, they build on one another. Before one can have a proper relationship with the unsaved, he must develop certain skills within the church. Thus, Paul presents us with a Christian growth chart, the pinnacle of which is the ability to make godly decisions. When Paul writes, "I beseech you therefore," it is not a command. We dedicate ourselves because we want to,

not because we have to. To "present your bodies" as "living sacrifices" invokes the imagery of the burnt offering of Leviticus 1. That offering is dead! It is chopped up! It is totally burned! It is voluntary! And it is all God's. We don't look at this as a waste of good meat. It is God's. Thus, even though we live, we live for God and God alone. This is how spiritual people successfully worship God. Paul does command us "be not conformed" or *pressed into the mold* of the world. Don't be "Jell-O" Christians. This is the "will of God." If we want God's will for our lives we need to begin right here! Verses 3 8 speak of exercising our gifts. We must learn our position in God's family (verse 3) and learn to behave as a responsible member of that family. Whatever talent God has given to us, it has been given to promote the welfare of the entire body, not to promote or advance ourselves.

LIFE STEP The great adventure of sanctification begins when we entrust ourselves entirely to God. Until that happens we will struggle at every turn.

ROMANS 12:9-21

WHAT IS THE WRITER SAYING?

HOW CAN I APPLY THIS TO MY LIFE?

PRAY Albania – Pray that Albania's government and business cultures might be positively influenced by the growing number of believers.

Paul has just spoken of using our gifts for the benefit of the whole body. The only way this will happen is if we let love govern our interpersonal relationships. Love is the glue that holds the family of God together. Just as we learn how to behave at home, so Christian graces must be learned within the protected environment of the church. What we learn at home we live out in public. Notice the characteristics that Paul assigns to love.

It devotes its time and energy to others and prefers (considers more important) one another. Love does not *look out for number one*. It does not seek to be number one. It always takes the feelings of others into consideration. It's enthusiastic. It handles hardship well. It always sees the silver lining and dismisses the clouds. It devotes time to prayer. Those we pray for are those we love. If we constantly pray only for ourselves, then we love only ourselves. Once we have learned to interact with the family of God, it is time to take this love to the world. Paul proposes at least five principles. First we must respond positively to negatives, not in kind, namely, "turn the other cheek." Forgiveness is always in order. Secondly, we must learn to empathize with others. The words of a wise man, given at the proper time and with the proper sensitivity, are very helpful. Thirdly, Paul says that we cannot be social snobs. Accept and treat all men equally. Fourthly, don't seek to get even! Be concerned about what others think; appearances are important. And finally we are responsible to show love; God will take care of punishment. Meting out justice is not a part of the believer's responsibility.

 LIFE STEP One of the last things that Christ said was, "Forgive them, for they know not what they do" (Luke 23:34). Even in His moment of greatest indignity and pain, He was not looking for payback. He kept reaching out in love even to those who crucified Him.

SUNDAY 34

ROMANS 13:1-14

WHAT IS THE WRITER SAYING?

HOW CAN I APPLY THIS TO MY LIFE?

PRAY New Zealand – For support to be raised to send pastors and missionaries to Bible schools.

When a child leaves his home he encounters the regulations of secular human government. Paul reminds us that believers are not exempt from the laws of secular society. He points out that God is ultimately responsible for all human authority. To rebel against any legitimate human authority is to rebel against God (v. 1). He further suggests that God has given governments the right to take human life (the sword). This would include the right to wage war and the right to use capital punishment (vv. 2-4). It does not necessarily demand that governments exercise this option but it certainly does make it available. Verse 5 suggests two reasons for obedience—punishment and conscience. We obey, not just to avoid punishment, but also because it is the right thing to do.

Verses 8-14 are a little difficult to categorize. It seems that Paul is speaking of the believer and his possessions. Verses 8-10 address material possessions and verses 11-14 non material possessions. He states first that we are not to take that which does not belong to us whether it be money, sexual benefits, or human life. Our lives should not be consumed in the attempt to acquire as much *stuff* as possible. Rather than looking for ways to take, we ought to look to protect our neighbor's possessions. The immaterial possessions Paul speaks of are our time and passions. God has given us all the time we have. Let's appreciate it and use it wisely. Our passions or emotions are also a gift from God. Let's use them for his honor and glory. If we allow them to go unrestrained, they will destroy us.

LIFE STEP We are stewards. Stewards are those who are responsible for the administration of that which belongs to someone else. "Well done thou good and faithful servant" (Matthew 25:21) are the words we want to hear someday.

ROMANS 14:1-12

WHAT IS THE WRITER SAYING?

HOW CAN I APPLY THIS TO MY LIFE?

PRAY Bolivia – For missionaries willing to serve in the remote villages of the Quechua and Aymara people.

Chapter 14 begins Paul's discussion of the believer and his decision-making process (14:1–15:13). Note that when it is a matter of right and wrong, there is no decision making process. Just do right! This passage refers to the neutrals of life, those areas that do not clearly fall into the categories of right or wrong. The issue in this case is meat offered to idols. A few definitions should be helpful. A *conviction* is any area where there is no direct biblical teaching but where we do have strong biblical evidence that this is a matter of right and wrong based on Biblical principles. A *preference* is a neutral area in which the believer is expected to develop a position, but not to force that position on others. A *legalist* is a professing believer who tries to force others to adopt his preferences. A *stronger brother* is one who, in good conscience, can exercise his Christian liberties as he determines his preferences. A *weaker brother* is a believer who can be influenced by a stronger personality to go against his conscience (his preferences). An *offense* is when a brother exercises his liberty in a situation where a weaker brother may be influenced to go against his conscience (his preferences).

In most ancient cities on festival days there would be a glut of fresh meat available to the public. Because it had been offered to idols, some believers argued that it was contaminated. Others said meat was meat. Paul declines to take sides but instead suggests that both sides have a right to their position. Paul's first principle for dealing with neutral areas is: *Never judge another brother based on your own personal preferences*. Where there is room for legitimate disagreement, there must also be willingness to respect.

LIFE STEP God expects us to develop godly behaviors in many of these neutral areas but He does not want us to use these preferences as a club to hammer our brothers.

ROMANS 14:13-23

WHAT IS THE WRITER SAYING?

HOW CAN I APPLY THIS TO MY LIFE?

Today Paul introduces the second principle for decision-making: *Let edification replace condemnation* (14:13 23). Rather than judging and discarding those who have arrived at a different opinion, we are challenged to be sensitive to their needs and opinions. We do this first of all by yielding our rights. If the exercise of my *rights* causes a brother to be harmed (encourages him to sin against his conviction or preference), I have sinned. If his conscience is convicted, I must yield. Paul wrote in 1 Corinthians that all things are lawful, but not all things are expedient. To exercise one's freedom in an irresponsible manner is not only contentious, it is dangerous to the spiritual welfare of others.

We must choose to do the thing that allows both parties to remain unharmed. If I am not convicted that I must do something,

the best solution is for me to yield. The stronger brother must always yield to the conscience of the weaker. Verse 23 is very clear concerning this. If our actions, even though they are scripturally allowable, cause a weaker brother to act in "doubt," we not only contribute to his sin, but we become accomplices and sin ourselves. We cannot allow things like meat to destroy the work of God. Many times it is the unimportant issues that divide the church. When we demand our rights at the expense of others' feelings, everybody loses. Only as we considerately exercise our freedom in Christ can we grow strong as the body of Christ. Mutual respect only comes when the stronger pick up their cross and yield their rights over and over again, seventy times seven if necessary.

LIFE STEP Jesus complimented the meek and said that they would inherit the earth (Matthew 5:5). Meekness does not exclude strength; it confirms it. The strong must be secure enough to submit their rights to the weak.

ROMANS 15:1-16

WHAT IS THE WRITER SAYING?

1 Kings 11:9
Rom 14:19

HOW CAN I APPLY THIS TO MY LIFE?

PRAY Pray for those who teach in your church to be faithful to the Word.

Today Paul introduces his third and final principle. The right way is always the love way. If we put the feelings and welfare of others ahead of our own desires, we will almost certainly do right. Love can be defined as putting the welfare of others ahead of ourselves regardless of the personal cost. That's what Paul is speaking of when he suggests that each one live to "please his neighbor." He is not asking us to be men-pleasers, but to consider the other person first in our decision-making process. Only when we have taken our fellow believers into consideration can we truly claim to be making wise decisions. And only when we consider them first can we claim to be exhibiting love.

True worship is not a matter of outward conformity, such as circumcision, but it is a matter of inward transformation. There will always be controversies regarding many of the outward matters that pertain to the faith. The one who eats by faith and the one who abstains by faith are equally pleasing to Him. It is the one who despises the faith of another, or mocks the faith of another who is a threat to the welfare of the body.

Remember, at issue here are matters that the Bible does not directly or indirectly address. In these areas where there is truly room for legitimate debate, we must willingly give ground. Should the circumcised despise those who are not circumcised? Should those who abstain from eating meat despise those who eat? Should those who observe a day despise those who do not? In all of these cases the answer is no. It is not what goes into a man that defiles him; it is what comes out of his heart.

LIFE STEP Submission is a tough concept. It runs contrary to everything that the natural man holds dear. We assume that surrender is something that losers do. But if we are not willing to surrender our rights, we will never experience true Christian living. "Whosoever shall lose his life shall preserve it" (Luke 17:33).

ROMANS 15:17-33

WHAT IS THE WRITER SAYING?

HOW CAN I APPLY THIS TO MY LIFE?

As Paul begins to wrap up this magnificent epistle he turns to personal news and plans. He explains why and on whose authority he writes such a letter to them. He says that he has written "boldly" to them, references his position as "the minister of Jesus Christ to the Gentiles," and points out that through "mighty signs and wonders by the power of the Spirit" his ministry has been authorized. All of these and similar comments serve to reinforce Paul's apostolic authority. It serves no purpose to write an epistle such as this to people who do not accept it for what it is—the Word of God.

We learn a whole lot about the apostle and his plans in this passage. Paul is at the end of his third missionary journey, probably in Corinth, preparing to travel to Jerusalem. From the Book of Acts we know that Paul is aware that he will be arrested and bound in that city, and yet he still continues to make plans for evangelizing parts unknown. Clearly he is not planning to spend a lot of time in Rome. The Lord would change Paul's plans by having him arrested in Jerusalem and eventually transported (free of charge!) back to Rome (see Acts 26-28). Notice the phrase, "much hindered," in verse 22. God's way of doing things was not always the way the apostle would have done it.

Verse 26 speaks of the offering that Paul collected throughout Macedonia and Greece for the saints at Jerusalem. The new believers in that region gave generously. Paul explains his responsibility to safely deliver this gift. By noting the generosity of the Greek and Macedonian Christians, Paul was perhaps hoping to encourage the believers in Rome to enthusiastically support his project to reach Spain with the gospel.

LIFE STEP The plans we make are never certain. All things do indeed work together for good, but the path we take to that destination often bears little resemblance to our original design.

FRIDAY 34

ROMANS 16:1-16

WHAT IS THE WRITER SAYING?

HOW CAN I APPLY THIS TO MY LIFE?

PRAY Honduras – For godly businessmen to establish enterprises to employ and evangelize the poor.

Chapter 16 opens with an incredible list of greetings. Paul had never visited this church and yet he knew many members who had moved there from other locations. The personal touch was always important to Paul. Our passage today is the beginning of Paul's concluding remarks. Note that a kiss was a common form of greeting in that day. It did not carry any of the overtones that it might in our culture. In North America we commonly shake hands. If Paul were writing us today he would have written, "Greet one another with a warm handshake."

Paul ended chapter 15 with prayer requests. Sitting in Corinth, Paul knew that there were problems on the horizon. He did not fear them, but he did fear that his ability to reach the lost with the gospel might be hampered. Notice his three requests. First he prayed that the unbelievers in Judea would not be able to silence him. He knew from previous experience (and his own pre-salvation attitude!) that they would stop at nothing to shut down the preaching of Christ. He further asks that the believers in Judea accept him and his financial gift. Some mistrusted Paul because of his former persecution of the church. Others were concerned that he was mocking the Law of Moses. Others thought he was denying the Jewish right to practice circumcision. His final request was that he might come to Rome in joy. Notice that he qualifies that last statement with the phrase, "by the will of God." Paul was not asking that they pray that his path be made easier, but that he might do all things God's way and have the right attitude about it.

 LIFE STEP Paul was a very intense person. It might have been difficult to get along with him because of his high ideals. However, notice his emphasis on people, prayer and interpersonal relationships. How are we doing in those areas?

SATURDAY 34

ROMANS 16:17-27

WHAT IS THE WRITER SAYING?

Rom. 16:19   simple concerning evil

aetv.com
Duck Dynasty

HOW CAN I APPLY THIS TO MY LIFE?

PRAY Pakistan – Pray for the government to have insight in how to deal with effort to impose shari'a law that appears impossible to root out.

The comments in verses 18-19 may at first seem at odds with Paul's teachings in Chapter 14. It must be remembered that in chapter 14 Paul is addressing the issue of preferences. Here he is speaking of those who deny and disobey the clear and direct teachings of Scripture. Excommunication is a biblical concept. It is to be used when a professing believer, after appropriate confrontation (see Matthew 18; 1 Thessalonians 5; and 2 Thessalonians 3), refuses to conform to biblical doctrine or biblical behavior. At such a point that person is to be noted and no one from the assembly is to interact socially with him. This also serves to protect the body at large from *wolves in sheep's clothing*. Discipline always seems hard for the moment but it will work to the benefit of all involved. Paul briefly mentions some of the saints who are with him at the time and wraps up his epistle with a doxology. There are some unique features to this word of praise. Notice the qualifiers that Paul uses. God is able to establish us only "according to my gospel." Paul's preaching of Jesus Christ is "according to the revelation of the mystery, which was kept secret since the world began." God is not limited by anything outside of Himself but He has chosen to limit Himself. God's blessing can only come according to the gospel that Paul has shared with us in this book we call The Book of Romans. Any other gospel is powerless. Any other salvation is fraudulent. Paul wants them to understand that his gospel is not *another* way to be saved, it is the *only* way to be saved – past, present and future. There are many worship systems but there is only one gospel.

LIFE STEP There is only one road that leads home to heaven. Therefore an understanding of everything associated with that one road is crucial. Christians must be experts in the gospel road! How's your GPS?

EZEKIEL

Dr. Tom Davis

Ezekiel's name means *God strengthens*, a rather appropriate name for the ministry God called him to and the situation the people of Israel faced. He was a Zadokian priest, which was the priestly line of the high priest. The Babylonians took him into captivity in the second deportation in 597 B.C. He lived with the common Jewish captives about fifty miles from the capital city of Babylon, ministering to them for over twenty-two years. Daniel, by way of comparison, was taken in the first deportation in 605 B.C. and lived in the city of Babylon with a ministry to his captors. Jeremiah, the third influential prophet in this period, stayed in Jerusalem, ministering to the Jews left behind. All three prophets lived and ministered beyond the 586 B.C. destruction of the first temple (Solomon's Temple).

Ezekiel's wife died the year before Jerusalem was destroyed, and he was not allowed to mourn for her, just as God would not mourn the death of His wife, Jerusalem. Despite the horror of the deportation, once the Jewish people were established in Babylon, they eventually experienced a relatively pleasant life. They were free to build homes, write back to Judah, establish businesses, and enjoy their own Jewish culture. Their comfort in Babylon is illustrated in the fact that when they were allowed to return in 539 B.C., only 50,000 of the estimated 2.5 million Jews elected to go back to Jerusalem (see Ezra 2:64-65). Even though they were somewhat comfortable in Babylon, it was still a depressing thought to be uprooted from their homeland, as illustrated by the mournful words of Psalm 137:

"By the rivers of Babylon, there we sat down, yea, we wept, when we remembered Zion. We hanged our harps upon the willows in the midst thereof. For there they that carried us away captive required of us a song; and they that wasted us required of us mirth, saying, Sing us one of the songs of Zion. How shall we sing the LORD's song in a strange land? If I forget thee, O Jerusalem, let my right hand forget her cunning. If I do not remember thee, let my tongue cleave to the roof of my mouth; if I prefer not Jerusalem above my chief joy.

Remember, O LORD, the children of Edom in the day of Jerusalem; who said, Rase it, rase it, even to the foundation thereof. O daughter of Babylon, who art to be destroyed; happy shall he be, that rewardeth thee as thou hast served us. Happy shall he be, that taketh and dasheth thy little ones against the stones."

The theme of Ezekiel is *The Glory of the Lord*. By way of comparison, the other three Major Prophets have similar themes: Isaiah, *The Salvation of the Lord*; Jeremiah, *The Judgment of the Lord*; and Daniel, *The Sovereignty of the Lord*.

The outline of Ezekiel is organized by topic and time:

- Before 586 B.C.: Ezekiel's call 1-3
- Before 586 B.C.: Ezekiel's condemnation of Judah 4-24
- In 586 B.C.: Ezekiel's condemnation of the nations 25-32
- After 586 B.C.: Ezekiel's country restored 33-48

There are a number of famous passages in the book:

- The wheel within the wheel vision: chapter 1
- Messianic passages: 17:22-24; 21:26-27; 34:23-24
- The Battle of Gog and Magog: chapters 38-39
- The Millennial Temple: chapters 40-48

Finally, there are several key points of theology that the book addresses. Ezekiel tells the people that Jerusalem *can* fall (as opposed to the supernatural deliverance they experienced from Sennacherib in 701 B.C.). As the Jews are taken to Babylon, God promises and demonstrates that He is still with them and that He is not just a local deity.

In the book of Ezekiel, God is the source of spiritual life. Just as God breathed into Adam the breath of life, likewise He will give His people a new heart (chapter 36); He will resurrect their dead bodies from the Valley of Dry Bones (chapter 37); and He will cause a life-giving river to flow from the new temple in the New Jerusalem (chapter 47).

SUNDAY 35

EZEKIEL 1:1-14

WHAT IS THE WRITER SAYING?

HOW CAN I APPLY THIS TO MY LIFE?

PRAY Sweden – Pray for a new awakening for this spiritually struggling nation; recent signs are that young people are moving back toward more traditional values.

In chapters 1-3 we see Ezekiel's call to his ministry. He is thirty years old, the typical age that priests would begin their priestly duties. He was from a priestly family, in fact, the family from which the high priests also came (the line of Zadok). Notice that Christ also waited until thirty years of age to begin His public ministry.

Ezekiel had been deported five years earlier with King Jehoiachin (also called Jeconiah or Coniah), which was the second Babylonian deportation in 597 B.C. This then dates the vision to 592 B.C.

The vision that follows is the famous "wheel within the wheel" vision that is popularized in the old folk song. While we can speculate on the exact appearance of this contraption, we do not have to guess at the purpose for it. By the time we get to the end of the chapter, it is clear that this is God's glorious chariot throne. Just as ancient kings had servants and special vehicles for transportation, so also does the great God of Israel. The characteristics of the throne underscore His attributes of omnipotence, omnipresence, and omniscience.

The servants are "cherubs," according to a later reference (Ezekiel 41:18). This name means *watchers*, which implies that they are guardians of the holiness of God. This category of angel occurs ninety times in Scripture. They appear to be the same as the "seraph" (burning one) of Isaiah 6, but "seraph" only appears that one time in the Bible.

The vision left quite an impression on Ezekiel, as it is mentioned again in 3:23, 8:4, and 43:3. Each animal is the *best* in his or her category. They may have been the animals on the four tribal standards (flags) in the wilderness wanderings. Some see parallels to the four Gospels of Christ's life.

LIFE STEP The Greek word for "fire" is *puros,* from which we get the word *pure*. The presence of God purifies us if we allow it; we must stay in His presence.

EZEKIEL 1:15-28

WHAT IS THE WRITER SAYING?

Matthew- king - Jews - lion - genealogy to Abraham
mark- servant - Romans - ox - no genealogy for servants
Luke- greatest man - Greeks - man's face - genealogy to Adam
John- God of very God = all men - eagle - no genealogy -

HOW CAN I APPLY THIS TO MY LIFE?

God always was!

The angelic creatures (called "beasts" in the parallel passage in Revelation 4) are *blockheads*—all four faces are on each of the four creatures. This apparently ensures that all four faces can be viewed from any angle. The lion parallels the gospel of Matthew, where Christ is presented as the king of Israel ("the lion of the tribe of Judah"). Mark, who was writing to Romans who appreciated servants, presents Christ as the obedient, diligent servant, which is pictured by the ox. Luke, writing to Greeks, presents Christ as the greatest man who ever lived (the face of the man). John presents Christ in His soaring majesty as God of very God (the eagle). Matthew gives Christ's genealogy back to Abraham through the kings of Judah. Luke gives Christ's genealogy all the way back to Adam. Mark gives no genealogy, for it doesn't matter for a servant. John gives no genealogy, for God has always existed.

The wheels appear to be designed to demonstrate mobility; God can go wherever He needs to. The angels and the throne do not need to turn in order to go in a particular direction. Perhaps there were four pairs of wheels, one pair under each angel, with the wheels at right angles for this multi-directional capability.

The multiple sets of wings on creatures are found elsewhere in Scripture (Isaiah 6:2). In addition to implying mobility, the wings are used to show respect by covering certain parts of the body.

Notice all the impressive colors. Fire is yellow. In Hebrew, amber refers to a bright metallic shine. Crystal is clear but sparkling. The rainbow has multiple colors. Beryl is golden brown, and sapphire is blue. The net effect: Ezekiel's God is an awesome God.

LIFE STEP The ancients saw God and revered Him. We don't see God. How do we honor Him in our thoughts and prayers?

EZEKIEL 2:1 - 3:7

WHAT IS THE WRITER SAYING?

HOW CAN I APPLY THIS TO MY LIFE?

Chapter two contains Ezekiel's charge to his ministry. In 2:1-2 he is indwelt for power. In 2:3-5 he is informed for confidence. In 2:6-7 he is encouraged for endurance, and in 2:8-10 he is programmed for success. Notice that God commands Ezekiel to stand on his feet to receive his charge, but the Spirit enters and lifts Ezekiel to his feet. Apparently our spiritual life is so empowered by God that we need to only assent to what He wants to do through us, not work up the courage, wisdom, and strength to do so. As God gets Ezekiel ready, He does not hide the difficulties that Ezekiel will face. By this time, Jerusalem has already been attacked twice by the Babylonians. You would think that the Jews left behind would have been desperate to win God's favor. But one of the characteristics of sin is that it blinds the perpetrator to his or her faults. The majority of the Jewish people had centuries earlier abandoned pure Jehovah worship for a syncretism of Biblical and pagan theology. It was not that they rejected Jehovah outright— they just wanted Him plus all the other gods and goddesses. God steels Ezekiel for the negative reception and encourages him with the thought that it is not crucial that he be popular to successfully convince people to repent. He is merely required to deliver the message, and God will see to it that they recognize the message as having come from a prophet of God. (This should not be interpreted as the right of a preacher/ witnesser to be rude to get a sinner's attention!)

The scroll represents the information that Ezekiel internalizes, then to deliver it. There is an abundance of it ("within and without," 2:10), and it is sweet since it is God's Word, but bitter because it is a word of judgment.

LIFE STEP Why do we believe, but so many others don't? How can we be more effective spokespersons for God? Why should we share when they reject?

EZEKIEL 36:1-15

WHAT IS THE WRITER SAYING?

HOW CAN I APPLY THIS TO MY LIFE?

PRAY Cuba – Fruitfulness and a greater area of outreach for the Christian radio feeds out of Latin America.

God promises to bring the Jewish people back and bless them once again in their ancient homeland. When this takes place, they are told that never again will the nations harm them, nor will they ever be scattered again.

Within seventy years of the writing of this prophecy, close to fifty thousand Jews had returned to Jerusalem, and the second temple had been built. Every step of the way was filled with opposition, however, by the local Gentiles. Besides this, only fifty thousand of an estimated 2.5 million Jews had returned. From 516 B.C. to the time of Christ, conditions continued to be severe, and at no time could we say the Jews had been *re-gathered* and were under the watchful care of a *good shepherd*. When their *good, great and chief shepherd* appeared to them on Palm Sunday around A.D. 30, they did not recognize Him, and they rejected Him. In A.D. 70, the Romans destroyed the second temple, 1.2 million Jews were killed, and the rest were scattered once again.

In other words, the promises here in Ezekiel have never been fulfilled. There are evangelical Christians who are comfortable with the idea that God will not fulfill these promises to national Israel, saying they have forfeited the right to receive them because they have rejected Jesus Christ. This overlooks the fact that the promises God made to Abraham were unilateral—only God was making the pledge. If any one generation of the Jews wanted to be blessed, they had to obey to receive the blessing, but the ultimate fulfillment was always based on the sovereign plan of God. He will see to it that the terminal generation believes, obeys, and is worthy to receive the promises.

LIFE STEP

Trust and obey for there is no other way to be happy in Jesus, but to trust and obey.

THURSDAY 35

EZEKIEL 36:16-25

WHAT IS THE WRITER SAYING?

HOW CAN I APPLY THIS TO MY LIFE?

PRAY Romania – Pray for the church to remain grounded in biblical truth amidst the swings of new freedoms.

God affirms that He judged the nation of Israel for her gross sins—particularly the sins of murder and idolatry. When He scattered the people of Israel to the nations, it was like when a woman was declared "unclean" and separated from her people in Jewish society due to childbirth or the monthly menstrual period. Before a woman could return to worship in the temple she had to undergo a ceremonial bath (Hebrew: *mikveh*) in running water (the "baptisms" mentioned in Hebrews 6:2). The "sprinkling" of verse 25 refers to a similar process of ceremonial cleansing (see Leviticus 14:1-7). The important emphasis in this chapter is that God intends to return the Jewish people to their homeland, not because of their behavior but for His great name's sake. God has made promises, and He knew when He made those promises what the response of the people would be—their failures did not catch Him off-guard.

He predicted to Abraham, even as He was giving him the Promised Land, that Abraham's descendents would spend four hundred years in Egypt (Genesis 15:13). When God affirmed His covenant with Abraham in Genesis 15, He alone walked between the pieces of the sacrificed animals, binding Himself, and not Abraham, to the ultimate fulfillment of the covenant. In Jeremiah 31, where the new covenant is announced, God concludes the chapter with a reminder that as long as the earth rotates on its axis, and as long as it revolves around the sun, His covenants with Israel still stand. In fact, even after the Jewish people had rejected Jesus and the Gospel had gone to the Gentiles (with the church being defined and explained by Paul, the Apostle to the Gentiles), Paul still insists that God is not done with national Israel, and that one day all Israel will be saved (Romans 11:26).

 LIFE STEP The gifts and calling of God are without repentance (Old English phraseology). Modern version: *God keeps His promises*. We can count on it!

FRIDAY 35

EZEKIEL 36:26-38

WHAT IS THE WRITER SAYING?

HOW CAN I APPLY THIS TO MY LIFE?

PRAY Thailand – For pastors to accept their responsibility to lovingly confront believers engaging in sin.

Once again, God promises to bless Israel for His glory, so the heathen nations will know that He is the one true God. This passage is a repeat of the famous *new covenant*, which is first explained in Jeremiah 31. The Old Testament law was given to illustrate the sinfulness of man and to provide a fence to protect the chosen people of Israel from the perversion of the pagan nations surrounding them. It was not a way to live to merit salvation (salvation is always a gracious gift from God appropriated by faith). Rather it was a guide to the people's spiritual development as they grew in their relationship with their God (sanctification). The weakness of the Mosaic Law was that it provided guidance, but it did not give the power for the sinful human nature to do what it requested. The *new covenant* is superior because the Holy Spirit of God takes up residence within the believer, and in the process, provides an inner sense of God's will while also empowering the believer to obey. This inner sense is directly connected to the believer's ongoing study of God's Word, which the Spirit helps us understand and apply. These features of the new covenant have been enjoyed by the Church ever since the Holy Spirit came in Acts 2, however, the nation of Israel must also receive this blessing in order for the new covenant to be fulfilled. This will take place during the tribulation period and millennial reign of Christ. This increased closeness to God and empowering from God may explain why King David fell so hard morally, while the New Testament heroes didn't.

LIFE STEP God justly desires that His greatness be published and acknowledged by His creatures. A *secret* of a successful prayer life is to figure out what would bring God glory in any situation and then ask Him to help you accomplish that.

EZEKIEL 37:1-14

WHAT IS THE WRITER SAYING?

HOW CAN I APPLY THIS TO MY LIFE?

PRAY Finland – That widespread evangelism would neutralize the rapid growth of the Muslim faith and cults.

Chapter 37 pictures the resurrection of the nation of Israel. The bones in the valley have obviously been there for a while. The bodies have decayed, wild animals have separated the bones, and the bones are bleached white in the hot sun. Ezekiel and the Israelites had every reason to feel hopeless now that their capital city had been defeated, their temple destroyed, and their people uprooted from their homeland. Ezekiel had already recorded messages of renewed blessing, but when asked by God if these bones could live again, Ezekiel could not respond with confidence. God tells him to command the bones to come together. In a rather long process, including several commands and activities by the prophet and God, the skeletons are reassembled, the flesh comes back upon the bodies, and there are now corpses in the desert.

Since the late nineteenth century, Jewish people from around the world have moved back to Israel. Not only were they coming to renew an independent Jewish state that had not existed for over two thousand years (Israel was annexed by Rome in 63 B.C.), but they also resurrected the Hebrew language that had not been used as a spoken language for over two thousand years. Never in the history of the world has a dead language been resurrected to become the mother tongue of a nation. Ezekiel 37:8 illustrates the current situation of Israel. She has come back to her homeland in unbelief. Israel is a complete but spiritually lifeless nation. The breath of God will come into them, and like Adam, they will become a spiritually alive nation. This evangelistic event will take place during the tribulation period.

LIFE STEP With God there is always hope. Even when we are in the tomb, all is not lost. God has been in the tomb once before and knows the way out!

EZEKIEL 37:15-28

WHAT IS THE WRITER SAYING?

HOW CAN I APPLY THIS TO MY LIFE?

PRAY Pray for unity among the staff and the membership of your local church.

When Solomon was king, he violated the commands of the Lord not to multiply horses (for military purposes), wealth (for self-sufficiency and decadence), or wives (for international treaties, and lest they entice the king with their gods) (Deuteronomy 17:14-20). Unfortunately, despite Solomon's good start, he eventually violated all three of these principles. He especially allowed his wives to influence his spiritual life to the point that eventually he placed idols right next to the temple of Jehovah. For that reason, God decided to punish Solomon by dividing his kingdom in two. At his death, this happened, with ten tribes forming the Northern Kingdom of *Israel* with a capital at Samaria and two tribes forming the Southern Kingdom of *Judah* with a capital at Jerusalem. (The tribal designations are approximations, for actually the Jews had moved freely around the Promised Land. The *two tribes* were technically Judah and Benjamin, but Simeon also was represented in the Southern Kingdom, as were the Levites.) The Northern Kingdom never had a godly king, and its inhabitants were taken into captivity by the Assyrians in 722 B.C.

This passage looks forward to the day when members of all twelve tribes are returned and united in Israel. "Judah" and the "children of Israel" in verse 16 refer to the Southern Kingdom. "Joseph" and "Ephraim" (the son of Joseph and the largest tribe and home of the capital of the Northern Kingdom) refer to the Northern Kingdom. This passage promises eternal peace and blessing, which indicates that the prophecy still awaits fulfillment.

LIFE STEP History contains thousands of years of unnecessary suffering due to man's rebellion. An incredible day is coming when rebellion ceases and God is free to bless.

EZEKIEL 38:1-12

WHAT IS THE WRITER SAYING?

HOW CAN I APPLY THIS TO MY LIFE?

This passage envisions a time when Jewish people have gathered back to Israel and are at peace, not needing walls for protection (v. 11). A number of nations join with *Gog and Magog* for this attack. Some are well-known today (*Persia* is modern Iran and *Libya* is modern Libya). Others are slightly changed (*Ethiopia* is modern Sudan). Others cannot be identified with a particular modern nation with certainty (*Meshech* may sound like Moscow and *Tubal* may be the root of Tobulsk, but language scholars conclude that there is no provable connection). In Genesis 10, Magog, Meshech, Tubal, and Gomer are all identified with nations to the north of Israel, in Turkey and southern Russia. Whoever these enemies may be when this prophecy is fulfilled, it is clear that they come not just from the immediate north of Israel (such as modern Lebanon and Syria) but rather from the "far north" (Ezekiel 38:6,15; 39:2). As to the timing, the passage indicates (v. 8) that it will take place "after many days," in the "latter years," when the Jews have "gathered from many people (nations)." Ezekiel 38:16 adds that this will take place "in the latter days," a reference to the events leading up to the messianic kingdom.

From the time the prophecy was written until now, Israel has not dwelt securely in unwalled towns (v. 11). This must refer to the time during the tribulation period when Israel finally achieves security under the protection of the Antichrist. Perhaps he will even have a regional capital in Jerusalem. The Gog and Magog attack would then be against Israel and the Antichrist. After an initial defeat, the Antichrist recovers (Daniel 11:40-45) and God destroys Magog, leaving a power vacuum in which the Antichrist can then pursue world domination.

LIFE STEP Israel had great promises, but the road to the Promised Land was difficult, as the path to future blessing will be as well.

EZEKIEL 38:13-23

WHAT IS THE WRITER SAYING?

HOW CAN I APPLY THIS TO MY LIFE?

PRAY Malaysia – Pray for wisdom and fearlessness for Christians seeking to share the good news with Muslims.

"Sheba and Dedan" (v. 13) refer to Arab tribes that moved freely throughout the Middle East as caravan operators, traders, and herders. "Tarshish" is the city in Spain, not Asia Minor. It was also known for its accomplishments in the area of seafaring and trade (see 2 Chronicles 9:21). In verse 13, both of these groups of people would naturally be inquisitive about a traveling group looking for financial advantage. Some have argued that the *lion* refers to Great Britain and the *cubs* would be her colonies, including the United States of America. This is highly unlikely since Tarshish was a known entity in Ezekiel's day and Great Britain was not at that time known as a *lion*.

Gog is most likely the leader of Magog. In Ezekiel 38:2, some translations refer to him as the prince of *Rosh. Rosh* does not refer to Russia (although the country might actually turn out to be Russia). *Rosh* is the Hebrew word for *head* and is used metaphorically for *head of state*. Gog, therefore, is the *chief* prince of Magog.

God says that the prophets of old had talked about Magog. From Ezekiel's day, those prophets of old would be the prophet Isaiah and countries prior to the current Gentile enemy, Babylon. Assyria is a good candidate for this *enemy of old*. As the Bible looks forward to the tribulation period, it uses old enemies of Israel as metaphors for future enemies, such as the kingdom of the Antichrist being called "Babylon" in Revelation and Magog being "Assyria" here in Ezekiel. Since *Russia* is in the *remote parts of the north* in today's geo-political world, she and her Muslim allies would most naturally fulfill the role of Magog.

LIFE STEP God's payday is coming someday. He will use nations to accomplish His will but still holds them responsible for their behavior.

EZEKIEL 39:1-16

WHAT IS THE WRITER SAYING?

HOW CAN I APPLY THIS TO MY LIFE?

PRAY United Kingdom – Over 40% of evangelical churches have no one under the age of 20 in attendance. Pray for a harvest of souls among young people.

In chapters 38-39, the armies of Magog are pictured as unprecedented in size. Apparently this attack will be even greater in scope than the attacks by Assyria and Babylon. The horsemen and soldiers will cover the land of Israel. *Horses* seem strange in the modern context. Certainly modern military equivalents would not be excluded by the lack of mention, but due to the terrain from the Russian steppes down to Jerusalem, horses cannot be excluded.

Magog thinks she is acting under her own genius and power. God brought her to Israel (38:4). He uses her to upset the Antichrist and rattle Israel. Then He rains destruction upon her armies in Israel as well as her homeland. Certainly this could be literal fire and weather patterns sent by God. God can also use secondary means to accomplish His work, which could include man-made weapons. In Revelation 13, the Antichrist calls fire down from Heaven, imitating the powers of the two witnesses of Revelation 11 and perhaps implying that it was he who destroyed Magog on the mountains of Israel.

We are told that the people of Israel will burn the weapons left behind for seven years. Some have argued that this requires the battle to take place before or at the start of the seven-year tribulation period. While certainly possible, there is no obligation to fit the period of cleanup entirely in the tribulation period. As an event that sparks the rise of the Antichrist to international dominance, a mid-tribulation battle of Gog and Magog makes sense. Even today, the Israelis have specially trained inspectors to clean up all human remains after terrorist attacks. Likewise, God will have His people cleanse His land of these enemy bodies.

 LIFE STEP The Bible and tomorrow's news—despite the horror, it is realistic, and we can imagine CNN reporting on site. Even so, come, Lord Jesus!

THURSDAY 36

EZEKIEL 39:17-29

WHAT IS THE WRITER SAYING?

HOW CAN I APPLY THIS TO MY LIFE?

PRAY South Africa – For the church to cultivate multi–racial relationships and to model unity in Christ.

Revelation 19:9 announces the *marriage supper of the Lamb*, the great banquet that will inaugurate the millennial reign of Christ. Here we have the *marriage supper of Gog and Magog* as the birds of the air and the beasts of the field are invited to eat the bodies of the fallen on the hills of Israel. Since this same imagery is used of the Battle of Armageddon, some have argued that *Gog and Magog* refer to the Antichrist and his defeat at the Battle of Armageddon. Similar imagery does not prove identical events. Likewise, Revelation 19 refers to another *Gog and Magog* event, which will happen at the end of the millennial kingdom. Here again, we don't have to conclude that the events are one and the same but that the one event illustrates the other. For instance, when we say, "He met his Waterloo," we are not saying that person was in France with Napoleon and

was defeated by the British, but rather *Waterloo* stands for any frustrating setback based on Napoleon's experience there. From Ezekiel's day until now, no enemy has come against Israel and been defeated in the way described in these chapters.

Notice that in the aftermath of this episode, all the Jews will return to Israel, and "none" will be left in the nations (v. 28). This also specifies that the Jews have returned from multiple nations (in Ezra, the return under Zerubbabel was from one nation—Persia).

When all the Jews return from many nations, God will pour out His Spirit upon them (v. 29). This is one of the features of the day of the Lord in Joel 2:28-32. During the tribulation period, many Jews (and Gentiles) will be born again, and the Spirit of God will be evident in their lives and testimonies.

LIFE STEP Even in the world's darkest hours, God will be gracious, and many will come to Him for eternal safety.

FRIDAY 36

EZEKIEL 43:1-9; 44:1-4

WHAT IS THE WRITER SAYING?

HOW CAN I APPLY THIS TO MY LIFE?

Ezekiel chapters 40-48 describe *kingdom blessings*, particularly, worship of the Messiah during that time. The year is 573 B.C., thirteen years after chapter 39. Israel was still languishing in captivity. God had already predicted her national resurrection (chapter 37). Now He shows them their new temple— the focus of Jewish national life. The temple described in Ezekiel 40-48 is significantly different from Solomon's Temple. There would be none of the following: Ark of the Covenant, table of shewbread, menorah, veil, high priest, feast of Pentecost, Day of Atonement or evening sacrifice. The temple complex will be located outside the walls of Jerusalem, about twenty miles to the north near ancient Shiloh (Hebrew for *he to whom it belongs*), one of the early sites of the tabernacle.

When the people returned in 536 B.C. and built a new temple, however, it was not patterned after Ezekiel's Temple. Clearly the Jews considered Ezekiel's Temple to be a messianic temple.

In Ezekiel 11, Ezekiel witnessed the Shekinah glory of God leaving the temple. To date, He has never returned other than temporarily on Palm Sunday in the person of Jesus Christ. Now, as the Messianic Age has dawned, Ezekiel views the return of the glory of God to His special city. The passage describes God's delight in Jerusalem and Israel. Once He has entered the temple by the Eastern Gate, the gate is shut and no human will use it, although the political leader will be privileged to eat and meet with the Lord at the Eastern Gate.

 LIFE STEP For all of human history to date, God's creatures have defied Him. What a great day when all rational creatures join to honor their Creator and worship Him. Righteousness and knowledge of the Lord will cover the earth like the waters cover the seas.

EZEKIEL 47:1-12

WHAT IS THE WRITER SAYING?

HOW CAN I APPLY THIS TO MY LIFE?

PRAY Peru – For churches as they seek to meet the needs of their congregations in which up to 70% percent of attendees are unemployed.

A river will flow from the temple to Jerusalem and then to the Mediterranean and Dead Seas, causing the northern half of the Dead Sea to come *alive* (v. 9). As strange as this may seem, the modern state of Israel has already contemplated building a *Med/Dead Canal* for the purpose of hydroelectric power and restoring the level of the Dead Sea. The land of Israel will be distributed among the twelve tribes, from the Euphrates River in the north to the eastern branch of the Nile River in the south. Earthquake activity associated with the judgments of the tribulation period and the return of Christ will create a plateau on the former mountains of Judea, covering fifty square miles for a *holy precinct* for Jerusalem, the temple, and priests. The city is described to be about ten miles square (100 square miles).

Some would argue that the death of Christ abolished the need for animal sacrifices, but the book of Hebrews warns against practicing animal sacrifices in the Church Age, not the Millennium. The sacrifices in the Millennium will be used to atone (apologize) for violations of messianic law, symbolize the substitutionary death of Messiah, and provide meat for the priests (Ezekiel 44:29). They will be a memorial looking back at the sacrifice of Christ, just as our communion service is today. During a period in which death and suffering will be severely limited by the blessings of God, perhaps God wants a graphic reminder of the horror of sin and the price paid by His Son. Four other prophets also mention a millennial temple (Zechariah, Isaiah, Jeremiah, and Daniel). We actually have more details about this temple than Solomon's. Revelation 22 uses similar imagery for Heaven, but this does not require that Ezekiel is describing Heaven.

 LIFE STEP Ezekiel's final verse is the ultimate statement about the nature of the messianic era: "the name of the city (Jerusalem) … shall be, *The Lord is there*" (48:35). Nothing could make any place or situation any better!

REVELATION

Dr. Tom Davis

John the Apostle wrote the Book of Revelation around A.D. 95 during the reign of the Roman emperor Domitian (A.D. 81-96). John was in exile on the Isle of Patmos (a four by eight mile island that served as a penal mining colony located sixty miles southwest of Ephesus). Tradition states that John was released under Emperor Nerva, who reigned A.D. 96-98.

In harmony with Christ's statement to Peter in John 21 and according to church history, John was the only apostle to live to old age (although he also died a martyr's death). It is believed that the Gospel of John and the epistles of 1, 2, and 3 John were also written in the A.D. 90's so we can't say dogmatically that Revelation was the last book written, but certainly it logically concludes the information given in both testaments. John was the *beloved disciple*. He was a member of Jesus' inner circle of disciples along with Peter and James. He was with Christ on the Mount of Transfiguration. He took Peter to the high priest's home for Christ's first trial, as apparently John knew that influential family. He alone of all the disciples is mentioned at the crucifixion, as Christ asked him from the cross to take care of Mary. By A.D. 95 he would have been serving Jesus for almost seventy years. What memories would have enriched his mind as he received the amazing information contained in the Book of Revelation. Of all the New Testament authors only Luke and Paul provide more written Scripture.

"Revelation" is the translation of the Greek word *apocalypse*. Both refer to an *unveiling*. While we normally associate the *unveiling* of future events (prophecy) with the book, actually the word is referring to the revelation of the person of Jesus Christ, who is both the main subject and the *spirit* of future events. Revelation 1:19 provides a nice outline of the book in three tenses. John was told to write the things which "thou hast seen" (past tense – chapter 1), "the things which are" (present tense – chapters 2-3), and "the things which shall be hereafter" (future tense – chapters 4-22). We could also consider the way in which the book presents Jesus. In chapters 1-3, He is pictured as the *Lord over the churches*. In chapters 4-20, He is presented as the *Lion over the nations*. In chapters 21-22, He is viewed as the *Lamb of eternity*.

The book is highly symbolic. Some of the symbols are explained in context. Most of the symbols have precedents in the Old Testament. We must be careful not to force statements introduced by "like" or "as." They indicate comparison, not identification.

Historically, there have been four ways to approach the book. In the "Preterist Theory," the predictions are thought to apply to events surrounding the A.D. 70 destruction of Jerusalem by the Romans. In the "Historical Theory," the predictions are thought to cover all of world history from John's day until the end of time. In the "Idealist Theory," it is thought that the book teaches principles, not specific events. The fourth view, which is the view affirmed in this commentary, is the "Futurist Theory." It holds that chapters 4-22 still lie in the future.

REVELATION

There is an amazing use of numbers in the book ("seven" appears 50 times!). Scholars have noted over 550 allusions to the Old Testament with 278 of the 404 verses containing references to Old Testament ideas. Daniel 2 is alluded to ten times and Daniel 7 has thirty parallels. The Greek text contains many irregularities in grammar that can only be explained by John's intense excitement as he received and recorded the information.

The book presents the final struggle of God the Father, Son, and Holy Spirit against the father (Satan), son (Antichrist), and unholy spirit (false prophet). Revelation concludes with *newness*: the new heaven and earth, new people, a new bride, a new home, a new temple, and a new light. It is the answer to the tragedy of Genesis 1-3 with paradise regained for redeemed humanity. Revelation is the only book in the Bible that promises a blessing for those who read it. Yet for most of church history it has been ignored as being too hard to understand. Perhaps Daniel 12:4 indicates that in the end times, Christians would become knowledgeable in prophecy. ("But thou, O Daniel, shut up the words, and seal the book, *even* to the time of the end: many shall run to and fro, and knowledge shall be increased.")

REVELATION 6:1-17

WHAT IS THE WRITER SAYING?

HOW CAN I APPLY THIS TO MY LIFE?

Revelation 6:1–8:1 describes the seven seal judgments. As each seal is opened on the scroll, John witnesses a prophetic event. The first four seal judgments are also known as the *four Horsemen of the Apocalypse*. Notice that the four living creatures of chapter 4 call these horsemen forth. The thunderous voice of the first living beast implies judgment. The color white speaks of victory and perhaps counterfeit purity. While the horse and bow are both instruments of ancient warfare, perhaps the absence of arrows implies a political conquest (see Daniel 7:8, 24). It says that the rider of the white horse "was given" his authority ("crown"), indicating that these events are initiated from the throne of God, and therefore would be classified as God's wrath being poured out on the sinful earth as a judgment.

While no specific chronological markers are given here in chapter 6, both Daniel and Matthew associate war with the entire seven years of the tribulation period. Therefore, we could suggest that the opening of the seals begins shortly after the Rapture of the church and that the white horse represents the beginning of the Antichrist's rise to world dominance. The red horse speaks of the bloodshed of war. The black horse represents the famine that comes in the wake of war. The voice that describes the symbolism of the third horse is God's (from the midst of the four living creatures), indicating once again that this is God's judgment on sinful mankind. Wheat is more nutritious than barley. The prices mentioned indicate tenfold price inflation. Since olives and grapes grow wild, these items are not immediately affected. The famine is limited and the wealthy still have their food. The last horse is yellowish green (the word is *chlorine* in Greek). It represents death in general (*green around the gills*). "Hell" (actually *hades*, representing the grave) is like the hearse, bringing up the rear. The sixth seal (vv. 12-17) parallel the signs of the times in Matthew 24.

LIFE STEP If this happened tomorrow, 1.5 billion people would die. Are your friends safe?

REVELATION 7:1-17

WHAT IS THE WRITER SAYING?

HOW CAN I APPLY THIS TO MY LIFE?

The seventh and final seal is not opened until 8:1. In chapter 7, we take a break from the chronological sequence and step back to fill in details of some of the other things that God is doing during the first half of the tribulation period. In 7:1-8 we are introduced to the 144,000 sealed Jews who are protected from the divine judgments and apparently become the evangelists on the planet after the Rapture of the church. Ancient Jewish superstition claimed that winds blowing from the "corners" (east-northeast, etc.) of the compass were harmful. The direction of the rising sun (east, v. 2) is associated with the following positive concepts in Scripture: paradise; the direction that the Shekinah glory of God takes when returning to the temple; the Magi; and the messianic title, "Dayspring" (Luke 1:78). God is called the "living God" as contrasted with the *dead* gods of paganism.

The ancient world was familiar with tattoos and distinctive cuttings in the flesh for tribal, military, trade guild, or religious purposes. In Revelation 13 we will be introduced to the infamous "mark of the Beast," 666. Here, as in a parallel situation in Ezekiel 9, the individuals are marked on the forehead. In Ezekiel 9:4 the "mark" was actually the Hebrew letter *tav* or *t*. At that time, the Hebrew letter even looked like a small cross! In the Bible, there are many different arrangements of the "12 tribes of Israel." In addition to the original twelve sons of Jacob, we have the two sons of Joseph, Ephraim and Manasseh. Levi is left out in some lists since as priests they were given cities throughout the country and not territory. Joseph is left out in many lists to make room for his sons. In this list, Dan and Ephraim are missing. Perhaps Dan is missing because that tribe left the original tribal allotment in the south, moved to the extreme north, apostatized, and was absorbed into Syrian paganism. Perhaps Ephraim is missing because that tribe opposed Judah and David. Verses 9-17 indicate that many people will be gloriously saved during this time.

LIFE STEP God does dangerous things, but always with great care for those who are part of His master plan.

REVELATION 8:1-13

WHAT IS THE WRITER SAYING?

HOW CAN I APPLY THIS TO MY LIFE?

PRAY Mexico – For the full implementation of religious freedom at the national and local levels.

Chapter 8 begins with the opening of the seventh and final seal. All of heaven is shocked into adoring silence with the realization that the title deed to Planet Earth is now back in the hands of the rightful owner and the official copy is now open in the heavenly court with the breaking of the last seal. Satan, the usurper, is in the process of being defeated and expelled from his squatter claim. Adoring silence as a mode of worship is observed in other passages such as, "Be still and know that I am God" (Psalm 46:10). In biblical times, trumpets were used to get attention, call people together, and announce important events. Both metal and ram's horn trumpets (the *shofar*) were known and used. It is not clear here what type is being used. "Thy kingdom come" is probably the most frequently uttered prayer. The altar of incense symbolizes the prayers of the saints going up to God. Here, the coals from that altar are also symbolic of the judgment to fall upon the rebellious earth in the process of establishing that kingdom.

The accompanying physical traumas heighten the judgmental aspect of these trumpets. Note that the seventh seal is not a specific judgment, but rather contains all seven of the judgments in this next series of judgments. The first four trumpet judgments fall on nature and indirectly attack man. The first trumpet judgment attacks green vegetation. The second trumpet judgment affects the salty sea. The third trumpet judgment attacks fresh water. Wormwood is *absinth*, a bitter chemical used to kill intestinal parasites. Amazingly, it is also the meaning of the name Chernobyl, the city in the Ukraine with the tragic nuclear reactor malfunction. The fourth trumpet judgment affects the heavenly light. A similar phenomenon took place in one of the ten judgments upon the Egyptians and also the day Christ died.

LIFE STEP "God is great and God is good." Here His greatness is on terrible display.

REVELATION 9:1-21

WHAT IS THE WRITER SAYING?

Chart p. 1930

HOW CAN I APPLY THIS TO MY LIFE?

PRAY Brazil – Pray for the millions of people practicing spiritism to be delivered by salvation.

At the end of chapter 8, John is told that there are three more trumpets to sound and that they will be the three final woes to fall upon mankind. Actually, this is a very accurate statement as the third woe (seventh trumpet) is in fact the final series of judgments, the vial (bowl) judgments. The devastation these judgments bring is cataclysmic. If you take one-fourth of a number (the fourth seal judgment) and then one-third of the remainder (the sixth trumpet judgment) the result is half of the original number. There are over seven billion people on the planet today. This would represent a death toll of over 3.5 billion people!

The "star" (v. 1) represents a spirit being. He has authority to open the bottomless pit. Smoke comes out, darkening the sun and also mimicking the darkening of the sun produced by a great swarm of locusts. These are not normal locusts but demonic locusts. Instead of eating vegetation, their *diet* is human flesh. Their *sting* is like that of a scorpion.

Some scorpions have deadly stings but these do not. The sting of a scorpion has been described as the equivalent of being stung by two wasps at the same time. Torment for God-haters is the stated mission for these horror-film creatures. That they would do so for five months is significant because that is the length of the lifespan of a normal locust. It is not clear why these tormented men cannot commit suicide. Perhaps it means that they are in so much pain they wish and think they should die from the stings but don't. Both "Abaddon" and "Apollyon" mean the same thing, *Destroyer*. Verses 13-21 continue with another scourge of demonic creatures. Some have speculated that the fanciful description of these demonic beings was the best John could do in describing weapons of modern warfare. While God can use modern equipment to produce such torment, it would not be surprising if this were a literal description of the fearful appearance of these bizarre creatures.

LIFE STEP

We have a choice. We can fear God now in reverential awe that leads to eternal salvation, or we can fear Him later in stark terror.

REVELATION 11:1-14

WHAT IS THE WRITER SAYING?

HOW CAN I APPLY THIS TO MY LIFE?

Some theologians argue that the Book of Revelation was written prior to the A.D. 70 destruction of the temple and that most of the prophecies herein were fulfilled in A.D. 70. They see no future Jewish Temple. However, in 2 Thessalonians 2:4, Paul envisions worship of the antichrist in the temple. Since this did not happen in A.D. 70, it must be a future event. "Measuring" implies ownership and authority. God lays claim to the temple even while predicting its desecration. It would seem that the "forty two months" refers to the second half of the Tribulation while the "1260 days" refers to the first half. For the first 3½ years of the Tribulation, the two witnesses will preach in Jerusalem. This is the same length of time as Jesus' public ministry. They will be invincible until it is God's time for their martyrdom by the Antichrist as he dominates Jerusalem for the second half of the tribulation. Verse 4 uses the imagery of Zechariah 4:1-14. Elijah announced a drought on Israel and called fire down from heaven. He is also the predicted forerunner of Christ (Malachi 4:5). Moses is also mentioned in Malachi 4:4 along with "Mt. Horeb" (Mt. Sinai) which both men visited in their ministries. Both men also appeared with Christ on the Mount of Transfiguration. They are good candidates for the two witnesses. The "beast" is defined as the antichrist in Revelation 13:1-18. The abyss defines his satanic origins and perhaps a resurrection from a mortal wound. The whole world will know of the two witnesses' death and will rejoice. Today satellite TV makes this possible. In earlier times, ambassadors in Jerusalem from every nation would have made this possible. They do not rise until the fourth day proving that indeed they were dead and that this is a supernatural resurrection.

LIFE STEP
Why does the world hate us so much? It is because their father, Satan, hates our Savior, Jesus Christ.

FRIDAY 37

REVELATION 12:1-17

WHAT IS THE WRITER SAYING?

HOW CAN I APPLY THIS TO MY LIFE?

PRAY Israel – Pray that the gospel may be understood as a fulfilment of their Jewish heritage, and pray that a widespread turning to their Messiah might come.

Chapter 12 adds more actors and activities to the Tribulation story. The man-child is obviously Jesus, so the woman would then represent the nation of Israel. This is affirmed by the twelve stars, which would represent the twelve tribes of Israel. In the Joseph story in Genesis, the sun and moon represented Joseph's father (Jacob) and mother (Rachel). The red dragon is obviously Satan (and so identified in v. 9). He appears as a serpent in Genesis. The color red may reflect Egyptian mythology that featured a fearsome red crocodile. The "stars" swept from heaven may refer to the angels that joined Satan's rebellion (v. 9). If so, then we would have the added bit of information that 33% of the angels followed Satan, becoming *demons*.

Revelation 12 is the first of several passages that speaks of Satan's end-time kingdom as composed of ten or seven countries/kings. Daniel 7:7-8 teaches that ten confederated kings will be dominated by Satan's antichrist, who eliminates three of them leaving seven kings over ten territories. In a parallel description in Revelation 13:1 there are ten horns, seven heads, and ten crowns instead of the seven crowns mentioned here in Revelation 12.

Another important observation from this chapter is the freedom with which the prophecies jump around the timeline. For instance, from verse 5a to verse 5b we jump from Jesus' birth to His ascension (33 years). From verse 5b to verse 6 we jump over the entire Church Age (1980+ years) to the tribulation period. We can conclude that biblical prophecy does not have to be strictly chronological or inclusive. Verses 7-9 would seem to be a mid-tribulation event, providing the reason why the second half is more intense than the first half of the tribulation. "Devil" means *slanderer*. "Satan" means *accuser*. He is the original and master deceiver. Verses 6-17 describe what Israel does to escape the dragon, namely, hide in the wilderness for the last half of the tribulation.

LIFE STEP

God has a master plan and He is in control of even His enemies.

REVELATION 13:1-18

WHAT IS THE WRITER SAYING?

HOW CAN I APPLY THIS TO MY LIFE?

Here in chapter 13 the word "sea" is used instead of the *bottomless pit* (abyss) of Revelation 11:7 and 17:8 as the *home* of the beast. In Luke 21:25 the "sea" is a symbol of the Gentile nations in sinful turmoil. In Revelation 21:1 we are told that there is no "sea" in the new earth (no more wickedness). The beast is a symbol of both the kingdom of the antichrist and the Antichrist himself. That the beast comes out of the sea indicates its Gentile (European) roots. The ten horns and crowns refer to the ten European (former Roman Empire) nations that the Antichrist controls.

"Blasphemy" refers to the Antichrist's claim of deity. Even in Roman times the emperors were worshiped as gods. The Emperor Domitian called himself "Dominus et Deus noster" (*Our Lord and God*). The description of the beast in verse 2 is similar to the description of the terrible fourth composite beast in Daniel 7:7. "Deadly" (v. 3) is the same word describing the slain lamb in Revelation 5:6. It can refer to the death of the Antichrist or a crushing military defeat from which he miraculously recovers. This "resurrection" would be at the midpoint of the tribulation period as he then is dominant for the next forty-two months (v. 5, see 11:2).

The book of life (v. 8) is patterned after the typical citizens' lists of the ancient cities. All citizens were listed until they died, and then their names were erased. Verse 9 contains a sentence repeated seven times in Revelation 2-3, but now has one phrase missing, "…what the Spirit saith unto the churches." This strongly implies that the church is no longer on the planet and that these saints should be identified as *Tribulation* "saints," not *church* "saints." The "mark… of the beast" represents Satan's *unholy trinity*, using the number one less than God's number (6 instead of 7).

LIFE STEP Even in the world's darkest hour it is clear that God is still in control and that His people will be remembered and protected.

REVELATION 14:1-13

WHAT IS THE WRITER SAYING?

HOW CAN I APPLY THIS TO MY LIFE?

PRAY Hungary – For the Church to mature in its ability to evangelize and overcome feelings of inferiority that restrain boldness in its witness.

In answer to the questions, Who is like unto the beast? Who is able to make war with him? (13:4) Revelation 14 presents the 144,000. Instead of the mark of the beast (13:16) they have God's name on their forehead. The lamb with them would be the "lamb as it had been slain" of Revelation 5:6. "Sion" refers to the temple mount specifically but Jerusalem in general. Powerful sounds emanate from heaven honoring their testimony. The four beasts (cherubim) and twenty-four elders (representative Old Testament and New Testament saints) of Revelation 4 are there, worshiping. The 144,000 are called "virgins" (v. 4). This could be physically true, although since Hebrews 13:4 says that the marriage bed is "undefiled," this might be a reference to spiritual purity. They did not defile themselves by association with Jezebel (see 2:20). They are "first fruits." This is a reference to the religious practice of giving some of the first grain to ripen to the Lord as thanks for the full harvest to follow. These 144,000 do not represent all the humans who are saved during the tribulation period, but rather the first group to be saved with many more to come. Deceit does not exist in their lives (as opposed to Satan). They are blameless (as opposed to the beast and false prophet).

The word "gospel" means *good news*. There are several "gospels" in the Bible. For salvation effectiveness they all rely on the cross work of Jesus Christ. However, they emphasize different aspects of God's good news for humanity. The gospel of the kingdom in Matthew is "Repent: for the kingdom of heaven is at hand." The Gospel of the Church Age is the death, burial, and resurrection of Jesus Christ (1 Corinthians 15:3-5). Here, the emphasis of the gospel of the tribulation period is *Repent, you have offended the Creator God*.

LIFE STEP

What a rude awakening when arrogant sinners are brought face to face with God their Maker!

REVELATION 14:14-20

WHAT IS THE WRITER SAYING?

HOW CAN I APPLY THIS TO MY LIFE?

PRAY Paraguay – For new believers to sever all ties to former religious practices and superstitions.

Chapter 14 is basically an overview of the entire tribulation period and concludes with the battle of Armageddon at the second coming of Jesus Christ. The "white cloud" and title "Son of Man" come from Daniel 7:13-14. "White" speaks of purity. "Clouds" are often associated with the glory of God. "Son of man" was Christ's favorite title for Himself. He used it twice as often as any other title (such as, "Son of God"). "Son of" means *characterized by*. This is demonstrated in the response the Jews had to Christ's claim to be the "Son of God" (namely, *characterized by deity*). They hated Him for making that claim and called it blasphemous. "Son of Man" identifies Jesus with us; he is a man like we are.

God the Father in the heavenly temple sends an angel to tell Jesus to start the final harvest. "Ripe" (v. 15) is the word for *over-ripe* such as sun-dried *golden waves of grain*. The "sickle" (v. 16) would be the large instrument used for harvesting grain. The next "sickle" (v. 17) would be a smaller instrument, designed for cutting grape stems. "Fully ripe" (v. 18) means *peak condition* and for grapes would mean *full of juice*. The juicy clusters of grapes represent sinful humanity with their life-preserving blood. In ancient times, grapes were thrown into large stone vats with a framework overhead from which straps hung. The unmarried men and women would remove their sandals, hike their robes, hang onto the straps, and crush the grapes as they joyously stamped to music. In this final judgment, the blood of Christ's enemies will flow the entire length of the land of Israel (about two hundred miles). A horse's bridle stands about 4.5 feet from the ground. Assuming a literal river of blood about five feet wide, these dimensions would require about one billion people.

LIFE STEP While God is a loving God, He also is a just God. While gruesome, the judgment of sinners is legally and eternally just for they deserve the punishment that they receive.

REVELATION 15:1-8

WHAT IS THE WRITER SAYING?

HOW CAN I APPLY THIS TO MY LIFE?

Chapter 15 re-introduces the last series of judgments. In Revelation 10:6 and 7 we were told these judgments will come quickly, be intense, and climax the tribulation period. However, as a literary device, God keeps us in suspense through chapters 11-14. The sea of glass would magnify all the colors and lights in heaven. That "fire" is reflected from the sea of glass heightens the sense of impending doom and judgment. The martyrs sing the "song of Moses." Moses created two songs in his public ministry. Exodus 15 praises God for the safe and miraculous exodus from Egypt. Deuteronomy 32 covers all of Israel's history up to Moses' day. Here they not only praise God for His attributes, but as fitting to the context, they specifically praise Him for His intent to judge their enemies. John sees the temple in heaven open. The inside is described as the "tabernacle." This word means *tent* or *dwelling place*. It underscores the fact that in the tabernacle and later in the temple built by Solomon, God dwelt with His people. He was present in the Holy of Holies, residing above the Ark of the Covenant (testimony) between the two sculpted cherubim. The top of the ark was called the mercy seat because on the Day of Atonement (Yom Kippur) the *covering* blood was sprinkled on the top and God was *satisfied* (*propitiated*) that the just price for sin had been paid. Here we see mercy and punishment emanating from the same location. The seven angels are dressed like priests indicating that their job of judging was a holy, priestly job. One of the four beasts (cherubim) passes out the seven bowls of wrath. The temple is filled with smoke, as it had been with God's glory cloud when Solomon dedicated his temple in his day (see 1 Kings 8:10-11). The temple is then closed until the job is complete.

LIFE STEP God's payday is coming some day. We might be frustrated now with the arrogance of sinful man, but God's longsuffering will come to an end.

REVELATION 16:1-11

WHAT IS THE WRITER SAYING?

HOW CAN I APPLY THIS TO MY LIFE?

PRAY Bahamas – Nearly a third of the population are bible-believing Christians. Pray these communities would grow in their love for each other and the lost.

The first four bowl judgments parallel the first four trumpet judgments, although they are more devastating. In the trumpet sequence, only one third of each category was damaged. In the bowl sequence there is total destruction in each category. The first bowl produces horrible skin eruptions on all the beast worshipers. The second bowl kills all life living in salt water by making the water coagulate like blood does. The third bowl kills all life living in fresh water by turning it into blood. The saints and angels in heaven find this particularly appropriate since the beast worshipers were so quick to shed the blood of God's saints. The fourth bowl intensifies the effects of the sun. This may just be increased heat or it could include the damage produced by unblocked ultraviolet light as well. Not only does ultraviolet light increase the incidences of skin cancer, but it also hastens cataract formation, inhibits crop growth, and damages plankton in the sea. Sinful humanity refuses to acknowledge God's hand in these events and repent. Perhaps they think these are natural disasters or the result of human (nuclear?) warfare. While perhaps not believing in God they still use His name in their curses!

The fifth bowl plunges the world into a tormented darkness. Perhaps the pain is psychological (fear and dread). Or maybe they stumble around hurting themselves even more. Or perhaps the darkness lets them sit still and concentrate on the pain of their existing wounds.

LIFE STEP One of the necessary features of *free will* is that it is free to be totally irrational. Man's depravity produces the most illogical response, which leads to eternal loss. Not only is hell eternal because sinful man has sinned against an infinite being which requires infinite punishment, but also because given a *second chance* sinful man would still arrogantly reject God!

REVELATION 16:12-21

WHAT IS THE WRITER SAYING?

HOW CAN I APPLY THIS TO MY LIFE?

The sixth bowl causes the great Euphrates River to dry up, allowing troops from the east to easily march to Israel. For years now Turkey has had the power to shut off the flow of the Euphrates with a system of hydroelectric dams. This is also predicted in Isaiah 11:15.

Frogs are *unclean animals* (Leviticus 11:10). These demonic frogs perform "sign-miracles" to convince the kings of the earth to come to Israel. The phrase "I come as a thief" is never used in Scripture of the Rapture. It always is used of the judgments associated with the day of the Lord in general or the second coming specifically ("great day of God Almighty" and Battle of "Armageddon," vv. 14, 16). The word "thief" refers to a *cat burglar*, not an armed robber (hence the popular phrase, "thief in the night"). The unsaved will be caught off-guard by the appearance of Christ, "the thief." "Armageddon" comes from two words, "Har" (*mountain*) and "Megiddo" (*place of troops*). Megiddo was the name of a strategic city that controlled the roadway through the Carmel mountain range into the huge Jezreel (*God Sows*) Valley. It is in the shape of a triangle about twenty miles on a side. It also goes by the name "Plain of Esdraelon" (Greek form of "Jezreel"). It has always been a fertile valley. The earliest battle in human history with recorded details (on the walls of the Temple of Karnack in Thebes, Egypt) occurred there between the Canaanites and Thutmose III around 1450 B.C. During the time of the judges, Barak and Deborah fought the Canaanites there, who were led by Sisera, the man eventually killed by Jael as she drove a nail through his head while he slept. Gideon also defeated the Midianites in this valley. The seventh bowl judgment caps all the judgments with the worst earthquake the world has ever seen. In addition, one hundred pound hailstones rain down on what remains of the earth.

LIFE STEP The final conflict leads to eternal victory for the people of God and His Christ.

REVELATION 17:1-8

WHAT IS THE WRITER SAYING?

HOW CAN I APPLY THIS TO MY LIFE?

PRAY Czech Republic – For the organization and funding needed to start a national Christian radio network.

In Revelation 13 the beast represents the Antichrist and his kingdom. Here a woman rides the beast, which is now described as a "scarlet" beast. Isaiah 1:18 likens the stain of sin to "scarlet" and "crimson." She is an immoral woman and has immoral connections with all the kings of the earth. She is symbolically named Babylon. In the Old Testament, God likened the pagan religions to strange lovers and accused Israel of spiritual adultery when she went after the other gods (see Ezekiel 23:37). The woman is dressed like royalty. Purple traditionally has been the color of kings because the color was so expensive to produce. It took ten thousand murex shellfish to produce one ounce of the colorfast purple dye. "Mystery" probably refers to the deceitfulness and treachery of false teaching. She is "the great" because of the size of her organization, activities and the extent of her apostasy. 2 Thessalonians 2:3 indicates that the revelation of the Antichrist will be accompanied by "<u>the</u> falling away (*apostasy*)." She is the "mother" of harlots and abominations as the source and greatest offender. In addition to false teaching and immorality, she is guilty of murdering those who love the Lord. John is puzzled and the angel begins to explain the scene. He first describes the beast. Satan loves to counterfeit Christ's program in an attempt to replace it. Note the similarities between Revelation 17:8 (describing the antichrist) and Revelation 1:18 (describing Christ). Both have a "death," *burial*, and *resurrection*. In the tribulation period, the Antichrist will start to organize his kingdom in the first half (v. 8, "was"). He will then be killed or suffer a devastating political setback ("and is not"). He will descend into Hades, be indwelt by Satan, and then "arise" to renew his goal of world domination ("and yet is").

LIFE STEP

Good people are not necessarily holy. Some of the greatest evils are done in the name of or hiding behind God.

REVELATION 17:9-18

WHAT IS THE WRITER SAYING?

HOW CAN I APPLY THIS TO MY LIFE?

PRAY Serbia – Due to political changes, there are many open doors for the Gospel. Pray that the church would seize this time in history to evangelize youth there.

Revelation 17:3 says that the woman is sitting on the beast with seven heads. Verse 9 says she is sitting on seven mountains. Both "heads" and "mountains" are used symbolically of kings or governments elsewhere (see Isaiah 14:13; Ezekiel 35:2; Daniel 2:44-45, 7:6). They could be simultaneous, and in fact the horns and crowns (12:3, 13:1) do seem to refer to contemporary associates of the Antichrist. They could also be sequential and that seems to be the case here. "Five are fallen" (v. 10) in Israel's history would be Egypt, Assyria, Babylon, Persia, and Greece. "One is" in A.D. 95 would be Rome. "The other is not yet come" would be the revival of Rome under the Antichrist. "He must continue a short space" refers to the first half of the tribulation before the Antichrist is *killed*. Notice that there is a connection between the "seventh" and the "eighth."

The Antichrist is also the "eighth" as the satanically indwelt *resurrected* wonder for the second half of the tribulation period.

The number ten is interesting. In Jewish thought, her enemies come in groups of ten (see Genesis 15:19-21; Psalm 83:6-8; Jeremiah 41:1). Revived Rome under the Antichrist will probably control the same territory as ancient Rome. Rome controlled all of Western Europe to the Rhine and Danube Rivers. She controlled northern Africa and the Middle East to Euphrates. The Mediterranean was the *Roman Lake*. The Antichrist and his associates use the woman until they have no more need for her and then they discard her. If she represents a false religious system, then her destruction would take place at the middle of the Tribulation when the Antichrist enters the temple for the world to worship him.

 LIFE STEP There was a time when the Vatican was the most powerful city in Europe. For a short time, another religious center will have political power.

SUNDAY 39

REVELATION 19:1-10

WHAT IS THE WRITER SAYING?

HOW CAN I APPLY THIS TO MY LIFE?

PRAY Pray that God will bless the ministry and outreach of your local Christian radio station.

"Hallelujah" ("alleluia") is such a popular word of praise that it is hard to believe that it only occurs in one chapter in all the New Testament: Revelation 19. There are four hallelujahs: one for salvation (v. 1), one for judgment (v. 3), one for worship (v. 4), and a final one for the sovereignty of God in all these judgments (v. 6). In these verses we have the answer to the question asked by the souls of the martyrs under the altar in Revelation 6:10, "And they cried with a loud voice, saying, How long, O Lord, holy and true, dost thou not judge and avenge our blood on them that dwell on the earth?" The twenty-four elders and four beasts of chapter 4 are still part of the story, here worshiping God in the courts of Heaven. We can't tell who the owner of the voice is. It could be one of the four beasts or an unnamed angel. "Our God" almost implies a human, which would be one of the twenty-four elders, but Revelation 7:12 has the four beasts using the phrase "our God" in worship. God's "omnipotence" (*all powerfulness*) is now an observable characteristic of human affairs. God is obviously on the throne and His will *will* be done on earth as it is in heaven. It is announced that the "marriage of the Lamb" is come. His bride is ready, not just willing but also spiritually qualified. She had been impure, but as a redeemed individual her past has been forgiven and forgotten. She is given white clothing to illustrate her purity. What does the fashion-conscious person wear in Heaven? They wear white trimmed with white and with white accessories! During the tribulation period, when someone shares the Gospel, he will be inviting that person to the "marriage supper of the Lamb"!

LIFE STEP Nothing can match the beauty and excitement of a bride on her wedding day. What a day that will be when our Savior we will see and our Bridegroom He will be.

MONDAY 39

REVELATION 19:11-21

WHAT IS THE WRITER SAYING?

HOW CAN I APPLY THIS TO MY LIFE?

PRAY Germany – Pray for theologically sound Bible schools and staff to emerge for the training of workers.

At the second coming of Christ, the bride of Christ will return to the planet to reign with Him. Those who accept Christ as their Savior during the Tribulation will be "friends of the bridegroom," a designation that John the Baptist used of himself (John 3:29). They will enter the messianic kingdom and rejoice, as the marriage supper of the Lamb will be the first order of business when the one thousand year reign begins. The "spirit" of prophecy refers to its ultimate purpose. The ultimate purpose of the "revelation" of Jesus Christ is the unveiling of His glorious person for all to admire and worship. Revelation 19:11-16 describes this wonderful person as He returns to take possession of His rightful property, Planet Earth. A secret name (v. 12) implies that even in the next mode of existence there will be mysteries to explore and learn. Christ returns to the planet like a Roman general in a triumphal parade of spoils before his adoring countrymen. He has His title on His thigh, where a Roman would wear his weapon, the sword.

In Revelation 19:9 we have an invitation to the marriage feast of the Lamb. In Revelation 19:17 there is an invitation to the marriage feast of the Antichrist! Humans are invited (16:14) but they are invited to be eaten, not eat. The Antichrist and false prophet escape becoming a meal only to find themselves cast alive into hell.

Revelation 19:14 pictures the armies of heaven following Christ back to the planet. Notice that only Christ does any fighting, and that by the spoken word. Satan, knowing that Christ will attempt to return to the planet, wants all available fighters present. He entices the kings of the east to attack the Antichrist. As they prepare to fight each other at Armageddon, they see Christ return and join forces against Him.

 LIFE STEP What a day that will be when the rightful heir returns to His throne.

REVELATION 20:1-15

WHAT IS THE WRITER SAYING?

HOW CAN I APPLY THIS TO MY LIFE?

PRAY Uganda – Pray for the continued and steady growth of the ministries in Uganda. For God to supply workers and open doors of opportunity.

As the mastermind, Satan is given the severest punishment. Revelation 20 is the first time in Scripture that the messianic reign is said to last for one thousand years. All statements prior to this point have been open-ended. This number is repeated six times in the chapter, leading us to conclude that it is to be taken as a literal, not symbolic figure. (Others have argued that the entire Church Age has been "the kingdom" and that in some fashion, Satan is currently bound.) Perhaps God's original perfect human lifespan was one thousand years. Adam sinned and died in the "day" (less than 1,000 years) that he sinned. Now as Christ returns there is a restoration of Edenic conditions, including the lengthening of the human lifespan. This is reinforced by Isaiah's contention that a human struck dead by Christ for disobedience at one hundred years of age has died tragically as a "child" (Isaiah 65:20). Christ will not tolerate any open rebellion. The Spirit will be poured out on all flesh, and holiness will be the hallmark of that time. Despite these great conditions, there will be humans born during this long period of history who will outwardly conform, but never truly acknowledge the Lordship of Christ over their personal life. At the end of this initial phase of the messianic kingdom, Satan will be released for a brief period, enabling him one final opportunity to spark a rebellion. While seemingly unbelievable, the father of lies will once again succeed in deluding men with their inherited sin nature into joining his cause. John views the final judgments that result in sinners of all ages receiving their fair trial and assigned degrees of punishment in hell.

LIFE STEP In Scripture there are only two options. Either we are saved and part of the "first resurrection" (Old Testament, New Testament, Tribulation and millennial saints) or we are unsaved and part of the "second death."

WEDNESDAY 39

REVELATION 21:1-8

WHAT IS THE WRITER SAYING?

HOW CAN I APPLY THIS TO MY LIFE?

PRAY Sudan – Pray that peace might prevail in this wartorn land and that those perpetuating violence and disorder may be stopped.

Human history is complete. Sinners and saints have been evaluated, rewarded, and placed in their respective eternal homes. Several passages describe the renovation of the physical universe to purge it of all vestiges of sinful humanity (see 2 Peter 3:10-13). Why would God's heaven need purging? Job 1 pictures Satan and his demons coming to the halls of heaven, so even God's abode will be renovated. John views no sea in the new earth. The "sea" speaks of sinful nations in turmoil. It was also the *front door* by which evil Gentile armies entered Israel. Instead of the false religious system, the harlot of Revelation 17, we now have the New Jerusalem as a bride. Psalm 37:29 promises, "The righteous shall inherit the land." For all eternity, "heaven" will be on earth. In the book of Hosea, God says that Israel will be "lo ammi" because of their rebellion. The phrase means, *not My people*. Now (v. 3) redeemed humanity will be "ammi" (*My people*).

The blessedness of heaven includes healed memories. Imagine the release a godly rape victim will experience when that horrible memory will no longer affect her. Some would argue that God has to wipe tears of regret from our eyes. Since this passage is 1007 years after the judgment seat of Christ, that would not be an appropriate conclusion. Even once safely entered into eternity, we are reminded that salvation is a free gift (v. 6). Being "fearful" (v. 8) does not seem like a gross sin worthy of eternal damnation. In context, it is referring to a lack of respect for God and the shame a sinner has in associating with Christ. This *fearful unbelief* condemns an individual to a Christless eternity. There are several words for afterlife punishment. "Sheol" (Hebrew) and "Hades" (Greek) are the terms for the current place of punishment. Gehenna (Hebrew), hell, and the lake of fire refer to the eternal place of punishment.

LIFE STEP Heaven will be greater and hell worse than we could ever imagine.

REVELATION 21:9-27

WHAT IS THE WRITER SAYING?

HOW CAN I APPLY THIS TO MY LIFE?

PRAY God's guidance for staff and candidates participating in the Word of Life Missionary in Training program.

Earlier in Scripture, the church is called the bride of Christ. Here the eternal abode of the church (the New Jerusalem) is called the bride. It is a glorious sight. John chooses the prettiest gemstones of his day to describe the beauty that he sees. "Jasper" usually has some color (light green) but here it is clear like crystal (no impurities, the impurities impart the color). The city is well protected. It has a high wall, gates, and guardian angels. It is laid out in a square with three gates in each wall. On each gate is inscribed the name of one of the tribes of Israel. Each gate is made of a single pearl (v. 21). The city has twelve foundations and on each is the name one of the twelve apostles. This very graphically indicates that while God has a separate program for Old Testament Israel and the New Testament church, both are treated equally as brothers and sisters in Christ for all eternity. The city is 1500 miles per side. The tabernacle Holy of Holies, where the Shekinah glory of God dwelt, was a cube. Perhaps the three equal dimensions are designed to remind us of God's holiness and His presence with His people. However, the text does not require a cube. It could also be describing a pyramid (which has a square base, v. 16, and in the center rises to the same height as the length and width). Physically, it would be impossible for the current earth to rotate with that lopsided weight, but of course this would be on the new earth designed for such a city. In the new heaven, there is no need for a temple. First, everyone is saved so there is no need for the atonement represented by the temple. Second, Satan is no longer entering the courts of heaven so all of heaven itself can now be the temple without fear of any contamination. In the new heaven there is no need for the sun or moon for God will provide the light from His person. "Gates" (v. 25) represent both access and safety.

LIFE STEP Eye has not seen nor ear heard all that God has prepared for His saints.

FRIDAY 39

REVELATION 22:1-9

WHAT IS THE WRITER SAYING?

HOW CAN I APPLY THIS TO MY LIFE?

PRAY Chile – Pray for a reverence and obedience to the Word and a rejection of sensationalized faith.

This sinful world is contaminated with a depressing amount of moral and ecological sewage. In heaven, the moral and ecological climate will be perfect, as pictured by the crystal-clear water flowing from the throne of God. One of the strong arguments for the intelligent design of the universe is the fine-tuning necessary to produce the narrow range of parameters in which biological life can exist. One of those important ingredients is water. A little closer or further away from the sun and our earth would not have water. A large percentage of our body mass is *just* water. We can survive for weeks without food, but only a few days without water. In our eternal home, life-giving water is in abundant supply. Apparently, our glorified bodies will process food. No mention here of beef steak, but twelve kinds of fruit sound refreshing. The tree reminds us of the Garden of Eden where man's moral problems began. One of the stated reasons for expelling fallen Adam and Eve from the garden was to prevent them from eating of the tree of life and thereby sealing themselves in their fallen state for eternity. Now the saints have returned to Eden and can profitably eat of the tree of life. The leaves are for "healing." If Heaven is perfect, why would there be a need for healing? "Healing" does not require a pre-existing sickness. It is a preventative or therapeutic health regimen.

God the Father and Jesus Christ the Lamb both have thrones and are a delight to the citizens of Heaven. We will see God face to face. He will be our light. His name, instead of the mark of the beast, will be on our foreheads. The saints will reign. What will they reign over? That is one of the mysteries not revealed in Scripture. Verse 6 begins the conclusion to the whole book. The trustworthiness of the information is affirmed. Christ speaks stating that He will come "quickly," meaning that He can come at anytime, unannounced. John then adds his testimony in verses 8-9.

 If these things are so, how then shall we live?

REVELATION 22:10-21

WHAT IS THE WRITER SAYING?

HOW CAN I APPLY THIS TO MY LIFE?

Verse 11 seems contradictory to God's normal challenge for sinners to repent. Perhaps it is phrased to warn that at any moment the world is liable to be swept into the final judgments and that if you want to be on the side of righteousness, you need to be there today. Tomorrow will be too late. Christ refers to Himself as "Alpha and Omega" (v. 13), a description that God the Father uses of Himself in Revelation 1:8.

The whole chain of Revelation starts with Jesus (v. 16), goes to an angel, then to John, next to the seven churches of Asia Minor, and finally, down through the centuries to us. In the Old Testament, "the branch" is a messianic title referring to the Messiah's connection with the *soil* of humanity in general and the family of David specifically (see Jeremiah 33:15). The "morning star" is the planet Venus because it is the brightest of the heavenly bodies after the moon and is often visible just before dawn. "Lucifer" is the Latin name for *morning star*, applied to Satan in Isaiah 14:12 (in the sense that he has attempted to usurp the title). The Messiah is the "light" to the Gentiles (Isaiah 9:1-2). The "Spirit" (v. 17) is the Holy Spirit. The "bride" is the New Jerusalem (as in 21:9), implying that the city calls out for more inhabitants. Verse 18 pronounces a curse on those who tamper with the material. Some commentators have tried to use this as proof that the Book of Revelation is the final book of inspired information in human history. However, the word "book" is the Greek word for *booklet* and therefore refers only to the Book of Revelation, not the whole Bible. In fact, an identical statement occurs in Deuteronomy 4:2 and 12:32. It obviously means that nothing should be taken away from or added to the information in that book. Only an unsaved person would do so, hence the warning of eternal damnation.

?

LIFE STEP

"Maranatha" (1 Corinthians 16:22) is Aramaic for *Our Lord Comes*!

There are times when all those theological maxims just don't cut it; times when the gap between what we know and what we feel is like a vast empty void; times when our soul wants to express itself to God but the words just don't seem to come. It is just for such times that the Wisdom books (Job, Psalms, Proverbs, Ecclesiastes, and Song of Solomon) were written.

These books deal with down-to-earth feelings and down-to-earth questions. They are concerned more with our physical and emotional welfare than they are with religious theories or systems. These are lessons for living, guidelines to godliness, schooling for success. Each of these five books deals with a different aspect of surviving on Planet Earth.

These books "breathe a certain universality. The problem of suffering, the conscience marred by sin, the transience of human life, and the passionate love of woman and man, to mention only a few of the matters dealt with in these books, cut across national and ethnic lines to include all of the human race. The spokesmen in these books formulate questions that have lain in man's subconscious mind, often without his having the courage to bring them to the surface." [C Hassel Bullock, *An Introduction to the Old Testament Poetic Books* (Chicago: Moody, 1979), 17]. Job, the first of these books, deals with the problem of evil and suffering.

The lifestyle and historic references in the book indicate that Job lived about the time of Abraham. It is the longest story in the Bible from the earliest period of biblical history. The book does not identify the author. It could have been Job himself or the relatively wise and godly young friend in the story, Elihu (*He is my God*). Certainly Moses is a candidate since God moved Moses to write other large portions of the biblical record. Since Solomon was known for his intense interest in wise sayings and theological and philosophical discussions, the Holy Spirit might have used him to record this story. If such were the case, it was well-known among the people and handed down from one generation to the next.

The book opens in Heaven with a discussion between God and Satan. There is no question that God instigates the ensuing discussion and draws Satan into a conversation about personal behavior and its relationship to adversity. This is the most fundamental dichotomy that exists in the created universe. There does not appear to be any immediate correspondence between righteousness and adversity. There is however a correlation between godliness and grief. The mistake that Job and his friends make is in trying to find a correlation between the former and ignoring man's responsibility to the latter. Men long to live in a world where fairness reigns. They want to be able to think that the *good* live long and prosper. But in reality it rains on the just and the unjust. The difference is not between the various life experiences, but rather the way in which we view these experiences.

The just man interprets the "rain" differently than the proud one. He looks at all of the events of life through the eyes of faith.

Job's journey is one of clarification. It is a journey into the depths of living by faith. It is a journey constructed by an omniscient God to bring His choice servant into a better understanding of a salvation that is by grace alone through faith alone, a salvation that means more than justification, a salvation that sustains a man in the greatest adversity that one could ever imagine.

The following outline is a helpful memory aid:

Job in the hands of Satan: 1:1–2:10
Job in the hands of Men: 2:11–37:24
Job in the hands of God: 38-42

JOB 1:1-12

WHAT IS THE WRITER SAYING?

HOW CAN I APPLY THIS TO MY LIFE?

The book opens with a description of Job. He was a wealthy land owner, but more than that, he was in God's words, "blameless and upright, and one who feared God and shunned evil." One would be tempted to think that such a man would be exactly the kind of person that God wanted him to be, a man that could put his feet up and enjoy the good life that God had given him. But that would be wrong. The journey we take in this life is one of reliance, not autonomy. The lessons to be learned are the lessons that only weakness can teach. Jesus put it succinctly, "The first shall be last and the last shall be first." This is not to say that Job was in any way deficient by human standards; it is only to say that spiritual growth is a privilege that never fades. It is a glimmer of light that shines brightest in a dark place.

Yes, God looked at Job and saw one awesome servant. He saw that Job had one awesome life but God knew something else. He knew that Job's life could shine brighter. He knew that Job and his friends were drawing the wrong conclusions about life. God knows life; He knows real life. So He turned to Satan and said, "Have you considered my servant Job?" Thus begins one of the most troublesome journeys to be found anywhere. This is not a punishment for Job. It does not happen because God wants Job to be *more* "upright." It happens because God loves Job and He wants Job to have the best life possible. When it comes to His children, God is always in the grace business. Man's problem is that he does not always believe that such is the case. We allow the trials of this life to become temptations and doubt God's love.

LIFE STEP Whenever Satan attacks believers, he has to go through the Lord first. The Lord only allows Satan to test us as a part of His gracious plan. If the rulers of this world would have known, they never would have crucified the Lord of Glory. (See 1 Corinthians 10:13.)

JOB 1:13-22

WHAT IS THE WRITER SAYING?

HOW CAN I APPLY THIS TO MY LIFE?

PRAY Portugal – For God to burden hearts with a passion to evangelize other Portuguese–speaking nations.

The series of *evils* that befall Job are hard to comprehend from a human perspective. It is even harder to believe that God has allowed Satan to do this. A life that had been so peaceful the day before turns into a nightmare for Job. A series of manmade and natural disasters take everything he holds dear. Even his family was not spared. The thought that begins to formulate in each of our minds is, *How could God allow that to happen*? God allowed Satan to kill Job's children. How can that be? Doesn't Job's righteousness count for anything? Here is the problem with these questions. Job had no righteousness. All the *real* righteousness he had was given to him by God. What Job was expected to have was faith. It is the unfairness of the events that draws us into the story, but it is also that supposed "unfairness" that God wants us to reconsider. If this were a fair world, would we not all be spending an eternity in the fires of Hell? Does God *owe* sinners anything? Did God *owe* Job anything?

The writer of this ancient book wants us to grasp this concept. He wants us to ask a different question: "Why would God take such interest in a single person and unleash a sequence of events that would overwhelm Job with His grace?" We might be tempted to ask how this qualifies as grace. But if it is not grace then what is it? Is God condemning Job? Is He unable to protect Job? Has His love for Job grown cold? Can God be anything but loving toward his children? The God who willingly gave Himself for Job would never allow anything to happen to Job that was not designed to bless Job. The true grace of God sometimes comes in strange packages.

LIFE STEP Life in God's family only gets better as the days go by. That can only be known by faith and that is why we are called believers. It's what we do.

JOB 2:1-13

WHAT IS THE WRITER SAYING?

HOW CAN I APPLY THIS TO MY LIFE?

Any one of us might be tempted to think that after such a devastating day the Lord would be inclined to give Job time to recover and perhaps even comfort him in his distress. Instead, at the next opportunity the Lord once again engages Satan in a conversation about Job. God invites Satan to respond. And again Satan claims that Job only worships Him because of all the protection and blessing that He provides. In the initial go round Satan was not allowed to touch Job's person, but now God gives Satan permission to harm Job physically without taking his life. Satan therefore covers Job with painful sores from head to foot.

It is worth noting that Satan did not ask for permission to enter Job in any form of *demon possession*. God did not allow Satan to enter Job or to influence him from an internal vantage point. This option was not on the table. In recent days there has been much talk about demon possession and demon bondage.

Since the focus of this book is about a case of extreme testing, one would think that if such were a possibility for a follower of God, then Satan would have brought it up. Satan can only attack the believer from the outside. He may be able to afflict the body but he cannot attack the soul of a child of God.

The arrival of Job's friends accomplishes two purposes. First, it serves to reinforce the intensity of Job's suffering. His friends were overwhelmed by Job's condition. Second, it moves the conversation from heaven to earth. Job's friends were not privy to the conversations that have just taken place. They are looking at these matters from only an earthly and human perspective. Their goal is simple: to make some sense from all that has just happened. The journey begins here, a journey that all of us will take at some point or points in our lives. A journey for answers to life's most perplexing problem: Why do righteous people suffer?

LIFE STEP As we read this account, we need to consider where we would look for such answers? Can we figure it out or does God have to show us in His Word?

JOB 7:1-16

WHAT IS THE WRITER SAYING?

HOW CAN I APPLY THIS TO MY LIFE?

PRAY Angola – Pray for the provision of funds, buildings, and above all, godly teachers for leadership training.

The thirty-five chapters of the second section of Job are a series of speeches by Job's three friends. Each is followed by a response from Job. There are three cycles of speeches. Elihu is only involved in the last cycle and Job does not respond to Elihu. Cycle one covers chapters 3-14 (Eliphaz, Bildad, Zophar); cycle two chapters 15-21 (Eliphaz, Bildad, Zophar); and cycle three chapters 22-37 (Eliphaz, Bildad, Elihu). Elihu gives four speeches in this final section.

In this first series of speeches Job's friends argue that God blesses the godly and punishes the ungodly. Satan has already given his assessment of the matter. He suggested that man's faith in God is directly related to services provided by God and man's prosperity. Eliphaz is the first to speak and suggests (Job 4-5) that man brings trouble upon himself because God is always fair. Our passage today picks up in the middle of Job's response to Eliphaz. Job's central thesis is not an uncommon one. He believes that he is justified in his complaint against God because he did nothing knowingly to deserve the severe trial that he is enduring. He refuses to blame God but he is still unwilling to accept his situation without some explanation. Job is willing to suffer but only on condition that he knows why. And he wants to know why so that he can correct his ways.

In today's passage Job points out the frailty of human life. He acknowledges the weakness of the flesh. He does this in order to strengthen his contention that all he wants is an answer. See 6:24, "Teach me and I will hold my tongue, cause me to understand wherein I have erred."

LIFE STEP It is not always sinful to ask the Lord why something has happened in your life (Jesus asked why from the cross). The issue comes when we demand such an answer as a condition for contentment. God only wants us to live by faith, to trust Him. He does know what He is doing.

JOB 9:1-20

WHAT IS THE WRITER SAYING?

HOW CAN I APPLY THIS TO MY LIFE?

PRAY For many young people to catch the excitement for Word of Life Youth Outreach student missions program.

In chapter 8 Bildad presents his analysis. He bases his argument on God's character. Because God cannot twist or pervert justice, he reasons, Job must have done something to *earn* this trial. These kinds of arguments continue to be made today. Well-trained scholars will sometimes pick an attribute of God and use that attribute to deny a rather clear teaching from Scripture. For example, using the love of God as a foundation, many try to maintain that those who have never heard the gospel will be give a second chance or simply accepted into God's kingdom. No man can fully understand the character of God or how his stated attributes interface. We can all agree that God is just, but does that force us to conclude that every trial is retribution? Maybe trials are good things designed to help us in some way.

In today's passage, Job answers Bildad. He correctly concludes that God's acts are all in keeping with God's character. He cannot deny Himself, but Job still maintains that he himself is guiltless. He knows that this tribulation is not condemnation for known sin, but he still cries out in frustration. Verse 19 sums up this frustration. Like Bildad, he uses God's attributes to frame his anxiety. God is omnipotent so there is no one to stop His purposes and He is also the supreme Judge so that there is no one who can force Him to give an accounting for that behavior. It seems that we just have to trust Him. Job has still not gotten to the point where he is willing to ask the right question. He still thinks that his suffering is a *bad* thing.

LIFE STEP Life often deals us some unexpected and painful blows. It sometimes seems that our whole world is coming apart at the seams. Is it possible that God had a discussion with Satan prior to our trial? More importantly, would that matter?

JOB 9:21-35

WHAT IS THE WRITER SAYING?

HOW CAN I APPLY THIS TO MY LIFE?

It is important for us to keep in mind the larger context from which this passage is taken. The issues we are dealing with are not going to be solved this early in the narrative. The thing to note is that all of the discussion to this point has originated from Job's deep depression and disillusionment. Job would have come to similar conclusions if this had happened to one of his friends. It is not that he does not believe the same things that his friends are saying. He is not denying the basic arguments; he is simply claiming that they do not apply in his case because he is guiltless. All of the discussion to this point is based upon the unimaginable emotional and physical pain that Job is enduring.

This is also the prevalent worldview that exists today. Pleasure is good; pain is bad. We determine the quality of our experience by how it feels. This is the frustration that Job faces. He knows God is a good God but he is unable to reconcile that with his day-to-day experience. He says that he is without guilt and that he hates his life. At the very core of this complaint is the greatest challenge that we face as believers. Will we believe what God tells us about the circumstances of life, or will we believe what our hearts tell us about these trials?

Job is struggling to answer the most difficult question that exists in our universe, the question of evil. But to this point all his attention is directed toward the trial. In effect, he is trying to insulate God from what he considers to be an injustice.

LIFE STEP It is very easy for man to worship God from the comfort of prosperity but do we respond the same way when the music dies and the world becomes cold and empty? Is God sufficient for the valley of the shadow of death? Here is an accurate saying: *Whatever controls how we feel is our god.*

SATURDAY 40

JOB 13:1-18

WHAT IS THE WRITER SAYING?

HOW CAN I APPLY THIS TO MY LIFE?

PRAY New Zealand – That there would be a spiritual awakening in New Zealand.

Job is in the middle of his response to Zophar in our text today. He points out to Zophar that he already knows that God judges sin (vv.1-2), duh! Job goes on to say that the only one who can give him satisfaction is God and God alone. He exclaims, "I would speak to the Almighty and I desire to reason with God." This may seem a little much to us but it is a very appropriate question. It is God's answers that matter. Truth cannot originate with the created because the creation is not eternal. Only the absolute can offer absolutes. Only God can answer the questions that man has about life because God is the Creator of that life. God knows life. God knows meaning. God knows best.

Job is respectful in his request. He is asking the right Person but he is not asking the right question. He cries out, "Though he slay me, yet will I trust in Him, but I will maintain (argue) mine own ways before him" (v. 15). This same scenario will unfold later in the Old Testament. In a similar fashion Habakkuk stands before the God of the universe and cries out for an explanation. "I will stand upon my watch, and set me upon the tower, and will watch to see what he will say unto me, and what I shall answer when I am reproved" (Habakkuk 2:1). Neither Job nor Habakkuk is given the explanation they request. God's answer to both Job and Habakkuk is as true today as it was the day it was given. It is the heart of Paul's message: "the just shall live by faith" (Romans 1:17). Faith is not a means for man to achieve a goal. It *is* the goal. The faith life is the only real life. Faith transforms living. It is a lifestyle. Real life is from faith to faith. Job wanted an answer to believe in; God wanted Job to believe in the promise that had already been given.

LIFE STEP Do you trust in the Lord when things go wrong? Tell the Lord today that you trust in Him and will continue to no matter what happens to you.

330

JOB 14:1-15

WHAT IS THE WRITER SAYING?

HOW CAN I APPLY THIS TO MY LIFE?

PRAY Italy – For youth ministries to have an effective outreach among the 1,800,000 university students.

In this passage Job presents the worldview of a sufferer. He compares his life with the rest of creation in an attempt to move God on his behalf. Job points out, for example, that when a tree is cut off it has the hope of being able to sprout. But it is not so with a man. "Man lieth down and riseth not, till the heavens be no more (v. 12)." At first glance one might be tempted to think that Job has no concept of an eternal life and an eternal home in the future. Some even suggest that in the Old Testament there was no understanding of life after death. Such thinking takes a very narrow view of this passage. It is true that Job did not have as complex an understanding of future events as we do, but that is because there was no need for this information at this point in the development of God's plan. It is the Church Age that triggers the need for further revelation about the mysteries of God's plans for the future. Job did understand that the present heavens and earth were not designed for eternal living and that when these were renewed so would he be renewed. He makes this hope clear throughout the book. He knew that sometime in the future there would be a new universe in which he and others like him would live forever.

He also understood that a man only gets one chance in this present world. He understood that once this life ends there will be no second chances. Before the new heavens and new earth come into existence there will be a judgment. Once a man, woman or child passes from this world, their destiny cannot be changed.

LIFE STEP The present is all we have. It is a gift. It is an opportunity. It is also a very fragile thing. There are no *mulligans* (do-overs) in life. Paul suggests that we redeem the time because the days are evil. Using the time wisely and knowing its value are how the wise conduct their lives.

JOB 17:1-16

WHAT IS THE WRITER SAYING?

HOW CAN I APPLY THIS TO MY LIFE?

PRAY Pray that God would increase your awareness of the lost and your boldness in sharing Christ's love.

Today's passage is taken from Job's second response to Eliphaz. Read verses 11-16 very carefully. These verses give us a clear picture of Job's despair. He has lost all sense of comfort and joy. He feels utterly abandoned. His pain has darkened his soul and Job sees no possible way that he will ever smile or laugh again in this life. For him life is over and he sees death as his only friend. Physical and emotional pain can do this to a man, even a great man like Job. Remember, he was the most upright man on the planet. The fact that these three friends were here to "comfort" him only added to the problem. Job knew that they were not as upright as he was. He feared greatly that men would think him a hypocrite (v. 8). Not only did he lose all that he held dear, but "upright" men would all assume that he must have gotten what he deserved. Why? Because that was how Job thought before all of this had happened to him. Now he was totally confused. It was all so unfair and pointless. His life was gone and so was his reputation.

It is interesting to note that the further Job walks down the *fairness* road the more depressed he becomes, and Job's friends keep bringing him back to that road. When Job centers his thoughts on God, he seems a little more objective, but when he considers his situation as compared to everyone else's, despair dominates his thinking. Job was not getting godly counsel and it was compounding the problem. Job seems to be getting more and more depressed as the conversations move along. He liked the fact that his friends cared enough to spend extensive time with him but their messages were not helping the situation. The fairness message is always counterproductive.

LIFE STEP We are told that there is wisdom in a multitude of counselors. But counsel can be a two-edged sword. Not all counsel is equal. Seek out godly counselors or the problem may get worse.

JOB 19:19-29

WHAT IS THE WRITER SAYING?

HOW CAN I APPLY THIS TO MY LIFE?

In chapter 18, Bildad tries repeatedly to get his point across to Job. Remember, he believes that because God cannot twist or pervert justice, Job must have done something to *earn* this trial. He tells Job that he is being disciplined, and that it will not stop until he repents and gets his life right with the Lord. Until he does this, he will continue to walk in darkness. We need to understand that discipline is not a bad thing. We are told in Hebrews 12 that the Lord disciplines those He loves. It is a part of God's parental responsibility to discipline His children. However, Bildad is using the concept to put Job down. Not all discipline is because of sin. We sometimes use discipline in a preventive way. We do not wait until a child plays in traffic to assert some effort to keep him in the yard. A fence takes away a child's freedom but it does so in order to protect that child. He or she may resent and despise the fence but it is still an act of love and protection. We see in today's passage a clear assertion by Job that he does not view the grave as the end of human existence or as the end of a flesh and blood reality. He knows that there will be new heavens and a new earth and that he will stand before God in that time and that place. He has hope about the future but takes no pleasure in the present. In fact, he warns his friends that given their reasoning, the same or a worse thing may happen to them.

LIFE STEP Job still sees no light at the end of the tunnel. He knows that his real problem is with God but he continues to argue with his friends. Until a man is right with God, he cannot expect to be at peace with his friends. Every joy in life is predicated upon a right relationship with God. The real question is, Are there really tunnels?

JOB 23:1-12

WHAT IS THE WRITER SAYING?

HOW CAN I APPLY THIS TO MY LIFE?

PRAY Papua New Guinea – Increased provision of aircraft and staff for missions reaching into remote areas.

Today we will look in on a part of Job's third response to Eliphaz. In chapter 20, Zophar gives his second speech. His basic argument continues to be that God cannot be tricked and that He knows sin when He sees it. Job responds to Zophar in chapter 21. In Chapter 22 Eliphaz tells Job that a person can get away with evil for a little while, but eventually it will catch up with him. He tells Job that if he will only repent, then God will build him up and that God will put evil away from his home (22:23).

In his answer, Job continues to stress that the trial he has suffered does not prove that he has sinned more grievously than those who accuse him. He wants only to have the opportunity to present his case before the Almighty. Job seems to be convinced that by doing this he will somehow be justified in the eyes of both men and God. Job does not want his stuff back; he wants his reputation back. Note what he says in verse 10, "But he knoweth the way that I take; when he hath tried me, I shall come forth as gold." Job does not despise the trial; he longs for the trial to conclude so that his (and God's) reputation will be restored.

He is still convinced that this ordeal has an attached good that will somehow outweigh the bad. He cannot bring himself to believe that this tragedy was in and of itself the true grace of God. Somehow it must be a blessing in disguise. Why does he believe this? Because he has convinced himself that he has the ability to determine what is good and what is evil.

LIFE STEP We tend to view faith as a means to an end. The *end* that we want is sight, which is by definition the opposite of faith. Initially this seems rather odd. However, if hope that is seen is no longer hope, the same is true of faith. No one can see God and live because the just shall live by faith.

JOB 38:1-18

WHAT IS THE WRITER SAYING?

HOW CAN I APPLY THIS TO MY LIFE?

PRAY Uruguay – For the spiritual awakening of a country that is disillusioned by secularism.

In chapters 33-37, Elihu gives four separate speeches. Job does not respond to any of the four. The central idea in these speeches is that God is refining the righteous. Of all the solutions this is the only one that does not discredit Job and, therefore, Job does not respond to it. Also, there is a sense in which Elihu does make a significant move in the right direction, but he does not take his solution to the place that God wants it to be. Yes, God is refining the righteous but the ends cannot justify the means. With God the process is as meaningful as the outcome. God does not want us to trust in just future blessing, He wants us to believe that we are blessed today.

God calls to Job out of the whirlwind. He questions Job's basis for assigning meaning to the events that have just taken place. Over the course of these eighteen verses God asks Job a stream of questions for which the answers are always, "No." The point that God is making has to do with foundation. Job and all of his friends have made a judgment about the series of tests that have just taken place in Job's life. Without exception they have considered these to be a misfortune. But on what basis are they suggesting that such is the case? A starving person would think that a peanut butter and jelly sandwich was a treasure. A wealthy ruler might be insulted if he were offered the same. God is asking Job how he as a mere human thinks that he can determine what is good and what is bad. All events of life only have the meaning that was intended by God. If God intended it for good, then who are we as mere men to argue with the Almighty?

LIFE STEP A sketch-book of drawings by Picasso is valued at over ten million dollars. Is it because of their excellence or because they are Picasso's? The events of life must be valued based on the Artist, not the appearance.

JOB 40:1-14

WHAT IS THE WRITER SAYING?

HOW CAN I APPLY THIS TO MY LIFE?

PRAY Austria – Pray for churches to reach the younger generation who are increasingly turning to cults.

After an extended series of questions (two chapters), the Lord finally draws the matter to a conclusion. Continuing in the same style, it is framed as a question. He basically asks Job, *The one who contends with God is the one who thinks that he can correct God. Are you seeking to correct me, Job?*

Job gets it. He now responds to God from a place of humility (vv. 3-5). Job realizes that he has gone much too far in his complaint. He crossed a line when he assumed that he was capable of judging an act of God. Job's problem ran much deeper than the words he spoke. It was an issue of the heart. Job thought that he knew what was best for him. God is not to be defined by the conditions that one experiences. The events are to be defined by the God that we serve. Life does not help us understand God; God helps us understand life.

God then instructs Job in the way he should walk. Can anyone of us by our own effort earn a moment of peace or joy? Is not every moment that we are not suffering in the fires of Hell a moment of pure grace? Are not the trials that we face in this life indescribable joy compared with the consequences that we would face without the grace of God? We live in days of incredible opportunity. What we complain about as annoying frustrations would be considered a moment of greatest joy by those who face the torment of eternal death. These are not things that we can know by sight. They are things that we must accept by faith. It always boils down to what or whom we are going to believe. Will we believe the pain we feel or the God we serve?

LIFE STEP We can only serve one God. Whoever or whatever controls how we feel is ultimately our God. If we don't allow God to tell us how to feel, then we are not allowing Him to rule our lives, either.

JOB 42:1-17

WHAT IS THE WRITER SAYING?

HOW CAN I APPLY THIS TO MY LIFE?

As we come to the end of the book of Job, we are left with more questions than answers. In fact, we are not given any specific answers. Job's response to God is simple; he changes his mind (repents) and despises (abhors) all of his questions. They no longer seem meaningful. Once he understands (sees) God, there are no questions left. He is content to live the rest of his life in whatever arrangement God deems appropriate. The point is, if God told Job the reason He allowed all that had happened, Job would be trusting in the explanation. With God it is never the *why* that matters; it is the *Who*.

The last part of today's passage wraps up a few loose ends. Job's three friends are rebuked by God because they did not speak correctly to Job. They totally misunderstood God's relationship to the circumstances of life. Elihu is not rebuked but neither is he commended. If his solution was the correct one, then God would have commended his words to Job, but He did not. We may suggest here that Elihu proposed a possible solution that honored both God and Job even though it was not the right solution. God does refine the righteous but that is only a small part of what God is doing when He brings trials into the life of a believer. This is still a why answer not a Who solution.

The key to understanding the book is found in the fact that Job was restored only after he served his friends by praying for them. Only an others-centered life is of value to this world. Love gives and love lights a darkened world.

LIFE STEP For 41 chapters everything focused on Job. Now Job gets it. His life only matters if it impacts others. Otherwise God would have just taken him to Heaven. Giving is living and the more we give the more we live.

The purpose statement for this letter is found in 5:12: *stand fast in the true grace of God.* In developing that theme Peter has three main points. Each contains distinct information about the true grace of God and encouragement to stand fast in it.

The immediate occasion for the letter seems to involve some sort of persecution that has left some believers puzzled. They are beginning to question whether their commitment to Christ is really worth it. They may even be about to give up. Peter's letter is designed to communicate spiritual truths about the true nature of these trials and to encourage all believers to stand firm, especially in times of injustice. Peter suggests that frequently believers have wrong expectations and are therefore unable to respond properly to the difficulties they are facing. Peter, like Paul and James, believes that tribulations are actually wonderful opportunities to experience the grace of God.

This tone is set from the very beginning of the letter. Peter uses what might seem to be an insulting name when he addresses the readers as "strangers." He does this since they felt rejected by their government, their families and their fellow-citizens because of their commitment to Christ. This introduction sets one of the key themes that repeat throughout the letter. Believers are indeed *strangers and aliens* and must accept that status proudly. We *do* have a new government, a new family and new friends. In fact, we can outline the letter around this very idea of alienation.

The Strangeness of Grace
1. A Grace Difference in Suffering (1:1–2:12)
2. A Grace Difference in Submission (2:13–3:22)
3. A Grace Difference in Attitude (4-5)

The first of the three major sections proclaims that what we now have is better than anything we might have *lost.* Salvation is better than citizenship. Truth is better than civil protection. And the body of Christ (the church) is better than friends or family.

The second section opens as did the first with a reference to "strangers" but adds the descriptor *aliens.* The emphasis in this second part of the book is on submission. The believer is not to fight back against the fiery ordeal that he might be experiencing. Rather, he is to submit to the various authorities in his life, even when they are treating him unjustly. The reason for this response is that it is right and that it will provide *seeking* opportunities for those who see the believer's conduct. The trial is never the problem. The problem is always our wrong response to God's gracious provision.

The third section of the book deals specifically with attitude, or approach toward life's frustrations. Peter argues that trials are not to be considered strange. They are always an opportunity for both personal growth and disciple making. Trials are our friends. They build into our lives the kind of character qualities that will bring honor to our Savior. They provide opportunity for leadership to shepherd, they provide opportunity for the believers to encourage, and they provide opportunity for all saints to overcome the evil one. We may be strangers in this world but trials are not to be considered a strange part of our experience. They are all part of God's gracious plan. God is too wise to make a mistake and too loving to be unkind in the final analysis.

1 PETER 1:1-8

WHAT IS THE WRITER SAYING?

HOW CAN I APPLY THIS TO MY LIFE?

PRAY Costa Rica – That the Costa Rican people will understand that salvation is not by works, but by faith.

In today's passage Peter reveals two of the several points that he is going to make in his introduction. After a brief salutation (vv. 1-2), he wants believers to grasp the Plan of Grace (vv. 3-5) and the Permanence of Grace (vv. 6-9). Given that we enjoy a "by grace" salvation, Peter knows that it is imperative for us to understand how such a grace should affect our worldview. In verses 3-5 he emphasizes God's design in salvation. In the past, God saved us and freely gave us the incredible gift of justification (v. 3). In the present, we are being prepared (our sanctification) for an inheritance that cannot be taken away or even tarnished. Earthly citizenship may be lost but not our home in heaven (v. 4). In the future, the exact nature of this salvation is going to be revealed in all its glory (our glorification). It cannot be fully understood until we experience it (v. 5).

We cannot allow present troubles to rob us of the joy that God has given to us through this salvation. It cannot be taken from us; we must relinquish it. Troubles or trials are designed to improve our faith and thereby the quality of our lives. *Under the sun* living is the result of a wrong response to trials; *in the Son* living is what comes from a right response to trials. If our focus is on Jesus Christ and the salvation that He has provided, we will have the ability to rejoice no matter what the trial. We must not focus on ourselves or our circumstances. The Old Testament prophets prophesied that such a salvation would come and that its details would be clarified by the Savior who brought it. We now understand what Old Testament saints longed to see. They looked forward by faith to the coming Messiah; we must live with that same looking-forwardness that they had.

LIFE STEP Faith is the answer to all of life's turbulence. Grace requires faith to be meaningful. God is always gracious but we miss the blessing if we do not exercise our faith.

1 PETER 1:9-16

WHAT IS THE WRITER SAYING?

HOW CAN I APPLY THIS TO MY LIFE?

Verses 9-12 imply that the Old Testament prophets and even the angels did not understand salvation. That is not the case. They understood the basics of a "by grace through faith" salvation. What they did not understand was how God would accomplish this incredible feat. Even among the angels there was a longing to understand exactly how God would work this out. Remember, if Satan, one of the most intelligent created beings, would have known, he would not have crucified the Lord of Glory (1 Corinthians 2:8).

Beginning in verse 13 Peter initiates his first major point. He tells his readers to "rest your hope fully upon the grace." The emphasis in this particular section is on their intellectual knowledge of the gracious salvation that God has provided for them. If the believer is to correctly interpret and respond to his present situation, he must have a clear understanding of the nature of his salvation. He then writes, "not conforming yourselves . . . but . . . be holy." Holiness needs to be understood in this particular case in the same way that it is used in the passage that Peter quotes (Leviticus 11:44). In that passage it is referring to non-moral issues such as food. It is not addressing the purity issues we often associate with holiness. Thus Peter is speaking not of moral purity but of a distinct or separate *worldview*. The believer, because of his salvation, cannot look at the circumstances that surround him in the same way that an unbeliever does. God wants the believer to see life the same way that He does. Peter considers this aspect of holiness to be the basis of our sanctification.

LIFE STEP No matter how dark the hour, the believer is always commanded to format his worldview (gird his mind) based on the fundamental dynamics of salvation, namely, God's grace!

1 PETER 1:17-25

WHAT IS THE WRITER SAYING?

HOW CAN I APPLY THIS TO MY LIFE?

PRAY Syria - Pray that believers might rediscover the zeal and faith of the New Testament Church of Antioch.

Peter wants the believer to live in such a way that his behavior reflects accurately the kind of salvation that he enjoys. It is more precious than silver or gold. Persecution was robbing those believers of the ability to accumulate wealth. Their citizenship was being taken from them. Peter points out that silver and gold cannot help the one who possesses it in any way. It only adds to the pain. Quality of life is determined by only one thing, *the quality of a person's relationship to God*. Our salvation is in a category all by itself. It is not just of future value. It is the only thing that can rescue a person from the tyranny of this present evil age. Given this understanding of "be ye holy," "obeying the truth" is probably a reference to worldviews. Peter is commanding that believers adopt a biblical worldview. This worldview is communicated through the Word. This new worldview is driven by a sincere "love of the brethren." It starts with a proper understanding of our salvation and matures with an appropriate commitment to fellow believers. The only way that believers can master this new way of living is to have their souls purged of the old way of thinking and living. The word of God gives a replacement model so that the believer is no longer conformed to the former passions. There can be no compromise. We must be born again . . . through the word "which lives and abides forever." This transformation of heart is so thorough that it is referred to as *rebirth*. The sense here is that the old must be completely abandoned. Peter speaks of it in the terms of new birth because even the natural bent of the human nature must be changed. Our salvation must penetrate to the very foundations of our thinking if it is to transform our behavior.

LIFE STEP Our salvation must work from the inside out. Merely changing how we live is an insufficient response to the awesome salvation God has provided for us. We must accept a total renewal of the whole person.

1 PETER 2:1-10

WHAT IS THE WRITER SAYING?

HOW CAN I APPLY THIS TO MY LIFE?

PRAY France – Outreach among the growing Muslim population. Islam is now the second religion of France.

Too often we view the analogy of "newborn babes" as referring to the eagerness of the infant rather than the submissiveness of the infant. Peter is arguing that believers must put aside the old man and all that he stands for and as a totally empty vessel be refilled with the biblical worldview. Newborns have no ulterior motives and are totally dependent upon and trusting of the one who feeds them. The milk of the word enables the believer to appreciate the kindness of the Lord. The kindness of the Lord cannot be experienced in this life if the believer continues to hold to his former worldview. Life must be understood according to the message of Scripture in order to be fully appreciated. The Lord's kindness is an anticipated reward for those who worship successfully in the period of biblical history in which they find themselves. This kindness is always available, but if we ignore it we will not get to enjoy it in the trials of life. Beginning with verse 4, Peter begins a series of analogies that use metaphors from the Old Testament to highlight the special make-up of the church. He moves from the rejected Christ, to the by-faith Christians, to the new spiritual household called the church. It is interesting that Peter is making a strong statement about this new thing in God's program that we call the church but never uses the word *church*! Christ was certainly the "corner stone" but He was also the stone at which the nation of Israel stumbled. They stumbled because they chose works over faith and their own worldview over that of Scripture. The one who believes is the one who experiences blessing. Blessing has always been available; it is faith that has been lacking. Church age saints must not stumble here.

LIFE STEP Israel understood the law as a *works document* but it was always a faith document (Deuteronomy 30:11-15). Because they disobeyed the true message of the law, they experienced the judgments which the law promised.

THURSDAY 42

1 PETER 2:11-17

WHAT IS THE WRITER SAYING?

HOW CAN I APPLY THIS TO MY LIFE?

PRAY Ukraine – Wisdom and courage for full-time workers hampered by restrictions that limit growth.

Peter uses the names *beloved* and *strangers and pilgrims* to mark verse 11 as the beginning of a new section. The believers in Asia Minor felt ostracized from someone or something. Based upon Peter's whole letter, I think that they had been excommunicated from the synagogue, the institution of their legal protection in the Roman Empire. Without the protection of the synagogue, they were now experiencing civil rejection and persecution as followers of an illegal religion. The synagogue had rejected the church, siding with Roman law. Peter seems to suggest that this oppressed Jewish-Christian minority should now focus upon the Gentiles. This rejection has provided a new opportunity for witness. Just as the early persecution in Jerusalem propelled missionaries throughout Judea, Samaria and the world, so this rejection was providing an opportunity for believers to shine before their Gentile neighbors and authorities. Beginning with verse 13, Peter suggests that the believers can do this if they continue to respect and show loyalty toward secular authorities. These were the very authorities that were persecuting them! We do not know how intense the persecution may have been but historical accounts of the period imply that it was brutal. Still, Peter insists that believers recognize that all authorities are put in place by God and are to be respected as such. The reason that we do this is because of the opportunity that it will provide. True freedom only exists when we are totally submitted to God and His all-encompassing purposes for Planet Earth.

Persecution is never pleasant, especially when it is unfair. And yet it is often in these kinds of situations that the believer is given the greatest opportunity to shine in this dark world.

1 PETER 2:18-25

WHAT IS THE WRITER SAYING?

HOW CAN I APPLY THIS TO MY LIFE?

PRAY Pray that the Lord might lead someone from your church into short – term or full – time missions work.

Government is not the only authority that exists for the believer. In today's passage, Peter suggests two additional *authorities* the believer must consider if he is to live with excellence among the Gentiles. In verses 18-20 he speaks of economic authorities and in verses 21-25 he refers to circumstances as an authority. The economic authorities of that day would be the "masters." Times have changed but whether the relationship is employer/employee or master/slave, the mandate is the same. If we react as the world would react, we will not advance the cause of Christ.

In verse 21 Peter lays out the heart of the matter. Believers were *called for this purpose.* (See also 3:9). The nasty turns of life can be interpreted in one of two ways. We may view them as the enemy of our spiritual life or we may view them as a friend. Peter points to Christ and His acceptance of providence as God's calling in His life. Christ provided more than spiritual wealth; He provided an example of how we ought to walk in this world. He did not view His mission here as a minor inconvenience to be endured until His glorification. He lived His life just as we should live ours and He gave His life just as we should give ours as living sacrifices. He "committed Himself" to the Father. Christ lived a life of total dependence upon the Father and He expects us to live similar lives. It is not enough to submit to the authorities that God has placed in our lives, we must also submit to the circumstances that swirl around us. Left to our own resources we will always stray like sheep and wander from the path that God wants us to walk.

LIFE STEP

Only by entrusting our welfare to our Shepherd and Guardian can we ever hope to experience the quality of life that God would have us to live. Trials make that kind of life possible.

1 PETER 3:1-7

WHAT IS THE WRITER SAYING?

HOW CAN I APPLY THIS TO MY LIFE?

PRAY Spain – Praise – Successful use of music in evangelization. Pray for more musicians and opportunities.

The final area in which the believer must practice submission is the family. Peter expects the wife to submit to her husband. This is not a concession to that ancient culture. Note that when Peter forbids the "arranging the hair" etc., he is not necessarily forbidding all outward beautification. What he is forbidding is an exclusive focus or over-emphasis on beauty. Humans have a tendency to focus on outward beauty and dismiss those heart traits that God admires. This is in keeping with the emphasis on worldview change seen throughout the letter. We must understand that the wife finds contentment by being in a right relationship with her husband. When we ignore these established proper human relationships, God cannot bless us as He would like. Suffering occurs when we leave the protection of God's divinely authorized institutions (such as *the home, the state* and *the church*).

Husbands are exhorted to live with their wives in an understanding way. This is not a part of the submission topic, but Peter feels obligated to recognize that the husband has a different but equally compelling role in the family. Husbands and wives have different roles but they do not have different value in the household of faith. Husbands need to keep these two distinct relationships in perspective as they strive to love their wives as Christ loved the church. Only when both parties accept their God-ordained responsibilities can the family produce the kind of blessing that God wants for His children. Each partner in the husband/wife relationship is expected to enthusiastically carry out their responsibility regardless of their partner's compliance.

 LIFE STEP Love is not a two way street. Peter does not want us to have a conditional commitment to the family. Each one of us must act in response to God's love, not our partner's behavior.

1 PETER 3:8-12

WHAT IS THE WRITER SAYING?

HOW CAN I APPLY THIS TO MY LIFE?

PRAY China – For the failure of all government attempts to impose false doctrine on registered churches.

The next major section opens with a paragraph exhorting brotherly love (3:8) and closes with a similar exhortation (4:8). In verse 8 "finally" is the Greek word *telos*, which emphasizes *end*, as in *goal to which we move*. It indicates that Peter is focusing on the primary purpose of our salvation. The *telos* of our salvation is the *present*, not just the eternal salvation of our souls. That happens when we experience harmony, brotherhood, kindness and humility. When we live this way we not only are a blessing to others, but we also receive a blessing. We are debtors, as Paul mentioned in Romans 1:14. This deep obligation must be based on God's treatment of us, and it is always shown by extending similar grace to others. We don't return evil for evil or just good for good; we should always treat others the way God has treated us. We are truly blessed only when we are a living and contributing member of the household that God is building on Planet Earth. Peter is talking about the church as an institution of fellowship, not just as an institution of salvation. Present salvation is only available to those who are totally committed to God and to His program. Love God. Love one another. That's all there is. We were called for this very purpose. We were not called to be miserable. True, we were called to experience difficult circumstances, but difficult circumstances have no power to diminish blessing. If God sends them, then they are to be welcomed. We will then inherit a blessing. There is no question that the central issue addressed by this letter has to do with blessing. The believers in Asia Minor were taking an escapist attitude and counting entirely on the soon return of the Lord to solve their problems. Peter tells them that blessing is available here and now, no matter how dark the trial may be.

LIFE STEP Never give up on the present. Never throw in the towel. Life only has value when it is given in the service of others.

1 PETER 3:13-22

WHAT IS THE WRITER SAYING?

HOW CAN I APPLY THIS TO MY LIFE?

PRAY Moldova – Moldovans have an open door to share the Gospel since a democratic government was appointed. Pray that they will be bold in their witness.

Worldviews are seldom shaped by faith; they are usually shaped by experience. That is why many believers continually stray like sheep from the pastures that God has chosen for them. It goes against our nature to be happy when we suffer, but God does not want us to be intimidated by the fears of this life. We are intimidated by the world when we let the people or circumstances that we encounter shape our worldview. We fail to experience the full joy of this life because we have neglected a vital part of our great salvation. What we worship controls our life. If we worship our friends, fear of our friends' opinions controls our life. We are told to "sanctify the Lord" in our hearts. Worship of Christ must dwell alone in the believer's heart. All other concerns must shrink to nothingness in His presence. If we rejoice in hardships, we are sure to get questions about our behavior. These questions will give opportunities for the believer to share his faith with at least some of his persecutors. The issue is never the nature of the circumstance that one faces; the issue must always be the source of the circumstance. Should one consider the trial to be an independent entity or should one see it as it really is, a part of God's plan? The trial that Christ experienced was certainly undeserved; it occurred not for Christ's benefit, but for ours. Since His pain took care of the sin issue, all present trials are for our improvement, not punishment. His fleshly ordeal provided spiritual renewal. New life could not be provided unless old life was retired. God is in the process of effecting new living. The more we hang onto the old, the more pain we feel at its removal. Life hurts when we hang onto death.

 LIFE STEP No matter how dark the hour, the proper response is always to trust the Lord and demonstrate that trust by our attitude, actions and words.

1 PETER 4:1-6

WHAT IS THE WRITER SAYING?

HOW CAN I APPLY THIS TO MY LIFE?

PRAY El Salvador – For those taking Bible correspondence courses to gain a passion for studying the Word.

When Peter states that Christ has "suffered… in the flesh," he is referring back to the previous verses and is speaking of His death. The believer must prepare himself to weather the storms of life with the same mentality that Jesus had in His struggles. Because Christ died on our behalf, we must consider ourselves to be dead as well. This is the essential equipment for dealing with sinful responses to God-sent trials. Obviously dead people (those who "suffered" in the flesh) no longer sin. They cannot respond to influences from this world. In the same way the believer can reckon the old worldview to be dead and accept the worldview that God wants to superimpose on our minds and hearts. That new worldview can only function when the old is no longer at work. Believers have a choice about the quality of life that they experience in this world. Outside influences can only control us to the degree that we offer ourselves to them. The time has come to offer our lives fully and permanently to God for His use. The choice is simple. The believer can accept God's will for his life or he can bang his head against a brick wall. Those who fight God pay a severe price. There is a flood today. Not a flood of water but a flood of moral filth. We are protected from that flood if we commit ourselves to God and to His present program, the church. Those who fail to participate are often drowned, not physically but spiritually. There is no victorious Christian living apart from the divine provision for victorious Christian living. Past generations of believers have come and gone. Their "flesh" has been judged, but they live on as forever-spirits, awaiting the day of bodily resurrection.

LIFE STEP The believer cannot escape the damage that sin in general has done to our bodies but we can avoid the further immediate damage of present sin. We can also sow to the Spirit and reap the fruit of the Spirit here and now, as well as in Heaven.

1 PETER 4:7-11

WHAT IS THE WRITER SAYING?

HOW CAN I APPLY THIS TO MY LIFE?

In these verses, Peter shares the provisions God has made for life on Planet Earth. The believer must understand that the "end of all things is at hand." All physical things will end. Death of the flesh is not a tragedy. Why all the panic? This is God's will. Since this is true, we need to have a proper perspective: "sober and watch unto prayer, …have fervent charity." The instruction here is specific. We must be serious about the decisions we make. We must pray in a way that demonstrates a measured understanding that God is in control and that all circumstances are under His providential supervision. Finally we must see life from a group (church) perspective, not from an individual perspective. Hurt in my life may be preparation for bringing joy to someone else. We must be good stewards of the manifold grace of God. The testings of life are a part of His grace. They come for divine reasons. We need to be good stewards of these precious opportunities. We turn ourselves over to God's care. God also turns His grace over to our use. How will we speak of this grace? Will we complain? Will we take the glory when we succeed? What kind of stewards will we be? Good stewards recognize that they must access the strength that God supplies. No trial can overcome us that God has not also provided the strength to not only survive, but thrive. If we falter, it is not due to a lack of provision; it is due to lack of acquisition. God has freely provided all that we need to thrive and reproduce here in this world. The key to unlocking that strength is to recognize that it is only given to those who desire to love their neighbor. Love covers a multitude of sins.

LIFE STEP Love always gives and never takes, but the one who loves always ends up more blessed than the hoarders will ever know. The way of love begins on the road to Calvary.

THURSDAY 43

1 PETER 4:12-19

WHAT IS THE WRITER SAYING?

HOW CAN I APPLY THIS TO MY LIFE?

PRAY Argentina – Pray that the Church will have a vision to impact their communities and do more to address the enormous poverty in the city.

Peter has yet to actually address what he considers to be the appropriate response to fiery ordeals. He does so in this section. Our response to trials is a measure of our relationship with Christ. There is no doubt that this was an intense ordeal. Peter is not talking about some personal inconveniences. This is severe testing. They were concerned that they were becoming strangers and aliens in their own country. Peter says, *Praise the Lord. That's exactly what you are!* They considered the trials to be unnatural intrusions, but they weren't. Trials are to be counted as friends. God only sends friendly fire into our lives. It is always designed to improve. Peter tells believers to keep on rejoicing; he views rejoicing as a permanent state for the believer. This is not a *rejoice in spite of trial*; it is a *rejoice because of trials*. Those who suffer for evil behavior should not expect to rejoice.

As with the previous segments, Peter speaks of the return of Christ at the beginning of this the third section. We are to rejoice today so that we will rejoice then. It must be counted as a blessing to suffer for Christ. To respond in any other way is to fight the work of God's Spirit in our lives. "Judgment must begin at the house of God." This need not be a negative concept. Believers will only be rewarded at the Judgment Seat of Christ. The believer has been given the opportunity to experience God's blessing in a time of fiery persecution. We must be armed with the mind of Christ to view trials this way. Since only the grace of God stands between humans and utter despair, the unbeliever or double-minded believer has no hope to weather the storms of life until they believe.

 LIFE STEP In the final analysis what really counts is where one's trust is anchored. Blessing is available to those who trust God's grace and not their own ideas of how life should be.

351

FRIDAY 43

1 PETER 5:1-7

WHAT IS THE WRITER SAYING?

HOW CAN I APPLY THIS TO MY LIFE?

PRAY For the many summer children's camp leadership and staff, as they share the Gospel with hundreds of children.

Life was always meant to be shared, and that sharing begins with shepherding the flock or investing in the lives of other believers. This sounds a lot like the discussion that Jesus had with Peter in John 21. Left on our own, we believers will wander through a wide range of emotions when responding to the trials of life. We need shepherding. Believers are not born with a biblical worldview. We need to be taught and shepherded into right thinking. We need to be transformed by the renewing of our minds. Once we are strong enough to count trials as our friends, we can then begin to minister to others.

Younger men are exhorted to learn from those who have had more experience in the pastures of God's grace. This requires a humble heart and a willingness to serve and grow together. Remember, when

Peter exhorts us to humble ourselves, the immediate context is trials. When we make grandiose proclamations about fairness and grudgingly accepting God's will, we fail miserably in our mission. God's grace should always be prized. It must be received with a grateful and humble heart in order to be maximized. The *fiery ordeals of life* are distributed by the mighty hand of God. No circumstance of life is so powerful that it can overcome the mighty hand of God and inflict injury on even the weakest of God's children. We choose to respond improperly. All testing is providential. There is no personal or impersonal agent that is anywhere close to being in the same class as God. He rules all matters and expects His children to respect His decisions. This, Peter reminds us, is the true grace of God.

LIFE STEP God expects us to drink in the new information that he has provided as newborn babes drink milk. Without this nourishment we will certainly starve to death spiritually.

I PETER 5:8-14

WHAT IS THE WRITER SAYING?

HOW CAN I APPLY THIS TO MY LIFE?

PRAY
Pray for summer camp counselors, supervisors, and teen staff to serve Christ wholeheartedly.

Peter does take a moment to put the adversary into perspective. God's grace does not alleviate personal responsibility. Even though God may intend something for good that does not mean that the personal agent executing the "grace" is not guilty. Yes, the devil is our adversary and yes, he seeks victims. However, he can be resisted. Don't fall into his trap and begin to fear him or his associates. The only power that he has to hurt us is the power that we give him when we give our hearts over to anger and bitterness. God is "the God of all grace." There is no ungracious part in God. For this present existence all that He does is grace and purely grace. There is no duplicity. He offers grace and what we get is simply that – grace. He called us to "eternal glory." Like eternal life, this does not begin when we die. It starts the day we come to know Him as our personal Savior. The question has never been whether or not we have this eternal weight of glory; the question has always been whether we will become submissive enough to enjoy it now. Will we let God change how we think?

Peter wraps up the letter with a mention of "Silvanus, our faithful brother." This is Silas, Paul's former traveling partner. He appears to be the secretary for this letter. Peter concludes by restating his theme. This letter is about "the true grace of God" and how we are to *stand firm in it*. True grace is not to be free from the fiery ordeals of life, but rather to experience the joy that only God can provide in the midst of those trials.

LIFE STEP

When we understand this grace, we acquire personal and present peace. Paul opens all his letters with "grace and peace." Peter spends the whole of this first letter telling us what grace and peace truly mean. Grace is always there; it is our responsibility to accept it and then experience peace.

The titles of these two books comes from the Hebrew tradition of naming a book after its first word or phrase, which in this case is "Now King …, " which identifies the focus of the two books, an evaluation of the spiritual lives of each of Israel's kings. The Hebrew canon presents 1 and 2 Kings as a single writing with the same text as found in our Bibles. 1 and 2 Kings were first divided into two books when the Old Testament was translated into the Greek language (the Septuagint Translation), which takes up more space than does Hebrew!

The author of 1 and 2 Kings is unknown but Jewish tradition says the author was **Jeremiah**, which is a credible tradition. As such, **Jeremiah** would have been the compiler and editor of pre-existing materials to which he added his own comments. Note that the author tells us he made regular use of existing written, historical, governmental, records, such as the ancient court records called "*The Acts of Solomon*," "*The Chronicles of the Kings of Judah*," and "*The Chronicles of the Kings of Israel*" (1 Kings 11:41; 14:19, 29; 15:7, 23, 31; 16:5, 14, 20; etc.).

While **1 and 2 Samuel** tell the story of the first kings of Israel, Saul and David (1050 to 971 B.C.), **1 and 2 Kings** tell the majority of the history of the kings of Israel and Judah (385 years!), beginning with the death of David (971 B.C.) until after the end of the Kingdom of Judah when it was exiled to Babylon in 586 B.C. Historically, the events of 1 and 2 Kings can be summarized as follows:

1 Kings 1–11   **United Kingdom** (continuing)

1 Kings 12–2 Kings 17   **Divided Kingdom** (Judah and Israel)

2 Kings 18–25   **Remaining Kingdom** (Judah).

Since the book of **2 Kings** ends with an account of the last king of Judah who was then in exile at Babylon after the destruction of Judah, Jerusalem and the Temple, we see the writer's perspective at the time of his writing **1 and 2 Kings**:

- He was writing a history of the Hebrew people from the time of the death of **King David** through to the time when the kings of Israel and Judah *cease to control their own nation*. He is answering the question, **How could this great catastrophe have happened?**

- He was also writing to point out that God, throughout this time period, had been actively seeking to draw Israel and Judah back to a holy walk before Him. This is especially seen in the extensive emphasis in 1 and 2 Kings upon two of God's prophets, **Elijah** and **Elisha**, who were sent by God to minister to Israel's kings.

- Finally, we note that the author in 1 and 2 Kings wanted to provide a brief and selective history of the spiritual standing of each of Israel's and Judah's kings. Thus, consistently we find an evaluation of each king with the use of the words "he did that which was **evil** in the sight of the LORD" or "he did that which was **right** in the sight of the LORD."

Concerning King Solomon, who is the central figure of the first half of 1 Kings, the Bible scholar Scroggie says, "Solomon was a strange character, and he may be regarded in various ways; personally, officially and typically. Viewed personally, he was characterized by wisdom and wickedness; greatly gifted intellectually, yet he was very weak ethically. His mind and his morals were not on the same level. Viewed officially, his great work was two-fold: the material development of the Kingdom, and the building of the Temple. Viewed typically, it is not difficult to see an anticipation of Christ's Millennial Kingdom, when, after the extirpation of all His foes, there will be peace."

A Survey of the Books of 1 Kings and 2 Kings:

- **1 Kings 1:1–2:11**
  The Death of King David
  (United Kingdom)
- **1 Kings 2:11–11**
  The Reign of King Solomon
  (United Kingdom)
- **1 Kings 12–22**
  The Divided Kingdom, presented as a parallel history of the kings of **Israel** and of **Judah**.
  – *1 Kings 17–22*
    The Ministry of the Prophet Elijah.
- **2 Kings 1–17**
  Continuation of the parallel history of the kings of **Israel** and of **Judah**.
  – *2 Kings 2–13*
    The Ministry of the Prophet Elisha.
- **2 Kings 18–25**
  The last kings of Judah
  (Judah goes into captivity)
  (Northern Kingdom of Israel is destroyed)

1 KINGS 1:15-18, 29-37

WHAT IS THE WRITER SAYING?

HOW CAN I APPLY THIS TO MY LIFE?

PRAY Cameroon – Pray for deep repentance, true revival, and restoration of Bible reading, preaching and holiness among the many Christians in Cameroon.

1 Kings begins with the story of the transfer of leadership from King David to his tenth son, Solomon (1 Chronicles 3:1-8). Several years earlier the Lord had revealed to David that Solomon was to be the next king over Israel (1 Chronicles 22:9) and then David had told Bathsheba, his eighth wife (1 Kings 1:13, 17). Apparently David had not publicly crowned Solomon as Israel's next king. Thus, with King David dying, his fourth and oldest surviving son, Adonijah, who considered the kingdom his by birthright, makes a move to capture the monarchy. Adonijah *exalts* himself before the people with a triumphal parade (v. 5) and a great public feast (v. 9). Adonijah even wins over the support of Joab, David's nephew and chief general, and Abiathar, the high priest at the Temple (v. 7).

Plainly, Adonijah saw Solomon and his supporters, Nathan the prophet, Zadok the priest, and Benaiah, commander of David's bodyguard, as his rivals (v. 8) that needed to be out-maneuvered so he might become king. Adonijah also intended to put Solomon and his mother, Bathsheba, and their supporters to death once power had been secured (vv. 11-12).

Because of this emergency situation, Nathan urges Bathsheba to speak to David concerning Solomon's and her peril (v. 21). Nathan also asks David why the people at the public feast were declaring, "God save King Adonijah" (v. 25). At this point David powerfully declares that Solomon would reign as king by the LORD's own appointment (v. 30).

David skillfully defuses the situation. Solomon was to ride on David's mule (identifiable by its trappings) through Jerusalem protected by David's "servants," namely, *David's Mighty Men* (v. 33). Solomon was to be brought to the spring at Gihon, where Zadok and Nathan would anoint him king. Then a horn was to be blown accompanied by the shout, "God save King Solomon" (v. 34). By these activities the people would know that David was supporting the LORD's choice of Solomon as Israel's next king.

LIFE STEP Just as David wisely planned events to defuse a dangerous situation, how might you ask God for the wisdom to defuse a difficult situation in your own life?

1 KINGS 2:1-12

WHAT IS THE WRITER SAYING?

HOW CAN I APPLY THIS TO MY LIFE?

This chapter gives David's final charge to Solomon just prior to David's death (v. 10). David wanted to reassure Solomon, a young man of perhaps twenty years who was to reign over God's people, with several guiding principles of life:

Verse 2a: Solomon was to be **strong**. This word pictures a particular type of strength; *be like an ever-flowing stream in the desert*. Thus it is urging, *don't just be a stream that flows in the rainy season; be a source of spiritual influence when times are hard!*

Verse 2b: Solomon was to **show himself a man**. Even as a young ruler, he must be God's *image bearer* who reflects God's own regal character.

Verse 3a: Solomon was to **keep the charge of the LORD** concerning kings (see Deuteronomy 17:14-20). He was to faithfully study and adhere to God's Word in the Scriptures.

Verse 3b: Solomon was to **walk in God's ways**. He was to move forward in his own life displaying a consistent pattern of conduct that reflects **God's ways**. Solomon's **walk** was to be a source of **leading** and **guiding** of others by his own choices in conduct.

Verse 3c: Solomon would **prosper** in life by keeping this charge! Notice that this **prosperity** had to do with how to apply wisdom, knowledge, and justice.

Much unfinished royal business was to be attended to by Solomon regarding Joab (vv. 5-6), Shimei (vv. 8-9) and the sons of Barzillai (v. 7). The first two were to be dealt with severely, whereas mercy was to be shown to the sons Barzillai in that he had provided sustenance for David and his men when they were fleeing from Absalom (2 Samuel 19:31-39). Note that David comments on his confidence that Solomon will exercise *wisdom* (vv. 6, 9) and *kindness* (v. 7).

LIFE STEP What kind of *prosperity* are you seeking in life? Are you a source of influence? Do you reflect Christ's image? Are you paying close attention to your Bible? Is your walk a godly pattern to follow?

1 KINGS 3:1-15

WHAT IS THE WRITER SAYING?

HOW CAN I APPLY THIS TO MY LIFE?

PRAY Jordan – Pray for the freedom to proclaim the gospel and for followers of Jesus to be able to remain in Jordan.

In today's passage we find the defining statement for Solomon's early reign as king of Israel, "*Solomon loved the LORD*" (v. 3). His earlier years were years of obedience to the Lord. This statement is the definition for three issues here that could be mistakenly construed as compromises:

- Solomon's marriage to an Egyptian princess (v. 1) – In light of his love for the LORD, we must conclude that she was not a spiritual distraction; rather she must have adopted the Hebrew faith as did Ruth and other women who became a spiritual part of Israel.
- Solomon continued to allow people to sacrifice at various "high places" (v. 2, Hebrew worship sites around Israel). We must remember that as yet there was no recognized center of Jewish worship.
- Solomon himself brings a great offering to the LORD at Gibeon (v. 4). Yet we notice a strange situation that

continued; the *Ark* (v. 15, at Jerusalem) was not with the *Tabernacle* and the *Altar of Sacrifice* (v. 4, at Gibeon), even though the *Ark* was intended to symbolize God's presence at the time of Israel's sacrifices! Remember Solomon would shortly resolve this absurd situation.

After Solomon's great sacrifice, the Lord promised to give Solomon whatever he asked for (v. 5). We see that Solomon had noted the devoted *walk* of his father, David, as he ruled with *righteousness* and *uprightness* over Israel (vv. 6-7)! Solomon knew he was too young and inexperienced to complete the assignment which the LORD had given him, so he asked for an "understanding heart to judge" (v. 9).

God honored Solomon and gave him both his request and those things for which he didn't ask (vv. 11-13). Solomon is told to walk like his father and obey the Word. Blessing was assured.

 LIFE STEP Just as Solomon had noticed his father's walk, there will be those who will notice your godly walk and desire for righteousness and uprightness! Take a minute and write out a prayer to the Lord asking Him to give you the wisdom needed to have a godly walk of your own!

1 KINGS 3:16-28

WHAT IS THE WRITER SAYING?

HOW CAN I APPLY THIS TO MY LIFE?

PRAY Poland – Summer camp ministries safety, salvation decisions, and consecration commitments.

This paragraph provides an illustration of the fulfillment of the LORD's promise to give wisdom to Solomon (3:5-15). Solomon was personally administering justice in a public court when two prostitutes stood before him with a grave problem. One of their children had been accidentally killed (v. 19). The dead child's mother then switched children with the second woman (v. 20). Now both stood before Solomon, claiming the living child.

Since there were no witnesses or evidence to prove who was telling the truth, Solomon showed an understanding of human nature when he suggested that the child be cut in half so that each woman could have half of the child (v. 25). By this means Solomon was able to test their hearts to determine which was the real mother. One of the women – the real mother – cried out, from the depth of her being, that the child should not be divided (v. 26a). So then without a witness or other evidence, Solomon determined the real mother by bringing to light a truth that could not be seen. By this God established the reign of Solomon since people saw that God's special hand of blessing was upon him (v. 28).

We are reminded of the One who is "greater than Solomon" (Luke 11:31), that is, Jesus Christ, who has come into the world to rule as our righteous king. Gaebelein writes of Solomon, "In his wisdom he is a type of our Lord Jesus who is the wisdom of God. And the justice Solomon administered in his earthly kingdom is typical of the righteous judgment of our Lord when he rules as King over the earth." The day is coming when Jesus will likewise bring to light those failures we think we have hidden in darkness when we Christians stand before Him to give an account of our lives at the Judgment Seat of Christ (2 Corinthians 5:10)!

LIFE STEP Why not ask the Lord Jesus to give you a measure of Solomon's wisdom; that is, (1) an ability to know, as did Solomon, the human heart, be it good or evil; (2) an ability to judge rightly and wisely in those difficult matters that come before you in life? Also, how can you be an example of the life that demonstrates honesty, truthfulness, genuine love, and right choices which are often missing in times of hardship?

1 KINGS 4:20-34

WHAT IS THE WRITER SAYING?

HOW CAN I APPLY THIS TO MY LIFE?

PRAY Hungary – The rise in materialism over the past 20 years has led to an increase in atheism. 45% of Hungarians are atheists. Pray for revival in Hungary.

Today we focus on the *wise* administration of the young king, Solomon, over the Kingdom of Israel, which was the result of God's blessing Solomon with a "wise and understanding heart" (3:12). The earlier portions of this chapter can be summarized as follows:

4:1-6 – Solomon's *ministers of state*; his priests, recorders (scribes), commanders, advisors, and overseers are named.

4:7-19 – Solomon's *twelve governors* and *administrative districts*. This new division of the kingdom reflects the large territory controlled by Solomon. Each district was taxed in food commodities one month per year to feed Solomon's large administrative staff.

Today's passage focuses on the national blessings that had come upon Israel as a result of the reigns of David and now his son, Solomon. The blessings were to be a reminder of God's covenant promises:

- Israel's *population* had become as the *sands of the sea*, verse 20, see Genesis 22:17.

- The *boundaries* controlled by Israel – from the River of Egypt to the Euphrates River, verse 21 (see Genesis 15:18). Note that Israel received annual taxes or tribute from a number of foreign kingdoms.
- Israel was enjoying peace and prosperity, verses 22-25 (see Genesis 22:17).
- For the first time in Israel's history, Solomon maintained large, permanently-activated army detachments of chariots and horsemen.
- The last paragraph (vv. 26-34) notes that a new dimension was added to Solomon's accomplishments – he became internationally known (v. 34) for his great wisdom and writings [3000 proverbs and 1005 songs (v. 32)], which show his wisdom in various affairs of life.
- Solomon also spoke concerning trees, plants, animals, birds and fish (v. 33). This is a link back to Adam! It is saying that Solomon had a great intellect, like Adam, who tended the plants in the Garden and named the animals after their character (Genesis 2:16-20).

LIFE STEP Clearly the *faithfulness of God* is to be seen here as He keeps, and will continue to keep His promises (Genesis 15:3-6; 18-21). How has God shown His faithfulness and goodness to you?

1 KINGS 6:1-14, 38

WHAT IS THE WRITER SAYING?

HOW CAN I APPLY THIS TO MY LIFE?

Today's passage establishes a timeline for early events of Israel's history. The fourth year of Solomon's reign (v. 37), when the building of the Temple began, has been established archeologically at 966 B.C. In turn, this places Israel's crossing of the Red Sea at 1446 B.C. The author was pointing out that the building of the Temple was as important as the birth of the nation of Israel. Both would define Israel and the LORD her God! The author is also declaring the faithful working of God in history to bring fulfillment of His promise, such as Deuteronomy 12:5, *God will choose [a place] to put His name and make his habitation.*

Practically, the Temple became a permanent Tabernacle. Everything said about the Tabernacle, as the dwelling place of the Lord, would now be applied to the Temple. For several years, with God's blessing, Kings David and Solomon had been preparing to build this permanent Tabernacle. In fact, David drew up the plans that "he had by the Spirit" and then he "gave his son Solomon the plans" (1 Chronicles 28:11-19).

The Temple was about twice the size of the Tabernacle. It was ninety feet long, thirty feet wide and forty five feet high (v. 2). It was like a three-story building with 2,700 square feet of floor space. While it was not huge, it was beautifully adorned with white limestone, cedar, and gold. It also had a front porch adding fifteen more feet to its length (v. 3). On either side of the Temple were three floors of dormitories (vv. 5-6) that would be used by various priests during their rotation of service at the Temple.

Our passage ends with a historical perspective. After seven years of constructing the Temple (vv. 37-38), the LORD speaks to Solomon again. The LORD promises that He would "dwell among the children of Israel" (v. 13) as long as Israel and her king *walked* in God's truth. Remember, this book was written shortly after the Temple and Jerusalem were destroyed because the people of God had forgotten their responsibility to keep their *walk* pure, which had resulted in God removing His blessing upon Israel!

 LIFE STEP How important is it that our bodies (the temples of the Holy Spirit) and walks are *pure* in order to bring glory to the Lord! Is your body a holy place in which God may dwell? Is your walk pure so that God's blessings are not withdrawn from your life?

1 KINGS 11:1-13

WHAT IS THE WRITER SAYING?

HOW CAN I APPLY THIS TO MY LIFE?

For the first twenty years (9:10) of his reign, Solomon built the Temple (chapter 6) and improved the economy of Israel (chapters 4, 9). Yet here Solomon begins to undo the value of his spiritual accomplishments in Israel. He also, by his subsequent deeds, "turned away his heart" from the LORD (v. 2). He fails to heed the earlier warnings given to Israel's future kings, such as Deuteronomy 17:14-17: no king was to (a) "multiply horses" (10:25), (b) "multiply... silver and gold" (10:25), or (c) "multiply wives" (11:3).

After everything the Lord had done for Solomon, how could Solomon have allowed his heart to be *not perfect with the Lord* (vv. 4, 6, that is, allowing other gods to stand as equals to the true God, Jehovah)? Likewise, how could Solomon have been drawn away from the LORD, so that he himself "went after" these other gods (vv. 5-6)?

The answer is given in our passage: Solomon *justified personal compromise* (politically arranged marriages to foreign women who continued to worship their "foreign" gods, v. 8) to gain an advantage in his kingdom's commercial and political dealings. First, he was willing to *tolerate* such an inconsistency in his household. Soon he became *accustomed* to it and then *comfortable* with it. Lastly, we are here told that Solomon "did evil" (v. 6) as he was drawn to these other gods by his wives so that he himself "went after" these gods in *open involvement*, even building "high places" for their worship (v. 7). While Solomon didn't totally renounce the Lord, he was no longer fully devoted to God. Instead of being a king who wholly did what was right, Solomon became an example of one who compromised and drew away from God.

Again we must ask, how could this be? This is a common way that sin works deeper into our lives. First, it finds a way to insert the thin end of its wedge into our lives. Then, it works to insert itself further into our lives, creating a greater opening and greater compromise.

LIFE STEP

We are not all that different from Solomon, we too are often willing to justify compromise with evil things to gain some worldly advantage. We need to "take heed lest we fall" (1 Corinthians 10:12). Have you become comfortable with or involved in evil things?

1 KINGS 11:41 - 12:15

WHAT IS THE WRITER SAYING?

HOW CAN I APPLY THIS TO MY LIFE?

PRAY Bahrain – Pray that Christians would be able to have the courage and sensitively to share the love of Christ with others despite rules against evangelism.

We begin by noting that Solomon's son, *Rehoboam,* intending to be crowned as Israel's next king, had to come to Shechem in northern Israel (12:1; see Genesis 12:6; Joshua 20:7; 24:1), not at Jerusalem, the capital city. Apparently the northern tribes of Israel were of a mind to submit to Rehoboam as their next king if their demands were met! The people were obviously tired of Solomon's heavy taxes and the strenuous labor necessary for his many building projects.

The Request, 12:3-5 – Next we note that *Jeroboam* was recalled from exile in Egypt to represent the northern tribes. He had previously been the governor over the northern tribal areas, but he had "lifted up his hand" against King Solomon and was forced to flee into exile (11:26-40). So now Jeroboam, again representing the northern tribes, respectfully requested that their heavy yoke be lightened.

The Counsel, 12:6-11 – First Rehoboam consulted the old men who had advised Solomon. They advised that if he would be a servant to the people and speak good words to them then the tribes would submit to his rule (v. 7). Then he took counsel of the young men who were his friends and whose advice he prized! Note the change from the word *"I"* (v. 6) to the word *"we"* (v. 9) in his responses to the two groups of advisors.

The Foolish Response, 12:12-15 – Rehoboam, no doubt desiring to stress his power and absolute authority over the people, responds by threatening and menacing the people into submitting to his rule over them. Rehoboam and his young counselors foolishly put their own ambitions ahead of wisely complying with the requests of the people.

The Sovereignty of God, 12:15 – While Rehoboam was responsible for his own actions, here we are reminded of the sovereign workings of God (see 11:29-35), who intended to "rend the kingdom ...of Solomon" into two pieces. Ultimately God was overseeing the events that resulted in the dividing of the kingdom.

 LIFE STEP From whom do you seek advice, counsel, and direction? As with Rehoboam, your friends may not be your best advisors! Ask the Lord to give you wisdom as you seek out godly advisors

1 KINGS 12:16-30

WHAT IS THE WRITER SAYING?

HOW CAN I APPLY THIS TO MY LIFE?

PRAY Pray that the Lord will give you the strength to overcome temptation (Matthew 26:41).

Rehoboam's harsh and ill-advised answer to the requests of the northern tribes of Israel has triggered a revolt! Apparently the leaders met to agree upon a response to Rehoboam. so they "answered the king" (v. 16). They had decided to stand apart from Judah (v. 16b); they were going to form their own nation, Israel, instead of submitting to the rule of the house of David (of Judah, v. 20). Also, they had determined that Jeroboam, their former governor, would be their king (v. 20).

At this point Rehoboam sent his tax collector and foreman of forced-labor projects, Adoram (v. 18a), to enforce his earlier threats (v. 14). Since the people's response was to immediately stone Adoram (v. 18b), we can be sure that his previous methods were a source of their rebellion!

After fleeing back to Jerusalem (v. 18c), Rehoboam quickly assembled an army (v. 21) to put down this new rebellion by the northern tribes before they could organize their own fighting forces. But God interrupts, sending a prophet, Shemaiah, to Rehoboam, proclaiming that Judah was not to fight her brothers, the sons of Israel (vv. 22, 24).

The sinful character of *Jeroboam* is also seen here! First, he never acknowledges that God had fulfilled His promise to make Jeroboam king over the northern tribes (11:29-31). Also, he realized that he would not have permanent rule over the northern tribes as long as her people wanted to return to Jerusalem, in Judah, to worship God at His Temple (vv. 26-27). Thus Jeroboam deliberately altered Israel's worship of God by providing a substitute form of worship of the LORD. Jeroboam provided new sanctuaries for worship at the cities of Bethel and Dan (vv. 29, 31). He changed the religious symbols (v. 28, golden calves) used in their worship. He ordained different priests to lead in worship (v. 32b) and he established a new calendar for times of worship (v. 32a). By these things Jeroboam caused Israel to "sin" (v. 30) by false worship.

LIFE STEP Avoid being like sinful Jeroboam! When something good or important happens to you, do you take time to humbly acknowledge God's hand in working out the details of the blessings that have come your way? What aspects of your worship and meditation upon God must not be changed? What principles of worship are foundational to your Christian life?

TUESDAY 45

1 KINGS 13:1-10

WHAT IS THE WRITER SAYING?

HOW CAN I APPLY THIS TO MY LIFE?

PRAY Cuba – Increased freedom in the areas of Bible printing, importation and distribution.

Our passage begins with the arrival of a prophet from God who interrupts King Jeroboam, of the Northern Kingdom of Israel, just as he was preparing to burn incense as an offering to God. Jeroboam was functioning as the high priest at his counterfeit worship center he had built at Bethel (about twelve miles north of Jerusalem and just across the border from Judah).

This unknown man of God appeared on the scene crying against the idolatrous altar itself as he makes an astounding prophecy (v. 2). He predicts the continuation of the "house of David," in that, a son of David, Josiah, would bring God's judgment upon this altar and its false priests. Thus the man of God was declaring that true worship was found only at the Temple, which God Himself had directed to be built at Jerusalem. Additionally, to declare that the bones of these priests would be burned on this altar was to assert God's abhorrence of their actions of false worship that sought to draw believers away from true faith in God! This passage was fulfilled 360 years later by King Josiah (see 2 Kings 23:15-16)!

When Jeroboam heard of this thing, he put forth his hand from the altar and pointed at the man of God saying, "Lay hold on him (v. 4)." Immediately his hand was dried up! Entreating the prophet for help, his hand was restored. Wouldn't you think that when Jeroboam heard the message, attested by a miracle, that he would have given heed? He was more interested in his own will than in the revelation from God!

Apparently grateful for the healing he invited the prophet to his house and assured him of a reward. The answer was a definite "no." He insisted that he wouldn't be identified with Jeroboam and that he must obey God rather than man. We read, "So he went another way" (v. 10). The prophet was courageous in such a response. He was faithful to the trust the Lord had given him.

LIFE STEP The prophet's response challenges our hearts. How important it is to obey God's Word regardless of what is being offered. Often, we too must *go another way.* Perhaps you are being confronted with difficult choices. How can you choose to obey God's leading?

WEDNESDAY 45

1 KINGS 13:11-25

WHAT IS THE WRITER SAYING?

HOW CAN I APPLY THIS TO MY LIFE?

PRAY Senegal – Pray for Dakar, the capital city with many evangelical churches, to become a source of gospel light for the whole country.

A new person is now introduced to us, an *old prophet* in Bethel who had been told by his sons what had happened. We are told about him:

- First, he had stayed at Bethel after King Jeroboam built his idolatrous center for worship there! Thus the old prophet was giving tacit approval of this wicked, rebellious worship.
- Then the *old prophet* twists a half-truth as he seeks to convince the man of God to return to his home to eat with him. He says "an angel spake unto me" (v. 18), knowing his sons had been the *messengers* (a *lower* but *alternate meaning* of angel!) who came to him.
- When the man of God said he could not do so, the old prophet said, "I am a prophet also as thou art (v. 18)." By these words the old prophet was seeking to disguise his misdirection of the man of God. We can assume the old prophet had once been a true prophet of God.
- Likely the old prophet was seeking to

display his allegiance to King Jeroboam, who had been publicly reproached by the man of God.

Sadly, the man of God, by eating with the old prophet, was disobedient to the word of the Lord (vv. 1, 17). Therefore he became complicit in the abomination he had earlier courageously denounced! The man of God should have questioned the old prophet's claim to have new orders from a higher source and thus avoid the deceitful trap set for him.

By pronouncing sentence upon the man of God who had been seduced into disobedience by the old prophet's lie (vv. 20-22), God had the old prophet reinforce the man of God's proclamation that God stands against those who reject His word! Then by a cluster of miracles that surround the death of the man of God (vv. 23-29), God further reinforced His displeasure with, and implied future judgment upon, anyone associated with the false worship of King Jeroboam.

 LIFE STEP One lesson for us today from these strange events is that God still stands against all who disobey the "the word of the Lord," which today is the Bible. Is there some teaching of the Bible that you are knowingly violating by your conduct? What can you do to correct your life style before God brings retribution upon you?

1 KINGS 16:29 - 17:7

WHAT IS THE WRITER SAYING?

HOW CAN I APPLY THIS TO MY LIFE?

Today we jump ahead to the seventh king of the Northern Kingdom of Israel, *Ahab*, who was "evil ... above all" (v. 30). *Ahab* is known for fortifying Israelite cities and its new capital, Samaria (v. 34, 22:39), for selecting the Phoenician princess, Jezebel (v. 31), for his wife, and for building a temple with an altar of sacrifice (v. 32) to the Phoenician god, Baal. He also built an Asherah "Grove" (v. 33), a garden with a pole carved with images of Baal's wife, Ashtoreth, a fertility goddess.

Ahab hated the worship of Jehovah. It seems that he intended for Jezebel to assist him in supplanting the worship of the LORD with a counterfeit worship of the "LORD" at Ahab's two golden calves. We are given this background information (16:29-33) to see why God now brings *Elijah* onto the scene, a prophet of the LORD God of Israel (17:1). Suddenly and with minimal introduction, Elijah appeared before King Ahab boldly proclaiming that he represented the living LORD God of Israel and that there would be no dew or rain until Elijah himself released the rains (v. 1b)! It is important to note that Baal was the Canaanite god of thunder and rain, thus the LORD God was challenging Baal's supposed strength!

After Elijah's sudden announcement, he is told by the LORD to conceal himself by the mountain stream, Cherith, a tributary of the Jordan River, which runs down off the Gilead plateau and flows a few miles north of Elijah's home village of Tishbe (vv. 2-3). Clearly, the LORD God's challenge, that He alone controlled the weather, rain, and harvests, was going to take some time to display. Also, the worshippers of Baal would need time to become convinced that Baal was not able to provide the necessary rains needed by his worshippers. God kept Elijah safe from those who sought his death and miraculously provided food by some of His own creatures, the ravens (v. 6).

LIFE STEP Ahab's goal in life was to make Israel stronger militarily, commercially, and politically but he failed because he did not focus on the true worship of God. Does your life have a right focus? What must you do to refocus your ways so that you are truly living for God?

1 KINGS 17:8-24

WHAT IS THE WRITER SAYING?

HOW CAN I APPLY THIS TO MY LIFE?

Today's passage jumps ahead many months in Elijah's 3½ year drought (James 5:17). The brook Cherith in Gilead where God protected Elijah and provided him food and water (17:3) had dried up, so Elijah is directed to go north ninety miles to Zarephath (v. 9), a harbor town in the very heart of the territory controlled by Jezebel's father, King Ethbaal of Sidon (16:31), and the center for the worship of the god, Baal. Clearly God was *turning up the heat* on Elijah's situation. He was going to experience God's care while in the midst of the enemies of God's people! Zarephath means a *smelting furnace* and Elijah's situation there reminds us that God often puts His people through such crucibles in order to purify them (James 1:3; 1 Peter 1:7) and make them *prepared* for the master's use (2 Timothy 2:21).

Elijah is told to seek out a widow at Zarephath (v. 9). Upon meeting this woman of meager resources, who was gathering sticks for a cooking fire, Elijah asks her for a jar of water (v. 10). As she immediately goes to get him the water, he calls after her to also bring him a piece of bread (v. 11). The woman responds, "Surely as the LORD your God lives, I do not have a piece of bread – just a handful of flour and a little oil which I intend to cook with these few sticks for our last meal."

The woman had already recognized Elijah as an Israelite and here she appeals to Jehovah, the God of the Israelites, in whom she believes as the true and living God (v. 12), to be her witness that she has no bread to share. Elijah, who had learned to trust in the LORD to deliver to him his daily food, now alleviates her fears by instructing her to first make him a little biscuit to eat and then to draw again from her container of flour and jar of oil to make additional biscuits for her son and herself. He also declares to her a promise that the God of Israel (v.14) would not allow the flour and oil to run out. And so it was day-by-day that the poor Gentile woman was able to feed Elijah and her little family (v. 16)!

LIFE STEP It is also true that the Lord Jesus wants to teach us to rely upon God for our daily care and food. How is God going about teaching you to trust in Him? Perhaps your life is like Elijah's, where God is *turning up the heat* in your life. How is God preparing you for His use?

1 KINGS 18:1-16

WHAT IS THE WRITER SAYING?

HOW CAN I APPLY THIS TO MY LIFE?

It was now the third year of the famine in Israel and the LORD tells Elijah to go to King Ahab because the LORD would soon send rain. It is interesting that most of our passage is a sideshow to the main story line of these chapters. We must conclude that God wanted us to consider the merits of a government official, *Obadiah*, who had quietly put his life on the line and, most likely, spent great sums of money to protect and feed one hundred of God's prophets during the severe famine (v. 4)! *Obadiah* was in a difficult position; he was a loyal and trusted overseer of affairs in King Ahab's palace (v. 3a) but he was a faithful follower of the LORD who "feared the LORD greatly" (v. 3b). It is obvious that he feared the LORD more than he feared Jezebel, who was seeking to put to death those who truly followed the LORD (v. 4). Yet Obadiah was trying to please both godly Elijah and evil Ahab. He was willing to be involved with the people of God (v. 4b) as well as with those against God (v. 5). Obadiah was seeking to protect his position in the world, while still risking much to serve God's people.

He was also fearful that Ahab would discover his compromising deeds. Clearly Obadiah expected Elijah to have heard of the one hundred prophets of God (v. 13). Word would have gotten out as contacts were made for food and water for the one hundred prophets. It seems Obadiah was worried that Ahab would also learn of his betrayal so he did not want to do anything to raise suspicions (v. 9).

While it would be easy to criticize Obadiah's actions as carnal compromises, we must be careful to remember that godly people facing difficult moral decisions, as was Obadiah, must seek God's leading as to the best path to follow. Remember, Obadiah had to protect his privileged position so that he might continue to shelter and feed the one hundred prophets!

LIFE STEP While Obadiah's trust in God is seen wavering in this story, remember he did deliver Elijah's message to King Ahab (v. 16). Perhaps you are facing difficult moral decisions yourself! How about spending some time talking with God about your options and plans so as to find a sense of His direction for the decisions you must make.

1 KINGS 18:17-29

WHAT IS THE WRITER SAYING?

HOW CAN I APPLY THIS TO MY LIFE?

PRAY Mozambique – Pray for the development of projects that build biblical knowledge among oral learners, who constitute the majority of the population.

When King Ahab and Elijah met, Ahab's first words were, "Is that you, O troubler of Israel (v. 17)?" Ahab did not admit that his own sin was the source of the troubles. Elijah immediately made it clear that Ahab and his father's house were guilty in that they had not only "forsaken the commandments of the LORD" (v. 18), but had also turned to follow after "Baals" (v. 18b; that is the false god, Baal, and his wife, Asherah).

The extent of Ahab's government's backing of the worship of Baal and Asherah is seen in that 850 of the prophets of these gods were retained and fed at the royal palace by Ahab's wife, Jezebel (v. 19b). No doubt these prophets functioned as chaplains and advisors to the government of the Northern Kingdom of Israel as well as being sent out to every part of the country to promote the worship of Baal and Asherah.

The fact that Ahab accepts Elijah's demand that the people of Israel be gathered to Mt. Carmel indicates the extent of desperation Ahab faced as a result of the ongoing drought. Also Ahab hoped to induce Elijah to pronounce the "word" (see 17:1) that would return the rains upon Israel.

The LORD's purpose was to make the wayward people of God see the error of their ways and be brought to repentance so they might turn again to a true walk with the LORD. Only then would the LORD's judgment of the drought be removed and the LORD's blessing returned. And so the LORD has Elijah put the LORD and Baal on a public trial before all the people and the king (v. 24).

Note his penetrating question to his own people, "How long halt ye between two opinions (v. 21)?" The people of Israel were divided. Some worshipped the LORD while others worshipped the "Baals." Clearly, many were sometimes worshipping the One and sometimes worshipping the others. They sought to balance their activities so as to satisfy both Gods! They were a people in compromise who were seeking to "serve two masters" (Matthew 6:24).

LIFE STEP Are you like these Israelites of old, sometimes serving God and sometimes serving modern false gods, such as money, possessions, popularity? What must you do stop living between "two opinions"?

1 KINGS 18:30-40

WHAT IS THE WRITER SAYING?

HOW CAN I APPLY THIS TO MY LIFE?

Elijah's Prayer

It had become obvious that the priests of Baal had failed (vv. 26-29), so Elijah begins his turn at the contest between the Gods. There already existed an altar on Mt. Carmel to the LORD which had been "broken down" (v. 30). Likely, Elijah directs it's rebuilding with twelve replacement stones (vv. 31-32) arranged on the broken stones of the original altar to show a continuity with Israel's past worship of the LORD. Also notice the mention of an important historical event, namely, the LORD's renaming of *Jacob* with the name, *Israel*, (*a prince with God*, v. 31b). This reinforced Israel's shame in their drifting away from their true God. To enhance God's greatness, Elijah has a trench dug around this altar that would hold about three gallons of water. Next Elijah directs that the altar, its wood, and the offering be drenched with water, three times! Everything was soaked and the trench was filled with water (v. 35).

Only now was Elijah ready to turn to the LORD in a public prayer. Note its content: (1) Elijah points out that the LORD was still the true God of Israel (v. 36b), (2) He points out that he was God's servant acting under God's orders (v. 36c), (3) His objective was for God's people to be convinced that the LORD was the only true God (v. 37a) and (4) as a result the people of Israel would *turn their hearts back again* to the LORD (v. 37b). We should also note the character of Elijah's prayer. It was not filled with theatrics or religious trappings – rather his prayer was a simple request by one person to another Living Person. Immediately "the fire of the LORD" fell upon the altar and all was consumed: the offering, the wood, the stones, the ground below the stones and all the water (v. 38; see Leviticus 9:23-24). The people respond with repentance, submission, and true faith in the LORD as their God (v. 39) and in the rejection of the prophets of the false god, Baal (v. 40).

LIFE STEP If we are to know the power of God as Israel did here, then we, too, need to turn back to our heritage of faith in the Lord Jesus Christ! Do you need to reject false and competing interests in life that have turned you away from serving the Lord Jesus?

TUESDAY 46

1 KINGS 18:41 - 19:7

WHAT IS THE WRITER SAYING?

HOW CAN I APPLY THIS TO MY LIFE?

PRAY China – Special need for study Bibles and children's Bibles and safety for those transporting them.

In today's passage first we see *Elijah at his best* when his thoughts were only on the anticipated work of God to again bring rain (18:41-46). But after the rains come, we see *Elijah at his worst* when his thoughts were only on himself and the threats made against him (19:1-3).

Elijah confident in God's promises: Consider briefly the elements of his time of successfully waiting for God's promise to restore rain:

18:42a – First of all, Elijah deliberately spent time away from others so that he might be alone in prayer with God.

18:42b – Elijah remembered he was but God's servant. So he humbly submits himself to God by bowing down as he prepares to pray.

18:43a – By sending his servant to look towards the sea, Elijah was confidently expecting God to answer his request to send rain.

18:43b – The answer, "There is nothing!", did not trouble him. He knew that a part of successful prayer was persistence! He just prayed again.

18:44 – Elijah confidently begins to act upon the first indication that God was setting into motion His answer to Elijah's prayer for rain. **Elijah depressed and inconsistent** (19:1-3): Elijah ran away from a confident walk of faith in God's protection. Elijah, after an incredible day of seeing the mighty hand of God, becomes inconsistent and desperate in his response to Jezebel, an enemy who was seeking revenge. What were the elements that played a part in Elijah's worst moment?

1.**Fear of Man** – Once we get our eyes off the Lord Jesus and begin to look at threats and dangers, we too are liable to be despondent.

2.**Feelings of Failure** – Elijah must have realized that he had failed to follow up on his divinely-gained advantage of leading the people to destroy the temple and worship of Baal in Israel (19:4).

3.**Need of Rest** – Elijah was physically exhausted and emotionally drained. Yet even here under these discouraging conditions God ministered to Elijah, allowing him to rest, eat, and drink.

 LIFE STEP At times we act as Elijah did here; one day we are spiritually confident and trusting God but then on the next day we forget our walk in God's care and we run from our troubles in the world! How can you stop running from your troubles and return to a walk of faith in the Lord?

1 KINGS 19:8-21

WHAT IS THE WRITER SAYING?

HOW CAN I APPLY THIS TO MY LIFE?

PRAY Pray that the married couples of your church will nurture and protect their relationships by a dependence upon God's Word.

Elijah, who was in the northern Sinai Wilderness near Beersheba (v. 3), is told to eat and drink of the food provided by God, for Elijah was to travel further into the wilderness for forty days to the mountains of Horeb, which includes Mount Sinai. Notice that Elijah, like the Children of Israel before him, had to learn of God's faithful care and provision.

After arriving at Horeb, the LORD asks Elijah, "What are you doing here (v. 9b)?" Elijah gives an answer that reveals his discouragement, loneliness, and fear. So God causes Elijah to experience the power of God by means of a great and terrifying wind, and then an earthquake and then a fire. Yet somehow God *was not in these* (v. 11) power displays. Rather, the LORD intended to make known to Elijah His immediate presence by means of a still, small voice (v. 12b).

Although Elijah showed a token return to faith in the LORD (v. 13), the LORD's repeating His question to Elijah (v. 13b) showed that Elijah was not yet convinced of God's control over Elijah's troubles. So the LORD sends Elijah to Israel's enemy, Syria, whose capital was at Damascus (v. 15). Elijah was to anoint Hazael to be king over Syria, Jehu to be king over Israel, and Elisha to be his successor (vv. 15-16). As God advanced these three men, Elijah would learn that God controlled the events around Elijah. Note that Jehu would execute God's judgment upon King Ahab (2 Kings 9:7ff). Hazael and the Syrians would waste and destroy Israel as a judgment from God upon unbelieving Israel. The seven thousand that the LORD had reserved for Himself in Israel (v. 18) were far more than Elijah had imagined. This encouraging declaration by the LORD was also an indication of the direction of Elijah's future employment by the LORD. Elijah would be needed to instruct and strengthen these and other Israelites who had recently repented from their idolatrous following of Baal in their upright walk with the LORD.

 LIFE STEP What must God do in your life to teach you to trust in His care and provision for you? It took Elijah a lot of walking in a hard wilderness to learn his lesson of trusting in God. Perhaps you are walking in some hard situations – then make a list of the several things God would want you to learn as He sustains you in your "wilderness"!

THURSDAY 46

1 KINGS 21:1-16

WHAT IS THE WRITER SAYING?

HOW CAN I APPLY THIS TO MY LIFE?

PRAY Estonia – Pray for a new vision for evangelism and revival to reawaken the nominal Christiain majority in the former-Soviet country.

In the previous chapter King Ahab of Israel received undeserved help from the LORD who sends prophets to announce God's help in coming battles with Israel's powerful enemy, King Ben-hadad of Syria. As a result the LORD gave Ahab two great victories over the Syrians (20:20-21, 29-30). Sadly, Ahab failed to *utterly destroy* the Syrians (20:42) as God had intended. Rather Ahab made a treaty with Ben-hadad (20:34).

Today we find evil King Ahab enjoying the prosperity following Israel's victories over the Syrians. We find Ahab at home with money in hand to expand the lands around his palace so that he might have the convenience of a kitchen garden (21:2a). Ahab's request to buy the vineyard of his neighbor, Naboth, seems at first fair and even honorable; namely, a trade for better lands or an outright purchase of the land (v. 2b).

Yet there was a problem, Naboth was a faithful follower of the LORD who understood that it would be a dishonor to the LORD if he sold his family's ancestral lands (Numbers 36:7-8; the land could only be leased for a time but not sold). Naboth was willing to speak up for his responsibility to keep God's Law even though he knew that King Ahab had deliberately broken God's Law! Naboth was not willing to sin against God's Word by selling his land to make a profit or to please the king!

In response, King Ahab lies down on his bed and pouts! When his wife, Jezebel, hears of it, she comes to him and he explains the situation but leaves off why Naboth had refused the king's offer (v. 6). Jezebel promises Ahab that she will get Naboth's vineyard for him.

Jezebel puts into motion a deceptive plan by forging letters in Ahab's name (v. 8). A religious fast was proclaimed, implying that the king had been outraged by the actions of sinful man. With Naboth placed on a trial platform before the people (v. 12), two worthless men gave testimony against Naboth. They said he had blasphemed God and the king. As a result, Naboth was convicted and stoned to death (v. 13).

LIFE STEP Doing what is right, as did Naboth, can be costly. Are you committed to making right choices that will keep you from making a profit or cause you to become the enemy to powerful people in your world? Take a minute and write our Lord a note explaining your commitment.

FRIDAY 46

1 KINGS 21:17-29

WHAT IS THE WRITER SAYING?

HOW CAN I APPLY THIS TO MY LIFE?

PRAY Kenya – For the believers to live an exemplary life and speak out against what is wrong.

Today we look at the conclusion of a tragic story. King Ahab, knowing his neighbor, Naboth, was dead (v. 15), has gone down to Naboth's vineyard to claim it as his own (v. 16). It is clear that Ahab didn't care how his evil wife, Jezebel, had secured the vineyard for his enjoyment; he just wanted this vineyard. As a result the LORD places the blame for Naboth's false conviction and wrongful execution upon King Ahab. God tells His messenger, Elijah, what he is to announce as God's judgment upon King Ahab (v. 19).

When Elijah meets Ahab in Naboth's stolen vineyard, Ahab speaks first saying, "Have you found me, O my enemy (v. 20a)?" Ahab did not feel guilt nor was he repentant upon seeing the man of God. Rather, he was outraged and likely afraid that God had so quickly sent a prophet to confront him about the killing of Naboth and stealing of his land. Elijah's response is straight to the point,

"I have found you because you have sold yourself to do evil (v. 20b, 25)," which is to say *you have totally surrendered yourself to the service of sin*. This idea comes from the ancient practice of slavery. A person who was sold into slavery lost all independence; no longer having a will of his own but rather was totally in submission to the power of another, which, in this case, is sin.

And so Elijah declares God's judgment upon Ahab, Jezebel, and his house (v. 22); all would be destroyed. The reaction of Ahab caused the Lord to temporarily stay Ahab's execution (v. 29). In spite of Ahab's great sin (v. 26), the Lord showed Himself to be gracious and ever-loving with boundless mercy. We are reminded of what Peter would later say. "The Lord is not slack concerning his promise, as some men count slackness; but is longsuffering to us-ward, not willing that any should perish, but that all should come to repentance." (2 Peter 3:9)

LIFE STEP God continues to be ever-loving with a readiness to grant mercy and extend His longsuffering! What sin is there in your life that you vainly hope God has overlooked? Must God send judgment upon you before you renounce your own slavery to sin? How much better it would be for you to forsake your sin and turn back to God in repentance!

1 KINGS 22:29-40

WHAT IS THE WRITER SAYING?

HOW CAN I APPLY THIS TO MY LIFE?

The verses preceding this paragraph point out that there was an unholy alliance between Jehoshaphat, King of Judah, and Ahab, King of Israel (22:2-4), to go up to battle again the Syrians. Yet the "hated" prophet, Micaiah (vv. 8, 14), prophesied defeat (v. 17). Micaiah says he had seen the LORD "sitting on His throne" (v. 19), which reminded the two kings that God was in charge of events in their lives. Micaiah warns that a "lying spirit" had been put on King Ahab's other prophets so that he might die in battle (v. 20). Ahab's response was to put Micaiah in prison.

Yet in spite of Micaiah's warnings, the two kings went to battle. Ahab went disguised as a charioteer (v. 30) and he asked Jehoshaphat to dress as a king and to ride in a king's chariot. Jehoshaphat almost died when an elite Syrian force attacked what they thought was Ahab's chariot! In 2 Chronicles we have these words. "But Jehoshaphat cried out, and the LORD helped him; and God moved them to depart from him." (2 Chronicles 18:31) Jehoshaphat, whose life is reviewed as

doing that which is "right in the eyes of the LORD" (v. 43), was here in sin. First, after calling for a *second opinion* from a prophet of God in whom he could trust (v. 7), he remains silent when Ahab punishes Micaiah for speaking truthfully (vv. 26-27). Second, in spite of Micaiah's warnings of certain defeat, Jehoshaphat willingly goes into battle with Ahab while disguised as Ahab!

So we see that the Lord was in full control. Even the "random" arrow that smote Ahab was not "random" at all (v. 34), but directed by God's plan. We are reminded that God had earlier predicted that Ahab would be slain, "Because thou hast let go out of thy hand a man whom I appointed to utter destruction, therefore thy life shall go for his life, and thy people for his people." (1 Kings 20:42) Even Ahab's insistence that his dying body be propped up in his chariot (v. 35) resulted in God's pronouncement coming to pass, "In the place where dogs licked the blood of Naboth shall dogs lick thy blood." (1 Kings 21:19 and v. 38)

LIFE STEP We too must learn the lesson taught by Micaiah; God sits on His throne and oversees the events of our lives! Do you have a situation that seems to be out of control? Take time to talk out your confusing circumstances and ask Him to guide you in the direction you should take!

SUNDAY 47

2 KINGS 1:1-18

WHAT IS THE WRITER SAYING?

HOW CAN I APPLY THIS TO MY LIFE?

Today we have an unusual story about King Ahaziah of Israel (his father, Ahab, had died in battle). Ahaziah had fallen through a window's lattice and suffered internal injuries (v. 2). So He sent messengers to the Philistine city of Ekron to enquire of the oracle of Baal-Zebub. Baal-Zebub was one of the several variations of the god, Baal; this one was thought to have healing powers. This is probably the Philistine god, Baal-Zebul, meaning "exalted lord" (Matthew 12:24, 27). No doubt Ahaziah had hoped to obtain healing by this god. Clearly this was a violation of the law, "thou shalt have no other gods before me" (Exodus 20:3).

Elijah is instructed by an angel to intercept these messengers and send them back with a prophetic declaration from the LORD God of Israel instead! Elijah declares the king would die (vv. 3-4). When the king hears of it, he deduces that it must have been Elijah, that troublesome "man of God" (note vv. 9, 11, 13). So the king sends an officer and fifty soldiers to arrest Elijah. The officer speaks to Elijah out of contempt and with no fear of the God of Elijah! So Elijah called down fire from heaven, consuming all the soldiers (v. 10). A second detachment of soldiers is then sent out to arrest Elijah only to meet the same fate (v. 12). By calling down fire, God through Elijah was demonstrating again that He alone was the true God of Israel. Apparently, the first time Elijah called down fire from God (see 1 Kings 18:32-39 where Elijah calls down God's fire upon his sacrifice) the rulers of Israel had failed to forsake their worship of Baal and so here we have an additional demonstration of God's true power and authority.

A third detachment is sent, but this time its officer drops to his knees out of fear and respect for LORD God of Israel and pleads for the lives of himself and his fifty men (v. 13). Elijah finally went with the men (v. 15) and declared again that the king would die (v. 16).

LIFE STEP Consider the people that know you claim to be one of God's own people. By what character qualities are you known? How do these represent the true God of Heaven? Do your life and character cause others to show contempt for God or to honor Him?

MONDAY 47

2 KINGS 2:1-11

WHAT IS THE WRITER SAYING?

HOW CAN I APPLY THIS TO MY LIFE?

PRAY Mexico – That the Mexicans find their identity in a personal faith in Christ.

We come to the final day in Elijah's life, his translation to Heaven (namely, conveyed to Heaven without death). His route is interesting: from *Gilgal* to *Bethel*, to *Jericho*, across the *Jordan* and then up to *Heaven* on a fiery chariot through a whirlwind into the presence of God!

While Elijah gives the appearance that he wanted to spend his last day alone so that he might remember the great events of Israel's history at these four locations, his true purpose was to put his successor, Elisha, to a three-fold test, as indicated by Elijah's three "*tarry here*" requests (vv. 2, 4, 6).

Since Elisha (and the *sons of the prophets*, vv. 3, 5, 7) knew that this was Elijah's last day, it would appear that Elisha was determined to be faithful to his spiritual mentor to the end and to be present to perhaps receive a "*double portion*" blessing (v. 9) as the spiritual *first son* of his *prophet-father*. Elisha was not going to accept Elijah's offer to stay behind while Elijah hiked some thirty miles over a long day!

So Elisha passed his final exam! Elijah was able to again see that Elisha was a disciple of great character: Elisha was dedicated to and affectionate towards Elijah. Also, Elisha was persistent and not willing to give up on his responsibilities to his teacher, Elijah.

Finally, at the end of a long day, Elijah asks what he could do for Elisha (v. 9). Elisha responds that he desired a *double portion of Elijah's spirit*. Notice that Elisha did not ask for material blessings, rather he asked to have the privilege to carry on Elijah's ministry with twice the heart of Elijah! Elijah responds that the request was a "hard thing" (v. 10) in that it was something that only God could grant. So Elijah gives Elisha a sign, if Elisha sees Elijah depart from this world then Elisha had his confirmation from God. Elijah leaving for Heaven on a chariot of fire in a whirlwind was a clear and dramatic affirmation from God.

LIFE STEP How has God been testing your own determination to serve Him? How has God been testing your *spirit*? Like Elisha, is there some decision you must make between an easy and comfortable life and a life of dedicated and persistent service to your Lord Jesus?

2 KINGS 2:12-22

WHAT IS THE WRITER SAYING?

HOW CAN I APPLY THIS TO MY LIFE?

"*And Elisha saw it*" – an important little phrase! Elijah's conditional response to Elisha's request for a "*double portion*" (v. 10) of Elijah's "*spirit*" is here met! Elisha knew his "*hard*" request had been granted. "*My father, my father, …*": Note Elisha's great love (v. 12b) for his spiritual father, Elijah! In spite of the wonders that accompanied Elijah being taken up to Heaven, Elisha deeply felt the loss of his mentor. Yet, Elisha immediately picked up Elijah's mantle (v. 13) to be his banner, declaring that he would be God's agent carrying forward the work of God!

Elisha performed his first miracle using Elijah's mantle to part the waters again and cross back over the Jordan River on dry ground. Elisha knew he would be God's new messenger, so Elisha publicly acts as Elijah had acted (v. 14a). While doing this Elisha declares, "*Where is the LORD God of Elijah?*" (v. 14b) The Hebrew text here clearly declares that Elisha was acting upon his faith in God's intent to work powerfully through Elisha. The Hebrew words are in an *emphatic form* giving Elisha's question the following intent, "Where is Jehovah, the God of Elijah? He is still with me: though Elijah is not here, the God of Elijah certainly is."

Since the *sons of the prophets* had seen Elijah cross over the Jordan River after hitting its waters with his rolled-up mantle, when they saw Elisha do the same, they said, "*The spirit of Elijah doth rest on Elisha*" (v. 15). These *preachers in training* had matured nicely in their training in that there is no pride or selfish desire for Elijah's power or authority.

Next the leaders of Jericho come to him (vv. 19-22), having heard of the miracles at the Jordan River. They tell Elisha that their spring had turned bad (perhaps brackish). Its water was causing their crops and animals' young to die. Clearly, Elisha adding salt to brackish water was not the means of the spring's healing! Rather it was an outward sign of God's blessing them by supernaturally cleansing their spring. The Lord was demonstrating that He desired to bless His people as they turned to Him!

LIFE STEP The *grace of God* was demonstrated by Elisha to Jericho when its people asked for God's help. Are you willing to similarly say to God, "I need *your grace* to cleanse and purify my life that is contaminated with sin"?

2 KINGS 4:1-17

WHAT IS THE WRITER SAYING?

HOW CAN I APPLY THIS TO MY LIFE?

PRAY Tunisia – Pray that Tunisian believers might overcome their fear of sharing their faith.

A series of miracles concerning little people are before us in chapter 4. Elisha was interested in widows and the needs of the students at the Bible school of the day, *the sons of the prophets*.

The first miracle involves a widow woman who was the wife of one of these students, probably a young woman left with a series of bills after her husband's unexpected death (v. 1). The creditor, in keeping with the law (Leviticus 25:39-40) was coming to take her two sons. Elisha didn't tell her to forget the debt, but rather showed her how it could be paid. This also reminds us to pay what we owe (Romans 13:8). He told her to get "not a few" vessels and fill them (vv. 3-4) while in a private room. God wanted to teach us that faith is often a *participatory activity*! The woman had to do her part while anticipating that God would do His part.

God's blessing was limited only by the number of vessels the woman would go out and collect! So it is with us. God will supply our needs, but the degree of supply is often determined by the measure of our faith; in this case, more vessels result in more oil. Then Elisha said, "Go, sell the oil, and pay thy debt, and live on what is left" (v. 7).

The next miracle involved a woman of Shunem (v. 8, a town in northern Israel). She is called a "great woman." This would mean that she had a great wealth and was interested in using her wealth in the service of others and in the honoring of the LORD. She recognized Elisha's greatness (v. 9) and so she and her husband built a guest chamber for the prophet (v. 10). Then we are told that Elisha announced that she was to have a child (v. 16). The woman believed it was hopeless to any longer expect children any longer, but God performed a miracle and the woman bore a son (v. 17). Here we see that God was great and merciful.

 LIFE STEP The woman of Shunem was of service to Elisha and by implication many others in her community. She was a woman of godly character and devoted to helping others. How can you imitate her qualities? How can you use your wealth to help someone else in their service for the Lord?

2 KINGS 4:18-37

WHAT IS THE WRITER SAYING?

HOW CAN I APPLY THIS TO MY LIFE?

PRAY Kazakhstan – Pray for further growth and maturation of the Kazakh church in this ninth-largest country in size.

Today's passage finishes the story of the "great woman" from Shunem (4:8). Her infant is now a child, perhaps six years old. All during this time, Elisha continued his regular circuit around Israel, visiting Mt. Carmel and the various schools of the prophets. Elisha, during these circuits, continued to use of the woman's guest room (v. 10).

The story picks up during harvest, a hot day in June. The child had joined his father and the reapers out in the fields (v. 18). Apparently the child suffered sunstroke, calling out "my head, my head" (v. 19). He was taken to his mother who tends to him until he dies at noon.

Remember, this was the son given by a miracle from the LORD (v. 17). Now, it looked like the Lord was taking away His blessing. The woman reminds Elisha of this very thing (v. 28). Note that while she didn't understand why this was all happening, she gives a clear demonstration of faith. Rather than preparing the child for burial (by custom, done within twenty-four hours), she unexpectedly places the child upon Elisha's bed in his guest room and she, with a servant, "runs" to Elisha at Mt Carmel (v. 22).

Elisha recognized her when she came, but did not know why she had come (v. 27). Elisha and the woman return to Shunem and the dead child upon Elisha's bed (v. 32). What a wonderful example is given when we read that Elisha's first response was to take the matter to the Lord in prayer (v. 33). Then Elisha seeks to "warm" the dead child by stretching himself on the child until the child is restored to life by God's great power. The child sneezed seven times and opened his eyes (vv. 34-35).

What joy must have filled that home for the rest of the day! Prayer had been made, God's power was manifested and life returned to the child. There are so many indications that the woman was a woman of faith (vv. 8-10, 21, 22, 24, 25, 27, 30, 37). Her faith was rewarded. This is one of the greatest miracles in the Old Testament.

LIFE STEP There are many troubles in life – unexpected and difficult circumstances beyond our understanding. How can you respond to such events with a measure of faith in God's ability to see you through puzzling events? We must remember "all things work together for good" (Romans 8:28) for them that trust in the Lord. He is still in control today.

2 KINGS 4:38-44

WHAT IS THE WRITER SAYING?

HOW CAN I APPLY THIS TO MY LIFE?

PRAY Philippines – For effective outreach to youth through evangelistic sporting events.

In today's passage we have two of the many *smaller miracles* which characterized Elisha's ministry. Both events took place during a famine in the land of Israel (see 4:38, 6:25; 7:4; 8:1) and both events display Elisha's fatherly care for the "sons of the prophets." Likely, these several events occurred during the seven years of famine referred to in 8:1.

The Deadly Stew (vv. 38-41) – During a visit to Bethel, Elisha was again the *visiting lecturer* at their Bible school. He intended on this day to present an *illustrated lecture*! With all the students gathered for class (v. 38b), some students, whose turn it was to prepare the meal, begin making a *vegetable stew* that would be shared with the other students.

Due to the famine, wild grains and plants were gathered to supplement limited supplies. A wild vine bearing a *cloak-full* of gourds was found and collected for their meal (these were something like wild pumpkins). When they ate the pumpkin stew they discovered that it was poisonous.

Many became ill and called out to Elisha, "There is death in the pot." Elisha responds by adding some flour to the stew resulting in it no longer being harmful. Obviously, the flour was not the agent that healed the stew but only the *visual aid* that pointed to God as the Healer of the stew. Elisha wanted them to see that God's goodness and sustaining hand was upon those who served Him, even in hard times (Psalm 37:19)!

The Feeding of the 100 – (vv. 42-44): Next, a godly farmer brings Elisha twenty small loaves of bread and a bag of grain as a "Firstfruits Offering" to God. When the student serving the meal is instructed by Elisha to give the loaves as a meal to the people gathered, he asks how he was to feed one hundred people with twenty small loaves. Elisha reassures the man that there would be plenty with food left over! This event certainly would have come to mind when Jesus instructed His disciples to feed five thousand men, plus women and children, with only five loaves and two fish (Matthew 14:17-21)!

LIFE STEP God has not changed! His goodness and sustaining hand will be upon Christians who serve Him faithfully as did these "sons of the prophets." How can God's sustaining hand be helpful to you during the troubles you face in your life today? How might God satisfy your needs?

2 KINGS 5:1-16

WHAT IS THE WRITER SAYING?

HOW CAN I APPLY THIS TO MY LIFE?

Today we see another miraculous event surrounding Elisha. We are introduced to Naaman, a captain of the Syrian army, of high moral character, and a warrior of valor who had been granted victories by the God of Israel, *but he was a leper*! Leprosy in the ancient world slowly caused its victims to degenerate and eventually proved fatal. There were no cures.

Naaman's wife had an Israelite servant girl (v. 2) whose responsibility was to wait on her. As a result she had developed a fondness for her new *parents*, which leads to her musing before her mistress concerning the cleansing of her master from his affliction (v. 3).

As young as she was, the servant girl had somehow come to know about the godly and kind deeds of the prophet of God, Elisha. While he had not cleansed any lepers, she was persuaded that he would be of a mind to extend God's healing upon her master, Naaman.

When word of these things came to the king of Syria (Ben-Hadad II; 860-841 B.C.), he encourages Naaman to go to this prophet and seek a cure. The king, with *wrong reasoning*, sends a letter of request (accompanied by a vast amount of silver and gold to buy the LORD's favor) to the king of Israel, Jotham (the *wrong instrument* of God). Soon word of Naaman's coming reaches Elisha, who has Naaman come to him (v. 8).

When Naaman comes to Elisha's home, he is given a message, "Go and wash in Jordan seven times" (v. 10). Naaman had the *wrong attitude*, one full of pride; Elisha has not come to me! And there were bodies of water "better than" the *Jordan River* like *Abana* and *Pharpar* in Syria (v. 12)!

Thankfully Naaman listened to *right counsel* from his servants (v. 13) that brought about Naaman's cleansing. The ultimate plan of God was a *right confession* from Naaman, "I now know that there is no God in all the earth, but in Israel" (v. 15) – and I desire to only worship Him (v. 17).

LIFE STEP One of the heroes here is the captive Jewish girl. Even though she had faced many difficult events at the hands of the Syrian army, she held no hard feelings for the army's commander, Naaman. Perhaps there are people in your life that you need to forgive for the difficulties they have caused you! How can you be of service to these same people, desiring to bring God's blessing into their lives?

SUNDAY 48

2 KINGS 5:17-27

WHAT IS THE WRITER SAYING?

HOW CAN I APPLY THIS TO MY LIFE?

PRAY Pakistan – Pray that Pakistan would be freed from spirits of lawlessness and violence that continue to bleed the nation.

Our passage focuses upon the Syrian commander, Naaman. We see his response to his new faith in Jehovah and his rejection of other gods, like Rimmon, a chief god of the Syrians (v. 18)! So he asks for "two mules' load of earth" (v. 17) with which he intended to make a patch of the LORD's land in Damascus, upon which he would then worship the LORD. Obviously Naaman wanted to honor the LORD, yet his reasoning was in error! In his mind, to worship the LORD, Naaman would have to be standing on the LORD's ground! He did not yet understand that the true God was all-powerful everywhere. Also, he did not understand that burnt offerings (17b) were to only be done at the LORD's temple at Jerusalem by a Levitical priest. The lesson here is that the LORD is understanding; He knew Naaman desired to honor the true God! This passage also gives us a contrast to Naaman's story of true faith taking its first steps! The story of Gehazi is a tragic display of greed, deception, lying, and a dishonoring of the gracious character of God. Surprisingly this man, who for a long time professed to be a true follower of the LORD, showed himself to be full of selfish lust.

Clearly Elisha refused to take the gift Naaman offered him (v. 15; likely the huge amount of silver and gold brought from Syria, v. 5) so as to teach Naaman that God gives free gifts of His grace and help to all those who seek. Yet after Naaman had left to return to Syria, Gehazi decided he would get some of the refused gift! So he ran after Naaman, saying Elisha needed some of the gift money for one of the sons of the prophets. After Gehazi returned home, Elisha asked where he had been. Gehazi said, "I went nowhere," a lie to cover up his other lies and deception. Elisha responds, "Is it a time to receive money?" meaning, *God had done all the work, and so all the glory should go to God, not Gehazi!* The result of Gehazi's sin was God's judgment upon Gehazi that caused him to *go out from Elisha's presence a leper as white as snow* (v. 27).

 LIFE STEP Be careful when responding to new Christians! They may be like Naaman, wanting to honor and serve the Lord Jesus but mis-stepping in their good-intentioned worship of our Lord. How can you guide a young believer in his walk with the Lord while avoiding harsh criticism?

2 KINGS 6:1-7

WHAT IS THE WRITER SAYING?

HOW CAN I APPLY THIS TO MY LIFE?

PRAY Pray that thousands will be reached with the Gospel of Jesus Christ in 2013 all across the world.

Today's passage presents another miraculous event that enriches our impression of the ministry of Elisha. Apparently one of the *schools of the prophets* had grown in attendance so that the students, called "the sons of the prophets" (v. 1), requested and received Elisha's permission to build a larger facility to hold their growing numbers. Perhaps they needed larger living quarters and a larger classroom. Scripture mentions several locations for the *schools of the prophets* with Jericho being the likely school referred to here. Note that the school's growth also implies that Elisha's ministry was having a successful impact, causing more people to want to study the Scriptures. Also note that all the students shared in the work and they even asked Elisha to join them in cutting wood beams from trees along the Jordan River (v. 3; likely cutting beams from willow trees which would overhang the river's edge). In the process of cutting down trees an iron axe head slipped off its handle and fell into the river water. The student who lost the axe head cries out to Elisha that it was a borrowed tool. This indicates that he, who had given up all sources of earning money to become a student, was worried about his responsibility to purchase another for its owner (v. 5).

Elisha asked where along the river the iron had fallen. He then cuts a stick and casts it into that location on the river. This resulted in the iron axe head popping to the surface of the water (v. 6). Elisha tells the worried student to retrieve it from the river. Clearly we again are expected to observe that Elisha's solution, throwing a stick in the water, was only a token of the miraculous work of the LORD to solve the dilemma at hand. Clearly this odd miracle was intended to teach the students an important spiritual lesson, namely, that the character of the Lord includes His interest in even the small problems of life. Also, God is able to assist and bless those who seek His help in all things! We must wonder at the future attitude of this student when he faced his next anxiety in life's array of difficulties!

LIFE STEP Christian friend, have you learned the lesson that the Lord is interested in helping you with all your worries, anxieties, and fears? Write the Lord a note detailing a present, troublesome situation in your life and then, in faith, wait for the Lord to assist and bless you in your situation.

2 KINGS 6:8-23

WHAT IS THE WRITER SAYING?

HOW CAN I APPLY THIS TO MY LIFE?

PRAY Bangladesh – Pray that the church may grow in this proverty-stricken land to which William Cary took the Gospel over 200 years ago.

Once again the king of Syria (Ben-Hadad II, 860-841 B.C.) went to war against Israel. The Syrians were conducting a series of raids into Israel (v. 10c). For each raid, the Syrians sent out soldiers to "camp" in ambush against the Israelites (vv.8-10). Each time the King of Israel, (Jehoram, 855-841B.C.), is warned so that Israel had a defensive force at the place where the Syrians were to cross into Israel (v. 10b).

Unknown to Ben-Hadad, Elisha, *the man of God* (v. 9) was passing on to Jehoram what God had revealed about the secret Syrian war plans (v. 12). When Ben-Hadad became convinced he had a spy in his midst, he was told that somehow Elisha, *the prophet in Israel*, was telling the King of Israel their secret plans (v. 12). Thus a great company of horsemen and chariots were sent to the town of Dothan where Elisha was staying.

Being surrounded by Syrians caused great fear in Elisha's servant! Yet Elisha *did not fear* (v 16), for he was counting on God's invisible armies for protection. So Elisha prays, "LORD, I pray thee; open my servant's eyes that he may see" (v.17a). Then the servant's eyes were opened and "behold, the mountain was full of horses and chariots of fire round about Elisha" (v. 17b). Remember, God continues to have His ways of protecting us Christians. Perhaps God has even sent guarding angels unknown and unseen to us (Psalm 91:11; Hebrews 13:2). Next Elisha prayed that the soldiers be blinded (v.18); then he led the soldiers into Samaria, capital of Israel (v. 19). Here their eyes were opened; they were fed and sent home, never to raid Israel again!

A key lesson from this study is: the Lord knows, and can easily defeat, the secret machinations of his enemies. Sadly, a second lesson is also seen: wicked people are sometimes willing to be counseled by the servants of God (as was King Jehoram) in their every-day concerns (and they experience the advantage of this counsel); but they will not take warning "to flee from the wrath to come" or be persuaded to renounce their favorite sins! (*Scott's Bible Commentary*)

LIFE STEP Remember to trust the Lord's protection, knowing that he watches over you and has a host of angelic helpers to guide and guard. How has the Lord aided you as you sought to be of service to Him?

2 KINGS 6:24-33

WHAT IS THE WRITER SAYING?

HOW CAN I APPLY THIS TO MY LIFE?

PRAY Nicaragua – Praise the Lord that the church has doubled in the last 10 years!

Several months have gone by since the "blinded" Syrian army had been allowed to return home. Yet Ben-hadad, king of Syria, again attacks Israel. This time the Syrians made a direct assault with their entire army upon Israel's capital city, Samaria (v. 24) and set up a siege. The siege soon caused a severe shortage of food and greatly inflated prices for what food remained. The head of a donkey (an unclean food source) was sold for eighty pieces of silver (1½ pounds!), and a cup of seed pods sold for two ounces of silver. The people of Samaria were so desperate for food that they turned to eating their own children (vv. 28-29).

One might ask why God allowed His people to suffer through such an awful situation. The answer is simple. The people had turned away from God and were worshipping false gods. They had refused to repent and turn back to God. Also note that this horrible calamity happened just as God had warned Israel, through Moses, if Israel turned against Him (Leviticus 26:29; Deuteronomy 28:49-53).

When the king of Israel, Jehoram, saw the awful results of the famine he rent his clothes and put sackcloth on his body – these typically were the actions of a repentant person. But his repentance was only outward, as he blames the whole thing on God's prophet, Elisha. Also, it is obvious that the king was angry with the Lord (v. 33). The language "Why should I wait for the Lord any longer" means *why should I wait for the Lord to do anything?* Such is the extent of his lack of faith in the Lord.

Jehoram placed blame for the siege upon Elisha (v. 31); this is likely due to an unrecorded warning by Elisha that a Syrian siege was coming due to Israel's lack of repentance. Perhaps the king also assumed Elisha could have given information to help the Israelite army thwart the plans of the Syrians. Since Elisha had done nothing, the king swears that Elisha, who was in the city of Samaria, would die that day (v. 31b).

 LIFE STEP Don't be like Jehoram or the people of Israel. Be careful that you walk with the Lord "in the light of his word" and then "trust and obey." Be careful that you don't walk in sin to the point where God must send judgment your way to turn your heart back to Him in repentance!

2 KINGS 7:1-11

WHAT IS THE WRITER SAYING?

HOW CAN I APPLY THIS TO MY LIFE?

PRAY Cyprus – Pray for this divided country (Turk and Greek) that old grievances and bitterness might be overcome by forgiveness.

Our passage begins with a Syrian army besieging Samaria, capital of Israel. Conditions within the city were terrible as famine gripped the city's inhabitants. Elisha, who was inside the city with the suffering people, then makes a phenomenal prophetic announcement; tomorrow the siege will be over, the famine lifted, and food prices will return to normal (v. 1b). Sadly, the king's chief adviser answers with disbelief and disdain (v. 2).

Apparently, there were four lepers in the city who had not heard Elisha's pronouncement (likely because lepers were quarantined from other citizens). These four decided to sneak out of the city and surrender to the Syrians so that they might ask them for food. Now the Syrians might kill these lepers rather that feed them, but it was clear to the lepers that staying in the city would soon mean their deaths. So the lepers had nothing to lose; either way they were going to die. However when they came to the Syrians' camp, they found the Syrians had hurriedly left; leaving behind all their tents, horses, donkeys, food, drink and silver.

Verse 6 makes it clear that the Lord had divinely intervened. The Syrians heard the noise of chariots and thought the king of Israel had joined hands with an unknown powerful ally and both were on their way to destroy the Syrian army. So the camp had been abandoned and all the supplies in it had been left behind.

After the lepers ate, drank and took valuables that had been left in the camp (v. 8), they realized that their actions were greedy and self-serving in that they had not told the incredible news to the Israelite king or the people of Samaria. So the lepers decided that they would tell the king that this was "a day of good tidings" (v. 9). Here again we have a beautiful application in the Gospel. Those of us who know Christ as Savior must remember that our day is also a day of good tidings. What a pity if we hold our peace and not tell others around us.

LIFE STEP Do you agree that the Lord has been gracious to you in allowing you to hear the message of salvation? Should we not want to share it with others? Do you know someone who is spiritually hungry for the Gospel of Jesus Christ? How can you talk with them today?

FRIDAY 48

2 KINGS 7:12-20

WHAT IS THE WRITER SAYING?

HOW CAN I APPLY THIS TO MY LIFE?

PRAY Sierre Leone – Pray for more attention from the worldwide community – especially from Christians – to address the desperate poverty and suffering of this country.

We pick up on yesterday's story with the city's gatekeepers shouting out to all those in the king's palace the report that had been given to them by the lepers. As a result, King Jehoram was awakened in the middle of the night. Yet Jehoram is convinced that the lepers had been deceived by the Syrians who must have set a trap by pretending to have left the camp but were really waiting in ambush for the starving people of the city to come out and claim the Syrians' food (v. 12). To determine the true nature of the lepers' report, one of the king's counselors advises the king to send out scouts on chariots to investigate the Syrian camp. The charioteers went through the Syrian camp and then followed the road which the Syrians had used in their hasty retreat. They found clothing and equipment as far as the Jordan River. They then returned and reported what they had seen to the king (v. 15).

All the starving people in the city began rushing out to the Syrian camp to find food and to take the valuables left behind by the Syrians. At this point the king sends his palace officer to the city gate to control the flow of people and goods (likely intending to tax the rich bounty of items being brought back to the city). However, the press of people was so great at the gate that the palace officer was trampled and he died (v. 17). The exact nature of the officer's death, when compared to Elisha's prophecy (see v. 2), was so memorable that the writer of the Books of Kings now repeats the telling of Elisha's prophecy along with the events of the palace officer's death (vv. 18-20 compared with vv. 2, 17).

Let's close by noting that this chapter ends with the fulfillment of what was said at its beginning:

V. 1, "Hear ye the word of the LORD …"

V. 16, "… according to the word of the LORD."

The writer does not want us to miss that the word of the Lord can be completely trusted! We can be confident in what God says He will do.

LIFE STEP We Christians also have many promises from the Lord. Are you having trouble believing those things the Lord has promised to do? Take a minute and write the Lord a note explaining which of his promises you have trouble acting upon. Then ask Him to strengthen your faith.

2 KINGS 9:1-10, 30-37

WHAT IS THE WRITER SAYING?

HOW CAN I APPLY THIS TO MY LIFE?

PRAY Venezuela – For missionaries to overcome the obstacles that make obtaining a visa a difficult process.

This chapter begins with God having Elisha instruct a student under Elisha's training to *tuck in his cloak* (namely, "get ready to travel quickly"), take a flask of oil, and go to Ramoth-Gilead (50 miles east of the city of Samaria). The student was to find Jehu, the commander of Israel's army, and anoint him with oil as Israel's next king. Jehu and the army of Israel, but not King Jehoram, were still at Ramoth, a city in northern Gilead, after a recent battle with the Syrians (8:28-29). Twenty years earlier, God had told *Elijah* to anoint Jehu (1 Kings 19:15-16) but apparently this was delayed due to God's postponement of judgment upon evil King Ahab, because of his repentance (1 Kings 21:27-29). Now Jehu was to be anointed the next king and commissioned to carry out God's judgment upon the remaining family members; Jezebel, Ahab's wife, and Jehoram, his son, who had not repented of their Baal worship and returned to God.

Also, the young prophet was to instruct Jehu that he was to bring God's delayed judgment upon the house of Ahab and avenge the blood of the servants of the Lord (v. 7). Jehu and his commanders eagerly accept God's promotion of Jehu as king (v. 13) and so begins a takeover of the Kingdom of Israel (v. 14).

In the second portion of today's passage we see God's instruction carried out (vv. 30-37). Jezebel, after her son's death (v. 28), was waiting for Jehu (v. 30). She taunted him, seeking to humiliate him by calling him "Zimri," a name synonymous with *assassin*. At the command of Jehu, the palace guards throw her down from a window and Jezebel was killed. Jehu left her there, but later decided that they should go back and give her a burial since she was a king's daughter. It was too late. As predicted by Elijah (v. 36; 1 Kings 21:23), dogs had eaten her flesh.

LIFE STEP Here we see that God is longsuffering and patient; He had given Jezebel twenty years to repent of her sin and turn to the Lord. We today must be careful not to equate God's patience in dealing with us as an indication of His being unable to bring His judgment upon our sin. Is there some sin in your life from which you need to repent and turn to the Lord?

2 KINGS 13:14-21

WHAT IS THE WRITER SAYING?

HOW CAN I APPLY THIS TO MY LIFE?

Today we jump ahead forty years to Joash, king of Israel (798-782 B.C.). Even though Joash did that which was "evil in the sight of the LORD" (v. 11), under his rule Israel recovered both militarily and economically.

While Joash (sometimes spelled, Jehoash) is a lesser-known king, he is best known for his visit to Elisha on his deathbed (v. 14). By this time Elisha was an old man, having ministered as a prophet of God for over sixty years! Now he had fallen sick and it was apparent that this illness would kill him. So King Joash visits Elisha. King Joash greatly esteemed Elisha, calling him "father" while weeping over his approaching death. Joash also acknowledges and praises him as the "chariot of Israel," which was saying that Elisha had been Israel's chief defender (v. 14). Thus it would appear that religiously, Joash was not in opposition to the worship of the LORD as had the kings of Israel before him. Yet he continued to worship the false gods that had been introduced into Israel and to walk in the sinful ways of Israel's earlier kings (v. 11b).

Elisha now gives to King Joash a prophecy as he directs the king to pick up a bow and arrow, open a window facing east, and then to shoot the arrow. With his hand on the king's hand, Elisha says, "The arrow of the LORD'S deliverance …" (v. 17), indicating that God would bless Joash as the instrument of Israel's victory over the Syrians, who occupied the eastern provinces of Israel (Gilead and Bashan, 10:33).

Elisha then directs Joash to pick up the quiver of arrows and use them militarily ("smite" implies "by shooting") (v. 18a). Joash obeyed; but rather than shooting five or six times, as Elisha had intended, he shot only three and stopped (v. 18b). This had been a test of Joash's eagerness to be God's champion in battle.

Joash thought this action was trivial, so he stopped at three. This showed his lack of faith and zeal in the LORD. Thus Joash would win three victories that pushed the Syrians out of Israel's territory. If Joash had earned five or six victories, he would have destroyed Syria (v. 25).

LIFE STEP How trusting in the Lord are you? How eager are you to serve the Lord? Write out a prayer to Jesus asking Him to give you the trust to rely upon Him and the heart to want to fully serve Him.

2 KINGS 17:6-23

WHAT IS THE WRITER SAYING?

HOW CAN I APPLY THIS TO MY LIFE?

PRAY Portugal – For a mighty work of the Holy Spirit in the predominantly Catholic provinces of the north.

Israel's Demise

This chapter records the final defeat and destruction of the Northern Kingdom of Israel. Israel had earlier lost her northern territories (Galilee) and her eastern territories (Bashan and Gilead) to the Assyrians. Now we read of their rebellion against and final destruction by the Assyrians.

The intent of the writer here is to show that it was not God's lack of interest in His people that caused Israel's downfall but rather to show that it was Israel's continual disobedience that brought about God's judgment (v. 18). A helpful outline for the first half of the chapter is:

17:1-6: The **political and military developments** that result in Israel's deportation to eastern areas of the vast Assyrian Empire.

17:7-17: The **spiritual reasons** that led up to Israel's destruction. This section lists eighteen different sins against God (v. 7). Notice the opening *transition* statement (v. 7a), "And this (vv. 1-6) came to pass because" (vv. 7-17). This portion divides as follows:

- Verses 7-12, a general overview of Israel's wickedness.
- Verses 13-15, the primary sin of Israel was that "they would not hear" the LORD's prophets who warned them to "turn from their evil ways." Instead, Israel "hardened their necks" against God.
- Verses 16-17, the paramount acts of Israel's sin whereby they "sold themselves to do evil." A total abandonment of God's ways to worship metal idols, or heavenly bodies, or the god, Baal. These were worshipped with human sacrifice and witchcraft.

17:18-23: Note that the beginning word "therefore" defines this section:

- *Therefore* the LORD was *very angry* with Israel (v. 18).
- *Therefore* the LORD *rejected all* the seed of Israel (v. 20).
- *Therefore* the LORD *removed Israel* out of His sight (v. 23).

 LIFE STEP Notice the intended warning to Judah, "Also Judah kept not the commandments of the LORD;" if Judah kept on sinning, as did her sister Israel, then they too could expect God's judgment. Similarly we Christians can expect God's chastisement if we live in sin. Are there sins in your life that need to be made right with the Lord?

2 KINGS 17:24-41

WHAT IS THE WRITER SAYING?

HOW CAN I APPLY THIS TO MY LIFE?

PRAY Japan – Praise the Lord for the new openness caused by economic, social, and natural disasters.

The king of Assyria, now in control of the Northern Kingdom of Israel, decided that he would repopulate Israel, called the province of Samaria, with non-Israelites which he brought from other provinces (v. 24) of his vast empire. This manner of mixing populations was used by the Assyrians to diminish the chances of rebellion by its subjugated people.

These pagan colonists had not been judged by the LORD when they worshipped idols in their own countries, but they now possessed the land upon which the LORD had placed His name. Thus the LORD was intent upon showing them two things: first, that Israel had not been defeated by the Assyrians because the God of Israel was weak and unable to defend Israel, but rather that the LORD Himself had "removed Israel out of His sight" (v. 23) because of their sin while using the Assyrians as His agents of judgment. Secondly, the LORD wanted these pagans to "fear" the God of Israel (v. 25a), Who was offended by their ignorance of Him (Romans 1:21-24) and their dreadful worship of false gods.

As a result, the LORD sent lions to threaten the colonists and to kill some (v. 25b). Soon they appealed to the king concerning Jehovah who had sent lions among them in so remarkable a manner that they were convinced that the God of the land was punishing them. The king's response was to send back a "priest of Samaria" (vv. 27-28). Likely this was a priest who had falsely worshipped the LORD at the golden calf that had been set up at Bethel (v. 28b). Clearly he was not of the family of Aaron who "taught" them from the Scriptures that Jehovah was the one, true, eternal, almighty and glorious Creator and Judge of the world (Scott's Commentary)! It is also clear that he taught them that Jehovah was like other gods who did not mind the worship of Him being mixed with the worship of other gods so long as God was appeased (v. 33a).

 LIFE STEP Christian, do you mix your worship and service of the Lord with the modern gods of money, popularity, possessions, and power? Ask the Lord to show you how to live your life today so that you are completely focused upon serving God alone!

2 KINGS 19:5-20

WHAT IS THE WRITER SAYING?

HOW CAN I APPLY THIS TO MY LIFE?

PRAY Morocco – Pray for a good balance in how and how much foreign believers interact with indigenous Christians.

During the first years of Sennacherib's rule over the Assyrian empire (705-681 B.C.) he had to put down a revolt in the east, centered in Babylon. Now in 701B.C., he turns west to put down a revolt by a coalition of nations, including Judah. First, he crushed the leader of the revolt, Tyre, and then he moved down the coast to defeat the Philistines. The Assyrians wanted to push south into Egypt and destroy the rebels being led by Tirhakah, an Ethiopian who would become king over all Egypt (v. 9). But he must first deal with Judah's rebellion on his exposed flank.

Thus he attempted to intimidate Hezekiah, king of Judah, into surrendering. After all, the rebel coalition would certainly lose to the Assyrians. So the purpose of the questions in the Assyrian letter (vv. 11-13) was to frighten and compel King Hezekiah (v. 8) to surrender. Sennacherib's final argument was that all the gods of other kingdoms had failed to stop the Assyrians and so Hezekiah was *deceived* if he thought his God would be able to "deliver" Judah (19:12-13).

We must commend Hezekiah for going to the prophet, Isaiah (vv. 2, 5, 6, 20), to determine what the LORD would want Hezekiah to do in this very difficult situation.

Hezekiah also prays to the LORD" (vv. 14-19). He begins by taking the scroll containing the Assyrian's threats (v. 14) and "spreading it out before the LORD." Hezekiah begins by reviewing the LORD's greatness (v.15); Jehovah "alone" is God, He is Creator, He is the only living God. The other gods that had been destroyed by the Assyrians had failed their peoples because they "were not gods" at all (v. 18). Hezekiah then asks the LORD to intercede in Judah's impossible situation and to "save" them so that "all the kingdoms of the earth may know" He "only" is God (v. 19).

 LIFE STEP Christian friend, we must learn from Hezekiah's example, when faced with a daunting situation the first thing he did was to take the matter to the Lord in prayer. Are you willing to come to the Lord today with your daunting situation and spread before Him your needs?

2 KINGS 19:35 - 20:11

WHAT IS THE WRITER SAYING?

HOW CAN I APPLY THIS TO MY LIFE?

PRAY Columbia – For boldness and perseverance among missionaries who live with the threat of violence.

From a stele (a monument carved with pictures and writing) found at the ruins of Nineveh, we understand that Sennacherib defeated the Ethiopian/Egyptian rebel army near the Philistine city of Ekron. Next his Assyrian army turned back upon Judah and he boasts on the stele that he took forty-six fortified towns in Judah, seizing 200,000 prisoners. He then marched to Jerusalem and began making preparations to assault it.

Our passage tells us, on the night following King Hezekiah's prayer (vv. 35, 15-19), God sent out "the angel of the LORD" who delivered God's judgment upon the Assyrian army so that 185,000 soldiers died. Not until the survivors awoke the next morning were they aware of this judgment from God (v. 35b). The Assyrian king, Sennacherib, lived to return home to Nineveh in disgrace only to be assassinated by his own sons (v. 37).

A second event is recorded in today's passage – Hezekiah's illness. God's advice was to "set your house in order" for Hezekiah would die. For a third time we see Hezekiah, when confronted with a difficult situation, taking his troubles to the LORD in prayer (v. 2; see 19:1, 15). The king prayed for an extension of life (v. 3) for he did not consider the LORD's pronouncement to be irreversible! Hezekiah understood that God hears the prayers of His people and also sees their tears (20:5). In answer to his prayer, the LORD added fifteen years to his life. The prophet Isaiah also had figs placed on the boil that was the source of Hezekiah's deadly disease as a token of God's power and might to heal the ailment (v. 7).

In response to Hezekiah's request for a sign that would verify God's promise of a lengthened life, God makes the shadow on the palace's sundial retreat ten degrees (perhaps the half-hour markings on the sundial). Our text does not tell us how God accomplished this miracle; there are a variety of miraculous ways that He could have done it.

LIFE STEP It would seem that Hezekiah needed God's miraculous reassurance before believing God's promise would occur. How much better it is for us Christians to trust God to do what He has promised us! Is there an uncertainty in your future about which you need to confidently trust God to deal with on your behalf? Write out a pledge to turn the matter over to Him so that you need not worry about it!

2 KINGS 20:12-21

WHAT IS THE WRITER SAYING?

HOW CAN I APPLY THIS TO MY LIFE?

PRAY Pray that your pastor will have God's wisdom and guidance in the area of counseling.

The event in today's passage occurs a few months after King Hezekiah's recovery from his deadly illness. A delegation was sent by the king of Babylon with the announced intention of congratulating him on his recovery (v. 12b, also Isaiah 39:1). The underlying reason was for Babylon and Judah to continue to collaborate in their efforts to cast off the over-lordship of the powerful Assyrian empire.

Likely the "present" sent by the Babylonian king were lavish gifts, which sealed his ongoing alliance against the Assyrians. In response, Hezekiah may have shown them all his treasures and military equipment out of pride in his wealth and newly-acquired world-wide fame, but primarily he wanted to emphasize that he was financially and militarily able to stand with Babylon in a revolt against the Assyrians.

Note that Hezekiah failed to point to the LORD as the source of his healing, wealth, and power. He clearly missed the opportunity of showing them that the LORD alone was the living and true God (2 Kings 19:15-19).

The prophet Isaiah then comes to King Hezekiah demanding answers. Note that Hezekiah does not answer the first question, "What did these men say?" (v. 14), since he was not willing to reveal the secret pact offered by the Babylonian (Hezekiah already knew Isaiah was opposed to any alliance with wicked and sinful nations; Isaiah 30:1-7; 31:1-3). He answers Isaiah's second question from a self-centered perspective – he was honor bound to show his own resources in response to the lavish gift they had sent. Isaiah then delivers the LORD's strong rebuke to Hezekiah, namely, the day would come when his nation, Judah, would be carried off to Babylon and nothing of its wealth would be left.

The chapter ends with references noting some of the achievements in the king's life. A water conduit is mentioned. It deals with the waters of the Gihon spring being redirected through a 1,777 foot-long tunnel under Jerusalem's walls to the pool of Siloam located inside the city's walls. It can be seen in Jerusalem even to this day.

LIFE STEP If Isaiah were to come to you today would he rebuke you for having sought out agreements with the powerful but evil people in your world? Ask the Lord how to trust in Him alone without evil alliances!

SATURDAY 49

2 KINGS 22:3-10; 23:1-3

WHAT IS THE WRITER SAYING?

HOW CAN I APPLY THIS TO MY LIFE?

PRAY Ecuador – Pray for church growth to continue to increase and for a renewed emphasis on evangelism.

Today we read of Judah's last "good" king, Josiah (22:1; 640-609 B.C.). We have skipped over some forty-five years of wicked reigns by Kings Manasseh and Amon. Josiah's reign marks a rare period of time when Judah did not face foreign military threats. The mighty Assyrian empire was in decline and was ruled by weak kings. Its vassal city-state, Babylon, would successfully rebel against the Assyrians in 625 B.C. and then advance on and take the Assyrian capital, Nineveh, in 612 B.C.

Scripture tells us that King Josiah himself, at age sixteen, began "to seek after the God of David his father" (2 Chronicles 34:3). At age twenty (628 B.C.), King Josiah began to purge the temple of all the idolatrous altars and graven images set up there by his grandfather (2 Kings 21:4-7). Josiah also needed to repair damage caused to the temple (2 Kings 22:3-6).

In the repairs, the high priest finds a copy of "the book of the Law" (v. 8) that had been hidden in the temple during the years of apostasy and neglect under Kings Manasseh and Amon. While our text does not define what was contained in this book (a scroll), Hebrew scholar Keil feels that this Hebrew phrase can only mean the "Mosaic books of the Law (the five books of the Pentateuch given to Moses by the LORD)." Traditionally, a copy of the Law had been kept at the temple for study and use by the priests (Deuteronomy 31:24-26). When a copy became old, it was incased in a clay jar and buried (likely one had been entombed in a wall of the temple so that it was now "found" during the temple's remodeling).

Apparently under the reigns of Manasseh and Amon, copies of Scripture had been destroyed so that the long-ignored "Book of the Law" was again discovered. The Law was read by the king and then read to the people. As a result, the Passover was again kept. Also the king and all the people renewed their covenant to keep God's commandments.

 LIFE STEP King Josiah realized the spiritual danger of neglecting the commands of Scripture (v. 13). Likewise we Christians must seek to put into practice those things our Lord has commanded us to do! What principles of Scripture are you neglecting in your daily life? Take a minute and write out an agreement with the Lord to keep His Word.

The Book of Acts is the history of the early church. Since the initial Christians were Jewish, they worshipped in the temple and synagogue as well as in their own house assemblies. These early believers did not understand that Christ fulfilled and put an end to the Old Testament worship system. Their belief in Christ as the Messiah, however, was sufficient to bring persecution that was so intense (Acts 8:4) that the believers fled Jerusalem and went everywhere preaching the Word.

Paul's part in the persecution of the church, as well as his conversion, are both recorded in Acts 9, along with his commission to preach the Gospel to both Jew and Gentile. The church confirmed his testimony and ministry and he made three notable missionary journeys. The first (Acts 13–15:35) is to Asia Minor accompanied by Barnabas and John Mark. The second (Acts 15:36–18:22) finds Paul and Silas crossing over into Europe after a brief visit to Syria. Timothy (at Derbe) and Luke (at Troas) join the team. In Greece, they visit Athens and Corinth where Paul meets Aquila and Priscilla. He then visits Ephesus (Acts 18) and after a brief time of reasoning in the synagogue leaves Aquila and Priscilla and continues his journey.

The third journey (Acts 18:23–21:14) finds Paul returning to Ephesus (Acts 19), where he remains for nearly three years in a teaching ministry. He finally departs to visit Macedonia and Greece, planning to return to Jerusalem for Pentecost (Acts 20:16). A very touching scene occurs in Acts 20 as he stops off at Miletus, some forty miles south, and calls for the elders of the Ephesian church. His visit to Jerusalem ends in his being arrested and finally brought to Rome as a prisoner in bonds. It is from Rome, as a prisoner under house arrest, that he writes the Ephesian epistle, and has it delivered by Tychicus, a "beloved brother" (Ephesians 6:21).

WHY THE EPISTLE WAS WRITTEN

The early church was not only persecuted (Acts 8:4), but was threatened by doctrinal heresies, including that of Gnosticism, which presumed to "know" and sought to thrust between the soul and God all sorts of human and angelic mediators. Paul's letter to the Colossians deals with this heresy and emphasizes the pre-eminence of Christ. In Him alone dwells all the fullness of the Godhead bodily. He sends that later letter by Tychicus and Onesimus, a fugitive slave from Colosse who was converted under Paul's ministry in Rome and is now sent back to his master Philemon with the letter that bears his name.

What Paul has to say to this church is appropriate for all churches, both then and now. In fact, numerous scholars are of the opinion that Ephesians was "a circular letter," a doctrinal essay in the form of a letter, to the churches in Asia Minor. Some old Greek manuscripts omit the words "at Ephesus" in 1:1.

Since Paul had worked at Ephesus for about three years, and since he normally mentioned many friends in the churches to whom he wrote, the absence of personal names in this letter strongly supports this idea. It was likely sent first to Ephesus by Tychicus (Ephesians 6:21:22; Colossians 4:7-8) and is probably the same letter that is called "my letter... from Laodicea" in Colossians 4:16 (Ryrie Study Bible).

Harry Ironside offers this note that "there are very remarkable correspondences between certain Old Testament books and New Testament epistles. The Epistle to the Romans, for instance, answers to Exodus; the letter to the Hebrews is the counterpart of Leviticus; and this Epistle to the Ephesians is the New Testament parallel to Joshua. In Joshua we have the people of Israel entering upon the possession of their inheritance. In Ephesians, believers are called upon to enter by faith now into the possession of that inheritance which we shall enjoy in all its fullness by-and-by. We are far richer than we realize. All things are ours, and yet how little we appropriate."

THE CONTENT OF THE EPISTLE

Some have called this epistle the "profoundest book in existence." The epistle is divided into two sections, the first doctrinal and the second practical, each taking three chapters. The church is viewed as the body of Christ in which God unites Jew and Gentile through whom He will manifest His purposes to the universe. The epistle stresses the unity of the church, the unity of Jew and Gentile in Christ and the unity of its members within the body. The key words in the epistle are "in" (93 times); "grace" (13 times); "spiritual" (13 times); "heavenlies" (5 times). Accompanying Paul's great emphasis upon unity, you will find him placing a heavy stress upon love in this letter. He uses the verb form of "love" (agapao) nine times, while only twenty three times in all his other writings. Here he uses it ("love") in noun form (agape) ten times, and only sixty-five additional times in all his other letters. Therefore, of the 107 times Paul uses the word for "love" (noun or verb), nineteen are here in Ephesians. Thus more than one-sixth of Paul's references to "love" appear in this brief epistle to the Ephesians. This letter begins with love (1:4, 6), and ends with love (6:23-24). Paul's encouragement in this vital area of interpersonal relationships should guide our churches as well.

EPHESIANS 1:1-6

WHAT IS THE WRITER SAYING?

HOW CAN I APPLY THIS TO MY LIFE?

PRAY Sri Lanka – Pray for inspired, thoughtful, biblical ways that Sri Lankan Christians can fellowship, worship, and witness.

Paul's opening words are magnificent. He introduces himself as Paul (using his Gentile name: *small*) not Saul (his Hebrew name: *to ask or pray*), and identifies himself as an apostle (one sent on a mission), in this case as an official ambassador of Christ. He uses his position to give the letter official character, for his apostolic appointment was "by the will of God" (v. 1).

He writes to "saints" (*set-apart ones*), set apart for God. From the same word comes the great doctrinal word, *sanctification*. At salvation the new believer becomes a "saint." This is positional sanctification to be followed by progressive sanctification, which is to be a life-long process until ultimate sanctification takes place in glory.

Paul describes these "saints" as "the faithful in Christ Jesus." Here the term *faithful* does not refer to lifestyle (though a saint should be faithful), but to the fact

that they had placed their faith in Christ. Others (pagans) were set apart to their gods; Paul's readers were set apart to Christ.

Other important words in this passage are "grace" and "peace" (v. 2); the former—God's steadfast love toward man; the latter—the relational state as a result of that grace. Verses 3-14 give us quite possibly "the longest sentence of connected discourse in existence" (Wuest). When Paul writes, "Blessed be the God," he uses the word *eulogetos*, the Greek word, which gives us "eulogize" – *Let our God be well-spoken of*. Other words to examine are *chosen*, *predestinated* and *adoption*. Nor should one overlook the truth that all of the "spiritual blessings" the believer receives are found "in Christ," a phrase or its equivalent used ten times in verses 3-13.

 LIFE STEP Let's live our lives in such a way that God is eulogized through them, and that our gratefulness for His grace and peace is obvious.

EPHESIANS 1:7-14

WHAT IS THE WRITER SAYING?

HOW CAN I APPLY THIS TO MY LIFE?

Paul's long sentence (vv. 3-14 are one long and magnificent sentence in the original Greek text) continues, as does his doctrinal dissertation of God's work on man's behalf. He directs our attention to our redemption (vv. 7, 14), *to deliver by paying a price*, and "the forgiveness of (our) sins," (Matthew 26:28), both secured "through His (Christ's) blood" (see Ephesians 2:13; 1 Peter 1:19) and was "according to the riches of his grace" (see Ephesians 1:7; 2:7).

In verses 8-10 we find that in God's grace the believer has the resources necessary to comprehend and understand God's will and purposes throughout the ages. Without God's gracious revelational input, all of this would have remained a "mystery" (v. 9, see 3:3, 4, 9; 5:32), namely, not something mysterious, but rather a secret hidden with God and held in reserve for its proper time of revealing.

Here the mystery is the New Testament church as one body composed of both Jews and Gentiles (3:1-12); and the church as the bride of Christ (5:23-32). The phrase beginning in verse 11 can be read two ways: "we have obtained an inheritance," or "we were made His inheritance." Both ideas are true. We, who were outcasts, are "heirs of God and joint-heirs with Christ" (Romans 8:17). Also, Christ, for the joy that was set before Him (that's us—we're His inheritance) endured the cross (Hebrews 12:2). Then, to ensure that this would take place, Paul tells his readers that God's will cannot be frustrated, nor will His purposes for His people be thwarted. Why not? Because once salvation has taken place, the believer is "sealed with the Holy Spirit" (v. 13), a mark of ownership and a pledge that our promised redemption will be completed.

LIFE STEP What a great salvation we have! Now redeemed by the blood of the Lamb (purchased from the bondage of sin into the freedom of grace), let us commit ourselves to the task of telling other slaves how to be set free.

EPHESIANS 1:15-23

WHAT IS THE WRITER SAYING?

HOW CAN I APPLY THIS TO MY LIFE?

PRAY Bulgaria – That Christians would be protected from the violent attacks of neo-Nazi groups.

Paul follows the normal letter-writing custom of including a word of thanksgiving upfront. Here his *thank you* is to God for the Ephesian saints' "faith in the Lord Jesus" (a vertical relationship), and their "love unto all the saints" (a horizontal relationship). The former is to lead to the latter, and in this case it did, hence Paul's word of thanksgiving, which he follows with prayer. He was concerned that his readers would fully comprehend what they had received in Christ . . . that God would continue to bestow upon them "the spirit of wisdom and revelation in the knowledge of him (v. 17)." Only with the help of the Holy Spirit would that take place (see 1 Corinthians 2:14).

Three areas of desired knowledge are addressed: The Past (v.18b), "The hope of His calling" (vv. 3-6), with the follow-up of 4:1 . . . "walk worthy of the vocation wherewith ye are called." The Future (v. 18c), "The riches of the glory of His inheritance in the saints." Here we see God's inheritance–the believers He purchased at great price (v. 7); earlier it was the believer's inheritance, the final redemption from sin's presence. The Present (vv. 19-23), "The exceeding greatness of His power toward us who believe." This power makes continued growth in the Lord possible. Four different Greek words in the final verses of the chapter explain how much power is available to the believer: *power* (inherent power), *working* (operative power), *mighty* (demonstrated strength), *power* (the possession of power). This power, available to the believer, was experienced by Christ in His resurrection (v. 20a), exaltation (v. 20b) and His headship of the church (vv. 21-23).

 LIFE STEP Paul wants redeemed people to understand the power we have to understand Scripture, overcome sin and share what we are learning with other humans. He is promoting spiritual steroids, with no dangerous side effects!

EPHESIANS 2:1-7

WHAT IS THE WRITER SAYING?

HOW CAN I APPLY THIS TO MY LIFE?

PRAY New Zealand – The need for focused Youth Pastors and leaders.

Chapter 2 presents a spiritual *before and after* picture. It shows some of the changes the Gospel makes in men, starting with the death-to-life experience. This death ("in trespasses and sins," verse 1) is spiritual death, separation from God. In that state the unsaved man (1) walks according to the <u>world</u>, his external enemy, (v. 2a); (2) is controlled by <u>Satan</u>, his infernal enemy, (v. 2b); and (3) dominated by the desires of the <u>flesh</u>, his internal enemy, (v. 3). The result: as unbelievers we are the children of disobedience (v. 2a), and wrath, (v. 3b).

God, however, has not left the believer at the mercy of these enemies. The same power that was manifest in Christ's resurrection and exaltation brings about new life in the one who trusts Christ for salvation (v. 1). Because that is true, we no longer have to live defeated in a devil-dominated world system, but can live victoriously. God, in His "great love" (v. 4), intervened in His mercy, and (1) implanted spiritual life in all who believe, meaning that we are no longer separated from God; (2) elevated them to a new level of life; and (3) permits them to enjoy a continuous relationship with Christ in this present earthly life (v. 5). All of this takes place by the grace of God (v. 7), (unmerited favor extended where wrath was deserved).

Verse 6 indicates the marked contrast between the former lost condition of believers and their present situation in Christ. Though still in human bodies on earth, they also participate in the resurrection life of Christ, being seated with Him in heavenly places (1:3). The emphasis here is on the believer's identification with Christ in His death (v. 5), resurrection (v. 6) and ascension (v. 6). Verse 7 shows the purpose behind God's actions: that throughout all eternity believers will be trophies of God's grace.

LIFE STEP WOW! That's what these verses scream out. They talk of His great love, grace and mercy, given to undeserving sinners. Take the time to thank Him. Meditating on the passage will provide inspiration.

THURSDAY 50

EPHESIANS 2:8-13

WHAT IS THE WRITER SAYING?

HOW CAN I APPLY THIS TO MY LIFE?

PRAY Bolivia – For youth outreach activities to the 53% of the population that is 19 or under.

In verses 1-10, Paul gives three reasons why God wants to save people: <u>first</u>, to show His love (vv. 1-6); <u>second</u>, to show His grace; and <u>third</u>, to show His workmanship by producing good works in our lives. The salvation His love provides is "by <u>grace</u> . . . through <u>faith</u>." That is spelled out in verse 5: "By <u>grace</u> ye are saved"; and amplified in verse 8: "For by <u>grace</u> are ye saved through <u>faith</u>." Furthermore, "it is the gift of God." Three key words should be noted: *grace* – the motivation behind the plan of salvation; *faith* – the instrument by which it is received; and *gift* – the nature of the transaction. The source of this grace is God Himself, and He gives it with no strings attached.

Paul makes it clear that boasting is eliminated because we cannot earn the gift (v. 9). However, good works always follow salvation as the result, proving that salvation has come. Believers are God's "workmanship," His *work of art* that began at salvation and is to continue for a lifetime. "Ordained" to "good works," we are "to walk in them." In fact, believers were "created in Christ Jesus" for that purpose. While works cannot bring salvation to a person, they are always to accompany salvation (see James 2:17).

Verses 1-10 have application to both Jews and Gentiles before conversion; verse 11 has special reference to Gentiles. Jews referred to them as the uncircumcision, those on the outside with no part in the Old Covenant. Even some Jewish believers were hesitant to treat them as equals in the faith. But now, says Paul, that great gulf that separated Jew and Gentile has been removed, and those Gentiles who were once "far off" and "having no hope" have been "made nigh" (brought near) "by the blood of Christ."

LIFE STEP This would be a good time to thank the Lord for His wonderful free gift of salvation and then to review your life to see if the verbal thanks are being followed up by a life of "good works."

EPHESIANS 2:14-18

WHAT IS THE WRITER SAYING?

HOW CAN I APPLY THIS TO MY LIFE?

Paul has noted that Jew and Gentile, once alienated, are now one in Christ (v. 13). He now goes on to state what is involved. First, the wall of enmity that once existed has been broken down (v. 14). The animosity that existed, which centered in the advantages God had given the Jew (and which the Gentiles resented, verse 15), was done away with in Christ. Now reconciled, the two have been made "one new man" (a reference to the church, 1 Corinthians 12:12-13; Ephesians 1:22-23).

That reconciliation (removal of enmity) was brought about by the death of Christ, because in His work on the cross He rendered the Law inoperative, taking it away, so that it was no longer a separator. Wiersbe states the tearing down was three-fold: Physically, for in Christ we are all one (Galatians 3:28-29); Spiritually, the "far off" Gentiles were brought "nigh" (v. 13); and Legally, Christ fulfilling the Law in Himself (by meeting all of its requirements and ending its reign at the cross).

Not only is there peace between Jew and Gentile (v. 14), but also between God and those who place their faith in Him (v. 16). (Paul writes of this latter reconciliation in Romans 5:10; 2 Corinthians 5:18-20; Colossians 1:20). The bottom line is this: whether Jew or Gentile, all believers have a common denominator – their new life in Christ. In it they find oneness that does away with that which had kept them apart. They have lost their separate identities in the church. Through His death on the cross (v. 16), Christ *proclaims* peace to all mankind (v. 17), and He *is* peace; for through Him all men have access to God by way of the Holy Spirit (v. 18).

 LIFE STEP Why not make your time in the Word today one of thanking the Lord for removing the barrier between Himself and you? Only His cross made the difference. Take time to reflect on and enjoy the peace that comes by faith.

EPHESIANS 2:19-22

WHAT IS THE WRITER SAYING?

HOW CAN I APPLY THIS TO MY LIFE?

With these verses, Paul changes the imagery from that of a body to that of a temple. These are climactic verses because in them we find a graphic picture (v. 21) of what the work of Christ will result in – a living temple built out of people who are called "living stones" (1 Peter 2:4-8). This would be appropriate imagery for both Jew (they greatly revered their temple in Jerusalem) and Gentile (for here in Ephesus was the great Temple of Diana).

Paul begins (v. 18) by making it clear that Gentiles in Christ (just like Jews in Christ) are secure, no longer strangers to God as outsiders. They are now fellow citizens, along with Jewish believers, set apart as members of the household of God. Both Jew and Gentile are on equal footing in the Church of Jesus Christ, which began at Pentecost and will continue on earth until the Rapture.

Besides being a secure structure, this temple is also solidly built (v. 20). The laying of the foundation was the responsibility of the New Testament apostles and prophets. The foundation is Christ (1 Corinthians 3:11), not the apostles or prophets themselves. Considering them to be the foundation stones would destroy the imagery of the context. Like all other believers, they are stones in the superstructure of the temple building. Christ is also the cornerstone, because every line in the temple building is aligned with Him.

This "building" (v. 21), this "habitation of God" (v. 22), is the place where God dwells while the church is in this world. In the Old Testament, God dwelt first in the tabernacle (Exodus 40:34), and then in Solomon's temple (2 Chronicles 7:1), in the Gospels in Christ Himself (John 1:14), and today in individuals (1 Corinthians 6:19-20) and the church (Ephesians 2:21). Exodus 25:8 reads: "Let them make me a sanctuary; that I may dwell among them." Today, He Himself is building that sanctuary. It is called the church.

LIFE STEP My heart, Christ's home! What a privilege to have God living in us. Does this concept alter any plans we have for today? Do others see Christ living in us? What about our church? Do we attract outsiders by our lifestyle?

SUNDAY 51

EPHESIANS 3:1-7

WHAT IS THE WRITER SAYING?

HOW CAN I APPLY THIS TO MY LIFE?

PRAY Sudan – Pray that the great hunger for Christian and educational reading materials might be met.

In the verses immediately preceding this passage (2:11-21), Paul briefly discussed the union of Jews and Gentiles in one body (v. 16), called the church. Now, as he was about to offer a prayer for these united believers, he stopped right in the middle of a sentence (end of 3:1), and then returns to his prayer in verse 14. In between, Paul inserts one long sentence in which he felt compelled by the Holy Spirit to explain in some depth the equality of position that Jews and Gentiles have in the church. Prior to his interruption he reminds his readers who he is – "the prisoner of Jesus Christ" (not of Rome, though detained by them), and was such "for you Gentiles." Then he begins to develop for them the ministry to which he has been called, that of "the dispensation of the grace of God" (v. 2). He was to make known to the world the meaning of the mystery God had revealed to him (vv. 3-4): the no-distinction union of Jew and Gentile in the New Testament Church. "Mystery" here is not something mystical, but incomprehensible until God chooses to reveal it, first to and through Paul, and then others ["Holy (*set apart*) apostles and prophets" (v. 5)].

In verse 6 Paul makes clear the meaning of the mystery in this context. It is not that Gentiles finally could be saved, for elsewhere Paul quotes Old Testament passages demonstrating God's past redemptive work among the Gentiles (Romans 9:24-33; 10:19-21; 15:9-12). It is that Gentile believers and Jewish believers are together (1) "fellow heirs," (2) of the "same body" and (3) "partakers of His promise" (a messianic promise) found "in Christ (see 2:12; Galatians 3:29) by the Gospel" (and that's good news). This joining together of Jew and Gentile into one was a revolutionary concept to both parties.

In verse 7 Paul shows clearly his attitude toward this great responsibility (of taking this mystery to the world) God had given him. He recognized that his position as a "minister," namely, a servant of God, was a "gift of the grace of God," and only through "His power" would he be able to fulfill his ministry.

 LIFE STEP God has been gracious to us as well, gifting us in many different ways to take the good news of the Gospel to a lost world. Let us live in such a way that we don't hinder the power He has made available to fulfill our personal ministries.

EPHESIANS 3:8-13

WHAT IS THE WRITER SAYING?

HOW CAN I APPLY THIS TO MY LIFE?

In verse 7 Paul noted his responsibility to God as a *minister* (servant) of the gospel, a task given to him by God's grace, and made effective by God's power. Here (v. 8) he articulates his personal feeling of unworthiness for such a task, saying he is "less than the least of all saints." No doubt his background of persecuting the church (Acts 9:5; 1 Timothy 1:13) contributed to that assessment, hence his genuine humility in being given the assignment of proclaiming to the world the "mystery" of the church.

He was to "preach among the Gentiles the unsearchable riches of Christ," riches *past finding out*, or *untraceable* (perhaps like a bird that leaves no tracks in the air), *not capable of being tracked by footprints*. Reason – it had, "from the beginning of the world...been hid in God" (v. 9). While just now being revealed, it had always been a part of God's eternal plan (see 1:4, 11). Paul's task was "to make all men see what is the fellowship of the mystery;" he is to *turn on the light* (from a word translated *photo*). He is to see to it that the entire world *gets the picture*, namely, that because of the grace of God, Jew and Gentile are now one body in Christ called the church, and through whom, of course, the world is to learn of the glories of the Gospel. But the Lord will also use the church to reveal the wisdom of God to angelic beings ("principalities and powers," 6:12). Comparing v. 10 with 1 Peter 1:12 we find that even angels did not previously know what God had planned for the Church Age, and only learned it when God chose to reveal it through Paul. As these angelic witnesses view the church, they must admit that having Jew and Gentile in one body is evidence of the "manifold wisdom of God" (v. 10).

Paul closes his interruption (begun in verse 1) by exhorting his readers to "faint not at (his) tribulations" which he suffered on their behalf. Instead, feel honored that in God's plan, their salvation was important enough for His servant to undergo such difficulties. While not glad he had to suffer, they could rejoice in its purpose and accomplishment.

LIFE STEP Paul was goal-oriented in his service for Christ. Neither his past life nor his current suffering took the goal out of focus. May we learn from, and follow, his example.

EPHESIANS 3:14-21

WHAT IS THE WRITER SAYING?

HOW CAN I APPLY THIS TO MY LIFE?

Paul's digression ends and he returns to the thought he had in mind as he began this chapter. "For this cause," namely, God's wonderful work of bringing Jew and Gentile together as one body in Christ, the apostle humbles himself before God in a great prayer for the church. This is the second of Paul's two prayers in this letter. The first (1:15-23) emphasized *knowledge*, this second prayer *lifestyle*. Paul wanted them to understand what they had and put it into practice. He prays for God's "whole family in heaven and earth" (v. 15). This verse is not teaching *the fatherhood of God* relative to salvation. That is based upon the crosswork of Christ. Instead, it is relative to creation, for all families of men and angels find their origin in God. He then lists his requests for God's people. (1) That they would be "strengthened… in the inner man" by the power of the Holy Spirit (v. 16). (2) That Christ may dwell (*feel at home*) in your hearts by faith – He would have *the run of the house* (v. 17). (3) That they "may be able to comprehend…and know the love of Christ, which passeth knowledge" –an appeal to an experiential knowledge of Christ's love which exceeds all theoretical and intellectual knowledge (for Christianity is far more than a series of doctrines, it is a life to be experienced) (vv. 18-19). (4) That believers "might be filled with all the fullness of God," or better, *with respect to all the fullness of God*. No believer could possibly contain all the fullness of God, but He is the unlimited source from which we draw for all of our needed spiritual resources. Verses 20-21 form a doxology, or praise, to God in which Paul notes that God can do "exceedingly abundantly (double compound word: *superabundantly*) above all that we ask or think." And He does it through the power that works in us – the Holy Spirit.

LIFE STEP Does Christ really have *the run of the house* as it relates to your life? If He doesn't, why not stop right now and make plans to *clean house*. Only then will He feel at home.

WEDNESDAY 51

EPHESIANS 4:1-10
WHAT IS THE WRITER SAYING?

HOW CAN I APPLY THIS TO MY LIFE?

PRAY Paraguay – For pastors to actively model the disciplines of prayer, Bible study, and witnessing.

Ephesians follows Paul's habit of beginning with doctrine and following with practice. Chapters 1-3 are doctrinal and 4-6 are practical. Following his doctrinal dissertation, Paul now tells the Ephesians to "walk worthy of the vocation wherewith ye are called," that is, the calling every believer has received and which brings to them the designation *saint*, one set apart to God (Romans 1:6-7).

This profession of sainthood will be marked by three qualities: (1) *lowliness* – true, not false, humility, in Greek culture thought of as a vice to be practiced only by slaves. Christ demonstrated genuine humility (Philippians 2: 6-8). (2) *Meekness* – gentleness, not weakness, but the ability to control one's emotions. Christ was meek (Matthew 11:29), but drove out the moneychangers from the temple (Matthew 21:12-13). (3) *Forbearing*, or forbearance, the ability to be patient with the weakness of others (all 3 in verse 2). Unity will not take place without these three qualities.

Paul lists (vv. 4-6) the seven-fold oneness believers share, and the impetus behind a unified walk. (1) *One body* – all believers from Pentecost to the Rapture, 1:23; 2:16; 3:6; (2) *one Spirit* – the indwelling Holy Spirit, 2:22; (3) *one hope* – an expectant attitude toward Christ's return and their personal future, 1 Peter 1:3; 3:15; (4) *one Lord* – Christ, the head of the church, 1:22-23; Colossians 1:18; (5) *one faith* – demonstrated by trusting Christ for salvation and life, Colossians 2:7; (6) *one baptism*, that of the Holy Spirit which all believers experience at salvation making them one, 1 Corinthians 12:13; (7) *one God and Father*, the relationship established when one trusts Christ, John 1:13; Galatians 3:26.

To accomplish the goal of walking in unity, God sovereignly bestows (spiritual) gifts upon all believers by the ascended Christ (vv. 7-9). How each believer uses these gifts will determine one's place of service during Christ's messianic, millennial reign.

 LIFE STEP You are a gifted believer. Do you know what your gifts are? Paul lists some in this chapter, others in Romans 12 and 1 Corinthians 12. Know what they are and use them for Him.

EPHESIANS 4:11-16

WHAT IS THE WRITER SAYING?

HOW CAN I APPLY THIS TO MY LIFE?

To serve Christ every believer has been spiritually gifted (1 Corinthians 12; Romans 12). For the church to accomplish its purposes, the Lord provides gifted men and places them providentially (Acts 11:23-26), or through His Spirit (Acts 13:1-2). He does so based on their gifting and upon the need of the church. Verse 11 lists four, or perhaps five, such men.

The first two, *apostles* and *prophets*, mentioned earlier (2:20; 3:5) are foundational gifts to the church. The former would include the Twelve Apostles, Paul and a handful of others, commissioned by the Lord to represent Him and deliver His message. The latter, strictly speaking, were those who were given direct revelation by God before the New Testament was written, to communicate to man. Being foundational in nature, neither has existed since the first generation of believers. *Evangelists* are preachers of the Gospel, helping to bring the lost into the body of Christ, while *pastors and teachers* (linked here, separate elsewhere, Romans 12:7; 1 Peter 5:2) are those who shepherd the flock and instruct them in their ministries. The goal of the church is outlined in verses 12-16. These gifted men are to (a) perfect (mature, prepare) *the saints* (by using their gifts) (b) so they (since all believers are gifted, *all* are to be involved) in turn will be able to *accomplish the work of the ministry*, (c) with the result of *edifying* – building up – *the body of Christ* (v. 12). Verse 13 makes it plain that spiritual unity and spiritual maturity are closely linked. The purpose of this linkage is described in verse 14, where the term *children* is applied to some believers. Spiritual children are often doctrinally insecure and can be "tossed to and fro," like a small boat in a storm, when false teaching comes along (v. 14). But when the "truth" is spoken in love (v. 15), "the whole body (no insignificant parts – 1 Corinthians 12:14-17) is joined together" (v. 16), resulting in an edified body, united to its head (Christ), one that functions as designed.

LIFE STEP A reminder – every believer is gifted, hence every believer is to be involved in Christian service, using one's gifts for Christ. Is that true in your life?

FRIDAY 51

EPHESIANS 4:17-24

WHAT IS THE WRITER SAYING?

HOW CAN I APPLY THIS TO MY LIFE?

PRAY That the leadership of your church will live justly, love mercy, and walk humbly with God (Micah 6:8).

Paul begins a long passage (ending at 6:9) in which he draws the logical conclusion in terms of life and morals that follow membership in the body of Christ. He challenges believers to "walk not as other (unsaved) Gentiles walk, in the vanity of their mind." The challenge suggests two things: one, they could walk that way; two, they did not have to. Though one's fallen nature is not eradicated at salvation, the believer, by receiving a new nature and the indwelling Spirit, no longer needs to be governed by it, though internal warfare between the two will be constant (Romans 7; Galatians 2:20; 5:13-26 etc.).

Those "other Gentiles" have had their "understanding darkened" (v. 18) and are "past feeling" (v. 19). They have no sense of shame, the result of years of sin and debauchery, and "have given themselves over unto lasciviousness" (sensuality), which leads to all types of "uncleanness" that goes deeper and deeper because it is never satisfied. Three times in Romans

1 Paul says that God gave them over to something: first, to sinful desires (1:24); second, to shameful lusts (1:26); third, to a depraved mind (1:28). Result – (1) live right, (2) love right or (3) think right. "But ye have not so learned Christ." These Ephesians no longer existed in this state of ignorance and separation from God. Paul knew that, having been their teacher. They were taught the truth about Jesus and salvation took place, yet even with that great event in their past, they still had the responsibility of discarding their old way of life ("put off" – verse 22), denying the appetite of their old sinful nature (Romans 6:13; Galatians 2:20; 5:13). The way that is done is by being "renewed in the spirit of your mind" (*continuously yielding to the Holy Spirit* verse 23) while at the same time "putting on" (v. 24) the "new man" – allowing the Holy Spirit to be the controlling force in one's life. Doing so manifests itself in "righteousness and true holiness" (v. 24).

 LIFE STEP The Christian's life is like stripping off the dirty clothes of a sinful past and putting on the snowy white robes of Christ's righteousness. Be sure to do it daily.

EPHESIANS 4:25-32

WHAT IS THE WRITER SAYING?

HOW CAN I APPLY THIS TO MY LIFE?

In Matthew 7:20, speaking of true and false teachers, Christ said, "…by their fruits ye shall know them." A similar application may be made relative to believers, for the fruit that comes from a person's life, his actions, will prove whether the individual is yielding to his old sinful nature or to the Holy Spirit. To illustrate, Paul uses four representative examples of problems present in his day and in ours. He underscores them all with a stern command: "grieve not the holy Spirit of God" (v. 30).

1. *Lack of Truthfulness* (v. 25) was common among the heathen, but because Christians are "members one of another," lying among them is unthinkable. Would one's foot lie to one's hand?

2. *Anger* (v. 26), which is sometimes justified by its cause, must not be permitted to stay and fester and give the devil an opportunity to gain a foothold in one's life.

3. *Stealing* (v. 28), of course, is wrong but was apparently being practiced by some believers who carried some of their old ways into their new lives, so Paul says, "Stop!" He then provides them with a practical antidote – work! That will not only meet their needs but also provide relief for others.

4. *Corrupt Communication* (foul speech) (v. 29), another *unthinkable* for the believer. The remedy is more positive than negative. Speak only "that which is good to the use of edifying." Let your language always build up, ministering "grace unto the hearers."

Finally, Christians are not to "grieve the Holy Spirit," remembering that the Spirit is a person, not an influence, and can be hurt when the believer turns away from His leading and follows the promptings of his flesh (some mentioned in verse 31). Paul closes this chapter with a number of positive characteristics that should mark all believers: kindness, a tender heart and forgiveness (v. 32).

 LIFE STEP Years ago, a song contained these words: "Accentuate the positive, eliminate the negative, and latch on to the affirmative." These would be good words to apply to this chapter. Put into practice, they will keep you from grieving the Holy Spirit.

EPHESIANS 5:1-7

WHAT IS THE WRITER SAYING?

HOW CAN I APPLY THIS TO MY LIFE?

The word *therefore* (or *wherefore*) usually refers one back to the previous passage. Not so here. Instead it is referring, as do other "therefores" (4:1, 17, 25; 5:14, 17) in this second half of the book (chapters 4-5) to the first half of the book (chapters 1-3). In other words, the *practical* follows the *doctrinal*. Aware of whom we are doctrinally (the church, the body of Christ), there is to be a lifestyle worthy of that relationship. *Therefore* in these final three chapters we see Paul exhorting his readers to live a life that differentiates them from their pagan world. The Temple to Diana was in Ephesus, where all sorts of vile sexual immorality, in the name of religion, took place. Paul warns the believers to avoid the pitfalls of the pagans, including "fornication" (sexual immorality); "uncleanness" (any kind of impurity); "covetousness" (greed), (v. 3); "filthiness" (shameless, immoral conduct); "foolish talking" (characteristic of an empty head); "jesting" (words with double meaning), (v. 4); for those who practice such things give evidence of an unchanged life and will have no place in God's kingdom, (v .5).

Positively, however, "Be followers (imitators) of God" (v. 1). No other New Testament passage gives such instruction directly (to imitate God). Believers are told to imitate *good* (1 Peter 3:13); *Paul* (1 Corinthians 4:16; 11:1); *godly men* (Hebrews 6:11-12); and *Christ* (by implication, 1 Corinthians 11:1). To do so may not be as unrealistic as supposed, for we are His "dear children" (v. 1), partakers of His nature (2 Peter 1:4); have access to Him (Romans 5:2); and fellowship with Him (1 John 1:3). Such a relationship makes possible a higher kind of life than the unsaved can know, a life whose behavior is ordered by "love" (agape); and, because "God is love" (1 John 4:8, 16), believers imitating Him will live a life that manifests that same love (1 Corinthians 13). The motivation for such a life is found in the sacrificial actions of Christ on the cross "for us" (for our benefit) (v. 2).

LIFE STEP In Paul's style, "therefore, brothers and sisters in Christ," let us live a life that so imitates God that others desire the same relationship. A life so lived will be "sweet-smelling" to the nostrils of God.

MONDAY 52

EPHESIANS 5:8-14

WHAT IS THE WRITER SAYING?

HOW CAN I APPLY THIS TO MY LIFE?

PRAY Peru – Apathy, doctrinal error, and cults are crippling churches. Pray for more trained Bible teachers.

Paul again points out some contrasts between the conditions of the unbeliever with that of the believer. An unbeliever is dead; a believer has a new life (v. 14). An unbeliever is asleep; the believer is awake to reality and truth (v. 14). An unbeliever is darkness (note: not *in* darkness, but darkness itself) while the believer is light. That darkness was once true of the believer (v. 5), but now he is numbered among those who are lights in the world (Matthew 5:14), and as such are to "walk as children of light" (keep their lights on), living lives reflective of their new life.

The parenthetical ninth verse explains that "the fruit of the light" (not Spirit according to most scholars), is "goodness and righteousness and truth," all desperately needed in a world of sensuality, sin and evil (vv. 3-5). "Light" comes from the Greek *photos* from which we get photography, etc. It is a common biblical expression, normally depicting the drastic difference between "what is acceptable unto the Lord" (v. 10), and that which is characteristic of a sinful life.

Verse 11 places upon the believer two responsibilities with respect to sin. First, no way is he to have "fellowship" or *to become a partaker with others* in the "unfruitful works of darkness." The second is to reprove such behavior by letting his life "show by contrast how dreary and futile these things are" (Phillips). By proper conduct, the believer living as a "child of light" will expose the deeds of other believers (not unbelievers – that is God's work – 1 Corinthians 5:12-13) who are not walking in the light. Their deeds were so vile that Paul hesitated to even mention them (v. 12), but "are made manifest" when "reproved by the light" (v. 13). Paul then appeals to the believer who is living inconsistently with his light position. "Be waking up the one who is sleeping, and arise from the dead, and there shall shine upon you Christ" (Wuest).

Little amplification is needed. You are a child of light. Keep on walking in it. And if you stumbled out of it, confess it. God does forgive and restore (1 John 1:9).

EPHESIANS 5:15-21

WHAT IS THE WRITER SAYING?

HOW CAN I APPLY THIS TO MY LIFE?

PRAY Gabon – Pray the evangelical growth in Gabon which has been steady and sustained for several decades will continue.

The issue is still Christian conduct. Paul urges the Ephesian believers to pay careful attention to their behavior, walking "circumspectly" (v. 15) or accurately. The path has been marked out (Psalm 37:23) and the believer is not to wander off course, being careful where he "walks." He is to walk "wisely," "redeeming" (*buying up*) the time for "the days are evil" (v. 16), or morally corrupt. In a once-born world, the twice-born Christian is to take every opportunity to shed light on an ever-darkening world.

Wherefore (noting the commands to "walk in light," verse 8 and in "wisdom,"v.15), "be ye not unwise" (*senseless*), but conduct yourself in a manner demonstrating an "understanding" of "the will of the Lord" (v. 17). The pagan cannot do so (1 Corinthians 2:14); believers can. They possess in Scripture the objective revelation of His will and the indwelling Holy Spirit to interpret it. And once He is known, for the Christian faith is not devoid of intellectual content, the Spirit will aid the believer in its application.

"Be not drunk with wine" (v. 18), a common sin among unbelievers in Paul's day, is one that Paul, quoting from Proverbs 23:29-32, warns against. It has no place among believers. Instead, the believer is to "be filled with the Spirit." Paul has already taught that *all* believers are *sealed*, once for all, at the point of salvation (1:13-14; 4:30), but *not all* believers are *filled*. Filling is commanded in Scripture and is dependent upon one's yieldedness to God's will (v. 17), thus differing from God's instantaneous act of sealing. It can be repeated according to Acts 2:4 and 4:31. All believers have the Spirit; the command here is that the Spirit is to have the entire believer. Only then will the wise walk with a verse 15 result.

Verses 19-21 advise as to how to carry out the command, <u>first</u>, through music (a) with other believers and (b) in your heart to the Lord (v. 19); <u>secondly</u>, through constant thanksgiving to God for all things (v. 20), and <u>thirdly</u>, through voluntary and willing submission to one another.

LIFE STEP The successful Christian life is dependent upon the filling of the Spirit. Evaluate your life. Is it measuring up to the command of verse 18?

WEDNESDAY 52

EPHESIANS 5:22-33

WHAT IS THE WRITER SAYING?

HOW CAN I APPLY THIS TO MY LIFE?

PRAY Nigeria – Pray that the churches in Nigeria would be more committed to ministering to their children and youth.

The key word is "submit" (v. 22), from a Greek word of military origin, emphasizing the *act of voluntary (not forced) submission to a proper authority.* Paul uses it as a basis for the relationships between husbands and wives, parents and children and masters and servants.

He deals first with the husband/wife relationship, it being the most fundamental. "*Wives*, submit… unto your own husbands," for that is your service "to the Lord" (cf. Colossians 3:18). God has made the husband the family's spiritual leader. His position is compared to Christ's headship over His church; Christ is the Savior of the body, the husband the protector of his wife. For her to fail in voluntary submission would be like the church usurping Christ's headship. She is to respond to his assigned position of authority. This is not a picture of superiority versus inferiority, but simply a role assignment.

"*Husbands*, love your wives," doing so as "Christ… loved the church and gave Himself for it" (v. 25). This is self-sacrificial love, giving of oneself for another person. When the husband practices such Christ-like love, willing submission on the part of the wife should not be difficult. Christ's death (v. 26) was to "set-apart" His bride (the church) for Himself, forever (cf. Hebrews 10:10, 14). He did so by cleansing her "with the washing of water by the word" (v. 26), especially the preached word (Ephesians 6:17; Romans 10:8; 1 Peter 1:25), in order to "present it to himself" (v. 27) in faultless condition.

Verses 28-30 apply the truths of verses 25-27. The church is the body of Christ, united to Him, its head. The wife is united to her husband, they become "one flesh" (v. 31), and men are to love their wives as their own bodies, a manner that precludes anything but the exceptional care Christ displayed for His body, the church.

LIFE STEP God's Word is a marriage manual, provided for family use. When the directions (such as above) are followed, so does blessing. Failure in following will negate the blessing. Don't let that happen to you.

EPHESIANS 6:1-9

WHAT IS THE WRITER SAYING?

HOW CAN I APPLY THIS TO MY LIFE?

Paul's discussion of personal relationships began in Ephesians 5:22 with husbands/wives. Now it continues with parents/children and slaves/masters. All three relationships require Spirit controlled lives (5:18), hence the instruction here is pointedly to believers. **Children/Parents (vv.1-4).** Even as wives are to be subject to their husbands, so children are to "obey" their parents, doing so "in the Lord." Such behavior "is well pleasing to the Lord" (Colossians 3:20), and is "right." The "submit" of wives implies voluntary action, but "obey" is much stronger, implying that parental direction is to be carried out regardless of the children's wishes. "Honor" goes beyond obedience itself to the heart attitude. *Obedience* is the duty (external); *honor* the disposition (internal). Attached to such positive behavior is a promise (v. 2), "…that you may prosper and live a long life on earth" (Williams Translation). (See the fourth commandment – Exodus 20:12 – the only one of the ten with a promise.) As for the parents, they are to earn such obedience and honor, hence the instruction: "Do not provoke (*exasperate*) to wrath, but bring them (the children) up in the nurture (*training*) and admonition (*instruction*) of the Lord," that is, not being unreasonable in their expectations of their children. They are to practice neither unlimited permissiveness nor spirit-breaking discipline (Colossians 3:21). Balance is the goal.

Slaves/Masters (vv. 5-9). These instructions apply today to employee/employer relationships. Employees are to carry out the orders of their employers (v. 5), understanding that no matter whom they serve in "the flesh," they are really serving Christ (v. 6), and their ultimate reward comes from Him (v. 8). Employers are to have similar attitudes, treating their employees fairly, for their ultimate responsibility is also to Christ. Both are to understand that God is impartial. Both are equal in His sight.

LIFE STEP Once again the directions are clear. In which category do you find yourself? And are you meeting your responsibilities?

FRIDAY 52

EPHESIANS 6:10-17

WHAT IS THE WRITER SAYING?

HOW CAN I APPLY THIS TO MY LIFE?

PRAY Myanmar – Pray for seemingly impossible ethnic harmony, effective federalism, and peace.

Paul now addresses the believer's warfare. Battlefield language is not uncommon to Paul, speaking often of the Christian life in military terms. This is more, however, than analogous language. The battle is real and no true soldier (cf. 2 Timothy 2:3) of Jesus Christ can expect to be immune from enemy attacks. And so, Paul exhorts the believers to "be strong in the Lord and in the power of His might" (v. 10). Victory will not be achieved on one's own; the believer needs the strength only the Lord can supply.

The "whole armor of God" is to be "put on" (v. 11). Paul is writing from prison. In full view would be fully armored Roman soldiers. That physical armor provides a picture of the spiritual battle facing the believer, a battle "not against flesh and blood," but against Satan, his strategies and his cohorts ("principalities... powers... etc." v. 12). In God's armor, victory is assured (v. 13), for it meets every need.

Briefly, here is what he is to put on (all of which are found in Christ): (1) the girdle of truth – tightened up it keeps everything else in place. Integrity is vital; union with the truth makes it possible (John 14:6); (2) the breastplate of righteousness – to protect the heart, imputed to the believer (2 Corinthians 5:21), demonstrated in life; (3) the shoes of peace – feet carry the soldier to battle, and the good news of salvation provides "peace with God" (Romans 5:1), and calmness for the conflict; (4) the shield of faith – to ward off the weapons of the enemy rendering them ineffective (1 John 5:4); (5) the helmet of salvation – to protect one's head (intellect) – "take it," says Paul. This salvation (all three tenses: *past*, from the penalty of sin; *future*, from the presence of sin; and *present*, from the power of sin) is a free gift. With it God provides victory. Finally, put on (6) the sword of the spirit – God's Word, to defend oneself against the thrusts of the enemy and attack his false teachings.

LIFE STEP Step in front of God's spiritual mirror (His Word) and see what you look like. You're a soldier in His army. Is the armor in place?

EPHESIANS 6:18-24

WHAT IS THE WRITER SAYING?

HOW CAN I APPLY THIS TO MY LIFE?

PRAY Costa Rica – For a new generation of godly, effective leaders for the churches that will commend the Gospel.

Having dealt with the proper equipment for the battle (vv. 10-17), Paul now deals with the equally important proper attitude, one of prayerfulness and watchfulness in this spiritual conflict. As to prayer, two different words are used: *prayer* (prayers in general – the necessity of a consistent prayer life) and *supplication* (special requests), both to be offered "in the Spirit." *Watching* means to be sleepless, always awake, characteristic of a reliable soldier. Having the proper attitude in spiritual warfare cannot be overemphasized. The conflict is real, the enemies spiritual, but a proper attitude will avail itself of that which God has provided and is necessary for victory. Prayer is to be constant ("always") and for "all saints," for they are all in the same battle (v. 18).

Paul's request for himself was more ministerial than personal. Even in prison his request was not for ease or prosperity, but that God would give him the ability to preach the Gospel with boldness (v. 19).

That was always Paul's chief aim in life. He considered himself an "ambassador in bonds," representing his Lord at all times.

Verses 21 and 22 are similar to Colossians 4:7-9. Recognizing that Paul's readers would want to know how he and his associates were doing ("*our* affairs," v. 22), Paul sends them this letter by the hand of Tychicus to provide that information and to "comfort" their "hearts" (v. 22). He doesn't name his associates, perhaps indicating that this letter was to be circular in nature, one intended for a number of churches around Ephesus.

Paul's closing benediction utilizes some of the same terms he used in beginning this letter, including "peace," "love" and "grace," all of which find their source in God, and which he desired for his brothers (and sisters) in Christ, for they are all "members one of another" (4:25).

 LIFE STEP It is checkup time. In this book the doctrinal (chapters 1-3) are followed by the practical (chapters 4-6). Belief is to dictate practice. You know what you believe. Does your practice demonstrate it? That should be your goal.

QUIETIME

ONE-YEAR
DAILY
DEVOTIONAL
WITH
COMMENTARY

The following chart applies to all Word of Life Quiet Times so that all ages will be on the same passage each day.

week 1	Aug 27 - Sep 2	Psalms 104:1–105:45
week 2	Sep 3 - Sep 9	Psalms 106:1–108:13
week 3	Sep 10 - Sep 16	Psalms 114:1–119:8
week 4	Sep 17 - Sep 23	Psalms 119:9–119:72
week 5	Sep 24 - Sep 30	Psalms 119:81–119:176
week 6	Oct 1 - Oct 7	Philippians 1:1–2:23
week 7	Oct 8 - Oct 14	Philippians 2:24–4:23
week 8	Oct 15 - Oct 21	Exodus 1:1–4:17
week 9	Oct 22 - Oct 28	Exodus 4:18–8:15
week 10	Oct 29 - Nov 4	Exodus 8:16–11:10
week 11	Nov 5 - Nov 11	Exodus 12:1–14:14
week 12	Nov 12 - Nov 18	Exodus 14:15–17:16
week 13	Nov 19 - Nov 25	Exodus 19:1–32:6
week 14	Nov 26 - Dec 2	Exodus 32:7–40:38
week 15	Dec 3 - Dec 9	2 Timothy 1:1–2:26
week 16	Dec 10 - Dec 16	2 Timothy 3:1–4:22
week 17 Start	Dec 17 - Dec 23	Nahum 1:1–Malachi 4:6
week 18	Dec 24 - Dec 30	John 1:1–1:51
week 19	Dec 31 - Jan 6	John 2:1–4:15
week 20	Jan 7 - Jan 13	John 4:16–5:47
week 21	Jan 14 - Jan 20	John 6:1–6:71
week 22	Jan 21 - Jan 27	John 7:1–8:20
week 23	Jan 28 - Feb 3	John 8:21–9:34
week 24	Feb 4 - Feb 10	John 9:35–11:29

week 25	Feb 11 - Feb 17	John 11:30–12:43
week 26	Feb 18 - Feb 24	John 12:44–14:14
week 27	Feb 25 - Mar 3	John 14:15–16:33
week 28	Mar 4 - Mar 10	John 17:1–19:22
week 29	Mar 11 - Mar 17	John 19:23–21:25
week 30	Mar 18 - Mar 24	Romans 1:1–3:20
week 31	Mar 25 - Mar 31	Romans 3:21–6:23
week 32	Apr 1 - Apr 7	Romans 7:1–9:33
week 33	Apr 8 - Apr 14	Romans 10:1–12:21
week 34	Apr 15 - Apr 21	Romans 13:1–16:27
week 35	Apr 22 - Apr 28	Ezekiel 1:1–37:14
week 36	Apr 29 - May 5	Ezekiel 37:15–47:12
week 37	May 6 - May 12	Revelation 6:1–13:18
week 38	May 13 - May 19	Revelation 14:1–17:18
week 39	May 20 - May 26	Revelation 19:1–22:21
week 40	May 27 - June 2	Job 1:1–13:18
week 41	Jun 3 - Jun 9	Job 14:1–42:17
week 42	Jun 10- Jun 16	1 Peter 1:1–3:7
week 43	Jun 17 - Jun 23	1 Peter 3:8–5:14
week 44	Jun 24 - Jun 30	1 Kings 1:15–11:13
week 45	Jul 1 - Jul 7	1 Kings 11:41–18:16
week 46	Jul 8 - Jul 14	1 Kings 18:17–22:40
week 47	Jul 15 - Jul 21	2 Kings 1:1–5:16
week 48	Jul 22 - Jul 28	2 Kings 5:17–9:37
week 49	Jul 29- Aug 4	2 Kings 13:14–23:3
week 50	Aug 5 - Aug 11	Ephesians 1:1–2:22
week 51	Aug 12 - Aug 18	Ephesians 3:1–4:32
week 52	Aug 19 - Aug 25	Ephesians 5:1–6:24